THE LANGUAGE OF LEARNING

Vocabulary for College Success

THE LANGUAGE
OF LEARNING

Vocabulary for College Success

Jane Hopper
Cypress College

Jo Ann Carter-Wells
California State University, Fullerton

Wadsworth Publishing Company
Belmont, California
A Division of Wadsworth, Inc.

Editorial Assistant: Sharon Wallach
Production Editor: Jerilyn Emori
Managing Designer: Donna Davis
Print Buyer: Barbara Britton
Designer: Juan Vargas
Copy Editor: Evelyn Mercer Ward
Cover: Donna Davis

Printed in the United States of America   14
    2 3 4 5 6 7 8 9 10—92 91 90 89

Library of Congress Cataloging-in-Publication Data

Hopper, Jane.
    The language of learning.

    Includes index.
    1. Vocabulary.   2. Universities and colleges—
Glossaries, vocabularies, etc.   I. Carter-Wells,
Jo Ann.   II. Title.
PE1683.H67   1988   428.1   87-23098
ISBN 0-534-08940-2

CONTENTS

PREFACE

This book is the result of a project that began about ten years ago when we were teaching a university vocabulary class. Because the class offered general education credit, students from many majors and from all class levels enrolled. We planned to improve the students' vocabularies in four areas of language development: listening and speaking, reading and writing. The listening and speaking vocabulary activities took place in small groups, much like groups used to develop foreign language skills. Reading vocabulary developed through reading materials in the course syllabus that contained readings from "classical" works in the various disciplines, such as Adam Smith's *The Wealth of Nations.* Writing vocabulary words were supplied by the students from their own college reading. They selected and defined words that were new to them; they wrote sentences and essays using context clues; and we gave feedback. That activity eventually led to this text.

Over the semesters we observed that whereas students and textbooks change, the words do not vary a great deal. We began to collect words and to organize them according to source (academic discipline, fields related to an academic discipline, literature, and so on) and according to the selector (age, year in school, major). We collected thousands of words; some of them appeared many times. A number of those words appear in this book. Naturally we could not use them all. Some of the more difficult are not included because any appropriate context could be very difficult indeed.

Our purpose in writing this book is twofold: to introduce some of the words that our students found essential and to give students the necessary skills to increase their vocabularies throughout their lives. Fundamental to our purpose is knowledge of the dictionary. Therefore we devote time to its description and use, and we include actual entries. We find that few students are able to use the dictionary efficiently, in part because most vocabulary texts supply definitions rather than requring students to seek them in a dictionary format. (In a survey of former students, we found that learning to use the dictionary in our class rated high and was "of continuing importance to vocabulary growth.")

We structured the book so that it can be used independently, with context clues and several exercises for each word. We provide a variety of evaluation measures and answer keys for immediate feedback. We cover a number of academic disciplines and include an overview of each discipline to increase student awareness. We emphasize the importance of creating a personalized concept of a word, because we know that even a hard-working, determined student cannot remember irrelevant words. Current research in vocabulary instruction supports these methods.

The book is divided into four sections. Part One provides information useful to the vocabulary student and necessary to the successful completion of the text. Part Two introduces general words from our student-supplied pool in a context useful to college students. Part Three introduces academic words in reading selections about the disciplines. Each word introduced has its separate exercises, accompanied by its dictionary entry. Instructions are repeated frequently so that the units can stand alone. If students have not mastered a word, the posttests alert them to this and instructions return them to the exercises for more careful study.

The fourth section, the appendixes, includes a segment giving the etymologies of the words introduced, for those who prefer more emphasis on word origins; an overview of the sources of the English language, which adds crossword puzzles as a benign evaluation measure; lists of additional academic words; the framework for developing self-selected vocabulary lists; and pretest and crossword puzzle answer keys.

The instructor who prefers to do so can use this text as an adjunct, providing little assistance beyond making sure students understand how to use it, evaluating the posttests, and, perhaps, using the section mastery tests supplied in the Instructor's Manual. An instructor who prefers to give more direction can select the areas to be studied and assign the words to be mastered. The text can be used by individuals, in small groups, or with whole class instruction, depending on the instructor's teaching style and the nature of the group. Our prime hope is that this text will help its users develop the abilities necessary to increase their vocabularies continuously and to become more skillful communicators in an ever more complex world.

ACKNOWLEDGMENTS

We are indebted not only to the hundreds of students who provided the academic terms over the years but also to those students and faculty who assisted in the development of the reading selections. We would like especially to thank the following for their contributions:

Art: April Licata, California State University, Fullerton

Biology: Shari Aube and Kenneth Goodhue-McWilliams, California State University, Fullerton

Business Administration: James W. Anderson, Fullerton College

Chemistry: Joan Burt, Saddleback Valley Unified School District

Communications: Nicholas King, Jr., California State University, Fullerton

Economics and Accounting: Dennis Leahy, California State University, Fullerton

History: Jerald Hopper, Saddleback Valley Unified School District

Mathematics: Cynthia Skogen and Gerald Gannon, California State University, Fullerton

Political Science: Mark Brashear and Keith Boyum, California State University, Fullerton

The faculty who reviewed our material also assisted in refining our ideas to make this text more meaningful for students in the classroom. We are grateful for the guidance of Lyn Becktold, Saddleback Community College; Patricia Desmond, Middlesex County College; Marya M. DuBose, Augusta College; Maurice Kaufman, Northeastern University; Robert Kopfstein, Saddleback Community College; Judy Kuppersmith, St. Petersburg Junior College; and Maureen Stradley, Community College of Allegheny County.

Our colleagues, family, and especially our husbands, Jerald Hopper and Donald Wells, have provided support and encouragement during the nurturing and writing stages of this project. In addition, we wish to express special appreciation to The World Book, Inc., for their comments and recommendations in the completion of the exercises related to the dictionary entries.

Finally, we are most thankful for the wisdom, perseverance, and foresight of John Strohmeier, former English Editor, and for the patience and meticulous attention to detail of Jerilyn Emori, Production Editor, both of Wadsworth Publishing Company, who helped translate our dream into reality!

THE LANGUAGE
OF LEARNING
Vocabulary for College Success

PART ONE

INTRODUCTION

CHAPTER ONE

HOW TO USE
THIS BOOK

The vocabulary words in this book were selected by college and university students like you. For each discipline, they chose the words they felt were essential to their learning and success as students. These choices of words do not necessarily represent the core vocabulary of a particular discipline, but they are words that are useful when reading a textbook or listening to a lecture in a particular field. Because these student-selected words have been collected by the authors over many years, the words will be more meaningful and useful than those generally found in college-level vocabulary texts. The vocabulary words in this book are used in context in reading selections. This provides interest and also helps you develop knowledge of a specific academic field as well as familiarity with important or key terms. Most of the reading selections were written by faculty and others with expertise in their disciplines. Although the selections were developed to present particular issues or concepts you might encounter in your introductory-level classes, the selections are primarily meant to serve as a vehicle for introducing the student-selected academic vocabulary.

This book is divided into four sections. Part I provides background information that will help you use this book, including dictionary usage, context clues, and verbal analogies. Part II introduces student-selected general vocabulary words focusing on the theme of becoming successful as a college student. Part III presents student-selected academic words from four major schools of study and thirteen separate disciplines. There is also an overview of each discipline that includes what you would typically study, what careers you would be prepared for, and how the textbooks are usually structured. The Appendixes contain supplemental activities, including Latin and Greek word roots, additional academic words as identified by students over the years, and some "just for fun" readings and crossword puzzles. A unique addition is the self-selected vocabulary worksheets that you can use to add your own words to this text.

You can select those chapters and academic areas you wish to study, or complete the ones as directed by your instructor. Before you work with the words, you will be able to identify those in your working, or production, vocabulary (words you know and use) and those in your recognition, or reception, vocabulary (words you recognize but do not actively know or use). The words are then used in reading selections to give you useful information. Pretests will help you find out what you know. Exercises focused toward various levels of thinking will give you practice where you need it. Posttests will let you evaluate your progress.

We have organized the book this way because we have found that students learn and remember best when they become *personally involved* with each new word and use it as often as possible in speech and writing. We have also found that most students *want* to learn, to become knowledgeable, and to demonstrate the extent of their knowledge. It is with this thought in mind that we provide the information in this book, some of which is expressed directly (as in the exercises) and some of which is expressed less directly (as in the chapter reading selections). You will find that some of the exercises have more than one correct answer. They are designed to make you think carefully about the meaning of each word.

You will probably know some of the words introduced. However, we hope that when you have completed this book, you will know and use *all* of the words. What is more important, you will know how to use context clues to help you understand new words. You will also know how to create a concept for a new word so that you can continue to increase your vocabulary throughout your life.

We think that this book can add to your success in your college endeavors, in your personal life, and in your chosen career. To summarize: In this book you will learn how to

- use context clues to understand unknown words
- create concepts for words in order to learn and remember them
- understand and use dictionaries
- reason through verbal analogies

You will also learn about

- efficient reading and learning strategies
- using your time and energy wisely
- using the resources of the library

Finally, you should learn more about

- various fields of study
- typical information or content in a field of study
- textbook structure
- sources of additional vocabulary words

Here's to your college and life success!

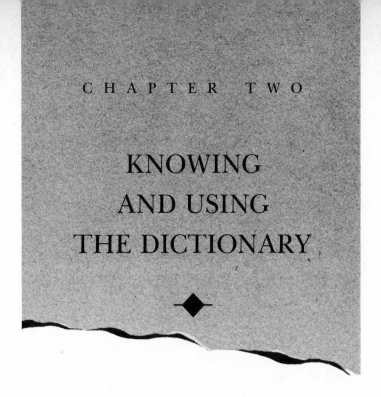

CHAPTER TWO

KNOWING AND USING THE DICTIONARY

Think of the dictionary as a tool. True, it is only one of the tools of the language user, but it is the most fundamental. Like all tools, the dictionary performs better as its user becomes more skilled. Prior to this time you may only have used the dictionary to verify the spelling or to find the meaning of a word. Now, however, you need to become more skillful. You are about to become an expert. You need to be aware of how a dictionary sets out its information and to realize that there are different types of dictionaries that offer different kinds of information in varying degrees of complexity. The brief outline that follows should help you to select the best tool for your job.

TYPES OF DICTIONARIES

Special Dictionaries

There are dictionaries that specialize in the vocabularies specific to the various disciplines, for example the *Harvard Dictionary of Music* and Taber's *Cyclopedic Medical Dictionary*. Such dictionaries give more limited definitions than regular dictionaries. That is, they list only those definitions that pertain to the specific field, and they include words that often will not be found even in an unabridged volume. Use such a dictionary when you cannot locate a word in a good unabridged dictionary. There are dictionaries specific to almost every field.

Oxford English Dictionary

Of the general dictionaries, the most complete is the *Oxford English Dictionary* (usually referred to as the OED), which consists of ten volumes covering the alphabet, with four volumes of updating information. The first portion of this extraordinary work was published in 1894, the ten volumes completed in 1928. The final volume of updating was completed in 1986. In addition to the usual information given for an entry—the pronunciation, part(s) of speech, etymology (history), and definition(s)—examples of usage over time are provided. For an enlightening view of how usage changes over time, look up a word of your choice. Don't forget to investigate the updating volumes also; the word you select might be "new."

Unabridged Dictionaries

Next in order of complexity are the unabridged dictionaries. These works list all (or nearly all) the words in the language. Volumes are not reprinted at each updating, so new words are often added as addenda in a separate section. These volumes give the word (called a main entry) with its derivatives (those words similar to it with different endings), the pronunciation(s), the part(s) of speech, and a full array of definitions accompanied by examples of usage where appropriate. Synonyms are given as well as references to related words.

Not all unabridged dictionaries are of the same quality. Size does not always indicate quality. One way to check the quality of a dictionary advertised as unabridged is to look up several words, ranging from easy to difficult, and see if full information, including examples, is given. The etymology, or history of the words, should be listed in some detail. Note, however, that dictionaries have strict space limitations and do not list the same information over and over. The complete etymology of a word usually appears only once—at the entry considered to be the base entry. Recommended unabridged dictionaries on the market are the Merriam-Webster *Webster's Third New International Dictionary*, the unabridged edition of the *Random House Dictionary of the English Language*, and *The World Book Dictionary*.

Desk Dictionaries

Next in size and complexity are the desk volumes, in some cases based on an unabridged work but with fewer words and examples of usage. A good desk volume will supply thousands of words, each with its pronunciation(s), part(s) of speech, derivatives, and definition(s). The definitions may not be as extensive as in an unabridged work, and examples of usage and usage notes may be limited. The etymology, however, should be as complete as that shown in the larger work. Desk volumes most suitable for college use are the Merriam-Webster *Webster's New Collegiate* (copyright 1977 and later), *The American Heritage Dictionary of the English Language, Webster's New World Dictionary of the American Language,* and the college edition of the *Random House Dictionary of the English Language. Webster's New World* is also available in paperback at a slightly reduced price.

Publishers update desk volume dictionaries regularly. You will want to use one that is no more than ten years old. In another analogy (comparison), we can say that a dictionary is a picture of the language as it exists at a given moment. And language is not a permanent thing but rather changes with use over time. You do not want to rely on an out-of-date "snapshot" as a reference tool.

A word of caution: The name *Webster* is in the public domain and may be used by anyone who produces a dictionary or reference work. Don't be fooled into thinking you are purchasing a quality work merely because it is called Webster's. Before you purchase, look at the work carefully to see if it offers all of the features listed above with reasonable completeness.

Paperback Dictionaries

Next in size and quality are paperback dictionaries. These usually provide information limited to pronunciation(s), part(s) of speech, and selected definitions. A few provide limited etymological information. Because college work requires a full range of definitions, paperback works are not recommended. They seldom include examples of usage or point out special usage problems. Also, as you become more skilled, you will need etymologies to help develop your concepts for the words. Most paperback dictionaries are not adequate tools for the serious college student. (However, as noted above, some standard desk dictionaries are available in paperback and should not be confused with the smaller paperbacks.)

The Thesaurus

Another tool often used by writers is the thesaurus. A thesaurus is a dictionary of synonyms and is labeled such by some publishers. Some thesauri are printed in alphabetical order, while others are grouped according to a classification system devised early in the nineteenth century by Peter Mark Roget. Whichever one you select is a matter of personal preference, but two comments are in order. First, the name *Roget* is in the public domain (like the name *Webster*), so even an inadequate work may carry that title. Second, a thesaurus provides *synonyms only, no definitions.* This means that if you are searching for synonyms of the word *passage,* you must recognize that they will be different depending on whether you mean "navigation" or "conversation." A thesaurus can be useful when used correctly, but do not try to use one as a substitute for a dictionary.

WHICH DEFINITION IS BEST?

Words by themselves have no meaning but only take on meaning as we attach concepts to them. That is, the word *chair* is only a sound until we have a picture in our minds of "chairness" and attach that picture, or concept, to the sound. If you already have the concept for a word in your mind, it is not too difficult to match the agreed-on word with that concept. Having once seen a table, you need only to be told what it is called, and that word becomes part of your vocabulary. One reason is that a table is a concrete object. It is more difficult to create concepts for abstract things, like faith or regret, particularly if you have never experienced them. To add to the problem, some concepts are varied and extensive. For example, some of the concepts (or definitions) of a simple word like *charge* are "to entrust with a duty," "to blame," "to postpone payment," "to attack violently," "to load (a gun)," "to excite or intensify," and "to fill." There are more verb definitions and even more noun definitions of *charge!* Attaching concepts to words can be very complicated indeed! All of this is not intended to discourage you but is intended to show you how you must form narrow or broad concepts and, in some instances, stretch your imagination to encompass the variety of ideas included within the word.

When you look up an unknown word in the dictionary, your task is to carefully examine the context that surrounds the word, then read all the recorded definitions and select the one that most nearly fits the author's use. If you are not sure of the author's meaning after one reading, read the material again until the likely meaning becomes clear. You cannot be sure you have the author's exact meaning, but you can proceed with thought and logic. So the answer to the question raised above is: *The best definition is the one that best fits the individual author's use.*

DENOTATIONS AND CONNOTATIONS

Although it is your responsibility as a user of language to form concepts for the words you use, you must be careful to not go beyond the definitions listed in the dictionary. A good dictionary will include the variety of agreed-on denotations of a word. *Denotations* are meanings "officially" attached to words. But many words also have *connotations*, or meanings that are suggested by a word and "unofficially" attached to it. Consider the word *work*. Although most dictionaries list many definitions for this word, it is safe to say that each individual attaches even more concepts to it! What do you think of when you think of work? Another example of the differences between denotations and connotations might be found in the word *football*. Denotations from the dictionary refer to games played by kicking and sometimes carrying a ball and include American football, British rugby, and soccer. Connotations of the word *football* may include thoughts of games attended in person or watched on television, so that football can come to mean excitement. Or if the thought of football fills you with boredom or annoyance, these may be the word's connotations for you.

But connotations are not attached to words only by individuals. Some groups of people have generally accepted connotations for certain words. For instance, in some societies the idea of fat has positive connotations. Fat people are considered more attractive, and body fat is a sign of prosperity and wealth. In other societies, fat has a negative connotation. A person who is fat is considered unfashionable, and body fat is thought to be a sign of poor health. Remember then, as you create concepts for new words or attach words to previously established concepts that you must take care to distinguish between the official definitions, or *denotations,* and the unofficial "tag-ons," or *connotations.*

USING THE DICTIONARY

The information on the following pages will help you interpret the dictionary definitions that accompany each of the words you will study so that you can work efficiently in this book.* Dictionaries differ somewhat in the way they present material, and the entries here may be slightly different from those in the dictionary you have been using. Look these pages over carefully and return to them if you experience any problems with the dictionary portion of the exercises.

Etymologies

One thing you may not have experienced previously is reading the history of the word, or the *etymology*, which is found between square brackets [ ]. Reading the information between the brackets will tell you the "family tree" of the word. (In the dictionary used here, the etymology appears at the end

---

*Dictionary entries given with the exercises for each word are taken from the text of *The World Book Dictionary* as needed, with the word being introduced given first and other pertinent or necessary words added after. Wherever possible, an etymology is included. If, in the etymology of a word, we are directed to "see etym. under _____," and we feel it would be useful to you, we have added that etymology to this text. Occasionally, the dictionary directs us to a synonym study with the indication "**SYN:** See syn. under _____." If we believe this synonym study might be useful to you in the exercises we provide, we include it also. All rearrangements of *The World Book Dictionary* text are made by special permission of World Book, Inc.

of the definitions.) Because a great number of English words have Latin and Greek roots, many people find that learning roots (nouns, verbs, or adjectives in the original language) and prefixes (usually prepositions) creates a basic core of knowledge that is useful in analyzing unknown words.

Read the etymology of each word carefully. When you note the meaning of a root or prefix, try to select an easy word to serve as a "seed word" in your memory. For example, in looking up the word *deposition* (the giving of testimony under oath), a careful reading of the etymology shows that the word comes from Latin. *De* means "down" and *pos* means "to put or place." It comes from the Latin verb *ponere*, which has the forms *pon-*, *pos-*, and *posit-*. (Compare this with English verbs that also have other forms, such as *sing, sang, sung* or *eat, ate, eaten* and so on.) You might use *deposit* as your seed word, since it is easy to remember. Then, if you were to come on the sentence

> The author's granddaughter selected Oxford's Bodleian Library as the *repository* for his works,

you would know that the word had something to do with "putting or placing," and by adding other clues from the reading, you can deduce the meaning of the sentence.

You can begin creating your core of knowledge in this book by reading the etymology when it is included with the introduced word. Use the information given to strengthen your concept of the word and other words related to it. In Appendix A you will find all of the Latin and Greek combining forms (the roots and prefixes) that are found in the etymologies of the 225 words introduced in this book. In some cases, the origins are other than Latin or Greek, and those prefixes and roots are also included. Use the material in Appendix A to help build concepts based on the family trees of the words.

HOW TO USE THE DICTIONARY
ENTRIES GIVEN IN THIS TEXT

Main Entry Main entries are words or phrases in heavy type that extend into the margin.

sub|li|ma|tion (sub´lə mā´shən), *n.* **1** the act or process of sublimating or subliming; purification: *This direct transition from solid to vapor is called sublimation* (Sears and Zemansky). **2** the resulting product or state, especially, mental elevation or exaltation: *that enthusiastic sublimation which is the source of greatness and energy* (Thomas L. Peacock). **3** the highest stage or purest form of a thing. **4** a chemical sublimate.

Pronunciation and Stress These are found in parentheses following the main-entry word. Be sure to

co|vert (*adj.* 1, *n.* 3 kō´vərt, kuv´ərt; *adj.* 2,3; *n.* 1, 2 kuv´ərt, kō´vərt), *adj.*, *n.* —*adj.* **1** kept from sight; secret; hidden; disguised: *The children cast covert glances at the box of candy they*

read the pronunciation key carefully. It is printed at the back of this book.

were told not to touch. SYN: concealed. See syn. under **secret**. **2** *Law.* married and under the authority or protection of her husband. **3** *Rare.* covered; sheltered.
—*n.* **1a** a hiding place; shelter. **b** a thicket in which wild animals or birds hide. **2** a covering. **3** = covert cloth.

Parts of Speech These are abbreviated and italicized following the pronunciation. The parts of speech and their abbreviations are as follows: noun, *n.*; verb, *v.*; transitive verb, *v.t.*; intransitive verb, *v.i.*; pronoun, *pron.*; adjective, *adj.*; adverb, *adv.*; preposition, *prep.*; conjunction, *conj.*; interjection, *interj.*

aug|ment (*v.* ôg ment′; *n.* ôg′ment), *v., n.* —*v.t.* **1** to make greater in size, number, amount, or degree; enlarge: *The king augmented his power by taking over rights that had belonged to the nobles.* SYN: amplify, swell. See syn. under **increase**. **2** to add an augment to. —*v.i.* to become greater; increase; grow; swell: *The sound of traffic augments during the morning rush hour.*
—*n.* **1** a prefix or lengthened vowel marking the past tenses of verbs in Greek and Sanskrit. **2** *Obsolete.* increase; augmentation.
[< Late Latin *augmentāre* < Latin *augmentum* an increase < *augēre* to increase] —**aug|ment′a|ble**, *adj.* —**aug|ment′er, aug|men′tor**, *n.*

Inflections These show any irregular endings. If a noun is made plural in any way except by adding an "s" or if the past tense and present participle of a verb are irregular, the dictionary will show the irregular endings. Comparative forms of adjectives and adverbs are also given.

com|pen|di|um (kəm pen′dē əm), *n., pl.* **-di|ums**, **-di|a** (-dē ə). a short summary of the main points or ideas of a larger work; abridgment; condensation. SYN: abstract, précis, epitome. [< Latin *compendium* a shortening; a weighing together < *com-* in addition + *pendere* weigh]

per|son|i|fy (pər son′ə fī), *v.t.*, **-fied, -fy|ing. 1** to be a type of; embody: *Satan personifies evil.* SYN: exemplify. **2** to regard or represent as a person. We often personify the sun and moon, referring to the sun as *he* and the moon as *she*. We personify time and nature when we refer to *Father Time* and *Mother Nature*. *Greek philosophy has a tendency to personify ideas* (Benjamin Jowett). [probably patterned on French *personnifier* < *personne* person + *-fier* -fy] —**per|son′i|fi′er**, *n.*

Definitions These are the meanings of the entries. Words that have more than one meaning have numbered definitions. When both a number and a letter are given, it means that the numbered definition is followed by one or more definitions that are closely related to it.

sol|vent (sol′vənt), *adj., n.* —*adj.* **1** able to pay all one owes: *A bankrupt firm is not solvent.* **2** able to dissolve: *Gasoline is a solvent liquid that removes grease spots.*
—*n.* **1** a substance, usually a liquid, that can dissolve other substances: *Water is a solvent of sugar and salt.* **2** a thing that solves, explains, or settles.
[< Latin *solvēns, -entis*, present participle of *solvere* loosen (used in *rem solvere* to free one's property and person from debt)] —**sol′vent|ly**, *adv.*

Illustrative Sentences and Phrases These are set off from the definition by a colon and help show the actual usage of the word.

in|dict|ment (in dīt′mənt), *n.* **1** a formal written accusation, especially on the recommendation of a grand jury: *an indictment for murder. When an indictment does come down, the accused individuals will have an opportunity at trial to defend their innocence* (New York Times). *I do not know the method of drawing up an indictment against a whole people* (Edmund Burke). **2** an indicting or being indicted; accusation: *Mr. Bond has written . . . a perfectly stunning indictment of the welfare state* (New Yorker).

Restrictive or Usage Labels These indicate that a particular word is not

sub|jec|tive (səb jek′tiv), *adj.* **1** existing in the mind; belonging to the person thinking rather than to the object thought of. Ideas and opinions

part of standard speech or writing or that it has special meaning in certain circumstances. Among the labels used in this dictionary are the following:

- *Archaic*—no longer in general use but found in special contexts such as law or scripture.
- *Foreign language*—such as Latin or French.
- *Obsolete*—words found only in writings of an earlier time or writings that imitate them.
- *Professional terms*—terms pertaining to arts, sciences, or technology.

Run-On Words These are formed by adding suffixes to the main-entry word. They appear in boldface type after the main-entry words from which they are formed. They are not defined because the meaning is clear from the main-entry definitions.

Etymology This traces the word's origin and development to its present use. In this dictionary, etymologies appear in square brackets following entry definitions. Two important symbols are <, meaning "derived from" or "taken from," and +, meaning "and." Some words are *doublets*, and this fact is noted in the etymology. (See Appendix B for more about doublets.)

are subjective; facts are objective. **2** about the thoughts and feelings, as of the speaker, writer, or painter; personal. Lyric poetry is subjective, expressing the feelings of the poet; narrative poetry is generally objective, telling a story. **3** *Grammar.* being or serving as the subject of a sentence; nominative. **4** *Psychology.* **a** originating within or dependent on the mind of the individual rather than an external object. **b** = introspective. **5** *Philosophy.* **a** of or relating to reality as perceived by the mind, as distinct from reality as independent of the mind. **b** influenced by an individual's state of mind: *a subjective perception or apprehension.* **c** having to do with the substance of anything, as opposed to its qualities and attributes. **6** *Medicine.* (of symptoms) discoverable by the patient only. **7** *Obsolete.* of or having to do with someone who is subject to rule or control. —**sub|jec′tive|ly,** *adv.* —**sub|jec′tive-ness,** *n.*

de|us ex ma|chi|na (dē′əs eks mak′ə nə), *Latin.* **1** a person, god, or event that comes just in time to solve a difficulty in a story, play, or other literary or dramatic work, especially when the coming is contrived or artificial: *There is … Ferral, a French representative of big business, whom Malraux uses as the novel's deus ex machina* (New Yorker). (*Figurative.*) *Mr. Galbraith rejects the notion that somewhere in Wall Street there was a deus ex machina who somehow engineered the boom and bust* (New York Times). **2** (literally) a god from a machine (referring to a mechanical device used in the ancient Greek and Roman theater by which actors who played the parts of gods were lowered from above the stage to end or resolve the dramatic action).

as|sid|u|ous (ə sij′ù əs), *adj.* working hard and steadily; careful and attentive; diligent: *No error escaped his assiduous attention to detail.* **SYN:** steady, unremitting, untiring. [< Latin *assiduus* (with English *-ous*) < *assidēre* sit at < *ad-* at + *sedēre* sit] —**as|sid′u|ous|ly,** *adv.* —**as|sid′u-ous|ness,** *n.*

vic|ar (vik′ər), *n.* **1** in the Church of England: **a** the minister of a parish, who is paid a salary by the man to whom the tithes are paid. **b** a person acting as parish priest in place of the actual rector. **2** in the Protestant Episcopal Church: **a** a clergyman in charge of a chapel in a parish. **b** a clergyman acting for a bishop, in a church where the bishop is rector or in a mission. **3** in the Roman Catholic Church: **a** a clergyman who represents the pope or a bishop. **b** the Pope, as the earthly representative of God or Christ. **4** a person acting in place of another, especially in administrative functions; representative; vicegerent. [< Anglo-French *vikere, vicare,* Old French *vicaire,* learned borrowing from Latin *vicārius* (originally) substituted < *vicis* change, alteration. See etym. of doublet **vicarious**.]

vi|car|i|ous (vī kãr′ē əs, vi-), *adj.* **1** done or suffered for others: *vicarious work, vicarious punishment.* **2** felt by sharing in the experience of another: *The invalid received vicarious pleasure* from reading travel stories. **3** taking the place of another; doing the work of another: *a vicarious agent.* **4** delegated: *vicarious authority.* **5** based upon the substitution of one person for another: *this vicarious structure of society, based upon what others do for us.* **6** *Physiology.* denoting the performance by or through one organ of functions normally discharged by another, as for example in vicarious menstruation. [< Latin *vicārius* (with English *-ous*) substituted < *vicis* a turn, change, substitution. See etym. of doublet **vicar**.] —**vi|car′i|ous|ly,** *adv.* —**vi|car′i|ous|ness,** *n.*

Definition of *doublet*:

(An asterisk * means that a word has an illustration.)

*dou|blet (dub′lit), *n.* **1** a man's close-fitting jacket, with or without sleeves. Men in Europe wore doublets from the 1400's to the 1600's. **2** a pair of two similar or equal things; couple. **3** one of a pair. **4** one of two or more different words in a language derived from the same original source but coming by different routes. *Example:* 1) *aptitude* and *attitude. Aptitude* came into English as a direct borrowing from Late Latin *aptitudo, aptitudinis.* However this Latin word was taken into Italian in the form *attitudine,* which was later further changed to *attitude* in French, from which it came into English. 2) *fragile* and *frail. Fragile* came into English as a direct borrowing from the Latin *fragilis.* However, the word *fragilis* changed to *frele* (or *fraile*) in French, from which it came into English in the form *frail.* **5** an imitation gem made of two pieces of glass or crystal with a layer of color between them. **6** *Printing, U.S.* a word or phrase set a second time by mistake. **doublets,** two dice thrown that show the same number on each side facing up. [< Old French *doublet* (originally) a "double" fabric < *doubler* to double + *-et* -et]

*doublet
definition 1

Synonyms These are words that have the same, or nearly the same, meaning. A synonym you can use in place of the word defined appears immediately after the definition and is labeled **SYN.** A synonym study that helps you select the best word is labeled *—Syn.*

ac|ces|si|ble (ak ses′ə bəl), *adj.* **1** easy to get at; easy to reach or enter: *tools readily accessible on an open rack. A telephone should be put where it will be accessible.* SYN: convenient. **2** that can be entered or reached: *This rocky island is accessible only by helicopter.* SYN: approachable. **3** that can be obtained: *Not many facts about the kidnaping were accessible.* SYN: available. **accessible to,** capable of being influenced by; susceptible to: *An open-minded person is accessible to reason.* —**ac|ces′si|ble|ness,** *n.* —**ac|ces′si|bly,** *adv.*

per|ti|nent (pėr′tə nənt), *adj.* having to do with what is being considered; relating to the matter in hand; to the point; relevant: *If your question is pertinent, I will answer it.* [< Latin *pertinēns, -entis,* present participle of *pertinēre;* see etym. under **pertain**] —**per′ti|nent|ly,** *adv.* —*Syn.* **Pertinent, relevant** mean relating to the matter in hand. **Pertinent** means directly to the point of the matter, belonging properly and fitting to what is being considered and helping to explain or clarify it: *A summary of the events leading up to this situation would be pertinent information.* **Relevant** means having some bearing on the problem or enough connection with it to have some meaning or importance: *Even incidents seeming unimportant in themselves might be relevant.*

Usage Notes This dictionary supplies notes to help clarify the use of some often misused words. Usage notes are indicated by a boldface arrow.

ad|ja|cent (ə jā′sənt), *adj.* lying near or close, or contiguous (to); neighboring or adjoining; bordering; next: *The house adjacent to ours has been sold.* ꜱʏɴ: abutting. [< Latin *adjacēns, -entis,* present participle of *adjacēre* lie near < *ad-* near + *jacēre* lie²] —**ad|ja′cent|ly,** *adv.*
▶**Adjacent** means lying near or neighboring, but not necessarily touching.

Figurative Usage Definitions and illustrative sentences or phrases are labeled "figurative" when the word defined is used out of its usual, matter-of-fact sense.

cat|a|clysm (kat′ə kliz əm), *n.* **1** a great flood, earthquake, or any sudden, violent change in the earth. ꜱʏɴ: calamity. **2** *Figurative.* any violent change or upheaval: *Atomic warfare between nations would be a cataclysm for all mankind. ... a day that has been designated by historians of the Wall Street cataclysm of that year as Black Thursday* (New York Times). [< Latin *cataclysmos* < Greek *kataklysmós* flood, ultimately < *kata-* down + *klýzein* wash]

CHAPTER THREE

CONTEXT CLUES
AND VERBAL
ANALYSES

◆

USING CONTEXT CLUES

Context clues are probably the most commonly used means of understanding unknown or partially known words. To use context clues effectively, you must try to understand the writer's point of view and his style as well as considering the subject matter of the written work. For example, the mournful tone of Edgar Allan Poe is unlike the brisk tone set by Rudyard Kipling. The vocabulary and sentence patterns used by Charles Dickens are different from those used by Ernest Hemingway. But the importance of style and vocabulary extend beyond literature. If you are reading a biology book and come to an unknown word, your guess about its meaning would be different from the guess you would make if you were reading an auto repair manual. Your use of the context clues will be influenced by your knowledge of the subject matter and your understanding of just how the author is trying to transmit his message to you.

In trying to grasp the meaning of an unknown word, you must look at all the other elements of the written work. Not all sentences give enough context clues to indicate the meaning of the unknown word, but you must use whatever clues are given. In the sentence

He had an obsequious manner,

the meaning of the word *obsequious* is not clear. It could refer to mood: Is he happy or sad? It could refer to style: Is he formal or informal? It could refer to conduct: Is he bold or shy? There are many possibilities. You cannot be sure from the sentence just what obsequious means, but you do know that it refers to some characteristic of a person. Other clues about the person would have to come from other sentences. If the sentence is changed to

> His obsequious manner made his superiors take advantage of him and made his comrades scornful,

you are now able to detect the negative qualities of the word and get a better picture of the person described.

TYPES OF CONTEXT CLUES

Context clues may be expressed in many ways. They may appear as *examples*, as in the sentence

> She dressed in a tawdry fashion, using cheap laces, glass beads, and poor-quality clothing.

Or they may *restate* or *reinforce*, as in

> He was a stentorian man, with a voice so loud that the neighbors complained.

Context clues may indicate *contrast*, as in

> John had sworn fealty to his master, so all were surprised when he refused to obey the order.

Another type of context clue is one of *general information,* or *experience*, where your knowledge, experience, or guesswork helps you get the meaning of the unknown word. In the sentence

> Jake is a debonair bachelor, enjoying the southern California good life,

you can use experience (if you have it) or your knowledge of southern California life-styles and of the life a bachelor is supposed to lead to deduce that debonair means lighthearted and carefree.

In addition to these meaning, or *semantic*, clues, *graphic* clues are often supplied. Occasionally the meaning of the word will be given and set off by commas or dashes. For example,

> Origami, the oriental art of paper folding, can be an interesting pastime.

In other cases, a capital letter may give you a clue that the word used is a proper, rather than a common, noun and so has special meaning. The sentence

Charles Bradlaugh was the most formidable atheist on the Secularist platform,

suggests that there was a political party (indicated by the word platform)
called "Secularist" (indicated by the capital letter) to which an atheist named
Charles Bradlaugh belonged.

As a reader, then, you must look for meaning in all of the words, using
whatever background information you possess. As a writer, you owe it to
your readers to supply enough context clues to show them clearly your
meaning. In this book you will use context clues both ways. In the reading
selections you must pick up every available hint, and in writing your own
sentences, you must give enough clues to show that you understand—and
are practicing—the meanings of the words. A good dictionary will show an
early definition of *clue* (also spelled clew) to be "a ball of thread or yarn to be
unwound to serve as a guide through a labyrinth or maze." The *Oxford
English Dictionary* includes examples of usage, one of which is meaningful to
us as readers and writers: "I will give you a clue of thread, and by that
perhaps you may find your way out again" (Kingsley, 1855). Be sure you
use the context clues given to you by the writers, and be sure you give them
to your readers!

CONTEXT CLUE EXERCISES

To give yourself some practice using context clues, complete the following
three exercises:

1. Try to define these words. Do not look them up in a dictionary.
   a. moiety
   b. eschew
   c. penultimate
   You can see that without any context to give clues, it is very hard
   to determine the meaning of a word.
2. Now try to define the same words after some context clues are
   supplied.
   a. John inherited the *moiety* of his grandfather's estate, while his
      sister inherited the other half.
      Meaning of *moiety* in this sentence: _____
   b. Convincing reports of the dangers of tobacco have led many
      smokers to *eschew* cigarettes.
      Meaning of *eschew* in this sentence: _____
   c. "Y" is the *penultimate* letter of the English alphabet.
      Meaning of *penultimate* in this sentence: _____

ANSWERS TO EXERCISE 2

In sentence *a*, *moiety* means "half." If John's sister inherited "the other half," John inherited the first half. *Moiety* can also mean "component" or "part," so you must use context clues to decide which meaning best fits the author's intent.

Eschew, in sentence *b*, means "to avoid habitually," or "to shun." Reports of the health hazards of smoking have made some smokers give up the habit.

Penultimate, in sentence *c*, means "next to last." You know that "z" is the last letter, so "y" is the next to last.

3. In the following sentences, a real word has been replaced by a nonsense word. Using the context clues supplied in each sentence, try to determine the meaning of the underlined nonsense word.
   a. The city council said today that a small chemical spill that occurred Tuesday probably would not glubblub the local water supply.
      Meaning of glubblub in this sentence: _____
   b. Mrs. Smith was found to be a dependable parent and so was awarded dreplam of the children.
      Meaning of dreplam in this sentence: _____
   c. If you want to succeed on this diet, you will have to give up chiduks such as pasta, bread, and breakfast cereal.
      Meaning of chiduks in this sentence: _____

ANSWERS TO EXERCISE 3

You can see that the meaning of glubblub in sentence *a* has something to do with damage. A better word for damage done to a water supply is pollution, so the verb that fits here is *pollute*.

Sentence *b* gives you only one choice: Mrs. Smith gets *custody* of the children.

Sentence *c* gives you examples of *carbohydrates*. If you have heard or read much about dieting, you probably know about these.

USING VERBAL ANALOGIES

An analogy is a resemblance, or a similarity. For instance, we say that the heart is a pump because there are certain similarities between the two entities; thus we make an analogy between a heart and a pump. In another analogy we say that an atom is a miniature solar system. This comparison helps us realize the great distances between the component parts of the atom, and thus the analogy is used to improve our understanding. It is essential that we recognize just what the resemblance is between the two items in an analogy; we must understand their relationship.

Although an analogy is a comparison, the meaning of *analogy* is some-what different; the concept is more specific. A comparison may include differences as well as similarities. An analogy is concerned only with similar-ities and, frequently, with a *single* similarity. To return to one of our exam-ples: We know that an atom is not really very much like the solar system. It would be a waste of time to compare them carefully, and yet we can gain understanding of the atom's structure if the analogy is presented to us.

In addition to general analogies, words may be set out in what are called "verbal analogies." *Verbal analogies* are words, set up in pairs, that have some kind of relationship. For example, the words *hot* and *cold* are opposites, and realizing this relationship, you would be able to select two more words that are also opposites; if given a word such as *up*, you could supply *down* to complete the analogy. Written in standard form, this anal-ogy would look like this:

hot : cold :: up : _____
a. warm   b. down   c. fall   d. temperature

You would, of course, select "b. down" from the supplied alternatives. Another way of setting out this verbal analogy is like this:

hot : cold :: _____ : _____
a. warm : hot   b. up : down   c. fall : down   d. water : wet

You would again select *b* as the correct answer, because it has the same *relationship* as the first two words. They, too, are opposites. A third way of setting out this verbal analogy would be like this:

hot : up :: cold : _____
a. warm   b. down   c. fall   d. temperature

Again the answer is *b*, and the relationship is the same, but the analogy is set up between the first word (*hot*) and the third word (*cold*), and then the second word (*up*) and the fourth word (*down*). Now you *might* see this relationship as one of description or analogy. (Yes, it's true. The relation-ship in a verbal analogy may be *analogy*.) When something is hot, we think of it as up (temperature), and when something is cold, we think of it as down. This relationship gives you the same answer, *b*. As you can imagine, there are a great many possible relationships.

IMPORTANCE OF VERBAL ANALOGIES

Understanding verbal analogies is important to you as a student. Being able to see relationships will strengthen your ability to reason, which is an essen-tial skill. In addition to increasing your general reasoning ability, you will want to understand verbal analogies in order to do well on tests that are used to evaluate your verbal skills. The ability to complete verbal analogies is learned. The less experience you have had, the more you will need to practice. Perhaps you can think of it as a mental tennis game. Practice will improve your score!

VERBAL ANALOGY EXERCISES

Some of the exercises in this book ask you to complete verbal analogies. To give yourself some practice, complete the following activities. (Answers follow each segment of the activity.)

Complete the following verbal analogies by placing the correct words in the blanks. In the first five verbal analogies, you need to add only one word to complete the relationship set up by the words in columns 1 and 2. Use the words supplied after number 5, labeled "column 4."

1		2		3		4
1. early	:	late	::	ahead	:	_____
2. fast	:	slow	::	run	:	_____
3. front	:	back	::	street	:	_____
4. light	:	dark	::	day	:	_____
5. past	:	future	::	before	:	_____

column 4—after, alley, behind, crawl, night

The first segment is fairly easy. In number 1, *early* and *late* are *opposite* elements of time that can also be expressed as the opposites, *ahead* and *behind*. In number 2, the relationship is again one of *opposites*, so the word in the blank should be *crawl*. The relationship in number 3 is that of *position*. A *street* is in *front*, and an *alley* is in *back*. Number 4 sets out a relationship of *characteristics*: *Light* is a characteristic of *day*, while *dark* is a characteristic of *night*. (If you think of these as opposites, this will give you the right answer, too, but you should be aware of the *characteristic* relationship.) Number 5 sets out a *sequence*. *Past* evolves into *future*, while *before* evolves into *after*. You might think of these as opposites also, but you should know that *sequence* is a possible relationship in verbal analogies.

In this second group, numbers 6 through 10, you must supply words in columns 3 and 4 that have the same relationship as the words in columns 1 and 2. Use the words supplied after number 10, labeled "column 3" and "column 4."

1		2		3		4
6. honey	:	bee	::	_____	:	_____
7. go in	:	go out	::	_____	:	_____
8. day	:	night	::	_____	:	_____
9. bottom	:	top	::	_____	:	_____
10. food	:	body	::	_____	:	_____

column 3—fuel, enter, below, book, dawn
column 4—above, writer, twilight, leave, engine

After practice on the first segment, the second segment should not be too difficult. In number 6, the relationship between *honey* and *bee* is that of *creation* and *creator*. Fill in columns 3 and 4 with *book* and *writer*. *You must not reverse these*. The relationship must be consistent from one pair to the other pair. The relationship in number 7 is *definition*. *Go in* defines *enter* and *go out* defines *leave*. In number 8, the relationship is of *sequence*. The beginning of *day* is *dawn*, and the beginning of *night* is *twilight*. Number 9 sets out a *position* relationship: *Bottom* is *below*, while *top* is *above*. *Food* is used by the *body* to produce energy, much like *fuel* is used by an *engine*, so the relationship in number 10 is *similar use*.

In the third group, 11 through 15, you must supply words in columns 2, 3, and 4. Using only the words supplied for the columns indicated, you must create an analogy on each line that has the same relationship for each pair of words.

	1		**2**		**3**		**4**
11.	ink	:	_____	::	_____	:	_____
12.	play	:	_____	::	_____	:	_____
13.	iron	:	_____	::	_____	:	_____
14.	knife	:	_____	::	_____	:	_____
15.	sand	:	_____	::	_____	:	_____

column 2—desert, pen, toy, cut, steel
column 3—gun, sand, paint, work, wax
column 4—brush, tool, candle, shoot, glass

In this last segment, you had many choices so you needed to think through all the possibilities before you made a final decision. The answers to number 11 are *pen*, *paint*, and *brush*. The relationship is *medium and implement*; we use ink in a pen and paint with a brush. In number 12, the answers are *toy*, *work*, and *tool*, showing the primary *function* of the object given. Number 13 deals with a *refinement process*: *Iron* is a raw product that can be refined into *steel*, while *sand* can be processed into *glass*. A *functional* relationship exists in number 14: A *knife cuts*, and a *gun shoots*. Using the only remaining words, we fill in number 15 with *desert*, *wax*, and *candle*. Do you see the relationship? It is *general–specific*. *Sand* is a general term, and *desert* is a specific kind of sand. *Wax* is a general term, and *candle* is a specific form of wax.

PART TWO

ESSENTIALS
FOR COLLEGE
SUCCESS

CHAPTER 4
EFFICIENT READING
AND LEARNING STRATEGIES

CHAPTER 5
LIBRARY RESOURCES AND THEIR USE

CHAPTER FOUR

EFFICIENT READING AND LEARNING STRATEGIES

◆

VOCABULARY SELF-EVALUATION

The following words will be introduced in this reading selection. Place a check mark (√) in front of any that you know thoroughly and use in your speech and writing. Place a question mark (?) in front of any that you recognize but do not use yourself.

_____ adhere	_____ deleterious	_____ linguistic
_____ articulate	_____ diligent	_____ optimum
_____ assimilate	_____ discern	_____ procrastinate
_____ cogent	_____ erudite	_____ proximity
_____ competence	_____ impediment	_____ retrieval

LEARNING TO READ CRITICALLY AND STUDY EFFECTIVELY

Succeeding in college requires more than just making good grades in high school and doing well on college entrance examinations. The academic environment in college is much different from that in high school, and therefore more efficient reading and learning strategies are crucial for success in college. Such strategies can help you approach learning systematically; as a consequence, you should become more successful and confident as a college student.

TAKING NOTES FROM LECTURES

Probably the most important activity of a student is to organize and retain information, or academic content, presented in a variety of formats. In many classes you will receive the majority of information from an erudite[1] professor in a scholarly lecture presentation. The professor is usually an expert in his field and knowledgeable about his subject, and therefore efficient note-taking strategies are essential. You will need to be diligent,[2] or careful, in listening to the professor and in organizing key information and ideas using a system that will provide for fast retrieval[3] and recall. You are usually required to know the information presented in the lecture and demonstrate your knowledge later on some type of examination.

We also know from learning theory that reviewing your lecture notes within twenty-four hours after the lecture will help you retain the information longer. Often students procrastinate[4] and delay reviewing their notes. Because of the principle of proactive interference in memory, it is more difficult to relearn old information because it has not been transferred to your long-term memory through reinforcement techniques such as recitation and regular review.

READING FROM TEXT AND THINKING CRITICALLY

Reading is a complex psychological and linguistic,[5] or language, process that incorporates prior knowledge, background, and experience. College reading, also known as "constructive reading," is an active process that requires you to relate what you learn to what you may already know.

Learning to discern[6] key ideas is an important skill when reading a textbook. Other crucial elements in learning from texts are recognizing the textbook structure, identifying important details, and relating the content to information you received in the lecture.

The optimum[7] learning situation is one in which the classroom lecture corresponds to the textbook chapters you have been assigned to read. Not every course is structured this way, however, and strategies that help you link information from a variety of sources—lecture, textbook reading, guest speakers, field trips, labs, and so on—will be most valuable.

Learning to be a critical thinker by analyzing the author's ideas, comparing and contrasting information in each paragraph, and making judgments on what you read will help you assimilate[8] ideas more effectively. A number of note-taking and textbook-mastery systems have been developed to help you organize course information. Or you may be able to develop your own systems once you have analyzed both your needs and the lecture and reading requirements. Most colleges and universities offer courses in academic reading and learning for this purpose.

PREPARING FOR AND TAKING EXAMINATIONS

There will be many opportunities for you to demonstrate your competence,[9] or ability, in a particular course. Occasionally you will need to clearly articulate[10] your ideas in an oral discussion or classroom presentation. Most often you will take written examinations. Many of these are the objective type, which include multiple-choice, true-false, short completion, and matching-item questions. At other times you will be tested in a subjective, or essay, format. Most essay examinations require that you can present your ideas about a topic with the vocabulary or terminology appropriate to the particular field of study. You will also need to present a cogent,[11] or valid, argument in your essay response to demonstrate your comprehensive knowledge of the issues related to the topic.

MANAGING TIME EFFICIENTLY

One of the most important strategies for the contemporary student is managing time efficiently. Most students today are combining their educations with jobs and therefore have multiple responsibilities. These additional responsibilities can create an impediment,[12] or obstacle, in achieving success in college.

Analyzing your time demands and then developing an efficient time-management system that you adhere[13] to on a regular basis can make you feel more in control of your life.

A large number of students are commuters who do not live in close proximity[14] to either their college campus or work location. For these students, commuting time would be an important factor to include in any time-management system and to consider when planning classes and study time.

Finally, devoting too much time to either school or work could be deleterious,[15] or harmful, to your health. Many students neither take care of themselves properly nor allow time for relaxing and exercising. Be sure to provide time on a regular basis for such activities, as this is one more way to help you develop the necessary strategies for success in the academic environment. ◆

PRETEST

Select words from this list and write them in the blanks to complete the sentences.

adhere	deleterious	linguistic
articulate	diligent	optimum
assimilate	discern	procrastinate
cogent	erudite	proximity
competence	impediment	retrieval

1. When you show how qualified you are, you are demonstrating your
   _____ .

2. It is difficult to _____ new information when you are
   sleepy or ill.

3. A learned or scholarly teacher is one who is _____ .

4. College and adult reading is a complex _____ process that
   demands sophisticated thinking skills on the part of the reader.

5. Having an apartment across the street from school is an example of
   living in _____ to campus.

6. A student who is hard working and persistent can be described as
   _____ .

7. Closely following a daily schedule that you have developed means that
   you are about to _____ to it.

8. A persevering student is one who can overcome the
   _____ to learning that can occasionally occur.

9. The _____ of important information from class lectures
   requires an efficient note-taking system.

10. It is not unusual to _____ when studying for an exam until
    the day before it is scheduled.

11. It is difficult to _____ the most important ideas in a class
    when you have had no previous experience with the subject.

12. Poor dietary habits and lack of sufficient sleep could prove to be
    _____ to your health.

13. Learning to _____ your ideas is important in classes that
    require student participation and interaction through group discus-
    sions and oral presentations.

14. A(n) _____ argument presented in an essay exam is one
    that is both valid and convincing.

15. The _____ arrangement is one that is the most favorable,
    such as a lecture that corresponds to the assigned readings.

Answers to this pretest are in Appendix E.

Unless your instructor tells you to do otherwise, complete the exercises for each word that you missed on the pretest. The words, with their
meanings and exercises, are in alphabetical order. The superscript numbers indicate where the words appeared in the reading selection so that you
can refer to them when necessary. There are several types of exercises, but
for each word you will be asked to write a sentence using context clues. (See
Chapter 3 if you need information about how to create context clues.) You
are also asked to perform some activity that will help you make your concept of the word personal. *Complete this activity thoughtfully, for creating a
personalized concept of the word will help you remember it in the future.*

Answers to all the exercises are at the end of the exercise segment.

EXERCISES

Adhere[13]

ad|here (ad hir'), *v.i.*, **-hered, -her|ing. 1** to stick fast; remain attached (to): *Mud adheres to your shoes. Paint adheres best to a clean, dry surface.* **SYN:** cling. See syn. under **stick**[2]. **2** to hold closely or firmly (to): *He adheres to his ideas even when they are proved wrong. We adhered to our plan in spite of the storm.* **SYN:** cleave, persevere. **3** to be devoted or attached (to); be a follower or upholder; give allegiance (to a party, leader, or belief): *Many people adhere to the church of their parents.* **4** *Obsolete.* to agree. [< Latin *adhaerēre* stick to < *ad-* to + *haerēre* cling] —**ad|her'er**, *n.*

1. Which of the numbered dictionary definitions of *adhere* best fits the word's use in the reading selection? _____

2. If you *adhere* to an idea, you probably
   _____ a. clarify a point.   _____ c. become attached to it.
   _____ b. reject it.   _____ d. discern its parts.

3. What might you most likely *adhere* to?
   _____ a. a schedule   _____ c. a chair or couch
   _____ b. food   _____ d. glue

4. Describe the time-management system that you *adhere* to on a regular basis. If you do not have one, do you plan on developing one? If so, what kind?

   _____

   _____

5. Write a sentence correctly using *adhere*. (Be sure to include context clues to show you understand the meaning of the word.)

   _____

   _____

Articulate[10]

ar|tic|u|late (*adj., n.* är tik'yə lit; *v.* är tik'yə lāt), *adj., v.,* **-lat|ed, -lat|ing**, *n.* —*adj.* **1** spoken in distinct syllables or words: *A baby cries and gurgles but does not use articulate speech.* **SYN:** clear, intelligible. **2** able to put one's thoughts into words easily and clearly: *Julia is the most articulate of the sisters.* **3** made up of distinct parts; distinct. **4** having joints; jointed; segmented. *The backbone is an articulate structure.*
—*v.t.* **1** to speak distinctly; express in clear sounds and words: *The speaker was careful to articulate his words so that everyone in the room could understand him.* **SYN:** enunciate. **2** to unite by joints: *The two bones are articulated like a hinge.* —*v.i.* **1** to express oneself in words: *Radio and television announcers are trained to articulate clearly.* **SYN:** enunciate. **2** to fit together in a joint: *After his knee was injured, he was lame because the bones did not articulate well.*
—*n.* any invertebrate having the body and limbs composed of jointed segments.
[< Latin *articulātus*, past participle of *articulāre* (probably) divide into single joints < *articulus* article] —**ar|tic'u|late|ly**, *adv.* —**ar|tic'u|late|ness**, *n.* —**ar|tic'u|la'tor**, *n.*

1. If you *articulate* an idea, you
_____ a. present it clearly.   _____ c. speak distinctly.
_____ b. clarify a point.   _____ d. ignore it.

2. Which professionals need to be able to clearly *articulate* their ideas on a daily basis?
_____ a. actors   _____ c. artists
_____ b. lawyers   _____ d. teachers

3. Select the synonym(s) of *articulate*.
_____ a. stress   _____ c. declare
_____ b. express   _____ d. speak

4. Write a sentence correctly using *articulate*. (Be sure to include context clues to show you understand the meaning of the word.)

_____

_____

5. In what learning situation was it especially important that you *articulate* your ideas correctly? What can you do to better *articulate* your ideas not only in the classroom but in the everyday life as well?

_____

_____

Assimilate[8]

as|sim|i|late (ə sim′ə lāt), v., **-lat|ed, -lat|ing,** n.
— v.t. **1a** to change (food) into living tissues; digest: *The human body will not assimilate sawdust.* **b** *Figurative.* to take in and make a part of oneself; absorb: *She reads so much that she does not assimilate it all.* syn: See syn. under **absorb.** **2** to make like the people of a nation or other group in customs, viewpoint, character, or other attribute: *We have assimilated immigrants from many lands. By living a long time with the Indians, he was assimilated to them in his thinking and actions.* syn: incorporate. **3** to make (a speech sound, usually a consonant) more like the sound which follows or precedes. syn: adapt. Consonants are frequently assimilated to neighboring consonants; *ads-* becomes *ass-; comr-, corr-; dist-, diff-.* See also **assimilation,** def. 4.
— v.i. **1a** to be changed into living tissue; be digested: *The woody fibers of plants will not assimilate into the human body.* **b** *Figurative.* to be taken into oneself; absorb: *After he has watched television all day, nothing will assimilate through his senses.* **2** to become like the people of a nation, or other group in customs, viewpoint, character or other attribute: *Many immigrants assimilate readily in this country.* **3** to become like.
— n. *Obsolete.* that which is like.
[< Latin *assimilāre* (with English *-ate*[1]), variant of *assimulāre* compare < *ad-* to + *simulāre* imitate]
—**as|sim′i|la′tor,** n.

1. Which of the numbered and lettered dictionary definitions of *assimilate* best fits the word's use in the reading selection? _____

2. Who might need to *assimilate* information?
_____ a. a professor preparing a lecture
_____ b. a politician coordinating an election strategy
_____ c. a student reviewing before an exam
_____ d. a weightlifter eating lunch

3. Select the synonym(s) of *assimilate*.
_____ a. adapt   _____ c. absorb
_____ b. differentiate   _____ d. convert

4. What are some strategies that you as a good student can do to best *assimilate* information learned in a class?

_____

_____

5. Write a sentence correctly using *assimilate*. (Be sure to include context clues to show you understand the meaning of the word.)

_____

_____

Cogent[11]

co|gent (kō'jənt), *adj.* **1** having the power to convince; forceful or convincing: *The lawyer used cogent arguments to persuade the jury that his client was innocent.* **SYN**: potent, compelling. See syn. under **valid**. **2** constraining; impelling; powerful: *The French Emperor . . . determined to insist in cogent terms* (Alexander Kinglake). [< Latin *cogēns, -entis*, present participle of *cogere* compel < *co-* together + *agere* drive] —**co'gent|ly,** *adv.*

1. The etymology of *cogent* shows that the word comes from the Latin words *co* (together) and *agere* (drive). Use this information and your background knowledge to match the following:

   _____ a. exigent   aa. to subject to smoke or fumes in order to exterminate vermin or insects

   _____ b. litigate   bb. able to move in a quick and easy fashion; active

   _____ c. fumigate   cc. requiring immediate attention or remedy; urgent

   _____ d. agile   dd. to subject to legal proceedings

   _____ e. navigate   ee. to control the course of a ship or aircraft

2. Select the synonym(s) of *cogent*.

   _____ a. impelling   _____ c. concur

   _____ b. valid   _____ d. convincing

3. Who would need to be able to present a *cogent* argument?

   _____ a. a student on an examination

   _____ b. a racecar driver

   _____ c. a politician defending new legislation

   _____ d. a lawyer during courtroom proceedings

4. Write a sentence correctly using *cogent*. (Be sure to include context clues to show you understand the meaning of the word.)

_____

_____

5. In what class did you present a *cogent* argument or position either on an examination or in class discussion? If you have not yet had the opportunity, in what situation do you think you will need to do so?

_____

_____

Competence[9]

com|pe|tence (kom′pə təns), *n.* **1** the quality or condition of being competent; ability; fitness; capacity: *No one doubted the guide's competence. The madwoman lacked the competence to manage her own affairs.* **2** enough money to provide a comfortable living: *He still thought how fine it would be to take one's ease with a rod by the lake ... now that his work was behind him and* he had his competence (Atlantic). **3** *Law.* legal power or authority. **4** *Geology.* the ability of a stream to carry and transport solid particles, pebbles, boulders, etc., measured by the size of the largest piece it can move. **5** *Embryology.* the ability of an embryonic tissue to react to various stimuli which can influence its development in particular directions.

1. Someone who has demonstrated *competence* would probably be
   - _____ a. a world-class gymnast.
   - _____ b. a college dropout.
   - _____ c. a president of a nation.
   - _____ d. a nationally known doctor.

2. Select the synonym(s) of *competence*.
   - _____ a. ability   _____ c. diligence
   - _____ b. capacity   _____ d. clarification

3. In which of the following sentences is competence used correctly?
   - _____ a. The student demonstrated his *competence* when he received an A in his seminar class.
   - _____ b. It is important to have competence when you eat apple pie.
   - _____ c. The president displayed competence when negotiating with the congressional representatives.
   - _____ d. The lawyer lacked competence when he won the difficult court case.

4. How can you demonstrate your *competence* on an essay examination? Have you ever felt concerned that you did not have the *competence* to perform a task? When?

_____

_____

5. Write a sentence correctly using *competence*. (Be sure to include context clues to show you understand the meaning of the word.)

_____

_____

Deleterious[15]

del|e|te|ri|ous (del′ə tir′ē əs), *adj.* causing harm; injurious: *'Tis pity wine should be so deleterious* (Byron). *The deleterious genetic effects [of radiation] would persist for hundreds of generations* (Bulletin of Atomic Scientists). **SYN:** harmful, noxious, pernicious. [< New Latin *deleterius* (with English *-ous*) < Greek *dēlētērios* < *dēlētēr* destroyer < *dēléesthai* hurt, injure] —**del′e|te′ri|ous|ly,** *adv.* —**del′e|te′ri|ous|ness,** *n.*

1. Complete the verbal analogy.
   adherence : cling :: *deleterious* : _____
   a. assimilate   c. hurt
   b. complete   d. discern

2. What might be *deleterious* to your health?
   _____ a. eating too much
   _____ b. driving during the night
   _____ c. studying for an exam
   _____ d. not getting enough sleep

3. Select the synonym(s) of *deleterious*.
   _____ a. closeness   _____ c. disadvantageous
   _____ b. harmful   _____ d. procrastinate

4. Write a sentence correctly using *deleterious*. (Be sure to include context clues to show you understand the meaning of the word.)

   _____

   _____

5. What activities might you or other students engage in that would be *deleterious* to your health? How could these be corrected?

   _____

   _____

Diligent[2]

dil|i|gent (dil′ə jənt), *adj.* **1** hard-working; industrious: *The diligent student kept on working until he had finished his homework.* **SYN:** assiduous. See syn. under **busy. 2** careful and steady: *The detective made a diligent search for clues.* [< Latin *dīligēns, -entis,* present participle of *dīligere* value highly, love < *dis-* apart + *legere* choose] —**dil′i|gent|ly,** *adv.*

1. Which of the following could correctly be called *diligent*?
   _____ a. a successful businessman
   _____ b. an incompetent policeman
   _____ c. a serious student
   _____ d. a student who drops out of school

2. Select the synonym(s) of *diligent*.

_____ a. hardworking   _____ c. illiterate

_____ b. lethargic   _____ d. assiduous

3. Which of the numbered dictionary definitions of *diligent* best fits the word's use in the reading selection? _____

4. In what situations have you had to be *diligent*? Classroom/school? Personal relationship? Job? Why?

_____

_____

5. Write a sentence correctly using *diligent*. (Be sure to include context clues to show you understand the meaning of the word.)

_____

_____

Discern[6]

dis|cern (də zėrn′, -sėrn′), *v.t.* to perceive; see clearly; distinguish or recognize: *Through the fog I could just discern a car coming toward me. When there are many conflicting opinions, it is hard to discern the truth. Not till the hours of light return, All we have built do we discern* (Matthew Arnold). — *v.i.* to distinguish; make a distinction; discriminate: *The Philosopher whose discoveries now dazzle us could not once discern between his right hand and his left* (William Ellery Channing). [< Old French *discerner* distinguish, separate, learned borrowing from Latin *discernere* < *dis-* off, away + *cernere* distinguish, separate] — **dis|cern′er**, *n.*

1. Complete the verbal analogy.

   linguistic : language :: *discern* : _____

   a. recognize   c. reclaim

   b. determine   d. defer

2. Select the synonym(s) of *discern*.

   _____ a. determine   _____ c. discharge

   _____ b. discuss   _____ d. discriminate

3. The etymology of *discern* shows that the word comes from the Latin words *dis* (off, away) and *cernere* (distinguish, separate). Use this information and your background knowledge to match up the following:

   _____ a. decree   aa. insecurity or instability

   _____ b. hypocrisy   bb. to engage or involve the mind or interest of

   _____ c. criterion   cc. insincerity

   _____ d. concern   dd. an authoritative order having the force of law

   _____ e. incertitude   ee. a standard, rule, or test on which a judgment or decision can be based

4. Write a sentence correctly using *discern*. (Be sure to include context clues to show you understand the meaning of the word.)

_____

_____

5. In what classes was it difficult for you to *discern* information? What did you or can you do in such a situation?

_____

_____

Erudite[1]

er|u|dite (er'ů dīt, -yů-), *adj.* having much knowledge; scholarly; learned: *an erudite teacher, an erudite book.* [< Latin *ērudītus,* past participle of *ērudīre* instruct < *ex-* away, out of + *rudis* rude, unskilled] —**er'u|dite'ly,** *adv.* —**er'u|dite'ness,** *n.*

1. Select the synonym(s) of *erudite*.

   _____ a. cultivated   _____ c. learned
   _____ b. ignorant   _____ d. scholarly

2. Complete the verbal analogy.
   ignorant : learned :: *erudite* : _____
   a. lazy   c. adhere
   b. keen   d. illiterate

3. In which of the following sentences can *erudite* be correctly placed in the blank?

   _____ a. The math professor presented information in an
   _____ manner.
   _____ b. He selected an _____ present for his mother at Christmas.
   _____ c. As the tutor discussed the science problem, the student looked _____ .
   _____ d. The student received an _____ book as a graduation gift.

4. Describe a person whom you've met who is *erudite*. Would you consider yourself to be *erudite*? Why or why not?

_____

_____

5. Write a sentence correctly using *erudite*. (Be sure to include context clues to show you understand the meaning of the word.)

_____

_____

Impediment[12]

im|ped|i|ment (im ped′ə mənt), *n.* **1** a hindrance; obstruction: *As an impediment to South American tourism, the expensiveness of getting to some places is being given serious study* (Newsweek). **2** some physical defect, especially a defect in speech: *Stuttering is a speech impediment. They bring unto him one that was deaf, and had an impediment in his speech* (Mark 7:32). **3** *Law.* a bar to the making of a valid marriage contract. [< Latin *impedīmentum* < *impedīre;* see etym. under **impede**]

1. Select the synonym(s) of *impediment*.
   _____ a. disadvantage   _____ c. exemption
   _____ b. competence   _____ d. obstruction

2. What could be an *impediment* for a college student?
   _____ a. living on the campus grounds
   _____ b. receiving high SAT or ACT scores
   _____ c. not knowing the vocabulary used in the classes
   _____ d. not having enough money for books

3. Complete the verbal analogy.
   competence : ability :: *impediment* : _____
   a. clarify   c. defer
   b. discern   d. hindrance

4. Write a sentence correctly using *impediment*. (Be sure to include context clues to show you understand the meaning of the word.)

   _____

   _____

5. What is an *impediment* to learning and receiving a degree that most students face? Finances? Working? Career decisions? Discuss what might be an *impediment* for you and how you plan to avoid or overcome it.

   _____

   _____

Linguistic[5]

lin|guis|tic (ling gwis′tik), *adj.* having to do with language or the study of languages. —**lin|guis′ti-cal|ly,** *adv.*

1. Who would most likely need to develop *linguistic* talents for their jobs?
   _____ a. an international politician
   _____ b. an administrator of an ethnically diverse school district
   _____ c. a postman
   _____ d. the ruler of a country

2. If you take a class where you do *linguistic* analysis, you would probably study

_____ a. the political characteristics of various cultural groups.

_____ b. the history and structure of language.

_____ c. issues related to health issues in society.

_____ d. basic units of language—phonemes and morphemes.

3. Select the synonym(s) of *linguistic*.

_____ a. speech   _____ c. diligence

_____ b. correctness   _____ d. language

4. How would a knowledge of *linguistic* differences help you as a student? As a citizen?

_____

_____

5. Write a sentence correctly using *linguistic*. (Be sure to include context clues to show you understand the meaning of the word.)

_____

_____

Optimum[7]

op|ti|mum (op′tə məm), *n., pl.* **-mums, -ma** (-mə), *adj.* —*n.* **1** the best or most favorable point, degree, or amount, for the purpose. **2** *Biology.* the degree or amount of heat, light, food, moisture, or other condition, most favorable for the reproduction or other vital process of an organism: *There is usually for each species a rather narrow range, the optimum, in which the organism lives most effectively* (Harbaugh and Goodrich). —*adj.* best or most favorable: *An optimum popu-* lation is one of a size and quality best fitted to achieve some social goal (Emory S. Bogardus). [< Latin *optimum,* neuter of *optimus;* see etym. under **optimism**]

from **optimism:**

[< French *optimisme* < New Latin *optimum* the greatest good (in Leibniz' philosophy); the best, neuter of Latin *optimus,* superlative of *bonus* good]

1. Complete the verbal analogy.

procrastinate : delay :: *optimum* : _____

a. cheerful   c. favorable

b. learned   d. freedom

2. The etymology of *optimum* (see at *optimism*) shows that the word comes from the Latin words *optimum* (the greatest good) and *optimus* (the best). Use this information and your background knowledge to match the following:

_____ a. copious   aa. to develop to the utmost

_____ b. optimist   bb. horn of plenty

_____ c. cornucopia   cc. characterized by great wealth; rich

_____ d. opulent   dd. a person who looks on the bright side of things

_____ e. optimize   ee. large in quantity; abundant

3. Use *optimum* in two sentences: one as a noun and one as an adjective. (See the dictionary entry if necessary.)

_____

_____

4. Write a sentence correctly using *optimum*. (Be sure to include context clues to show you understand the meaning of the word.)

_____

_____

5. What would you describe as an *optimum* learning situation for yourself? What type of instruction do you prefer? Why?

_____

_____

Procrastinate[4]

pro|cras|ti|nate (prō kras′tə nāt), *v.i., v.t.,* **-nated, -nat|ing**. to put things off until later; delay, especially repeatedly: *to procrastinate until an opportunity is lost.* SYN: defer, postpone. [< Latin *prōcrāstināre* (with English *-ate¹*) < *prō-* forward + *crāstinus* belonging to tomorrow < *crās* tomorrow] —**pro|cras′ti|na′tor,** *n.*

1. If you *procrastinate*, you might
   _____ a. hurry to complete an assignment.
   _____ b. postpone a decision.
   _____ c. act diligently.
   _____ d. wait to do something.

2. Select the synonym(s) of *procrastinate*.
   _____ a. defer   _____ c. determine
   _____ b. decide   _____ d. delay

3. Complete the verbal analogy.
   retrieval : reclamation :: *procrastinate* : _____
   a. continue   c. postpone
   b. hinder   d. retain

4. When do you usually *procrastinate*? Before an exam? Doing homework? Deciding on classes to take? Looking for a job? List a few examples.

_____

_____

5. Write a sentence correctly using *procrastinate*. (Be sure to include context clues to show you understand the meaning of the word.)

_____

_____

Proximity[14]

prox|im|i|ty (prok sim′ə tē), *n.* nearness; closeness: *She and her cat enjoy their proximity to the fire. Marriages in proximity of blood are amongst us forbidden* (John Florio). [< Latin *proximitās* < *proximus* nearest]

1. In which sentence(s) is *proximity* used correctly?
   _____ a. She lived in proximity to her job.
   _____ b. He needed proximity to complete the assignment.
   _____ c. Mary's aunt represents proximity in kinship.
   _____ d. Having proximity is important when completing an examination.

2. Select the synonym(s) of *proximity*.
   _____ a. closeness   _____ c. condition
   _____ b. relativity   _____ d. nearness in kinship

3. Select the antonym(s) of *proximity*.
   _____ a. retrieval   _____ c. distance
   _____ b. separation   _____ d. difference

4. Write a sentence correctly using *proximity*. (Be sure to include context clues to show you understand the meaning of the word.)

   _____

   _____

5. Why might it be important for a student to have *proximity* to his college campus? Do you live in *proximity* to your campus? How does this affect your life as a student? If you work, do you have *proximity* to either school or home?

   _____

   _____

Retrieval[3]

re|triev|al (ri trē′vəl), *n.* **1** the act of retrieving; recovery: *data storage and retrieval.* **2** the possibility of recovery.
re|trieve (ri trēv′), *v.,* **-trieved, -triev|ing,** *n.*
—*v.t.* **1** to get again; recover: *to retrieve a lost pocketbook, to retrieve information from the storage of a computer.* **syn:** See syn. under **recover.** **2** to bring back to a former or better condition; restore: *to retrieve one's fortunes.* **3a** to make good; make amends for; repair: *to retrieve a mistake, to retrieve a loss or defeat.* **b** to rescue; save: *to retrieve the nations sitting in darkness from eternal perdition* (William H. Prescott). **4** to find and bring to a person: *Some dogs can be trained to retrieve game.* —*v.i.* to find and bring back killed or wounded game.
—*n.* the act of retrieving; recovery, or possibility of recovery.
[< Old French *retruev-,* stem of *retrouver* < *re-* again + *trouver* to find] —**re|triev′a|ble,** *adj.*
—**re|triev′a|bly,** *adv.*

1. Complete the verbal analogy.
   erudite : scholarly :: *retrieval* : _____
   a. destroy   c. refer
   b. release   d. return

2. Which of the numbered and lettered dictionary definitions of *retrieval* best fits the word's use in the reading selection? _____

3. Select the synonyms of *retrieval*.
   _____ a. recovery   _____ c. cancellation
   _____ b. reclamation   _____ d. revelation

4. What are some study strategies that you have developed to help you in fast *retrieval* of course information when preparing for an examination?

   _____

   _____

5. Write a sentence correctly using *retrieval*. (Be sure to include context clues to show you understand the meaning of the word.)

   _____

   _____

ANSWERS TO CHAPTER 4 EXERCISES

Adhere: **1.** 1 **2.** c **3.** a, d
Articulate: **1.** a, c **2.** a, b, d **3.** b, d
Assimilate: **1.** 1b **2.** a, b, c **3.** a, c
Cogent: **1.** cc, dd, aa, bb, ee **2.** a, b, d **3.** a, c, d
Competence: **1.** a, c, d **2.** a, b **3.** a, c
Deleterious: **1.** c (characteristic) **2.** a, d **3.** b
Diligent: **1.** a, c **2.** a, d **3.** 1
Discern: **1.** a (synonym) **2.** d **3.** dd, cc, ee, bb, aa
Erudite: **1.** c, d **2.** d (antonym) **3.** a, d
Impediment: **1.** d **2.** c, d **3.** d (synonym)
Linguistic: **1.** a, b, d **2.** b, d **3.** a, d
Optimum: **1.** c (synonym) **2.** ee, dd, bb, cc, aa
Procrastinate: **1.** b, d **2.** a, d **3.** c (synonym)
Proximity: **1.** a, c **2.** a, d **3.** b, c
Retrieval: **1.** d (synonym) **2.** 1 **3.** a

If you missed any of the items in the exercises, return to the exercise and to the dictionary definitions to see where you went wrong. Remember: If you get something right, you only affirm that you knew it. If you get something wrong and understand why, *you have learned something*.

POSTTEST

Fill in the blanks with the words from this list.

adhere	deleterious	linguistic
articulate	diligent	optimum
assimilate	discern	procrastinate
cogent	erudite	proximity
competence	impediment	retrieval

1. _____ is the act of recovery.

2. *Defer* and *postpone* are synonyms of _____ .

3. _____ means "having to do with language."

4. *Scholarly* and *learned* are characteristics of a(n) _____ teacher.

5. To _____ something is to perceive, distinguish, or recognize it.

6. Something that is harmful, or injurious, is said to be _____ .

7. A(n) _____ argument is one that is convincing and forceful.

8. _____ means "to absorb, or take in and make a part of oneself."

9. *Cling* and *stick* are synonyms of _____ .

10. _____ means "to speak distinctly, or to express in clear sounds and words."

11. Ability, fitness, and capacity are indicators of a level of _____ .

12. A(n) _____ is something that is a hindrance, or obstacle.

13. Hardworking and industrious are characteristics of a(n) _____ student.

14. A(n) _____ condition means that it is the best, or most favorable.

15. _____ means "nearness and closeness."

Answers to this posttest are in the Instructor's Manual.

If you missed any of the words, you may need to return to the exercises and to the dictionary entries to see why your concepts for some words are incomplete.

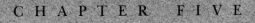

CHAPTER FIVE

LIBRARY RESOURCES AND THEIR USE

◆

VOCABULARY SELF-EVALUATION

The following words will be introduced in this reading selection. Place a check mark (√) in front of any that you know thoroughly and use in your speech or writing. Place a question mark (?) in front of any that you recognize but do not use yourself.

_____ abstract	_____ assiduous	_____ formidable
_____ accessible	_____ avid	_____ myriad
_____ adjacent	_____ compendium	_____ plagiarize
_____ adjunct	_____ copious	_____ replicate
_____ ancillary	_____ expedite	_____ stringent

LEARNING TO USE THE LIBRARY

The purpose of a college or university is to provide education beyond high school. It may prepare students for a profession as well as giving them a broader basis of, and appreciation for, knowledge. In order to carry out these functions, many institutions furnish ancillary[1] services in addition to the traditional lecture, laboratory, practice, and evaluation. For example, colleges may provide mental and physical health centers, tutoring and job placement services, special assistance for the handicapped, and so on. But the service most essential to the assiduous[2] student, and to the entire college community, is the library. Knowing how to use the library efficiently can greatly increase your chances of academic success.

LIBRARY ORGANIZATION

Even if you have used libraries previously, the college library can be a formidable[3] place. Yet while each library has its own arrangement, it also has certain standard features. There will be a central catalog, located in a prominent position, that serves as a compendium[4] of the entire collection. This catalog may be divided into sections according to author, title, and subject (and labeled as such) or unified into a single, alphabetical whole. More and more libraries are using computers to make the extent of their collections known to users. Instead of searching through the card catalog for materials written by an author or about a given subject, you need only put the necessary information into the computer terminal, and the titles in the collection, with the location of each, will be shown on the screen. Data may be called up using title, author, subject, or key terms.

At the time of this writing, most community and public school libraries in the United States use a classification (organization) system called the Dewey Decimal System, while colleges, universities, and (of course) the Library of Congress use a system called the Library of Congress Classification System. Each is based on the same principle, that is, of arranging materials according to subject matter. Things about the same topic are labeled alike and clustered together on the shelves. If you are accustomed to the Dewey system, you will immediately notice the differences in the call numbers with the Library of Congress system, but this should not keep you from locating the materials you need. Watch for the signs that indicate the floors and areas where the books are shelved. Signs will also tell you where to find the reserve room, the reference room, and periodicals.

Reserve Room

The reserve room houses special-assignment materials. Instructors frequently assign adjunct[5] readings and will place a few copies "on reserve." The avid[6] student will check these materials out promptly. If the professor does not tell you the identifying number of the material, you can find it in the nearby printout by looking up the class and instructor. Then you can give the identifier to the library clerk, who will retrieve the material from the shelves. Materials in the reserve room have more stringent[7] time limits placed on them than most other library materials. Frequently they may be checked out for as few as two hours.

Reference Room and Periodicals

In the reference room are myriad[8] reference works, such as almanacs, atlases, encyclopedias, dictionaries, technical books, and so on. Also included are indexes and abstracts,[9] which lead you to articles in periodicals and other publications. Often the works abstracted will not be available in the library, but if the data given indicate the material is useful, you can send for it. Once you know which periodical(s) you need, you can look in the printout of the holdings, usually to be found adjacent[10] to the periodical section. The list of holdings may also be on a computer or on microform, with a microform reader nearby. Many libraries keep the most recent periodicals on shelves, easily accessible[11] to readers, while back issues are on microform, usually in another area. Make a note of the call numbers in the printout and follow the maps and signs to the correct location. Microform (microcard, microfilm, or any other reduced-size) machines will be available and will permit you to read, and sometimes copy, the reduced-size material.

Interlibrary Loan

Occasionally the books and periodicals, as well as the abstract sources mentioned earlier, will not be housed in your college library, but in most cases they are still available to you. Most libraries are part of a system of libraries—other college libraries, a state or regional library system, and so forth—and can request the material you need from the larger collection. This is called interlibrary loan. Your school may also have a special name for this process, but the general term will communicate your need to the librarian. You will have to fill out a form, taking care to include all the necessary information to expedite[12] your request. You may also be able to use a system wherein you supply key terms referring to your subject, and the library, through its computer network, can search for works that relate to your topic. You can understand that these procedures take time, and so it is important to begin the research for a paper or project early.

USING THE MATERIAL

If you are using library materials to prepare a paper, be sure to take copious[13] notes or to replicate[14] the needed pages on a copy machine. Record the bibliographic material (the author, title, edition, publisher, place, and date of publication) carefully. You won't want to begin work, discover data are missing, and then have to locate your sources again! One important piece of advice: Do not plagiarize.[15] If you wish to use information directly from a source, quote it directly and give credit to the author. It is understandable to want to "borrow" a few words and ideas when there are so many before you, but *do* resist the temptation. It is academic dishonesty and, if it is discovered, may lead to an F on the submitted paper or to dismissal from the class. (Rules governing academic dishonesty are usually clearly set out in the college catalog so that students can be aware of them.) The library is full of a wide variety of information that can be used to stimulate your thoughts so that you can create a fine piece of writing of your own. ◆

PRETEST

Select words from this list and write them in the blanks to complete the sentences.

abstract	assiduous	formidable
accessible	avid	myriad
adjacent	compendium	plagiarize
adjunct	copious	replicate
ancillary	expedite	stringent

1. An abridgment of a larger work is a(n) _____ .

2. A synonym for *innumerable* is _____ .

3. A(n) _____ person is extremely eager.

4. If you are steady and untiring, you are _____ .

5. To take the ideas or writings of another and use as one's own is to _____ .

6. _____ is a synonym for *convenient*.

7. If you reproduce something exactly, you _____ it.

8. Something added but nonessential is a(n) _____ .

9. A(n) _____ rule is a strict rule.

10. If something is close or nearby, it is _____ .

11. Something _____ contains more than enough.

12. Something _____ is concerned with concepts rather than actual particulars.

13. A thing hard to deal with is _____ .

14. Something that assists is _____ .

15. If you make something easy, you _____ it.

Answers to this pretest are in Appendix E.

Unless your instructor tells you to do otherwise, complete the exercises for each word you missed on the pretest. The words, with their meanings and exercises, are in alphabetical order. The superscript numbers indicate where the words appeared in the reading selection so that you can refer to them when necessary. There are several types of exercises, but for each word you will be asked to write a sentence using context clues. (See Chapter 3 if you need information about how to create context clues.) You are also asked to perform some activity that will help you make your concept of the word personal. *Complete this activity thoughtfully, for creating a personalized concept of the word will help you remember it in the future.*

Answers to all the exercises are at the end of the exercise segment.

EXERCISES

Abstract[9]

ab|stract (*adj.* ab′strakt, ab strakt′; *v. 1, 3, 4* ab-strakt′; *v. 2, n.* ab′strakt), *adj., v., n.* —*adj.*
1 thought of apart from any particular object, real thing, or actual instance; not concrete: *Sweetness is abstract; a lump of sugar is concrete. Truth is an abstract concept.* **2** expressing or naming a quality, idea, or other concept, rather than a particular object or concrete thing: *Honesty is an abstract noun.* See also **abstract noun, abstract number**. **3** hard to understand; difficult; abstruse: *The atomic theory of matter is so abstract that it can be fully understood only by advanced students.* SYN: profound. **4** concerned with ideas or concepts rather than actual particulars or instances; not practical or applied; ideal or theoretical: *abstract reasoning, abstract mathematics.* SYN: visionary. **5** not representing any actual object or concrete thing; having little or no resemblance to real or material things, especially in art that avoids the use of ordinary conventional designs and the representation of material things, animals, or persons: *We saw many abstract paintings in the Museum of Modern Art. The interest of an abstract picture is exclusively decorative* (London Times). SYN: nonrepresentational, nonobjective.
—*v.t.* **1** to think of (a quality, such as color, weight, or truth) apart from any object or real thing having that quality or any actual instance: *We can abstract the idea of redness from the color of all red objects.* **2** to make an abstract of; summarize: *Try to abstract this story for a book report.* SYN: abridge. **3a** to take away; remove: *Iron is abstracted from ore.* SYN: extract. **b** to take away secretly, slyly, or dishonestly. SYN: steal, purloin. **4** to withdraw (the attention); divert. SYN: detach, disengage.
—*n.* **1** a brief statement of the main ideas or important points of an article, book, case in court, or other printed material; summary: *The students will write brief summaries of scientific treatises, earning $2.50 for each such abstract* (Wall Street Journal). SYN: abridgment, digest, compendium. **2** an abstract of title. *Abbr:* abs. **3** a work of abstract art; abstraction: *a geometric abstract in red and yellow.* **4** an abstract idea or term; abstraction: *the abstract called capitalism.*
in the abstract, in theory rather than in practice: *10 percent of society understands in the abstract the meaning of "freedom"* (Maclean's).
[< Latin *abstractus*, past participle of *abstrahere* draw away < *abs-* away + *trahere* draw] —**ab|stract′er, ab|strac′tor,** *n.* —**ab′stract|ly,** *adv.* —**ab′stract|ness,** *n.*

1. In which of the following sentences can *abstract* correctly be placed in the blank?

　　_____ a. Mary read the entire article and then wrote an _____ of it.

　　_____ b. Many modern artists create _____ paintings.

　　_____ c. Please _____ the main points of the story and hand them in.

　　_____ d. Concrete is too expensive, so we have decided to cover the driveway with _____ .

2. Place an "s" before any synonym and an "a" before any antonym of *abstract*.

　　_____ a. digest　　　　_____ d. abridgment
　　_____ b. concrete　　　_____ e. summary
　　_____ c. difficult　　　_____ f. representational

3. Which of the numbered and lettered dictionary definitions of *abstract* best fits the word's use in the reading selection? _____

4. What is your favorite candy bar? What is one of its *abstract* qualities?

_____

_____

5. Write a sentence correctly using *abstract*. (Be sure to include context clues to show you understand the meaning of the word.)

Accessible[11]

ac|ces|si|ble (ak ses′ə bəl), *adj.* **1** easy to get at;
easy to reach or enter: *tools readily accessible
on an open rack. A telephone should be put
where it will be accessible.* SYN: convenient.
2 that can be entered or reached: *This rocky island is accessible only by helicopter.* SYN: ap-
proachable. **3** that can be obtained: *Not many
facts about the kidnaping were accessible.* SYN:
available.
accessible to, capable of being influenced by;
susceptible to: *An open-minded person is accessible to reason.*
—**ac|ces′si|ble|ness,** *n.* —**ac|ces′si|bly,** *adv.*

1. If an object is *accessible*, it is

   _____ a. useful.   _____ d. portable.

   _____ b. easy to reach.   _____ e. hard to find.

   _____ c. convenient.   _____ f. in great demand.

2. Check any appropriate response to the following statement:
   "The counselor's office is *accessible* to students in the Learning Center."

   _____ a. They must not enter that office.

   _____ b. I'm happy they have made it so easy for the students.

   _____ c. Too bad it couldn't be better arranged.

   _____ d. How convenient!

3. Complete the verbal analogy.
   access : verb :: *accessible* : _____

   a. noun   d. adverb
   b. verb   e. conjunction
   c. adjective

4. Are you able to park your car (or bike) so that it is *accessible*? Where do
   you put it?

   _____

   _____

5. Write a sentence correctly using *accessible*. (Be sure to include context
   clues to show you understand the meaning of the word.)

   _____

   _____

Adjacent[10]

ad|ja|cent (ə jā′sənt), *adj.* lying near or close, or
contiguous (to); neighboring or adjoining; border-
ing; next: *The house adjacent to ours has been
sold.* SYN: abutting. [< Latin *adjacēns, -entis,*
present participle of *adjacēre* lie near < *ad-* near
+ *jacēre* lie²] —**ad|ja′cent|ly,** *adv.*
►**Adjacent** means lying near or neighboring, but
not necessarily touching.

1. In which sentence(s) can *adjacent* correctly be placed in the blank?
   _____ a. The horse stood in a field _____ to the highway.
   _____ b. Bring that _____ set of tools into the garage.
   _____ c. John's car was parked in the lot _____ to the school.
   _____ d. We plan to paint the front wall white and the _____ wall brown.

2. Which of the following might be *adjacent*?
   _____ a. a driveway and a street
   _____ b. the sun and the moon
   _____ c. a couch and a chair
   _____ d. a house and a garden

3. Things that are *adjacent* must
   _____ a. be near one another.
   _____ b. be touching.
   _____ c. be similar in nature.
   _____ d. be contiguous.

4. Write a sentence correctly using *adjacent*. (Be sure to include context clues to show you understand the meaning of the word.)

   _____

   _____

5. Name an object that is *adjacent* to the chair in which you are sitting.

   _____

   _____

Adjunct[5]

ad|junct (aj′ungkt), *n., adj.* — *n.* **1** something added that is less important or not necessary, but helpful: *A spare tire is a more important adjunct to a car than a radio.* SYN: accessory, auxiliary. **2** an assistant to, or associate of, a more important person. **3** a word or phrase that qualifies or modifies one of the essential elements of a sentence. Adjectives, adjectival phrases, adverbs, adverbial phrases, and some nouns used in a modifying or qualitative position are adjuncts. In "The tired man walked down the village street," *tired* is an adjunct to the subject *man, down the street* is an adjunct to the verb *walked*, and *village* is an adjunct to *street.* **4** *Logic.* a nonessential property or attribute. — *adj.* **1** subordinate: *adjunct arteries.* **2** accompanying: *adjunct military forces.* [< Latin *adjūnctus*, past participle of *adjungere* join to < *ad-* to + *jungere* join] — **ad′junct|ly,** *adv.*

1. In which of the following sentences is *adjunct* used correctly?
   _____ a. In the phrase "a beautiful sunset," beautiful is an adjunct.
   _____ b. Sue is taking Biology I and an adjunct class called "Reading Biology Textbooks."
   _____ c. Now semiretired, George works as Adjunct Professor of Psychology.
   _____ d. All they have for sale at that garage sale is a bunch of adjunct.

2. Check anything that might be an *adjunct*.
   _____ a. a class   _____ d. a textbook
   _____ b. a teacher   _____ e. a support group
   _____ c. an adjective   _____ f. life

3. Which of the numbered dictionary definitions of *adjunct* best fits the word's use in the reading selection? _____

4. What is your favorite *adjunct* to your daily diet?

_____

_____

5. Write a sentence correctly using *adjunct*. (Be sure to include context clues to show you understand the meaning of the word.)

_____

_____

Ancillary[1]

an|cil|lar|y (an′sə ler′ē), *adj., n., pl.* **-lar|ies.**
—*adj.* **1** subordinate; dependent; subservient. SYN:
subsidiary. **2** assisting; auxiliary: *an ancillary engine in a sailboat.* SYN: accessory.
—*n. British.* **1** a subordinate part; accessory. SYN:
subsidiary. **2** an assistant; helper. SYN: accessory.
[< Latin *ancillāris* < *ancilla* handmaid]

(Note: *Ancillary* and *adjunct* are very much alike. In fact, the dictionary gives each of them the synonym *accessory*, gives *adjunct* the synonym *auxiliary*, and uses *auxiliary* as a definition of *ancillary*. The words have in common the meaning of something secondary, rather than primary, in importance. To distinguish between them, it helps to look at the etymology of each word. *Adjunct* is something "added," or "joined," while *ancillary* comes from a word meaning "helper, or handmaiden." In some cases, these two words can be used interchangeably; but in other instances, where shades of meaning are important, one of them will fit the context better than the other.)

1. Check any appropriate response to the following statement:
   "John works in an *ancillary* position in the factory office."
   _____ a. He must be the president of the company.
   _____ b. Perhaps he can work his way up.
   _____ c. How wonderful to be on top!
   _____ d. I'm sure he makes a fine assistant.

2. Check any statement that describes something *ancillary*.
   _____ a. of primary importance
   _____ b. giving assistance
   _____ c. of secondary importance
   _____ d. independent

3. Complete the verbal analogy.
   church : churches :: *ancillary* : _____
   a. ancillarys   c. ancillarae
   b. ancillaries   d. ancillaris

4. Write a sentence correctly using *ancillary*. (Be sure to include context clues to show you understand the meaning of the word.)

_____

_____

5. What *ancillary* services do you use at your school? At work?

_____

_____

Assiduous[2]

as|sid|u|ous (ə sij′ü əs), *adj.* working hard and steadily; careful and attentive; diligent: *No error escaped his assiduous attention to detail.* SYN: steady, unremitting, untiring. [< Latin *assiduus* (with English *-ous*) < *assidēre* sit at < *ad-* at + *sedēre* sit] —**as|sid′u|ous|ly**, *adv.* —**as|sid′u-ous|ness**, *n.*

1. Check any appropriate response to the following sentence: "Mark is well known for his *assiduous* study habits."
   _____ a. He'd better get his act together or he'll flunk.
   _____ b. No wonder he gets good grades.
   _____ c. Maybe he would do better if he liked what he is studying.
   _____ d. I know. He works hard.

2. If someone is *assiduous*, he or she
   _____ a. works if he or she feels like it.
   _____ b. works carefully.
   _____ c. is steady.
   _____ d. keeps at the task.

3. Place an "s" by any synonym and an "a" by any antonym of *assiduous*.
   _____ a. careless   _____ d. untiring
   _____ b. unremitting   _____ e. lazy
   _____ c. diligent   _____ f. steady

4. Have you ever been *assiduous*? When? What were you doing?

_____

_____

5. Write a sentence correctly using *assiduous*. (Be sure to include context clues to show you understand the meaning of the word.)

_____

_____

Avid[6]

av|id (av′id), *adj.* extremely eager; greatly desir-
ous; greedy: *The dictator had an avid desire for
power. The miser was avid for gold.* **syn:** keen,
craving, covetous. [< Latin *avidus* < *avēre* desire
eagerly] —**av′id|ly**, *adv.*

1. If you had a friend who was *avid*, you might
   _____ a. tell him to take it easy.
   _____ b. have her divide the last piece of cake.
   _____ c. expect him to let you win at games.
   _____ d. find out she likes to win.

2. Which of the following might be *avid*?
   _____ a. a leader   _____ d. a town
   _____ b. a student   _____ e. weather
   _____ c. a child   _____ f. a tree

3. A person who is *avid* is
   _____ a. eager.   _____ d. greedy.
   _____ b. generous.   _____ e. craving.
   _____ c. covetous.   _____ f. disinterested.

4. Write a sentence correctly using *avid*. (Be sure to include context clues
   to show you understand the meaning of the word.)

   _____

   _____

5. Is there anything for which you are *avid*? Describe it.

   _____

   _____

Compendium[4]

com|pen|di|um (kəm pen′dē əm), *n., pl.* **-di|ums,**
-di|a (-dē ə). a short summary of the main points
or ideas of a larger work; abridgment; condensation. **syn:** abstract, précis, epitome. [< Latin *compendium* a shortening; a weighing together <
com- in addition + *pendere* weigh]

1. In which of the following sentences might *compendium* correctly be
   placed in the blank?
   _____ a. The instructor asked the students to make a _____
            of the class textbook.
   _____ b. A _____ of the novel could be found on the
            back cover.
   _____ c. Only the main points of the book are found in this
            _____ .
   _____ d. A _____ must contain every detail of the work.

2. Check any appropriate response to the following sentence:
   "Have you seen the *compendium* of Louis L'Amour's new book?"
   _____ a. Yes. We went to that movie last night.
   _____ b. I don't want to read it. I want to read the whole book.
   _____ c. Yes. I saw it in the book review section of the newspaper.
   _____ d. Yes, but it is longer than the book itself.

3. Complete the verbal analogy.
   wheel : round :: *compendium* : _____
   a. summary   d. short
   b. large   e. work
   c. abstract   f. précis

4. If you were to create a *compendium* of the happy times of your life, what are some of the things that you would include?

   _____

   _____

5. Write a sentence correctly using *compendium*. (Be sure to include context clues to show you understand the meaning of the word.)

   _____

   _____

Copious[13]

co|pi|ous (kō′pē əs), *adj.* **1** more than enough; plentiful; abundant: *copious tears. There was a copious supply of wheat in the grain elevators.* **SYN:** overflowing, ample. **2a** containing much matter; full of information. **b** containing many words; profuse; diffuse. **3** *Obsolete.* having or yielding an abundant supply. [< Latin *cōpiōsus* < *cōpia* plenty < *cōpis* well supplied < *co-* with + *ops* resources] — **co′pi|ous|ly**, *adv.* — **co′pi|ous|ness**, *n.*

1. Check any appropriate response to the following sentence:
   "Mary eats *copious* amounts of vegetables on her new diet."
   _____ a. She is likely to get very fat.
   _____ b. She probably gets lots of vitamins and minerals.
   _____ c. I'm going to tell her to eat more vegetables than that!
   _____ d. I like vegetables, so I may try that diet, too.

2. If something is *copious*, it is
   _____ a. abundant.   _____ d. ample.
   _____ b. full.   _____ e. simple.
   _____ c. limited.   _____ f. profuse.

3. Which of the numbered dictionary definitions of *copious* best fits the word's use in the reading selection? _____

4. Write a sentence correctly using *copious*. (Be sure to include context clues to show you understand the meaning of the word.)

_____

_____

5. Think of your bedroom. Is there a *copious* amount of anything there? What is it?

_____

_____

Expedite[12]

ex|pe|dite (eks′pə dīt), *v.*, **-dit|ed, -dit|ing,** *adj.*
— *v.t.* **1** to make easy and quick; help forward; hurry along; speed up: *Airplanes expedite travel. The telephone expedites business. If everyone will help, it will expedite matters.* **SYN:** accelerate, hasten, quicken. **2** to do quickly: *The manager had the ability to expedite all tasks assigned him.* **3** to issue officially; dispatch.
— *adj.* **1** (of a place, road, or way) clear of obstacles or impediments. **2** (of an action or motion) unrestricted; unembarrassed; easy; free. **3** (of persons) ready for action; prompt; alert; ready.

4 (of contrivances or instruments) ready for immediate use; conveniently serviceable; handy. **5** (of an action or process, a means, or remedy) prompt; speedy; expeditious.
[< Latin *expedītus*, past participle of *expedīre;* see etym. under **expedient**]

from **expedient:**

[< Latin *expediēns, -entis*, present participle of *expedīre* to free from a net, set right < *ex-* out + *pēs, pedis* foot]

1. In which of the following sentences is *expedite* used correctly?
   _____ a. The company will do well to hire John; he is an expedite worker.
   _____ b. A new highway across the foothills would expedite the flow of traffic to the beach.
   _____ c. The large budget for the navy will expedite its shipbuilding program.
   _____ d. You can expedite your raise in pay by doing all of your work carefully.

2. Place an "s" by any synonym and an "a" by any antonym of *expedite*.
   _____ a. hinder   _____ d. delay
   _____ b. accelerate   _____ e. hasten
   _____ c. quicken   _____ f. dispatch

3. Which of the numbered dictionary definitions of *expedite* best fits the word's use in the reading selection? _____

4. If you had the power to *expedite* one thing in your life, what would it be?

_____

_____

5. Write a sentence correctly using *expedite*. (Be sure to include context clues to show you understand the meaning of the word.)

_____

_____

Formidable[3]

for|mi|da|ble (fôr′mə də bəl), *adj.* hard to over-
come; hard to deal with; to be dreaded: *a formidable opponent. A long examination is more
formidable than a short test.* SYN: appalling, fear-
ful. [< Latin *formīdābilis* < *formīdāre* dread <
formīdō terror, dread] —**for′mi|da|ble|ness**, *n.*
for|mi|da|bly (fôr′mə də blē), *adv.* in a formidable
manner

1. If you have a *formidable* task to perform,
   _____ a. you can do it easily.
   _____ b. you may not want to do it.
   _____ c. you can do it with some extra effort.
   _____ d. no one can do it.

2. Check any appropriate response to the following sentence:
   "Driving a large truck would be a *formidable* task for Jim."
   _____ a. It should be easy for him to earn his living that way.
   _____ b. Those things would be hard for me to handle, too.
   _____ c. Oh, he's just lazy.
   _____ d. Since his accident he doesn't even like to drive a car!

3. Complete the verbal analogy.
   national : nation :: *formidable* : _____
   a. formidability   c. formidably
   b. formulation   d. formidableness

4. Write a sentence correctly using *formidable*. (Be sure to include context clues to show you understand the meaning of the word.)

   _____

   _____

5. Is there anything in your life that is *formidable*? Taking tests? A trip to the dentist? Going on a blind date? Explain.

   _____

   _____

Myriad[8]

myr|i|ad (mir′ē əd), *n., adj.* —*n.* **1** a very great
number: *There are myriads of stars. The grove
bloomed with myriads of wild roses* (Francis
Parkman). **2** ten thousand.
—*adj.* **1** countless; innumerable: *the City's moon-
lit spires and myriad lamps* (Shelley). **2** ten thousand. **3** having innumerable aspects or phases:
the myriad mind of Shakespeare or Da Vinci.
[< Late Latin *mȳrias, -adis* < Greek *mȳriás,
-ados* ten thousand, countless]

(Note: As a noun, *myriad* is usually used with *of* and often used in the plural.)

1. In which of the following sentences is *myriad* used correctly?
   _____ a. Sue has myriad problems, but she is usually cheerful.
   _____ b. I think my cat has myriads of fleas!
   _____ c. John's virtues are myriad, and his faults are few.
   _____ d. The valley is filled with myriads of colorful flowers.

2. Check any characteristic of the word *myriad*.
   _____ a. It means a very great number.
   _____ b. The plural is formed by adding an "s."
   _____ c. It has a noun and an adjective form.
   _____ d. It can function as a verb.

3. Which of the numbered dictionary definitions of *myriad* best fits the word's use in the reading selection? _____

4. There are *myriads* of books to be read. If you had the time, which ones would you read?

   _____

   _____

5. Write a sentence correctly using *myriad*. (Be sure to include context clues to show you understand the meaning of the word.)

   _____

   _____

Plagiarize[15]

pla|gia|rize (plā′jə rīz), *v.,* **-rized, -riz|ing.** — *v.t.* to take and use as one's own (the thoughts, writings, or inventions of another), especially, to take and use (a passage, plot, or the like) from the work of another writer: *I could not help plagiarizing Miss Hannah More's first line* (Harriet Beecher Stowe).
— *v.i.* to take ideas, passages, or the like, and represent them as one's own: *He even had doubts whether in 'The Silent Places,' he had been plagiarizing, more or less unconsciously,* from Henry James's 'Great Good Place' (H. G. Wells). — **pla′gia|riz′er,** *n.*

pla|gia|rism (plā′jə riz əm), *n.* **1** the act of plagiarizing: *If an author is once detected in borrowing, he will be suspected of plagiarism ever after* (William Hazlitt). **2** something plagiarized; an idea, expression, plot, or the like, taken from another and used as one's own. [< Latin *plagiārius* literary thief, kidnaper; earlier, plunderer (< *plaga* snare, net) + English *-ism*]

1. In which of the following sentences is *plagiarize* used correctly?
   _____ a. Sam and Joe plagiarized a small office of the Bank of America.
   _____ b. Bill discovered that someone had plagiarized his book and sold it to a publisher.
   _____ c. Mark Twain was once accused of plagiarizing Bret Harte.
   _____ d. To avoid plagiarizing, you must give credit to any source from which you copy.

2. If you *plagiarize* something,
   _____ a. you use someone else's written words or ideas without giving credit.
   _____ b. you commit literary theft.
   _____ c. you are being dishonest.
   _____ d. the instructor may give you an F.

3. Check any appropriate response to the following sentence:
"You do not *plagiarize* if you copy from the encyclopedia."

_____ a. Yes, you do! You must give credit even if you copy from that work.

_____ b. You can't take an idea from another source and present it as your own.

_____ c. It is okay to plagiarize if you don't get caught.

_____ d. Something like the encyclopedia belongs to everybody.

4. Write a sentence correctly using *plagiarize*. (Be sure you include context clues to show you understand the meaning of the word.)

_____

_____

5. Have you ever been tempted to *plagiarize*? What topic were you writing about?

_____

_____

Replicate[14]

rep|li|cate (*adj., n.* rep′lə kit; *v.* rep′lə kāt), *adj., n., v.,* **-cat|ed, -cat|ing. —*adj.* 1** exactly reproduced; duplicated. **2** folded back on itself: *a replicate leaf.*
—*n.* any exact reproduction or duplicate.
—*v.t.* 1 to copy exactly; reproduce; duplicate. **2** to say in reply. **3** to fold or bend back. **—*v.i.* 1** to reproduce oneself or itself: *When the cell reproduces by the process of division known as mitosis, these homologous chromosomes replicate and separate,* so that each of the two daughter cells has a full complement of 46 chromosomes (Scientific American). **2** to fold or bend back.
[< Latin *replicātus,* past participle of *replicāre* fold back; see etym. under **reply**]

from **reply:**

[< Old French *replier* < Latin *replicāre* unroll, fold back < *re-* back + *-plicāre* to fold]

1. In which of the following sentences can *replicate* correctly be placed in the blank?

_____ a. Taking great care, the scientist was able to _____ the experiment.

_____ b. If you _____ that page, we will have an exact copy.

_____ c. It is not unusual for some kinds of leaves to _____ .

_____ d. The TV movie "The Thorn Birds" was able to _____ the novel.

2. How might you *replicate* something?

_____ a. by carefully repeating each step

_____ b. by using a Xerox machine

_____ c. by making a general outline

_____ d. by tracing every part on another sheet of paper

3. Which of the numbered dictionary definitions of *replicate* best fits the word's use in the reading selection? _____

4. What was the last thing you had to *replicate*? How did you do it?

_____

_____

5. Write a sentence correctly using *replicate*. (Be sure to include context clues to show you understand the meaning of the word.)

_____

_____

Stringent[7]

strin|gent (strin′jənt), *adj.* **1** strict; severe: *stringent laws against speeding.* SYN: rigid, rigorous, exacting, binding. **2** lacking ready money; tight: *a stringent market for mortgage loans.* **3** convincing; forcible; cogent: *stringent arguments.* [< Latin *stringēns, -entis,* present participle of *stringere* bind, draw tight] —**strin′gent|ly,** *adv.*

1. In which of the following sentences is *stringent* used correctly?
   _____ a. The country must now follow stringent economic policies.
   _____ b. Joe cut his face while shaving and applied a stringent.
   _____ c. Some parents have stringent rules for their children.
   _____ d. His stringent comments made the information clear to all.

2. Place an "s" by any synonym and an "a" by any antonym of *stringent*.
   _____ a. lenient   _____ e. rigid
   _____ b. strict   _____ f. binding
   _____ c. mild   _____ g. severe
   _____ d. easygoing   _____ h. forcible

3. Which of the numbered dictionary definitions of *stringent* best fits the word's use in the reading selection? _____

4. Write a sentence correctly using *stringent*. (Be sure to include context clues to show you understand the meaning of the word.)

_____

_____

5. What *stringent* rule or law annoys you the most?

_____

_____

ANSWERS TO CHAPTER 5 EXERCISES

Abstract: **1.** a, b, c **2.** s, a, s, s, s, a **3.** *n.* 1
Accessible: **1.** b, c **2.** b, d **3.** c (part of speech)
Adjacent: **1.** a, c, d **2.** a, c, d **3.** a, d

Adjunct: **1.** a, b, c **2.** a, b, c, d, e **3.** *n.* 1
Ancillary: **1.** b, d **2.** b, c **3.** b (plural)
Assiduous: **1.** b, d **2.** b, c, d **3.** a, s, s, s, a, s
Avid: **1.** a, d **2.** a, b, c **3.** a, c, d, e
Compendium: **1.** a, b, c **2.** b, c **3.** d (characteristic)
Copious: **1.** b, d **2.** a, b, d, f **3.** 1
Expedite: **1.** b, c, d **2.** a, s, s, a, s, s **3.** *v.t.* 1
Formidable: **1.** b, c **2.** b, d **3.** d (noun form)
Myriad: **1.** a, b, c, d **2.** a, b, c **3.** *adj.* 1
Plagiarize: **1.** b, c, d **2.** a, b, c, d **3.** a, b
Replicate: **1.** a, b, c **2.** a, b, d **3.** *v.t.* 1
Stringent: **1.** a, c, d **2.** a, s, a, a, s, s, s, s **3.** 1

If you missed any of the items in the exercises, return to the exercise and to the dictionary definition to see where you went wrong. Remember: If you get something right, you only affirm that you knew it. If you get something wrong and understand why, *you have learned something.*

POSTTEST

Fill in the blanks with the words from this list.

abstract	assiduous	formidable
accessible	avid	myriad
adjacent	compendium	plagiarize
adjunct	copious	replicate
ancillary	expedite	stringent

1. A summary of a longer work is a(n) _____.

2. Something rigid, or severe, is _____.

3. _____ means "expressing a quality rather than a particular object."

4. To _____ is to commit literary theft.

5. _____ means "a very great number."

6. To copy exactly is to _____.

7. Something available is _____.

8. Something _____ is to be dreaded.

9. _____ means "keen, or craving."

10. _____ means "overflowing."

11. A thing subservient or dependent is _____.

12. _____ means "adjoining."

13. Something useful but not necessary is _____ .

14. To do quickly is to _____ .

15. To be _____ is to be diligent.

Answers to this posttest are in the Instructor's Manual.

If you missed any of the words, you may need to return to the exercises and to the dictionary entries to see why your concepts for some words are incomplete.

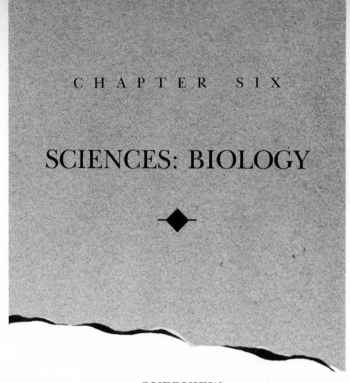

CHAPTER SIX

SCIENCES: BIOLOGY

◆

OVERVIEW

Biology is concerned with the relationship between structure and function in living systems. Biology has helped to solve problems in medicine, environmental resources, agriculture, and human ecology.

Emphases within the biological sciences include botany, zoology, microbiology, ecology, genetics, marine and medical biology, animal physiology, and neurobiology.

A wide range of job opportunities is available for students with a biology degree, including work as a public health microbiologist, laboratory technician, museum curator, science librarian, plant physiologist, forest ecologist, recreation specialist, park naturalist/ranger, entomologist, and fish and game warden. Biological training can also prepare students for advanced degrees leading to employment as research biologists, college and university professors, and medical and health professionals.

The introductory textbooks in biology are both expository and descriptive in that they explain broad concepts and generalizations as well as statements, ideas, and problems. Biology manuals are structured according to process analysis, with explanations of experimental procedures. There is usually visual reinforcement of concepts, provided through illustrations, photographs, charts, tables, classification systems, and structural formulas.

The vocabulary in biology is primarily specialized, with terminology unique to the field. Such terms as bacterium, mitosis, *and* metabolism *represent processes, structures, procedures, and theories within the field of biology and are usually Latin or Greek in etymology. You may add other terms you discover in your studies related to biology on the forms in Appendix D.*

VOCABULARY SELF-EVALUATION

The following words will be introduced in this reading selection. Place a check mark (√) in front of any that you know thoroughly and use in your speech and writing. Place a question mark (?) in front of any that you recognize but do not use yourself.

_____ bacterium	_____ eucaryote	_____ mitosis
_____ cytokinesis	_____ evolution	_____ mutation
_____ cytoplasm	_____ karyokinesis	_____ organelle
_____ diffusion	_____ membrane	_____ osmosis
_____ ecology	_____ metabolism	_____ photosynthesis

INSIGHTS INTO BIOLOGY

What does biology mean to you? Do you immediately picture a frog with its unidentified insides protruding onto a dissecting tray? Or perhaps your eyes burn in memory of time spent looking at yeast cells divide under a microscope. Although these experiences are part of biology, the field consists of much more. Biology is the study of life, and the smallest unit of life is the cell. Cells vary in size, shape, and function but exhibit similar traits that characterize them as cells.

All cells possess a plasma membrane,[1] a phospholipid or fat-like bilayer, that is differentially permeable to ions, water, and other molecules. In addition, those cells known as eucaryotes,[2] so termed because they have a visible nucleus, contain a membrane-bound organelle,[3] or spe-cialized part, that contains deoxyribonucleic acid (DNA). This DNA is enclosed in the nucleus in eucaryotes and has the necessary information to synthesize all the organic materials a cell needs for growth and reproduction.

While the nucleus is responsible for a cell's function and replication, it is in the cytoplasm,[4] or main body, of the cell that most of a cell's activity takes place. The cytoplasm consists of everything other than the plasma membrane and the nucleus and includes several organelles, such as mitochondria,* ribosomes,† and endoplasmic reticulum,‡ which are responsible for a cell's function and replication. Thus, the cell is the basic foundation for all biological studies.

---

* Mitochondria—organelles bound by a double membrane in which energy is captured in the form of ATP in the course of cellular respiration.

† Ribosome—small organelle composed of protein and ribonucleic acid; the site of protein synthesis.

‡ Endoplasmic reticulum—extensive system of double membranes present in most cells, dividing the cytoplasm into compartments and channels; often coated with ribosomes.

Many collegiate courses such as genetics, physiology, microbiology, and molecular biology concentrate on the study of cells and their functions. Cellular biologists seek to understand the basic chemical processes of protein synthesis, osmosis,[5] and diffusion[6] that allow cells to perform those various functions that ultimately maintain the organism's metabolism.[7] Cell membranes that are permeable allow the movement of water through them through the process of osmosis. And substances move within cells by the process of diffusion, which is the movement of suspended or dissolved particles from a more concentrated to a less concentrated region as a result of the random movement of individual particles. Cellular biologists also study the processes of cytokinesis[8] (cell division) and karyokinesis[9] (nuclear division).

An exciting topic in cellular biology is genetic engineering, a technique that alters the genetic constitution of cells by selective removal, insertion, or modification of nucleotide sequences (units of nucleic acid). One successful application of genetic engineering has been the splicing of nucleotide sequences responsible for insulin production to the normal genome of a bacterium.[10] (A genome is the sum of all the chromosomes within each nucleus of any species.) The bacterium now possesses the information to produce insulin.

Related cells divide by mitosis[11] and join together to form specialized tissues, which in turn form functional body organs. Organisms are thus composed of a number of organ systems. Botanists and zoologists are specialized biologists who study particular kingdoms of organisms. Botanists study plants and how they transform light energy and carbon dioxide into carbohydrates and oxygen through a process called photosynthesis.[12] Zoologists study the animals who use these carbohydrates and oxygen to respire and fulfill their metabolic needs.

The field of ecology[13] involves the study of plant and animal species and their interactions with the environment. These interactions may result from living factors—such as predation, competition, or mutualism—or from nonliving factors—such as climate, water availability, or natural disasters. One famous ecological study was how the pesticide DDT (dichloro-diphenyl-trichloroethane) affected the environment. Due to concentrated DDT at each trophic level, eagles who ate infected food laid thin, fragile, easily broken eggs. Eagle populations began diminishing and were rebuilt only after DDT was banned.

Another aspect of biology is evolution.[14] Evolution is genetic change over time, the mechanism that provides diversification of all living things. Genetic changes result from mutation[15] or genetic recombination. Although there is still controversy, students of Darwinian evolution believe that natural selection (survival of the fittest) is the mechanism for evolution. Organisms that are best suited for the environment, due to their superior genetic composition, survive to pass on their genes to their young. Over long periods of time, new species can and do result.

As you can see, biology isn't just concerned with formaldehyde-scented organs of lower vertebrates or the reproductive cycle of fungi. Biology as a field of study is as varied, intriguing, and dynamic as the world around us! ◆

BIOLOGY PRETEST

Select words from this list and write them in the blanks to complete the sentences.

bacterium	eucaryote	mitosis
cytokinesis	evolution	mutation
cytoplasm	karyokinesis	organelle
diffusion	membrane	osmosis
ecology	metabolism	photosynthesis

1. A cell or organism having a visible nucleus or nuclei is a(n)
   _____ .

2. _____ is the mixing together, or spreading into each other, of the atoms and molecules of different substances.

3. Living cells are enclosed in a(n) _____ through which they obtain their food.

4. A(n) _____ is a minute specialized part of a cell that carries out particular functions within the cell, such as providing energy for the cell's activities.

5. The tendency of a fluid of lower concentration to pass through a semi-permeable membrane into a solution of higher concentration is known as _____ .

6. _____ is the study of the interactions of organisms with their physical environment and with each other.

7. _____ means an alteration in the genes, which thereby affects biological evolution.

8. The sum of all chemical processes, such as energy production occurring within a living unit, is called _____ .

9. A(n) _____ is not only the oldest but among the most abundant organisms in the world.

10. _____ can be divided into four phases: prophase, meta-phase, anaphase, and telophase.

11. Darwin was known for his theory of _____ , which he described as a process of natural selection and survival of the fittest.

12. _____ , the conversion of light energy to chemical energy, takes place within cellular organelles known as chloroplasts.

13. The division of the cell nucleus is known as _____ .

14. All cells have a(n) _____ , which is the living matter of a cell excluding the nucleus.

15. In _____ , the cytoplasm of the parent cell is divided and packaged into two parts, each containing one of the nuclei.

Answers to this pretest are in Appendix E.

Unless your instructor tells you to do otherwise, complete the exercises for each word that you missed on the pretest. The words, with their meanings and exercises, are in alphabetical order. The superscript numbers indicate where the words appeared in the reading selection so that you can refer to them when necessary. There are several types of exercises, but for each word you will be asked to write a sentence using context clues. (See Chapter 3 if you need information about how to create context clues.) You are also asked to perform some activity that will help you make your concept of the word personal. *Complete this activity thoughtfully, for creating a personalized concept of the word will help you remember it in the future.*

Answers to all the exercises are at the end of the exercise segment.

BIOLOGY EXERCISES

Bacterium[10]

bac|te|ri|um (bak tir′ē əm), *n.* singular of **bacteria**. [< New Latin *bacterium;* see etym. under **bacteria**]

∗bac|te|ri|a (bak tir′ē ə), *n., pl.* of **bac|te|ri|um**. very tiny and simple plants, so small that they can usually be seen only through a microscope. Certain bacteria cause diseases such as pneumonia and typhoid fever; others do useful things, such as turning cider into vinegar. Bacteria consist of single cells that are rod-shaped, spherical, or spiral, and most kinds have no chlorophyll. Most bacteria multiply by splitting apart, some by forming spores. [< New Latin *bacteria,* plural of *bacterium* < Greek *baktērion* little staff, related to *báktron* stick, rod]

∗bacteria

bacilli cocci spirilla

1. Select the characteristics of a *bacterium*.
    _____ a. always harmful   _____ c. nonreproductive
    _____ b. single cell   _____ d. microscopic

2. The etymology of *bacterium* (see at *bacteria*) shows that the word comes from the Greek *backterion* (little staff) and is related to *baktron* (stick or rod). Use this information and your background knowledge to match the following:
    _____ a. debacle   aa. gem cut in the form of a narrow triangle
    _____ b. imbecile   bb. sudden disastrous overthrow or collapse; ruin
    _____ c. bacillus   cc. rod shaped
    _____ d. baguette   dd. deficient in mental ability; stupid
    _____ e. baculiform ee. rod-shaped bacterium; germ

3. What is the plural form of *bacterium*?
    _____ a. bacteriai   _____ c. bacterii
    _____ b. bacteria   _____ d. bacteriums

4. Write a sentence correctly using *bacterium*. (Be sure to include context clues to show you understand the meaning of the word.)

    _____

    _____

5. Is every *bacterium* harmful? Why or why not?

    _____

    _____

CHAPTER SIX

Cytokinesis[8]

cy|to|ki|ne|sis (sī′tō ki nē′sis, -kī-), *n.* the changes occurring in the cytoplasm of a cell during mitosis, meiosis, and fertilization.

1. In which of the following sentences can *cytokinesis* be correctly placed in the blank?
   _____ a. In _____ , the cytoplasm of the parent cell is divided into two parts, each containing one of the nuclei.
   _____ b. _____ usually begins during telophase of mitosis.
   _____ c. _____ is the fusion of two gametes and their nuclei.
   _____ d. In our own species, _____ takes place in the reproductive organs.

2. Complete the verbal analogy.
   organelle : specialized structure :: *cytokinesis* : _____
   a. bacteria production   c. osmosis
   b. cell division   d. mutation

3. Where does *cytokinesis* take place?
   _____ a. membrane   _____ c. cell wall
   _____ b. nucleus   _____ d. cytoplasm

4. How are cytoplasm and *cytokinesis* related? (See the dictionary entry if necessary.)

   _____

   _____

5. Write a sentence correctly using *cytokinesis*. (Be sure to include context clues to show you understand the meaning of the word.)

   _____

   _____

Cytoplasm[4]

from **cell:**

cy|to|plasm (sī′tə plaz əm), *n.* the living substance or protoplasm of a cell outside of the nucleus: *The main body of the cell, its cytoplasm, corresponds to the factory area where workers are manufacturing the specified product from incoming raw materials* (Scientific American). See picture under **cell.**

＊cell
definition, 3

animal cell   plant cell

1. Where is the *cytoplasm* located?
   _____ a. outside the cell wall   _____ c. within the cell
   _____ b. within organelles   _____ d. inside the nucleus

2. Select the synonym(s) of *cytoplasm*.

_____ a. living matter _____ c. diffusion

_____ b. gaseous substance _____ d. inorganic compound

3. In which of the following sentences is *cytoplasm* used correctly?

_____ a. Cytoplasm is the net movement of water through a membrane separating two solutions.

_____ b. All cells have a cytoplasm, which contains a large variety of molecules.

_____ c. The process by which plants manufacture their food is called cytoplasm.

_____ d. The process of glycolysis takes place in the cell fluid, or cytoplasm.

4. Write a sentence correctly using *cytoplasm*. (Be sure to include context clues to show you understand the meaning of the word.)

_____

_____

5. How is the *cytoplasm* different from the membrane of a cell?

_____

_____

Diffusion[6]

dif|fu|sion (di fyü′zhən), *n.* **1** the act or fact of diffusing; a spreading or scattering widely: *The invention of printing greatly increased the diffusion of knowledge. The spreading of patterns and traits from one group or area to another is known as cultural diffusion.* **2** a being widely spread or scattered; diffused condition. **3a** a mixing together of the atoms or molecules of substances by spreading into one another: *the diffusion of gases, liquids, or solids. An example of a new relation is found in the combination of diffusion and heat flow* (R. O. Davies). **b** the scattering of light resulting from its being reflected from a rough surface. See **scatter**. **4** the use of too many words; wordiness.

1. Which of the numbered dictionary definitions of *diffusion* best fits the word's use in the reading selection? _____

2. In which of the following sentences is *diffusion* used correctly?

_____ a. The loss of water vapor from a plant body is known as diffusion.

_____ b. Even distribution of molecules is a net result of the process of diffusion.

_____ c. The movement of water in diffusion is through membranes that are selectively permeable.

_____ d. Movement from a region of greater concentration to one of lesser concentration is a characteristic of diffusion.

3. Choose an appropriate synonym for *diffusion*.

_____ a. control _____ c. spread

_____ b. recede _____ d. clot

4. What is the difference between osmosis and *diffusion*? (See the reading selection if necessary.)

_____

_____

5. Write a sentence correctly using *diffusion*. (Be sure to include context clues to show you understand the meaning of the word.)

_____

_____

Ecology[13]

e|col|o|gy (ē kol ′ə jē), *n., pl.* **-gies**. 1 the branch of biology that deals with the relation of living things to their environment and to each other; bionomics: *Ecology . . . is likewise a composite of the fundamental biological sciences* (A. Franklin Shull). **2** the branch of sociology that deals with the relations between human beings and their environment: *Ecology, or the patterns of culture whereby a people adjust to their environment, undoubtedly plays a large role in the initiation of political systems and in some aspects of their further development* (Beals and Hoijer). **3a** the balanced or harmonious relationship of living things to their environment: *Spurred by mounting public alarm over smog-choked cities and a generally threatened ecology . . .* (Time). **b** *Figurative: The introduction of a comprehensive computerized data base into a large company could well upset the 'ecology' of the firm to such an extent that it could take ages to reestablish a stable balance* (Science Journal). [< Greek *oîkos* dwelling, habitation, house + English *-logy*]

1. Complete the verbal analogy.
   geology : rocks :: *ecology* : _____
   a. reproduction   c. environment
   b. photosynthesis   d. mutation

2. The etymology of *ecology* shows that the word comes from the Greek word *oikos* (dwelling, habitation, or house). Use this information and your background knowledge to match the following:

   _____ a. diocese   aa. an ecological community, together with its physical environment, considered as a unit

   _____ b. economy   bb. universal; worldwide

   _____ c. ecumenical   cc. destruction of the earth's environment through the uncontrolled use of pollutants

   _____ d. ecosystem   dd. district or churches under the jurisdiction of a bishop

   _____ e. ecocide   ee. making the most of what one has; avoiding waste; thrift

3. If you were studying *ecology*, you would probably be interested in
   _____ a. evolution and population genetics.
   _____ b. societies and social behavior.
   _____ c. human physiology and body structure.
   _____ d. the kinds and numbers of organisms in a community.

4. Write a sentence correctly using *ecology*. (Be sure to include context clues to show you understand the meaning of the word.)

_____

_____

5. Why do you think that the study of *ecology* is important for future generations?

_____

_____

Eucaryote[2]

eu|car|y|ote (yü kar′ē ōt), *n.* a cell or organism having a visible nucleus or nuclei: *If the first eucaryotes arose 1.2 to 1.4 billion years ago, there would be about half this time available for the evolution of soft-bodied multicellular organisms, since the first fossil animal skeletons were deposited around 600 million years ago at the beginning of the Cambrian period* (Scientific American). Also, **eukaryote**. [< *eu-* good, true + Greek *káryon* nut, kernel]

1. What is the unique characteristic of a *eucaryote*?
   _____ a. invisible nucleus   _____ c. visible nucleus
   _____ b. no membrane   _____ d. living matter

2. What part of *eucaryote* tells you that it has a "good," or "true," nucleus?
   _____ a. cary
   _____ b. eu
   _____ c. ote

3. In which of the following sentences can *eucaryote* be correctly placed in the blank?
   _____ a. _____ is a cell which has a true nucleus and inner membrane structure, or organelle.
   _____ b. Plants use _____ , water, and sunlight to make their food.
   _____ c. A _____ is the smallest indivisible particle of all matter.
   _____ d. A _____ is usually smaller than a prokaryote.

4. Describe the characteristics of a *eucaryote* in your own words. Then check the dictionary entry to see if your concept was correct.

_____

_____

5. Write a sentence correctly using *eucaryote*. (Be sure to include context clues to show you understand the meaning of the word.)

_____

_____

Evolution[14]

ev|o|lu|tion (ev′ə lü′shən), n. 1 any process of formation or growth; gradual development: *the evolution of the flower from the bud, the evolution of the modern steamship from the first crude boat.* 2 something evolved; product of development; not a sudden discovery or creation. 3 the theory that all living things developed from a few simple forms of life through a series of physical changes. According to evolution, the first mammal developed from a type of reptile, and ultimately all forms are traced back to a simple, perhaps single-celled, organism. ~~See picture below.~~ 4a a movement of ships or soldiers, planned beforehand; deployment. b any movement into a new formation, especially in marching. 5 a movement that is a part of a definite plan, design, or series: *A clumsy person could never achieve the graceful evolutions of that ballet dancer.* 6 a releasing; giving off; setting free, especially by chemical or physical change: *the evolution of heat from burning coal.* 7 *Mathematics.* the extraction of roots from powers. Finding the square root of a number is an example of evolution. 8 one of the regulated and recurring movements of a portion of a machine. 9 *Philosophy.* the theory that a process or progressive change, with the development of more complex entities, characterizes all force and matter in the universe: *Evolution is advance from the simple to the complex* (Edward Clodd). [< Latin *ēvolūtiō, -ōnis* < *ēvolvere;* see etym. under **evolve**]

from **evolve:**

[< Latin *ēvolvere* < *ex-* out + *volvere* roll]

1. Select the best synonym for *evolution*.

_____ a. transformation   _____ c. emergence

_____ b. genetic change   _____ d. gradual development

2. Which of the numbered dictionary definitions of *evolution* best fits the word's use in the reading selection? _____

3. The etymology of *evolution* (from *evolve*) shows that the word comes from the Latin words *ex* (out) and *volvere* (roll). Use this information and your background knowledge to match the following:

_____ a. voluble   aa. pass on, or delegate (authority, duty), to a successor or substitute

_____ b. volvulus   bb. fluent; loquacious; having a ready flow of words in speaking

_____ c. devolve   cc. revolve around a center, core, or axis

_____ d. obvolute   dd. obstruction in the intestine caused by inner twisting

_____ e. circumvolve ee. folded together with overlapping edges like petals and leaves in a bud

4. Write a sentence correctly using *evolution*. (Be sure to include context clues to show you understand the meaning of the word.)

_____

_____

5. How does the theory of Darwin (survival of the fittest) relate to the concept of *evolution*? (See the reading selection if necessary.)

_____

_____

Karyokinesis[9]

kar|y|o|ki|ne|sis (kar′ē ō ki nē′sis), n. *Biology.* the division of the cell nucleus, especially in mitosis. [< *karyo-* + Greek *kinēsis* motion < *kīneîn* move]

1. The process of *karyokinesis* occurs in the nucleus of the cell prior to cytokinesis. What part of the word relates to the nucleus?
   _____ a. karyo
   _____ b. kinesis

2. What happens as a result of *karyokinesis*?
   _____ a. cytoplasm and chromosomes divide equally
   _____ b. the cell nucleus divides
   _____ c. two new nuclei are formed
   _____ d. the cytoplasm divides

3. In what stage of cell division does *karyokinesis* occur?
   _____ a. mitosis   _____ c. mutation
   _____ b. cytokinesis   _____ d. osmosis

4. How are cytokinesis and *karyokinesis* different? (Review cytokinesis if necessary.)

   _____

   _____

5. Write a sentence correctly using *karyokinesis*. (Be sure to include context clues to show you understand the meaning of the word.)

   _____

   _____

Membrane[1]

mem|brane (mem′brān), *n.* **1** a thin, soft skin, sheet, or layer of animal tissue, lining, covering, separating, or connecting some part of the body: *Living cells are enclosed in membranes through which they obtain their food* (K. S. Spiegler). **2** a similar layer of vegetable tissue. **3** a similar layer of some synthetic substance. The semipermeable plastic sheets used in electrodialysis are called membranes. **4** a skin of parchment forming part of a roll. [< Latin *membrāna* a (covering) membrane of skin < *membrum* member]

1. Complete the verbal analogy.
   etymology : history :: *membrane* : _____
   a. hole   c. tissue
   b. gap   d. activity

2. Which of the numbered dictionary definitions of *membrane* best fits the word's use in the reading selection? _____

3. Which of the following is a synonym for *membrane*?
   _____ a. enclosure   _____ c. cavity
   _____ b. connector   _____ d. arrangement

4. Write a sentence correctly using *membrane*. (Be sure to include context clues to show you understand the meaning of the word.)

_____

_____

5. What organs in the human body are surrounded by *membranes*?

_____

_____

Metabolism[7]

me|tab|o|lism (mə tab′ə liz əm), *n*. **1** the process by which all living things turn food into energy and living tissue. In metabolism food is broken down to produce energy, which is then used by the body to build up new cells and tissues, provide heat, and engage in physical activity. Growth and action depend on metabolism. *Only living matter is able to carry on metabolism* (A. M. Winchester). **2** the metamorphosis of an insect. [< Greek *metabolē* change + English *-ism*]

1. In which of the following sentences can *metabolism* be correctly placed in the blank?
   _____ a. _____ provides another method for studying photosynthesis.
   _____ b. The part of the earth where life exists is called _____.
   _____ c. _____ is simply the sum total of all of the chemical activities of a living system.
   _____ d. The heart and lungs are important in maintaining the high rate of _____ of both birds and mammals.

2. Select the characteristics of *metabolism*.
   _____ a. energy production   _____ c. cell division
   _____ b. genetic change   _____ d. food conversion

3. The etymology of *metabolism* shows that the word comes from the Greek *metabole* (change). Use this information and your background knowledge to match the following:
   _____ a. catabolism   aa. brief story used to teach some moral lesson or truth
   _____ b. parole   bb. exaggerated statement used for effect and not meant to be taken literally
   _____ c. parable   cc. conference, or talk, to discuss terms or matters in dispute
   _____ d. hyperbole   dd. process of breaking down living tissues into simpler substances or waste matter, thereby producing energy
   _____ e. parley   ee. conditional release from prison before the full term is served

4. How can you characterize your own personal rate of *metabolism*? Fast? Slow? Why do you think so?

_____

_____

5. Write a sentence correctly using *metabolism*. (Be sure to include context clues to show you understand the meaning of the word.)

_____

_____

Mitosis[11]

mi|to|sis (mi tō′sis, mī-), *n. Biology.* the process by which a cell of a plant or animal divides to form two new cells, each containing the same number of chromosomes as the original cell; cell division. Mitosis is typically divided into four stages: *prophase*, in which the chromatin of the nucleus forms into a thread that separates into segments or chromosomes, each of which in turn separates longitudinally into two parts; *metaphase*, in which the nuclear membrane disappears and the chromosomes line up near the middle of the cell; *anaphase*, in which one chromosome of each pair moves toward each end of the cell; and *telophase*, in which the chromosomes lose their threadlike shape and again become chromatin, two new nuclear membranes form around the chromatin, and the cytoplasm draws together in the middle, divides, and two new cells exist. See diagram below. [< New Latin *mitosis* < Greek *mitos* thread + English *-osis*]

1. Complete the verbal analogy.
   bacterium : tiny plant :: *mitosis* : _____
   a. alteration   c. cell division
   b. environmental changes   d. gradual development

2. If an original cell has four chromosomes, how many does each of the new cells created during *mitosis* have?
   _____ a. two   _____ c. six
   _____ b. four   _____ d. eight

3. In which of the following sentences can *mitosis* be correctly placed in the blank?
   _____ a. Darwin's theory of _____ was concerned with hereditary changes.
   _____ b. In _____ the nuclear membrane breaks down, and after the chromosomes are divided equally, two new nuclei are formed.
   _____ c. The conversion of light into energy is the result of

   _____ .

   _____ d. _____ is the means or process by which organisms grow.

4. Write a sentence correctly using *mitosis*. (Be sure to include context clues to show you understand the meaning of the word.)

_____

_____

5. What are the four stages of *mitosis*? (Consult the dictionary entry if necessary.)

_____

_____

Mutation[15]

mu|ta|tion (myü tā′shən), *n.* **1** the act or process of changing; change; alteration: *The past is exempt from mutation* (Charles Brockden Brown). **2** a change within a gene or chromosome of animals or plants resulting in a new feature or character that appears suddenly and can be inherited: *Most mutations cause harmful effects, such as the reduction in the size of wings on a fly* (J. Herbert Taylor). *Many so-called gene mutations may actually be ultramicroscopic changes in* chromosome structure (The Effects of Atomic Weapons). **3** a new genetic character or new variety of plant or animal formed in this way; mutant: *It is claimed that the first of the small African violets came as mutations* (New York Times). **4** *Phonetics.* umlaut (def. 1): *Thus "man, men; woman, women;" ... show mutation, ... effected by an "i" or "j" in the succeeding syllable in Common Germanic* (Simeon Potter). [< Latin *mūtātiō, -ōnis* < *mūtāre* to change]

1. Which of the numbered dictionary definitions of *mutation* best fits the word's use in the reading selection? _____

2. The etymology of *mutation* shows that the word comes from the Latin word *mutare* (to change). Use this information and your background knowledge to match the following:

   _____ a. molt   aa. to substitute; exchange; interchange
   _____ b. commute   bb. change from one form to another; transform
   _____ c. transmute   cc. to shed part or all of a coat, or outer covering
   _____ d. permute   dd. change in a vowel sound
   _____ e. umlaut   ee. change the order of

3. In which of the following sentences is *mutation* used correctly?

   _____ a. In humans, a similar mutation can be expressed quite differently in different environments.
   _____ b. In the process of mutation, plants and animals use the energy of the sun to convert carbon dioxide and water into carbohydrates.
   _____ c. A mutation involves changes in the nucleotides of DNA.
   _____ d. X-rays, ultraviolet light, and other radiation have been shown to produce mutations harmful to organisms.

4. Do you think that a *mutation* is always harmful? Could it be beneficial? What would be an example (food production, new plants or flowers)?

_____

_____

5. Write a sentence correctly using *mutation*. (Be sure to include context clues to show you understand the meaning of the word.)

_____

_____

Organelle[3]

or|gan|elle (ôr′gə nel′), *n. Biology.* a minute specialized part of a cell, such as a vacuole in protozoans, analogous in function to an organ of higher animals.

1. Complete the verbal analogy.
   membrane : layer of animal tissue : *organelle* : _____
   a. chromosomes   c. fatty acid hormone
   b. organic substance   d. specialized structure

2. Which of the following are some functions of an *organelle*?
   _____ a. create mutations
   _____ b. make enzymes and other proteins
   _____ c. produce bacteria
   _____ d. provide energy for the cell's activities

3. In which of the following sentences is *organelle* correctly used?
   _____ a. An organelle provides energy for the cell's activities and makes enzymes and other proteins.
   _____ b. At the time of cell division, the organelle changes its appearance.
   _____ c. An organelle is the means by which an organism obtains the oxygen required by its cells and rids itself of carbon dioxide.
   _____ d. In an organelle, energy-rich molecules using oxygen are broken down and provide the energy for the cell's activities.

4. Write a sentence correctly using *organelle*. (Be sure to include context clues to show you understand the meaning of the word.)

   _____

   _____

5. What organ in the human body do you think is comparable to an *organelle*? Explain.

   _____

   _____

Osmosis[5]

os|mo|sis (oz mō′sis, os-), *n.* **1** the tendency of two fluids of different strengths that are separated by something porous to go through it and become mixed. Osmosis is the chief means by which the body absorbs food and by which fluid in the tissues moves into the blood vessels. Osmosis is specifically the tendency of a fluid of lower concentration to pass through a semipermeable membrane into a solution of higher concentration. **2** *Chemistry.* the diffusion or spreading of fluids through a membrane or partition till they are mixed. **3** *Figurative.* a gradual, often unconscious, absorbing or understanding of facts, theories, ideas, and the like: *to learn French by osmosis. A hilarious round of sport and pleasure which could only be described as the broadest education by osmosis* (Harper's). [Grecized variant (as in *endosmosis*) of *osmose* < French < Greek *ōsmós* a thrust]

1. Which of the numbered dictionary definitions of *osmosis* best fits the word's use in the reading selection? _____

2. If a friend said he received his education through *osmosis*, he meant that he

_____ a. paid for it.   _____ c. used telecommunication.

_____ b. studied diligently.   _____ d. unconsciously learned.

3. Select a synonym for *osmosis*.

_____ a. modification   _____ c. reduction

_____ b. mixture   _____ d. differentiation

4. Describe a function or activity in the body that is accomplished through *osmosis*. (See the dictionary entry if necessary.)

_____

_____

5. Write a sentence correctly using *osmosis*. (Be sure to include context clues to show you understand the meaning of the word.)

_____

_____

Photosynthesis[12]

pho|to|syn|the|sis (fō'tə sin'thə sis), *n.* **1** the process by which plant cells make carbohydrates from carbon dioxide and water in the presence of chlorophyll and light, and release oxygen as a by-product: *Photosynthesis, called by some the most important chemical reaction occurring in nature, takes place only in plants containing certain pigments, principally chlorophyll* (Harbaugh and Goodrich). **2** the process by which chemical compounds are synthesized by means of light or other forms of radiant energy.

1. In which of the following sentences is *photosynthesis* used correctly?

_____ a. Bacteria reproduce using the process of photosynthesis.

_____ b. The sun obtains its energy from photosynthesis.

_____ c. Chlorophyll is a key compound in the process of photosynthesis.

_____ d. A by-product of photosynthesis is the release of oxygen.

2. Which of the following derive energy from the process of *photosynthesis?*

_____ a. animals   _____ c. humans

_____ b. green plants   _____ d. algae

3. What is a by-product of *photosynthesis?*

_____ a. cell division   _____ c. carbon dioxide

_____ b. carbohydrates   _____ d. oxygen

4. Write a sentence correctly using *photosynthesis*. (Be sure to include context clues to show you understand the meaning of the word.)

_____

_____

5. Why is *photosynthesis* so important? What do you think is the relationship of *photosynthesis* to the food chain?

_____

_____

ANSWERS TO CHAPTER 6 EXERCISES

Bacterium: **1.** b, d **2.** bb, dd, ee, aa, cc **3.** b
Cytokinesis: **1.** a, b **2.** b (definition) **3.** d
Cytoplasm: **1.** c **2.** a **3.** b, d
Diffusion: **1.** 3a **2.** b, d **3.** c
Ecology: **1.** c (focus of study) **2.** dd, ee, bb, aa, cc **3.** a, b, d
Eucaryote: **1.** c **2.** b **3.** a, d
Evolution: **1.** d **2.** 3 **3.** bb, dd, aa, ee, cc
Karyokinesis: **1.** a **2.** a, b, c **3.** a
Membrane: **1.** c (synonym) **2.** 1 **3.** b
Metabolism: **1.** c, d **2.** a, d **3.** dd, ee, aa, bb, cc
Mitosis: **1.** c (definition) **2.** b **3.** b, d
Mutation: **1.** 2 **2.** cc, aa, bb, ee, dd **3.** c, d
Organelle: **1.** d (definition) **2.** b, d **3.** a, d
Osmosis: **1.** 1 **2.** d **3.** b
Photosynthesis: **1.** c, d **2.** b, d **3.** d

If you missed any of the items in the exercises, return to the exercise and to the dictionary definitions to see where you went wrong. Remember: If you get something right, you only affirm that you knew it. If you get something wrong and understand why, *you have learned something*.

BIOLOGY POSTTEST

Fill in the blanks with the words from this list.

bacterium	eucaryote	mitosis
cytokinesis	evolution	mutation
cytoplasm	karyokinesis	organelle
diffusion	membrane	osmosis
ecology	metabolism	photosynthesis

1. Having a visible nucleus is a characteristic of a(n) _____ .

2. The mixture of two fluids by passing through a membrane is a description of _____ .

3. A(n) _____ is a layer of animal tissue covering or connecting some part of the body.

4. *Change* and *alteration* can be used as synonyms of _____ .

5. A(n) _____ consists of a single cell that is rod shaped, spherical, or spiral and can only be seen through a microscope.

6. _____ is the theory that all living things developed from a few simple forms through a series of physical changes.

7. The division of the cell nucleus is called _____.

8. The change occurring in the cytoplasm of a cell is called

   _____.

9. _____ is the living substance, or protoplasm, of a cell outside of the nucleus.

10. The process by which plant cells make carbohydrates from carbon dioxide and water in the presence of chlorophyll and light and release oxygen as a by-product is called _____.

11. Cell division is known as _____.

12. _____ includes the process by which all living things turn food into energy and living tissue.

13. The branch of biology that deals with the relation of living things to their environment and to each other is _____.

14. A specialized part of a cell is called a(n) _____.

15. Spreading or scattering widely is a characteristic of the process of

   _____.

Answers to this posttest are in the Instructor's Manual.

If you missed any of the words, you may need to return to the exercises and to the dictionary entries to see why your concepts for some words are incomplete.

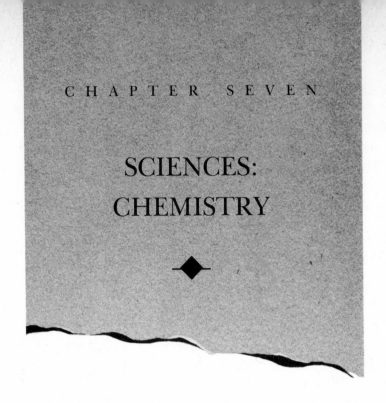

CHAPTER SEVEN

SCIENCES: CHEMISTRY

◆

OVERVIEW

Chemistry deals with the characteristics of simple substances (elements), the changes that take place when they combine to form other substances, and the laws of their behavior under various conditions. Research in chemistry has led to many advances in modern life through improvements in agriculture, drugs and medicines, the management of energy, and the production of consumer goods.

Four common fields of specialization in chemistry are analytical, inorganic, organic, and physical chemistry. Some specific course emphases include agricultural chemistry, biochemistry, clinical chemistry, forensic chemistry, and spectroscopy.

Students who receive degrees in chemistry can pursue careers in a variety of fields, including food processing, secondary education, technical sales, chemical patent law, forensic sciences, and environmental law. An emphasis in biochemistry is useful for students preparing for admission to the health professions—dentistry, medicine, pharmacology, or veterinary medicine. An emphasis on biochemistry is also valuable for students interested in graduate work in molecular biology, medical technology, or clinical chemistry.

Introductory chemistry textbooks are a combination of expository and process analysis. They explain broad concepts or generalizations, and there may be examples and illustrations in the form of charts, diagrams, and tables. Lab manuals are presented in an instructional format, with procedures for experiments and chemical analyses.

The vocabulary in chemistry usually consists of specialized terminology to represent substances, reactions, procedures, and so on and includes such terms as distillation, solvent, *and* induction. *You may add other terms you discover in your studies related to chemistry on the forms in Appendix D.*

VOCABULARY SELF-EVALUATION

The following words will be introduced in this reading selection. Place a check mark (√) in front of any that you know thoroughly and use in your speech or writing. Place a question mark (?) in front of any that you recognize but do not use yourself.

_____ alchemy	_____ equilibrium	_____ miscible
_____ amorphous	_____ evaporation	_____ solute
_____ aqueous	_____ induction	_____ solvent
_____ condensation	_____ kinetic	_____ sublimation
_____ distillation	_____ liquefaction	_____ viscosity

SOME PHYSICAL PROPERTIES OF MATTER

Chemistry is the branch of science that deals with the nature and composition of matter and the changes that matter undergoes. Although it has been a science in the modern sense for only two or three hundred years, historians generally agree that man's earliest involvement with changes in the composition of matter occurred when primitive man discovered fire and was thus able to change wood to gas and ash. Using fire, man was able to turn soil into pottery, to extract metals from soil, and to combine metals by smelting.

In the Middle Ages, the study of metals and their ability to combine became the "science" of alchemy.[1] The alchemist, observing the seemingly magical ability of metals to combine and change, became overly ambitious. He hoped to solve many problems of health and nature, to create gold and silver from base metals, and to produce precious stones from glass or quartz.

THE STUDY OF GASES

However, by the seventeenth century, scientists were better able to understand the physical properties of matter. Using a reasoning process called induction,[2] they collected evidence from specific cases and formed general rules. Evidence concerning odor, color, melting point, boiling point, and state (solid, liquid, or gas) could be observed without changing one substance to another substance. A number of discoveries were made through the study of gases, which could be easily and cheaply produced in the laboratory. Their weights and volumes could be measured with simple equipment, and because many gases are elements, the simplest form of matter, accurate general rules could be formed. Some of these "gas scientists" believed that matter was made up of tiny particles called atoms, even though the particles could not be seen. By experiment the scientists were able to determine that gas will expand to occupy any container into which it is placed and, unless contained, will escape into the atmosphere. Gas has both potential and kinetic[3] energy. (Energy is defined as the capacity or the ability to do work.) Both pressure and temperature affect the volume of gas. (Think, for example, of a balloon full of air. We can change the amount of space the air occupies by heating, cooling, or compressing the balloon.) When a gas is cooled to a specific temperature and compressed by a specific amount of pressure, it undergoes liquefaction.[4] The combination of temperature and pressure needed to produce this state differs according to the substances that make up the gas.

THE LIQUID STATE

Early studies of liquids revealed that some mix completely with others. These are said to be highly miscible.[5] (Liquids that will not mix are immiscible.) Liquids will also dissolve some solids. For example, water will dissolve salt. In such an aqueous[6] solution, the salt is called the solute[7] and the water is called the solvent.[8] Solutions have special properties. They do not "settle out," they can be filtered without being changed, and the solute is evenly distributed in the solvent. In our saltwater solution, for instance, the salt does not settle out of the water, it cannot be filtered out, and the water is as salty at the top of the container as it is at the bottom. The salt can be separated from the water again using a procedure called distillation.[9] If the molecules in a liquid have enough kinetic energy, they escape the attractive forces of the other liquid molecules and become gas, a process called evaporation.[10] The reverse of this process, called condensation,[11] occurs when the gas molecules return to the liquid state. When the number of molecules changing from liquid to gas is equal to the number of molecules changing from gas to liquid, a state of equilibrium[12] exists. Most substances change state in a progression from gas, to liquid, to solid, or the reverse: from solid, to liquid, to gas. In some cases, however, solid substances go directly from the solid state to the gaseous state without becoming a liquid, a process called sublimation.[13] Dry ice, which is solid carbon dioxide, is an example of a solid that sublimates.

Another observable characteristic of a liquid is its resistance to flow, or its viscosity.[14] Oil is more viscous than water, water more viscous than gasoline. We now know that viscosity is determined by differences in the attractions between molecules in the particular liquid.

THE SOLID STATE

Changes in solids could also be observed by early scientists, but there was no way to determine the reason for these changes. Later studies showed that solids exist in two principle types. One is the crystalline solid in which the molecules or atoms are in an ordered arrangement called a crystalline lattice. The second is an amorphous[15] solid in which the molecules or atoms are clumped together in a disordered fashion. A snowflake (a water crystal) is an example of a crystalline solid; common window glass is an example of an amorphous solid.

The changes discussed above are physical changes and do not involve changes in the molecules of the substances. If the molecules were to change—if, for instance, the water changed into its elements of hydrogen and oxygen—this would be a chemical change. Important to the understanding of both kinds of change is knowledge of atomic theory. Modern chemists know a great deal about the atom, the basic building block of nature, and about its composition, how it exists in elements and compounds, and how it undergoes changes. This knowledge has made modern living more comfortable through improvements in agricultural productivity, advances in drugs and medicines, the management of energy, and the production of an ever-wider variety of consumer goods. It is safe to say that the chemistry of today is as important to modern life as fire was to early man. ◆

CHEMISTRY PRETEST

Select words from this list and write them in the blanks to complete the sentences.

alchemy	equilibrium	miscible
amorphous	evaporation	solute
aqueous	induction	solvent
condensation	kinetic	sublimation
distillation	liquefaction	viscosity

1. Something _____ is made with water.

2. Reasoning from particular to general is called _____ .

3. Water and oil are not _____ .

4. The highest stage of something is _____ .

5. A(n) _____ is dissolved in a liquid.

6. The science of the Middle Ages was _____ .

7. The process of changing a vapor to liquid is _____ .

8. In _____ , opposing forces exactly balance.

9. Resistance of fluid to the motion of molecules is _____ .

10. _____ means "able to dissolve."

11. Something uncrystallized is _____ .

12. _____ has to do with motion.

13. Applying pressure and cooling to a gas results in _____ .

14. Changing a liquid into vapor is _____ .

15. _____ is a process of refinement.

Answers to this pretest are in Appendix E.
Unless your instructor tells you to do otherwise, complete the exercises for each word you missed on the pretest. The words, with their meanings and exercises, are in alphabetical order. The superscript numbers

indicate where the words appeared in the reading selection so that you can refer to them when necessary. There are several types of exercises, but for each word you will be asked to write a sentence using context clues. (See Chapter 3 if you need information about how to create context clues.) You are also asked to perform some activity that will help you make your concept of the word personal. *Complete this activity thoughtfully, for creating a personalized concept of the word will help you remember it in the future.*

Answers to all the exercises are at the end of the exercise segment.

CHEMISTRY EXERCISES

Alchemy[1]

al|che|my (al′kə mē), *n.* **1** a combination of chemistry, magic, and philosophy, studied in the Middle Ages. Alchemy tried to find or prepare a substance which would turn cheaper metals into gold and silver and which would also cure any ailment and prolong human life. *In its fullest sense alchemy was a philosophical system containing a complex and mobile core of rudimentary science and elaborated with astrology, religion, mysticism, magic, theosophy and many other constituents. Alchemy dealt not only with the* mysteries of matter but also with those of creation and life; it sought to harmonize the human individual with the universe surrounding him (Scientific American). **2** *Figurative.* a magical or mysterious power or process of transforming one thing into another: *the lovely alchemy of spring.* [< Old French *alkemie*, learned borrowing from Medieval Latin *alchimia* < Arabic *alkīmiyā'* < Late Greek *chymeiā* art of alloying metals < Greek *chýma* ingot < *cheîn* pour]

1. In which of the following sentences can *alchemy* correctly be placed in the blank?

   _____ a. Someone who believed in the promises of _____ might be cheated.

   _____ b. _____ is a modern science.

   _____ c. The solution to many of life's problems can be solved by _____ .

   _____ d. _____ was related to magic.

2. If you practiced *alchemy* during the Middle Ages

   _____ a. you might be honest but mistaken.

   _____ b. you might be trying to cheat people.

   _____ c. you might conduct careful "experiments."

   _____ d. you might have understood atomic theory.

3. Which of the numbered dictionary definitions of *alchemy* best fits the word's use in the reading selection? _____

4. Write a sentence correctly using *alchemy*. (Be sure to include context clues to show you understand the meaning of the word.)

   _____

   _____

5. Why do you think people might believe in *alchemy*?

_____

_____

Amorphous[15]

a|mor|phous (ə môr′fəs), *adj.* **1a** having no definite form; shapeless; formless: *The ghost was an amorphous being that drifted with mist.* **b** *Biology.* without the definite shape or organization found in most higher animals or plants: *An ameba is amorphous.* **c** *Geology.* occurring in a continuous mass, without stratification or cleavage. **2** of no particular type or pattern; anomalous; unclassifiable. **3** not consisting of crystals; uncrystallized; noncrystalline: *Glass is amorphous; sugar is crystalline.* [< Greek *ámorphos* (with English *-ous*) < *a-* without + *morphē* shape] — **a|mor′phous|ly**, *adv.* — **a|mor′phous|ness**, *n.*

1. Place an "s" by any synonym of *amorphous*.
   - _____ a. crystalline   _____ d. uncrystallized
   - _____ b. formless   _____ e. shapeless
   - _____ c. anomalous   _____ f. shaped

2. Which of the following would be *amorphous*?
   - _____ a. a cloud   _____ d. smoke
   - _____ b. an ameba (amoeba)   _____ e. sugar
   - _____ c. a snowflake   _____ f. glass

3. Which of the numbered and lettered dictionary definitions of *amorphous* best fits its use in the reading selection? _____

4. Unless you have special equipment, you cannot see *amorphous* matter in the sense that a chemist uses the word. You do, however, see objects that are *amorphous*. When you say the word, what do you think of?

_____

_____

5. Write a sentence correctly using *amorphous*. (Be sure to include context clues to show you understand the meaning of the word.)

_____

_____

Aqueous[6]

a|que|ous (ā′kwē əs, ak′wē-), *adj.* **1** of water: *aqueous vapor.* **2** containing water; made with water: *The druggist put the medicine in an aqueous solution.* **3** like water; watery: *Aqueous matter ran from the sore.* **4** produced by the action of water. Aqueous rocks are formed of the sediment carried and deposited by water. — **a′que|ous|ly**, *adv.* — **a′que|ous|ness**, *n.*

1. Check any appropriate response to the following statement:
   "An *aqueous* solution may contain many dissolved substances."
   _____ a. That helps to explain how water can become polluted.
   _____ b. That's because it is an acid.
   _____ c. Stirring will remove the substances.
   _____ d. Water solutions are very common.

2. Complete the verbal analogy.
   aqueousness : *aqueous* :: _____ : _____
   a. adj. : n   c. n. : v.
   b. adv. : adj.   d. n. : adj.

3. Which of the numbered dictionary definitions of *aqueous* best fits the word's use in the reading selection? _____

4. Write a sentence correctly using *aqueous*. (Be sure to include context clues to show you understand the meaning of the word.)

   _____

   _____

5. What is your favorite *aqueous* solution?

   _____

   _____

Condensation[11]

con|den|sa|tion (kon´den sā´shən), *n.* **1** the act of condensing: (*Figurative.*) *He [Goldsmith] was a great and perhaps unequalled master of the arts of selection and condensation* (Macaulay). **2** the state of being condensed. **3** a condensed mass. *A cloud is a condensation of water vapor in the atmosphere.* **4** the act or process of changing a gas or vapor into a liquid by cooling: *the condensation of steam into water. Condensation begins first on solid surfaces because these get colder than the general mass of air* (Thomas A. Blair). **5** *Chemistry.* a reaction in which two or more molecules unite to form a larger, more dense, and more complex molecule, often with the separation of water or some other simple substance: *the condensation of milk by removing most of the water from it.* **6** *Physics.* **a** an increase in density and pressure in a medium, such as air, due to the passing of a sound wave or other compression wave. **b** the region in which this occurs. **7** *Psychoanalysis.* the process by which images characterized by a common effect are grouped so as to form a single or composite image, as in dreams.

con|dense (kən dens´), *v.,* **-densed, -dens|ing.**
   —v.t. 1 to make denser or more compact. **SYN:** compress, contract. **2** to increase the strength of; concentrate: *Light is condensed by means of lenses.* **3** *Figurative.* to put into fewer words; say briefly: *A long story can sometimes be condensed into a few sentences.* **SYN:** reduce, shorten. **4** to change (a gas or vapor) to a liquid. **5** *Chemistry.* to cause to undergo condensation: *Milk is condensed by removing much of the water from it.*
   —v.i. 1 to become denser or more compact: *Each [theory] starts from the notion that stars condense from the matter scattered thinly through interstellar space* (W. H. Marshall). **2** to change from a gas or vapor to a liquid. *If steam touches cold surfaces, it condenses into water. If it is cloudy, rainy, or foggy, the water vapor in the air is condensing* (Beauchamp, Mayfield, and West). **3** *Chemistry.* to undergo condensation. [< Latin *condēnsāre* < *com-* together + *dēnsus* thick] **—con|den´sa|ble, con|den´si|ble,** *adj.*

1. In which of the following sentences can *condensation* correctly be placed in the blank?
   _____ a. Sometimes a magazine will print the _____ of a novel.
   _____ b. Vapor can change to liquid in the process of _____.

_____ c. Joe is not very tall; he is the _____ of his father.

_____ d. Canned milk is a _____ of regular milk.

2. Which of the following might undergo *condensation*?

_____ a. a gas   _____ d. a person

_____ b. a book   _____ e. a liquid

_____ c. an idea   _____ f. air

3. Which of the numbered and lettered dictionary definitions of *condensation* best fits the word's use in the reading selection? _____

4. You probably observe the result of *condensation* regularly. Can you say where? (Perhaps on the outside of a cold bottle or can of pop or beer.)

_____

_____

5. Write a sentence correctly using *condensation*. (Be sure to include context clues to show you understand the meaning of the word.)

_____

_____

Distillation[9]

dis|til|la|tion (dis′tə lā′shən), *n.* **1** the act of distilling: *the distillation of water to purify it.* (*Figurative.*) *Ordinarily, decisions which must be made when life and death are at stake require a profundity of reflection, a weighing of factors, and the eventual distillation of a choice* (Atlantic). **2** the process of distilling; heating a liquid or solid in a retort, still, etc., and condensing the vapor given off by cooling it in order to purify and condense the thing heated: *Distillation is important both in the laboratory and in industry* (William N. Jones). **3** something distilled; extract; the refined or concentrated essence: (*Figurative.*) *"Lover Man," written in 1941, [is] recorded by him for the first time on this disk with a simple, direct persuasiveness that can only be the distillation of 25 years of playing it in every conceivable fashion* (New York Times).

dis|till (dis til′), *v.*, **-tilled, -till|ing.** *— v.t.* **1** to make (a liquid or other substance) pure by turning it into a vapor and then cooling it into a liquid form again: *to distill water for drinking.* **2** to obtain by distilling; refine: *Gasoline is distilled from crude oil. Alcoholic liquor is distilled from mash made from grain.* **3** *Figurative.* to get out the essential principle; extract: *A jury must distill the truth from the testimony of witnesses.* **4** to give off in drops: *These flowers distill a sweet nectar.* **SYN:** exude. **5** to let fall in drops: *The sky distills the dew.* *— v.i.* **1** to fall in drops; drip; trickle: *Tears distilled slowly from her eyes.* **2** to undergo distillation. [< Late Latin *distillāre,* for *dēstillāre* < Latin *dē-* down + *stilla* drop]

1. Which of the following might be the result of *distillation*?

_____ a. a sandy beach   _____ c. perfume

_____ b. purified water   _____ d. liquor

2. Complete the verbal analogy.

fire : warmth :: *distillation* : _____

a. purification   c. heat

b. process   d. chemistry

3. Which of the numbered dictionary definitions of *distillation* best fits the word's use in the reading selection? _____

4. Write a sentence correctly using *distillation*. (Be sure to include context clues to show you understand the meaning of the word.)

_____

_____

5. The *distillation* of seawater for drinking purposes is possible. Do you think it should be widely practiced?

_____

_____

Equilibrium[12]

e|qui|lib|ri|um (ē′kwə lib′rē əm), *n., pl.* **-ri|ums**, **-ri|a** (-rē ə). **1** balance; condition in which opposing forces exactly balance or equal each other: *The acrobat in the circus maintained equilibrium on a tightrope. Scales are in equilibrium when the weights on each side are equal.* **2** the state of a chemical system when no further change occurs in it. **3** *Figurative.* balance between powers of any kind; equality of importance or effect among the various parts of any complex unity: *After a time which varies from a few to many years an equilibrium is established between parasite and host, so that both continue to survive* (Fenner and Day). **4** mental poise: *My mother does not let quarrels between my brother and me upset her equilibrium.* sʏɴ: stability. [< Latin *aequilībrium* < *aequus* equal + *lībra* balance]

1. In which of the following sentences can *equilibrium* correctly be placed in the blank?
   _____ a. In chemical _____, the rates of reaction between two solutions are the same.
   _____ b. I admire Mary's emotional _____.
   _____ c. _____ appears to be the absence of change.
   _____ d. In chemical _____, there is no movement of molecules.

2. Which of the following describe *equilibrium*?
   _____ a. unchanging   _____ d. balanced
   _____ b. stable   _____ e. unstable
   _____ c. equality   _____ f. varied

3. Which of the numbered dictionary definitions of *equilibrium* best fits the word's use in the reading selection? _____

4. Have you achieved a state of mental *equilibrium*? How? If not, how might you achieve it?

_____

_____

5. Write a sentence correctly using *equilibrium*. (Be sure to include context clues to show you understand the meaning of the word.)

_____

_____

Evaporation[10]

e|vap|o|ra|tion (i vap′ə rā′shən), *n.* **1** the act or process of changing a liquid or a solid into vapor; an evaporating: *Wet clothes on a line become dry by evaporation of the water in them.* **2** the state of being changed into vapor. **3** the removal of water or other liquid. **4a** the product of the evaporating process. **b** the amount evaporated. **5** *Figurative.* disappearance.

e|vap|o|rate (i vap′ə rāt), *v.*, **-rat|ed, -rat|ing.** — *v.i.* **1** to turn into vapor; change from a liquid or solid into a vapor: *Boiling water evaporates rapidly. Some solids, such as moth balls and dry*

ice, *evaporate without melting.* **SYN:** volatilize, vaporize. **2** to give off moisture. **3** *Figurative.* to vanish; disappear: *His good resolutions evaporated after New Year.* **SYN:** dissipate. — *v.t.* **1** to remove water or other liquid from, for example by heat, in order to dry or to reduce to a more concentrated state: *Heat is used to evaporate milk.* **2** to cause to change from a liquid (or less often, solid) into a vapor; drive off in the form of vapor: *Heat evaporates water.* [< Latin *ēvapōrāre* (with English *-ate¹*) < *ex-* out + *vapor* vapor, steam]

1. Check any appropriate response to the following statement: "During *evaporation*, molecules escape from a liquid."
   - _____ a. They become a gas.
   - _____ b. You have to pour them out of the container.
   - _____ c. It is the chemical opposite of condensation.
   - _____ d. The rate of evaporation can change with temperature.

2. Complete the verbal analogy.
   fishing : fish :: *evaporation* : _____
   a. change   c. liquid
   b. vapor   d. vanish

3. Which of the numbered and lettered dictionary definitions of *evaporation* best fits the word's use in the reading selection? _____

4. Write a sentence correctly using *evaporation*. (Be sure to include context clues to show you understand the meaning of the word.)

   _____

   _____

5. Are you aware of experiencing the process of *evaporation*? Describe the way your body is cooled in hot weather. Think about it the next time you perspire.

   _____

   _____

Induction[2]

in|duc|tion (in duk′shən), *n.* **1a** the process by which an object having electrical or magnetic properties produces similar properties in a nearby object, usually without direct contact; inductance: *Induction can give a conductor a permanent charge ... until it leaks off or is otherwise dissipated* (Scientific American). **b** a tendency exhibited by currents of electricity to resist change. **2a** reasoning from particular facts to a general rule or principle. **b** a conclusion reached in this way: *Every induction is a speculation and it guesses at a unity which the facts present but do not strictly imply* (J. Bronowski). **3a** the act of inducting; act or ceremony of installing a person in office; installation. **b** *U.S.* enrollment in military service. **4** the act of bringing into existence or

operation; producing; causing; inducing: *induction of a hypnotic state.* **5** the taking of the explosive mixture or air into the cylinder of an internal-combustion engine. **6** *Embryology.* the change in form or shape caused by the action of one tissue of an embryo on adjacent tissues or parts. **7** *Archaic.* an introductory statement in a literary work; a preface or prelude.
▶ See **deduction** for usage note.

from **deduction:**

▶**Deduction, induction** are names of opposite processes of reasoning, the two ways in which we think. *Deduction* applies to the process by which one starts with a general principle that is accepted as true, applies it to a particular case, and arrives at a conclusion that is true if the starting principle was true, as in *All female mammals secrete milk; this is a female mammal; therefore, this will secrete milk.* Induction applies to the process by which one collects many particular cases, finds out by experiment what is common to all of them, and forms a general rule or principle which is probably true, as in *Every female mammal I have tested secreted milk; probably all female mammals secrete milk.*

1. Check any appropriate response to the following statement:
   "He solved the problem by using *induction*."
   _____ a. Guesswork is sometimes the best way.
   _____ b. He established a general rule first.
   _____ c. He worked from individual items to a general rule.
   _____ d. Do you mean it was a chance discovery?

2. Which of the following might be interested in *induction*?
   _____ a. a waiter   _____ d. an army recruiter
   _____ b. a hairdresser   _____ e. a detective
   _____ c. a hypnotist   _____ f. a mechanic

3. Which of the numbered and lettered dictionary definitions of *induction* best fits the word's use in the reading selection? _____

4. *Induction* and *deduction* as reasoning processes are often confused. (Sir Arthur Conan Doyle added to this confusion in one of his Sherlock Holmes stories, "The Sign of the Four," with a chapter called "The Science of Deduction." Many people conclude from this that crime detection is carried out by *deduction*, rather than *induction*.) Take this opportunity to clarify for yourself the concepts of and differences between the two.

   _____

   _____

5. Write a sentence correctly using *induction*. (Be sure to include context clues to show you understand the meaning of the word.)

   _____

   _____

Kinetic[3]

ki|net|ic (ki net′ik), *adj.* **1** of or having to do with motion. **2** caused by or resulting from motion. **3** of or having to do with kinetic art; involving motion or the suggestion of motion produced especially by mechanical parts, colors, and lights. [< Greek *kīnētikós* < *kīneîn* to move] — **ki|net′i|cal-ly,** *adv.*

1. Complete the verbal analogy.
   attempt : try :: *kinetic* : _____
   a. motion   c. process
   b. energy   d. chemistry

2. Check any appropriate response to the following statement:
   "Tom is interested in *kinetic* theory."
   _____ a. He is taking dance lessons.
   _____ b. Perhaps he should run a restaurant.
   _____ c. No wonder he is studying chemistry.
   _____ d. Do you think he will run for political office?

3. Which of the numbered dictionary definitions of *kinetic* best fits the word's use in the reading selection? _____

4. Write a sentence correctly using *kinetic*. (Be sure to include context clues to show you understand the meaning of the word.)

   _____

   _____

5. The word *kinetic* comes from the same Greek root as *cinema*. Do you know how pictures appear to move?

   _____

   _____

Liquefaction[4]

liq|ue|fac|tion (lik′wə fak′shən), *n.* **1** the process of changing into a liquid, especially of changing a gas by the application of pressure and cooling. **2** liquefied condition.
liq|ue|fy (lik′wə fī), *v.t., v.i.,* **-fied, -fy|ing.** to change into a liquid; make or become liquid: *Liquefied air is extremely cold.* [< Middle French *liquéfier,* learned borrowing from Latin *liquefacere* < *liquēre* be fluid + *facere* make] —**liq′ue|fi′a-ble,** *adj.* —**liq′ue|fi′er,** *n.*

1. In which of the following sentences can *liquefaction* correctly be placed in the blank?
   _____ a. _____ occurs when a gas is cooled to a specific temperature and compressed by a specific pressure.
   _____ b. The combination of temperature and pressure needed for the _____ of a gas differs depending on the substances that make up the gas.
   _____ c. _____ occurs when the attractive forces between molecules overcome the forces of kinetic motion.
   _____ d. _____ is the formation of a gas.

2. The etymology of *liquefaction* (see at *liquefy*) shows that the word comes from Latin words, *liquere* (to be fluid) and *facere* (to make). Use this information and your background knowledge to match the following:
   _____ a. benefaction   aa. the liquid in which food is canned
   _____ b. liquor   bb. to make by hand or machine
   _____ c. malefactor   cc. fulfillment of desires
   _____ d. manufacture   dd. a criminal; evil doer
   _____ e. satisfaction   ee. kindly or generous action

3. Complete the verbal analogy.
   rose : flower :: *liquefaction* : _____
   a. liquefy   c. process
   b. Latin   d. pressure

4. You might have to make use of products that have undergone *liquefaction*. Liquefied gas fire extinguishers should be used on fires that involve combustible liquids such as cooking grease, gasoline, or oil, and on fires that involve motors, switches, or other electrical equipment. Where else might you see or use liquefied gas?

   _____

   _____

5. Write a sentence correctly using *liquefaction*. (Be sure to include context clues to show you understand the meaning of the word.)

   _____

   _____

Miscible[5]

mis|ci|ble (mis′ə bəl), *adj.* that can be mixed:
Water is not miscible with oil. [< Latin *miscēre*
mix + English *-ible*]

1. Check any appropriate reply to the following statement:
   "Oil and kerosene are *miscible* liquids."
   _____ a. I notice the price has gone down lately.
   _____ b. But oil and water are not.
   _____ c. Water and alcohol also mix.
   _____ d. Engines would miss them, all right!

2. Which statement(s) match(es) the following statement?
   "Two liquids that are infinitely soluble are said to be completely *miscible*."
   _____ a. Some liquids are partially miscible.
   _____ b. Any amount of water will dissolve in any amount of methyl alcohol.
   _____ c. Gasoline and oil are insoluble in water.
   _____ d. Gasoline and water are immiscible.

3. Complete the verbal analogy.
   opposition : cooperation :: *miscible* : _____
   a. mixable   c. soluble
   b. liquids   d. immiscible

4. Write a sentence correctly using *miscible*. (Be sure to include context clues to show you understand the meaning of the word.)

   _____

   _____

5. What *miscible* liquids make up your favorite beverage? Chocolate syrup and milk? Water and Kool-aid? Other?

_____

_____

Solute[7]

sol|ute (sol′yüt, sō′lüt), *n., adj.* —*n.* a solid, gas, or liquid that is dissolved in a liquid to make a solution: *Salt is a solute in seawater. Stems . . . act as channels through which water and solutes reach the leaves* (Fred W. Emerson).
—*adj.* **1** dissolved; in solution. **2** *Botany.* not adhering; free.
[< Latin *solūtus,* past participle of *solvere* dissolve, loosen]

1. Which of the following might be a *solute*?
   _____ a. sugar   _____ d. salt
   _____ b. carbon dioxide _____ e. oxygen
   _____ c. milk   _____ f. pepper

2. Which statement(s) match(es) the following statement?
   "One of the *solutes* in champagne is carbon dioxide."
   _____ a. Champagne contains water and alcohol.
   _____ b. Champagne is a solution containing a dissolved gas.
   _____ c. Champagne is an aqueous solution.
   _____ d. One of the solutes in champagne is sugar.

3. Complete the verbal analogy.
   branch : tree :: *solute* : _____
   a. solution   c. gas
   b. dissolve   d. solid

4. Do you add any *solute* to coffee or tea?

   _____

   _____

5. Write a sentence correctly using *solute*. (Be sure to include context clues to show you understand the meaning of the word.)

   _____

   _____

Solvent[8]

sol|vent (sol′vənt), *adj., n.* —*adj.* **1** able to pay all one owes: *A bankrupt firm is not solvent.* **2** able to dissolve: *Gasoline is a solvent liquid that removes grease spots.*
—*n.* **1** a substance, usually a liquid, that can dissolve other substances: *Water is a solvent of sugar and salt.* **2** a thing that solves, explains, or settles.
[< Latin *solvēns, -entis,* present participle of *solvere* loosen (used in *rem solvere* to free one's property and person from debt)] — **sol′vent|ly,** *adv.*

1. In which of the following sentences is *solvent* used correctly?
   _____ a. A solvent is a medium, usually a liquid, that dissolves another substance.
   _____ b. Water is a good solvent for many salts.
   _____ c. Through chemistry, many of the world's problems are solvent.
   _____ d. No solvent has been found for current banking problems.

2. Which of the following might be a *solvent*?
   _____ a. cold water   _____ d. sand
   _____ b. coffee   _____ e. alcohol
   _____ c. gasoline   _____ f. hot water

3. Which of the numbered dictionary definitions of *solvent* best fits the word's use in the reading selection? _____

4. Write a sentence correctly using *solvent*. (Be sure to include context clues to show you understand the meaning of the word.)

   _____

   _____

5. List at least five ways you use that most popular *solvent*, water.

   _____

   _____

Sublimation[13]

sub|li|ma|tion (sub´lə mā´shən), *n.* **1** the act or process of sublimating or subliming; purification: *This direct transition from solid to vapor is called sublimation* (Sears and Zemansky). **2** the resulting product or state, especially, mental elevation or exaltation: *that enthusiastic sublimation which is the source of greatness and energy* (Thomas L. Peacock). **3** the highest stage or purest form of a thing. **4** a chemical sublimate.
sub|lime (sə blīm´), *adj., n., v.,* **-limed, -lim|ing.**
—*adj.* **1** noble; grand; majestic; lofty: *Mountain scenery is often sublime.* **2** exalted; excellent; eminent; supreme: *sublime devotion. How sublime a thing it is To suffer and be strong* (Longfellow). **3** expressing lofty ideas in a grand manner: *sublime poetry.* **4a** of lofty bearing or appearance: *In his simplicity sublime* (Tennyson). **b** *Obsolete.* haughty; proud. **5** *Archaic.* set or raised aloft. **6** *Obsolete.* elated.
—*n.* **1** something that is lofty, noble, exalted, or majestic: *the sublime in literature and art. No, never need an American look beyond his own country for the sublime and beautiful of natural* scenery (Washington Irving). **2** the highest degree or example (of): *Your upward gaze at me now is the very sublime of faith, truth, and devotion* (Charlotte Brontë).
—*v.t.* **1** to make higher or nobler; make sublime: *A judicious use of metaphors wonderfully raises, sublimes and adorns oratory* (Oliver Goldsmith). **2a** to heat (a solid substance) and condense the vapor given off; purify; refine. **b** to cause to be given off by this or a similar process. —*v.i.* **1** to pass off as a vapor and condense as a solid without going through the liquid state; become purified or refined. **2** to be changed into a gas directly from the solid state.
from the sublime to the ridiculous, from one extreme to the other: *His writing is very uneven, running the gamut from the sublime to the ridiculous.*
[< Latin *sublīmis* (originally) sloping up (to the lintel) < *sub-* up + *līmen, -inis* threshold] —**sub|lime´ly,** *adv.* —**sub|lime´ness,** *n.* —**sub|lim´er,** *n.*

1. Check any appropriate response to the following statement:
   "The vaporization of a solid is called *sublimation*."
   _____ a. There is no liquid stage.
   _____ b. The solid must go directly into the gaseous stage.

_____ c. The solid becomes a liquid solution.

_____ d. This process does not occur in all solids.

2. Which statement(s) match(es) the following statement?
"Naphthalene (mothballs) will undergo *sublimation*."

_____ a. Mothballs melt to a sticky liquid.

_____ b. Mothballs change from solid to gas.

_____ c. The alchemists purified sulfur and arsenic by this process.

_____ d. Mothballs are made of naphthalene.

3. Which of the numbered dictionary definitions of *sublimation* best fits the word's use in the reading selection? _____

4. Have you ever seen the chemical process of *sublimation*? (If you have not seen dry ice, make it a point to see some.)

_____

_____

5. Write a sentence correctly using *sublimation*. (Be sure to include context clues to show you understand the meaning of the word.)

_____

_____

Viscosity[14]

vis|cos|i|ty (vis kos′ə tē), *n., pl.* **-ties. 1** the condition or quality of being viscous. **2** *Physics.* **a** the resistance of a fluid to the motion of its molecules among themselves. **b** the ability of a solid or semisolid to change its shape gradually under stress.
vis|cose¹ (vis′kōs), *n., adj. —n.* a thick, sticky substance made by treating cellulose with caustic soda and carbon disulfide. Viscose is used in manufacturing rayon and cellophane, for sizing, and for other purposes. *—adj.* having to do with or made from viscose. [< Latin *viscum* birdlime + English *-ose²* (because it is a syruplike material)]

1. In which of the following sentences can *viscosity* correctly be placed in the blank?

_____ a. _____ is the syruplike quality of a liquid.

_____ b. If a liquid is cooled, _____ increases.

_____ c. A fluid that has low _____ flows readily.

_____ d. Oil has higher _____ than water.

2. Place an "h" by substances with high *viscosity* and an "l" by substances with low *viscosity*.

_____ a. mustard   _____ d. milk

_____ b. tar   _____ e. soda pop

_____ c. hot tea   _____ f. whipped cream

3. Complete the verbal analogy.

warmth : fire :: *viscosity* : _____

a. liquid state   c. resistance

b. molecule attractions   d. coldness

4. Write a sentence correctly using *viscosity*. (Be sure to include context clues to show you understand the meaning of the word.)

_____

_____

5. List some occasions when you deal with the *viscosity* of a liquid. For example, when you try to get ketchup out of a bottle.

_____

_____

ANSWERS TO CHAPTER 7 EXERCISES

Alchemy: **1.** a, d **2.** a, b, c **3.** 1
Amorphous: **1.** b, c, d, e **2.** a, b, d, f **3.** 3
Aqueous: **1.** a, d **2.** d (parts of speech) **3.** 2
Condensation: **1.** a, b, d **2.** a, b, c, e, f **3.** 4
Distillation: **1.** b, c, d **2.** a (cause-effect) **3.** 2
Equilibrium: **1.** a, b, c **2.** a, b, c, d **3.** 2
Evaporation: **1.** a, c, d **2.** b (product) **3.** 1
Induction: **1.** c **2.** c, d, e, f **3.** 2a
Kinetic: **1.** a (synonym) **2.** c **3.** 2
Liquefaction: **1.** a, b, c **2.** ee, aa, dd, bb, cc **3.** c (specific-general)
Miscible: **1.** b, c **2.** b **3.** d (antonym)
Solute: **1.** a, b, c, d, e **2.** b **3.** a (part-whole)
Solvent: **1.** a, b, d **2.** a, b, c, e, f **3.** *n.* 1
Sublimation: **1.** a, b, d **2.** b **3.** 1
Viscosity: **1.** a, b, c, d **2.** h, h, l, l, l, h **3.** b (effect-cause)

If you missed any of the items in the exercises, return to the exercise and to the dictionary definition to see where you went wrong. Remember: If you get something right, you only affirm that you knew it. If you get something wrong and understand why, *you have learned something*.

CHEMISTRY POSTTEST

Fill in the blanks with the words from this list.

alchemy	equilibrium	miscible
amorphous	evaporation	solute
aqueous	induction	solvent
condensation	kinetic	sublimation
distillation	liquefaction	viscosity

1. _____ is the ability of a solid to change shape gradually.
2. In _____ , no chemical change occurs.
3. A liquefied condition is _____ .
4. A(n) _____ is an extract.
5. _____ is the removal of water.
6. A cloud is an example of _____ .
7. _____ means "without stratification."
8. Another word for installation is _____ .
9. Something suggesting motion is _____ .
10. _____ means purification.
11. Liquids that are highly soluble are completely _____ .
12. Something being dissolved is a(n) _____ .
13. _____ has to do with water.
14. A thing that solves or explains is a(n) _____ .
15. _____ is from the Greek meaning "the art of alloying metals."

   Answers to this posttest are in the Instructor's Manual.
   If you missed any of the words, you may need to return to the exercises and to the dictionary entries to see why your concepts for some words are incomplete.

CHAPTER EIGHT

SCIENCES: MATHEMATICS

◆

OVERVIEW

Mathematics is the study of numbers, measurements, and space. It is the science dealing with the measurement, properties, and relationships of quantities as expressed in numbers or symbols. The study of mathematics provides powerful intellectual tools that have contributed to advances in science and technology.

Curriculum offerings in mathematics include courses in calculus, trigonometry, analytic and plane geometry, probability and statistics, linear and abstract algebra, operations research, matrix analysis, linear programming, and differential equations. Coursework in mathematics prepares students for careers in applied mathematics, probability and statistics, or in teaching at the elementary or secondary levels. Computer science majors usually are required to take mathematics courses as part of their program also.

Introductory mathematics textbooks provide a combination of expository, problem-solution, and instructional material. They present theoretical concepts and accompanying examples, as well as problem sets with instructions on finding the problem solutions. Texts may contain historical notes and charts, as well as tables and figures that visually represent concepts.

The vocabulary in mathematics consists mainly of general vocabulary terms that have a specific meaning within the context of mathematics. Examples of such terms are range, function, *and* integral. *Specialized vocabulary unique to mathematics contains terms such as* calculus, decimal, *and* integer. *You may add other terms you discover in your studies related to mathematics on the forms in Appendix D.*

THEOREMS IN MATHEMATICS

Mathematics is the study of numbers, forms, or arrangements and their associated relationships. Thus mathematics is a form of reasoning, and mathematicians work from a set of fundamental rules or assumptions, also known as axioms,* that are accepted as true. A theorem[1] is another element in a mathematical system, since it is a statement that has been proved based on the assumed truth of the axiom(s) on which it was developed. Each of the following fields within mathematics—number theory, algebra, geometry, and calculus—contain theorems that have been proved through a logical deductive process, that is, through various levels of reasoning with statements and their proofs.

NUMBER THEORY

Number theory is a branch of mathematics concerned with properties of numbers. One collection of often-studied numbers is that of natural numbers; that is, 1, 2, 3, and so on. Interest in numbers is as old as civilization itself, and number theory grew out of the inexact sciences of numerology and astrology. Greek mathematicians, such as Eratosthenes and Euclid, were especially interested in investigating the properties of natural numbers.

One classification of natural numbers is even and odd numbers, and another classification consists of prime[2] and composite[3] numbers. A prime number is a natural number greater than 1 that has

---

* *Axiom* is introduced as word number 3 in Chapter 16.

exactly two divisors, itself and 1, namely, 2, 3, 5, 7, 11, and so on. The fourth-century B.C. mathematician Euclid proved that the number of prime numbers is infinite. A composite number, on the other hand, is a natural number greater than 1 that is not a prime number and thus has more than two divisors, such as 4 (which is divisible by 1, 2, and 4).

The fundamental theorem of arithmetic states that any natural number greater than 1 is prime or can be expressed as a product of prime numbers. This fundamental theorem also relates to the concept of the factor[4] of a number, that is, a composite number is a product of prime factors. For example, the prime factors of the composite number 21 would be 3 and 7, since both 3 and 7 are prime numbers and $21 = 3 \cdot 7$. For 30, it would be 2, 3, and 5, since they are prime numbers and $30 = 2 \cdot 3 \cdot 5$.

The early Greek mathematician Eratosthenes designed a technique called the "sieve of Eratosthenes" for finding primes smaller than some given number. And in 1640 the French mathematician Pierre de Fermat developed a test for primes that is still used today. In 1876, the English mathematician E. Lucas developed a test to discover a certain type of prime number. The test was refined in 1930 by the American D. H. Lehmer. It was used in 1986 in a large computer to discover a prime number that was so large it contained over 65,000 digits!

Finally, another concept in number theory concerns real numbers and integers. Integers are whole numbers, and real numbers include a decimal (44 is an integer, while 4.4 is a real number). Both real numbers and integers can be written in scientific notation, which expresses numbers in multiples of 10 to an exponent.[5] An exponent is a number placed at the upper right of a number to show how many times it is to be used as a factor. For example, 5,642 can be expressed in scientific notation as 5.642×10^3 or $56.42 \times$

10^2; the superscripts 3 and 2 to the right of 10 are both exponents.

ALGEBRA

Algebra is one of the chief branches of mathematics and is basic to more advanced study in higher mathematics, statistics, and computer technology. In algebra, symbols, usually letters of the alphabet such as x and y, represent numbers or members of a specified set of numbers. Such a symbol is also called a variable.[6]

Many early civilizations, such as the Chinese, Persians, Indians, and Babylonians, used a rudimentary form of algebra. A Greek mathematician, Diophantus (c. A.D. 200), has been called the "father of algebra" for his use of quadratic equations and symbols for unknown quantities. The Hindus, Arabs, Italians, and French (including René Descartes) have also contributed to the development of algebra. The term *algebra* is an Arabic word meaning "reduction" in the sense of solving an equation.

An example of an algebraic expression is $x - 3$, with x as the variable assigned to represent any element of the set N. The set N is therefore called the domain[7] of the variable. In an algebraic equation with two variables, such as in $x + y = 6$, x is the first variable and y is the second variable. The name given to the replacement set for y is called the range.[8]

When two variables are related so that for each value assumed by one there is a value determined for the other, this is known as a function.[9] An example of a function would be $y = 6x + 2$, with the value of y depending on the value of x. As different replacements are made for x, y will have a different value.

Finally, an example of a theorem in algebra that has been proved by application of logic to certain axioms is: If x and y are numbers greater than zero and $x > y$, then $y - x$ is a negative number. An application of this theorem would be the following: x is 10 and y is 5, then $5 - 10$ is a negative number, in this case, -5.

GEOMETRY

Geometry is the mathematical study of the shapes and sizes of figures. The term *geometry* comes from the Greek words *geo* (earth) and *metr* (measure). There is evidence that the Egyptians and Babylonians used a type of geometry in architecture, engineering, and astronomy. Early Greek mathematicians, including Thales of Miletus, Pythagoras, Euclid, and Archimedes, developed elementary geometry to a higher degree. The first book on analytic geometry, published in 1637 by the French mathematician René Descartes, showed a relationship between geometric figures and algebraic equations.

Geometry is based on assumptions (also known as axioms or postulates)[10] that are accepted as true without proof. Geometry is designated Euclidean if the postulates of Euclid (from his book *Elements*) are involved, and non-Euclidean if a change has been made in one or more of these postulates. An example of a Euclidean postulate is Postulate 1: A line can be drawn from any point to any other point.

Other geometric concepts include that of congruent and similar figures. Geometric figures are said to be congruent[11] when they have the same size and shape and are symbolized by $\cong$. On the other hand, the symbol $\sim$ is used to represent similar figures, those that have the same shape (see Figures 1 and 2).

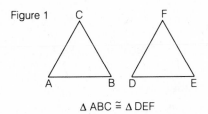

Figure 1

$\triangle\,ABC \cong \triangle\,DEF$

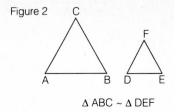

Figure 2

$\triangle\,ABC \sim \triangle\,DEF$

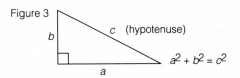

Figure 3

$a^2 + b^2 = c^2$

Finally, a famous theorem in geometry is that proposed by Pythagorus (c. 500 B.C.) and concerns the triangle. This theorem states that the sum of the squares of the lengths of the sides of a right triangle is equal to the square of the length of the hypotenuse[12] (see Figure 3).

CALCULUS

Calculus is an important tool in higher mathematics as well as in business, computer science, engineering, the physical sciences, and many other fields. The development of calculus in the 1660s marks a turning point in the history of mathematics. Both Isaac Newton and Gottfried Leibniz, working independently, in two different countries and on totally separate problems, developed calculus at about the same time.

Calculus is divided into two main branches of study: differential calculus and integral calculus. Differential calculus studies small, subtle changes, while integral calculus studies total change. The entities involved in calculus are functions. In differential calculus, functions are differentiated to obtain new functions called derivatives.[13] A derivative can be defined as the instantaneous rate of change of a function with respect to a variable through obtaining the slope of the line tangent to the graph of the function at that point.

In integral calculus, functions are integrated to obtain new functions called integrals.[14] By evaluating an integral at the endpoints of an interval in the domain of the function, we sometimes obtain the area of the region between the graph of the function and the horizontal axis on that interval. Integrals are often used in finding areas and volumes.

Differentiation and integration are inverse[15] operations, since integrating a function then differentiating the resulting integral yields the same function back again. For example, if $f(x)$ is $3x^2 - 6x + 5$, differentiation yields the new function $6x - 6$, while integrating $6x - 6$ can bring one back to $3x^2 - 6x + 5$. Prior to the development of calculus, the methods for finding tangent lines and areas were very different. Thus it was truly remarkable to find the derivative and the integral to be related. Newton was the first one in history to exploit this inverse relationship, but it was Newton's teacher Isaac Barrow who discovered and proved the amazing theorem that differentiation and integration are inverse operations in the fundamental theorem of calculus. The formal realization of this relationship can be said to mark the true birth of calculus. ◆

MATHEMATICS PRETEST

Select words from this list and write them in the blanks to complete the sentences.

composite	factor	postulate
congruent	function	prime
derivative	hypotenuse	range
domain	integral	theorem
exponent	inverse	variable

1. Correspondence between two sets of elements is sometimes called a(n) _____ .

2. A superscript number written above and to the right of a quantity to show how many times the quantity is to be used as a factor is a(n) _____ .

3. A(n) _____ number has no common integral divisor but one and the number itself.

4. _____ is the instantaneous rate of change of a function with respect to its variable.

5. _____ refers to a quantity that can assume any of the values in a given set of values or a symbol representing this quantity.

6. Something taken for granted or assumed as a basis for reasoning is a(n) _____ .

7. The set of all the values a given function may take on is called the _____ .

8. _____ refers to an operation that cancels what another operation does.

9. The number ten is a(n) _____ number, since it is a number exactly divisible by some whole number other than itself or 1.

10. A(n) _____ is a statement that can be proved or that has been proved.

11. Any one of the numbers or expressions that produce a given number or quantity when multiplied together is a(n) _____.

12. _____ is the set of all numbers that can be assigned to the algebraic variable x in an equation with two variables.

13. The side of a right triangle opposite the right angle is a(n) _____.

14. Triangles with the same size and shape are said to be _____.

15. The result of an integration in calculus is a(n) _____.

Answers to this pretest are in Appendix E.

Unless your instructor tells you to do otherwise, complete the exercises for each word that you missed on the pretest. The words, with their meanings and exercises, are in alphabetical order. The superscript numbers indicate where the words appeared in the reading selection so that you can refer to them when necessary. There are several types of exercises, but for each word you will be asked to write a sentence using context clues. (See Chapter 3 if you need information about how to create context clues.) You are also asked to perform some activity that will help you make your concept of the word personal. *Complete this activity thoughtfully, for creating a personalized concept of the word will help you remember it in the future.*

Answers to all the exercises are at the end of the exercise segment.

MATHEMATICS EXERCISES

Composite[3]

com|pos|ite (kəm poz′it), *adj., n.* —*adj.* 1 made up of various parts; compound: *The photographer made a composite picture by putting together parts of several others.* 2 belonging to the composite family.
—*n.* 1 any composite thing: *English is a composite of many languages.* SYN: combination, compound, complex. 2 a composite plant. 3 = composite number.

[< Latin *compositus*, past participle of *compōnere* < *com-* together + *pōnere* put. See etym. of doublet **compost, compote**.] —**com|pos′ite|ly**, *adv.* —**com|pos′ite|ness**, *n.*
composite number, a number exactly divisible by some whole number other than itself or one. 4, 6, and 9 are composite numbers; 2, 3, 5, and 7 are prime numbers.

1. Complete the verbal analogy.
   prime : first :: *composite* : _____
   a. premier   c. complication
   b. posterior   d. combination

2. The etymology of *composite* shows that the word comes from the Latin *componere* (*com* means "together" and *ponere* means "to put"). Use this information and your background knowledge to match the following:

_____ a. impose
aa. to put between; insert

_____ b. preposition
bb. to put out of office or a position of authority, especially a high office like that of a king

_____ c. repository
cc. to put (a burden, tax, or punishment) on something

_____ d. interpose
dd. a place or container where things are stored or kept

_____ e. depose
ee. a word that shows certain relations between other words

3. In which of the following sentences is *composite* used correctly?

_____ a. A mosaic is a composite of small pieces of glass.
_____ b. The numbers 3, 7, and 11 are composite numbers.
_____ c. This poem is like a composite of images describing a beautiful sunset.
_____ d. The numbers 15, 25, and 40 are composite numbers.

4. Write a sentence correctly using *composite*. (Be sure to include context clues to show you understand the meaning of the word.)

_____

_____

5. List five numbers that are *composite* numbers. How are they different from prime numbers? Explain.

_____

_____

Congruent[11]

con|gru|ent (kong′grů ent), *adj.* **1** *Geometry.* exactly coinciding: *Congruent triangles have the same size and shape.* **2** *Algebra.* producing the same remainder when divided by a given number. **3** in harmony; agreeing. **SYN**: harmonious, accordant, congruous. [< Latin *congruēns, -entis,* present participle of *congruere* agree, correspond with] — **con′gru|ent|ly,** *adv.*

1. Select the synonym(s) of *congruent*.
   a. accordant   c. opposing
   b. harmonious   d. dissimilar

2. Which of the numbered dictionary definitions of *congruent* best fits the word's use in the reading selection? _____

3. Which of the following is an example of a *congruent* figure?

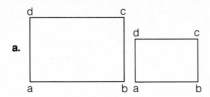

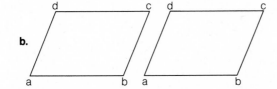 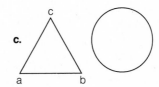

4. With whom do you experience *congruent* attitudes, perceptions of the world, or life goals? Explain.

_____

_____

5. Write a sentence correctly using *congruent*. (Be sure to include context clues to show you understand the meaning of the word.)

_____

_____

Derivative[13]

de|riv|a|tive (di riv′ə tiv), *adj., n.* —*adj.* 1 not original; derived: *derivative poetry.* 2 of derivation; derivational.
—*n.* 1 something derived: *Many medicines are derivatives of roots and herbs. They spoke a derivative of the Malay language* (Harper's). 2 a word formed by adding a prefix or suffix to another word. *Quickness* and *quickly* are derivatives of *quick.* 3 a chemical substance obtained from another by modification or by partial substitution of components: *Acetic acid is a derivative of alcohol.* 4 *Mathematics.* **a** the instantaneous rate of change of a function with respect to its variable. **b** a function derived from another in differential calculus; differential coefficient. —**de|riv′a|tive|ly,** *adv.* —**de|riv′a|tive|ness,** *n.*

de|rive (di rīv′), *v.,* **-rived, -riv|ing.** —*v.t.* 1 to obtain from a source or origin; get; receive: *He derives much pleasure from reading adventure stories.* 2 to trace (a word, custom, or title) from or to a source or origin: *The word "December" is derived from the Latin word "decem," which means "ten."* 3 to obtain by reasoning; deduce. 4 to obtain (a chemical substance) from another by substituting a different element. 5 *Obsolete.* to lead; bring; direct.
—*v.i.* to come from a source or origin; originate: *This story derives from an old legend.*
[< Old French *deriver,* learned borrowing from Latin *dērīvāre* lead off, draw off (water) < *dē-* off + *rīvus* stream] —**de|riv′er,** *n.*

1. In which of the following sentences is *derivative* used correctly?
   _____ a. A derivative is the center line to which parts of a structure or body are referred.
   _____ b. The inverse operation of multiplication yields a derivative.
   _____ c. The derivative of a function tells how the dependent variable tends to change with respect to the independent variable.
   _____ d. A derivative is the focus of study in differential calculus.

2. Which of the numbered dictionary definitions of *derivative* (as a noun) best fits the word's use in the reading selection? _____

3. Besides the mathematical meaning related to calculus, *derivative* can also mean "a word formed by adding a prefix or suffix to another word" (definition #2). Select the derivatives of *happy*.

_____ a. unhappy   _____ c. happily
_____ b. happiness   _____ d. happier

4. Write a sentence correctly using *derivative*. (Be sure to include context clues to show you understand the meaning of the word.)

_____

_____

5. *Derivative* in the specialized field of mathematics is the "instantaneous rate of change of a function with respect to its variable." In a general context, *derivative* means "something derived" or "obtained from a source or origin" (from *derive*). What, then, might be a *derivative* of oil?

_____

_____

Domain[7]

do|main (dō mān′), *n.* **1** the lands under the rule of one ruler or government: *Great Britain is a large island domain under the Crown of England.* SYN: realm, dominion. **2** land owned by one person; estate. SYN: manor. **3** *Law.* the absolute ownership of land. **4** *Figurative.* field of thought or action; sphere: *the domain of science, the domain of religion. Edison was a leader in the domain of invention.* SYN: province. **5** a region within a ferroelectric or ferromagnetic crystal, spontaneously polarized in a single direction. A crystal contains many domains polarized in a variety of directions, offsetting one another's energy. When domains are placed in a magnetic field, those favorably directed in respect to the field tend to grow at the expense of those unfavorably directed. **6** *Mathematics.* the set of all numbers which can be assigned to the algebraic variable x in an equation with two variables. Since the members of such a set may serve as replacements for the variable in a given relation, the set is sometimes called *replacement set.* [< French *domaine* < Old French *demaine,* earlier *demeine,* learned borrowing from Latin *dominium* < *dominus* lord, master < *domus* house. See etym. of doublet **demesne.**]

1. Select the synonym(s) of *domain*.

_____ a. axis   _____ c. function
_____ b. realm   _____ d. province

2. The etymology of *domain* shows that the word comes from the Latin *dominus* (lord or master) and *domus* (house). Use this information and your background knowledge to match the following:

_____ a. dominate   aa. power or right of governing and controlling; rule; control

_____ b. domicile   bb. political theory that if one country falls to an expansionist power, the next countries will inevitably fall in turn

_____ c. predominate   cc. to control or rule by strength or power

_____ d. domino   dd. to be greater in power, strength, influence, or numbers

_____ e. dominion   ee. dwelling place, house, home; residence

3. Which of the numbered dictionary definitions of *domain* best fits the word's use in the reading selection? _____

4. *Domain* in the context of mathematics refers to the set of all numbers that can be assigned to the algebraic variable *x* in an equation of two variables. *Domain* in the figurative sense can mean "field of thought or action" or "sphere." In this reading selection, Isaac Barrow was a leader in the *domain* of calculus because of his discovery of integration and differentiation as inverse operations. In what *domain* would you like to be known as a leader in your lifetime?

_____

_____

5. Write a sentence correctly using *domain*. (Be sure to include context clues to show you understand the meaning of the word.)

_____

_____

Exponent[5]

＊ex|po|nent (ek spō′nənt), *n.* **1** a person or thing that explains or interprets. **2** a person or thing that stands as an example, type, or symbol of something: *Abraham Lincoln is a famous exponent of self-education.* **3** a person who argues for a policy, program, etc.; advocate. **4** *Algebra.* a small number written above and to the right of a symbol or quantity to show how many times the symbol or quantity is to be used as a factor; index. *Examples:* $2^2 = 2 \times 2$; $a^3 = a \times a \times a$. [< Latin *expōnēns, -entis,* present participle of *expōnere;* see etym. under **expound**]

＊exponent
definition 4

$$a^2 = a \times a$$

$$2^4 = 2 \times 2 \times 2 \times 2$$

$$2^3a^2 = 2 \times 2 \times 2 \times a \times a$$

from **expound:**

[< Anglo-French *es-poundre,* Old French *espondre* < Latin *expōnere* < *ex-* forth + *pōnere* put.]

1. Which of the following are examples of an *exponent*?
   _____ a. $b(a + c)$ _____ c. 4^3b^2
   _____ b. 3^2 _____ d. $3xy + 5bc$

2. Which of the numbered dictionary definitions of *exponent* best fits the word's use in the reading selection? _____

3. Identify the synonym(s) of *exponent*.
   _____ a. advocate   _____ c. prime
   _____ b. index   _____ d. symbol

4. Write a sentence correctly using *exponent*. (Be sure to include context clues to show you understand the meaning of the word.)

_____

_____

5. Have you ever been an *exponent* of a political cause either on your campus, in your community, or at work? Explain.

_____

_____

SCIENCES: MATHEMATICS

Factor[4]

fac|tor (fak′tər), *n., v.* —*n.* **1** any one of the causes that help to bring about a result; one element in a situation: *Ability, industry, and health are factors of his success in school. Endurance is an important factor of success in sports.* **2** any one of the numbers or expressions which produce a given number or quantity when multiplied together: *5 and 2 are factors of 10.* **3a** a person who does business for another; an agent; commission merchant. **b** an agent managing a trading post: *[He] so impressed Hudson's Bay officials in London that he was transferred out of Labrador to Montreal as the company's chief factor* (Maclean's). **4** *Biology.* a gene: *The terms gene, factor, and determiner will be used as synonyms to designate the units responsible for* the transmission of hereditary characters (Harbaugh and Goodrich). **5** *Scottish.* a person who manages an estate; steward; bailiff. **6** *Law.* a person appointed to manage property that is forfeited or taken away. **7** an agent or company that lends money to a firm which has not yet collected its bills. When the bills are collected, the firm pays the factor a commission on the bills paid and interest on the loan.
—*v.t.* **1** to separate or resolve into factors; factorize. **2** to buy and collect the receivable accounts of (a business).
—*v.i.* to be a factor; act or serve as a factor.
[< Latin *factor, -ōris* doer < *facere* make, do. See etym. of doublet **faitour.**]

1. Select the synonym(s) of *factor*.
   _____ a. determiner   _____ c. agent
   _____ b. composite   _____ d. cause

2. Which of the numbered dictionary definitions of *factor* best fits the word's use in the reading selection? _____

3. The etymology of *factor* shows that the word comes from the Latin *facere* (to make or do). Use this information and your background knowledge to match the following:

   _____ a. malefactor   aa. an exact copy or likeness; perfect reproduction

   _____ b. faction   bb. a criminal; evil doer

   _____ c. facsimile   cc. a person who has given money or kindly help

   _____ d. benefactor   dd. anything made by human skill or work, especially a tool or weapon

   _____ e. artifact   ee. a group of people in a political party, church, club, or other body or organization who stand up for their side or act together for some common purpose against a larger group

4. What are the *factors* of the following numbers: 10, 20, 30? Why? Explain.

   _____

   _____

5. Write a sentence correctly using *factor*. (Be sure to include context clues to show you understand the meaning of the word.)

   _____

   _____

Function[9]

func|tion (fungk'shən), *n., v.* —*n.* **1a** proper work; normal action or use; purpose: *The function of the stomach is to help digest food. The great general functions of plant parts ... are conduction, support, storage, protection, and secretion* (Fred W. Emerson). **b** a duty or office; employment. SYN: province, task. **2** a formal public or social gathering for some purpose: *The hotel ballroom is often used for weddings, anniversaries, and other functions. He ... set out to attend the last gathering of the season at Valleys House, a function ... almost perfectly politi-* cal (John Galsworthy). **3a** *Mathematics.* a quantity whose value depends on the value given to one or more related quantities: *The area of a circle is a function of its radius; as the radius increases so does the area.* **b** anything likened to a mathematical function. **4** *Grammar.* the way in which a word or phrase is used in a sentence. —*v.i.* to work; act; perform a function or one's functions: *One of the older students can function as teacher. This old fountain pen does not function very well.* SYN: operate. [< Latin *fūnctiō, -ōnis* < *fungī* perform]

1. Select the synonym(s) of *function*.
   _____ a. operate   _____ c. provide
   _____ b. object   _____ d. task

2. Which of the numbered dictionary definitions of *function* best fits the word's use in the reading selection? _____

3. The etymology of *function* shows that the word comes from the Latin *functio* and *fungi* (perform). Use this information and your background knowledge to match the following:

   _____ a. defunct   aa. person who has certain duties to perform; an official

   _____ b. functionalism bb. of such a nature that one instance or portion may be replaced by another in respect of function, office, or use

   _____ c. perfunctory   cc. done merely for the sake of getting rid of the duty; mechanical; indifferent

   _____ d. functionary   dd. regard for the function and purpose of something as the primary factor in regulating its design

   _____ e. fungible   ee. no longer in existence; dead; extinct

4. Write a sentence correctly using *function*. (Be sure to include context clues to show you understand the meaning of the word.)

   _____

   _____

5. Why is a *function* also called a "rule of correspondence between two sets"? Give an example. (Use the dictionary entry and context in the reading selection.)

   _____

   _____

Hypotenuse[12]

✱**hy|pot|e|nuse** (hī pot′ə nüs, -nyüs; hi-), *n.* the side of a right triangle opposite the right angle. Also, **hypothenuse**. [< Late Latin *hypotēnusa* < Greek *hypoteínousa* stretching under, subtending, feminine present participle of *hypoteínein* < *hypo-* under + *teínein* stretch]

✱**hypotenuse**

1. To what theorem does a *hypotenuse* relate?
   _____ a. Euclidean
   _____ b. Hippocrates
   _____ c. Pythagorean

2. The etymology of *hypotenuse* shows that the word comes from the Greek *hypo* (under) and *teinein* (to stretch). Use this information and your background knowledge to match the following:

   _____ a. tendon   aa. to stretch out by pressure from within; swell out; expand

   _____ b. contend   bb. to claim falsely

   _____ c. pretend   cc. to continue or prolong in time, space, or direction

   _____ d. extend   dd. to work hard against difficulties; to fight or struggle

   _____ e. distend   ee. a tough, strong band or cord of tissue that joins a muscle to a bone or some other part and transmits the force of the muscle to that part

3. In which geometric figure would you find a *hypotenuse*?
   _____ a. rectangle   _____ c. circle
   _____ b. right triangle   _____ d. square

4. Draw a geometric figure that includes a *hypotenuse*. Label the part that is the *hypotenuse*.

   _____

   _____

5. Write a sentence correctly using *hypotenuse*. (Be sure to include context clues to show you understand the meaning of the word.)

   _____

   _____

Integral[14]

in|te|gral (in'tə grəl, in teg'rəl), *adj.*, *n.*
—*adj.* 1 necessary to make something complete; essential: *Steel is an integral part of a modern skyscraper.* 2 entire; complete. **SYN:** unbroken. 3 made up of parts that together constitute a whole. 4 *Mathematics.* **a** having to do with an integer or whole number; not fractional. **b** of or involving integrals.

—*n.* 1 a whole; a whole number. 2 *Mathematics.* **a** the result of an integration in calculus; the quantity of which a given function is the differential or differential coefficient. **b** an expression from which a given function, equation, or system of equations can be derived by differentiating. [< Late Latin *integrālis* < Latin *integer;* see etym. under **integer**] —**in'te|gral|ly,** *adv.*

1. Complete the verbal analogy.
   derivative : differential calculus :: *integral* : _____
   a. differential calculus   c. derivatives
   b. functions   d. integral calculus

2. Which of the numbered dictionary definitions of *integral* (as a noun) best fits the word's use in the reading selection? _____

3. An *integral* can often be used to find

_____ a. areas.   _____ c. volumes.

_____ b. changes.   _____ d. speed.

4. Write a sentence correctly using *integral*. (Be sure to include context clues to show you understand the meaning of the word.)

_____

_____

5. How are a derivative and an *integral* related? (See the reading selection and dictionary entry.)

_____

_____

Inverse[15]

in|verse (in vėrs′, in′vėrs), *adj., n., v.,* **-versed, -vers|ing.** —*adj.* **1** exactly opposite; reversed in position, direction, or tendency; opposite in nature or effect: *DCBA is the inverse order of ABCD. The reigning taste was so bad, that the success of a writer was in inverse proportion to his labor, and to his desire of excellence* (Macaulay). **2** turned upside down; inverted: *I saw a tower builded on a lake, Mock'd by its inverse shadow* (Thomas Hood). **3** *Mathematics.* of or having to do with an inverse or an inverse function: *an inverse operation, inverse elements.* —*n.* **1** something reversed: *The inverse of ¾ is* ⁴/₃. **2** the direct opposite: *Evil is the inverse of good.* **3** *Mathematics.* **a** an operation which cancels what another operation does: *The inverse of addition is subtraction.* **b** = inverse function. **c** either one of two elements in a set that by combining in a binary operation yield the identity element of the set. —*v.t.* to invert; reverse. [< Latin *inversus,* past participle of *invertere;* see etym. under **invert**] —**in|verse′ly,** *adv.*

from **invert:**

[< Latin *invertere* < *in-* in, on + *vertere* to turn]

1. Complete the following statement:

"The *inverse* of addition is _____ ."

_____ a. replication   _____ c. multiplication

_____ b. subtraction   _____ d. division

2. The etymology of *inverse* shows that the word comes from the Latin *invertere* (to turn). Use this information and your background knowledge to match the following:

_____ a. transverse   aa. go back; return

_____ b. versatile   bb. abnormal condition characterized by feeling of whirling in space; dizziness; giddiness

_____ c. revert   cc. turn aside

_____ d. vertigo   dd. able to do many things well

_____ e. divert   ee. lying or passing across

3. Which of the numbered dictionary definitions of *inverse* (as a noun) best fits the word's use in the reading selection? _____

4. Why are differentiation and integration called *inverse* operations? (See the reading selection if necessary.)

_____

_____

5. Write a sentence correctly using *inverse*. (Be sure to include context clues to show you understand the meaning of the word.)

_____

_____

Postulate[10]

pos|tu|late (*n.* pos′chə lit; *v.* pos′chə lāt), *n.*, *v.*, **-lat|ed, -lat|ing.** —*n.* something taken for granted or assumed as a basis for reasoning; fundamental principle; necessary condition: *One postulate in geometry is that a straight line is the shortest distance between any two points. The underlying postulate . . . was that knowledge is good and that those who advance knowledge need no further justification for their existence* (Bertrand Russell). **syn:** hypothesis.

—*v.t.* **1** to assume without proof as a basis of reasoning; take for granted; require as a fundamental principle or necessary condition: *Geometry postulates certain things as a basis for its reasoning.* **2** to require; demand; claim. [< New Latin *postulatum* < Latin *postulāre* to demand] —**pos′tu|la′tion,** *n.*

1. Select the synonym(s) of *postulate*.
   - _____ a. hypothesis
   - _____ b. delay
   - _____ c. conclusion
   - _____ d. claim

2. Which two of the following would *most* likely use a *postulate* in their professions?
   - _____ a. a businessman
   - _____ b. a church official
   - _____ c. a mathematician
   - _____ d. a truck driver

3. In which of the following sentences is *postulate* used correctly?
   - _____ a. A postulate was presented to the research group after extensive study and experimentation.
   - _____ b. At the Sunday service, the minister discussed the postulate that each human being has a soul.
   - _____ c. Based on the evidence presented in court, the lawyer outlined a postulate in defense of his client.
   - _____ d. The early mathematicians developed a postulate in geometry that is still used today.

4. Write a sentence correctly using *postulate*. (Be sure to include context clues to show you understand the meaning of the word.)

_____

_____

5. What is the relationship between *postulate* and theorem? (Check the reading selection if necessary.)

_____

_____

Prime²

*prime¹ (prīm), *adj., n.* —*adj.* **1** first in rank or importance; chief: *His prime object was to get enough to eat. The community's prime need is a new school.* **SYN:** principal. **2** *Figurative.* first in time or order; primary; fundamental; original: *the prime causes of war.* **SYN:** primordial. **3** first in quality; first-rate; excellent: *prime interest rates, a prime cut of meat.* **4** having no common integral divisor but 1 and the number itself: *7, 11, and 13 are prime numbers.* **5** having no common integral divisor but 1: *2 is prime to 9.* **6** ranking high or highest in some scale or rating system: *prime borrowers, prime time on television.* **7** (of beef and veal) being the best grade of meat; having red flesh that is firm, flavorful, and somewhat fatty. [partly < Latin *prīmus* first, partly < Old French *prime,* learned borrowing from Latin] —*n.* **1** the best time; best condition: *A man of forty is in the prime of life.* **2** the best part. **3** *Figurative.* the first part; beginning: *We see how quickly sundry arts mechanical were found out, in the very prime of the world* (Richard Hooker). **4** springtime: *And brought him presents, flowers, if it were prime, Or mellow fruit if it were harvest time* (Edmund Spenser). **5** early manhood or womanhood; youth: *They were now in the happy prime of youth* (Hawthorne). **6** Also, **Prime.** the second of the seven canonical hours, or the service for it, originally fixed for the first hour of the day (beginning at 6 A.M.). **7** = prime number. **8a** one of the equal parts into which a unit is divided, especially one of the sixty minutes in a degree. **b** the mark indicating such a part, also used to distinguish one letter, quantity, etc., from another. B′ is read "B prime." **9** *Music.* **a** the same tone or note in another octave. **b** the octave or octaves between two such tones or notes. **c** the tonic or keynote. **10** the first defensive position in fencing. **11** = prime rate: *Banks hiked their best corporate interest rate to 20%, their ninth increase in the prime since the first of the year* (Time). [Old English *prīm* (noun definition 6); later, the first period (of the day) < Late Latin *prīma* the first service < Latin *prīma* (*hōra*) first hour (of the Roman day)] —**prime′ness,** *n.*

1. Which of the numbered dictionary definitions of *prime* best fits the word's use in the reading selection? _____

2. Select the synonym(s) of *prime.*
   _____ a. best   _____ c. chief
   _____ b. last   _____ d. composite

3. The etymology of *prime* shows that the word comes from the Latin *prima* (first). Use this information and your background knowledge to match the following:

   _____ a. primeval   aa. the condition or fact of being the first born among the children of the same parents

   _____ b. primer   bb. first in rank or importance

   _____ c. premier   cc. any of the highest order of mammals, including human beings, apes, monkeys, and lemurs

   _____ d. primogeniture dd. of or having to do with the first age or ages, especially of the world

   _____ e. primate   ee. the first book in reading

4. List five numbers that are *prime* numbers. List five numbers that are *not* prime numbers. What is the difference?

   _____

   _____

5. Write a sentence correctly using *prime* (as a noun). (Be sure to include context clues to show you understand the meaning of the word.)

   _____

   _____

SCIENCES: MATHEMATICS

Range[8]

range (rānj), *n., v.,* **ranged, rang|ing,** *adj.* —*n.*
1 the distance between certain limits; extent: *a range of colors to choose from, range of prices from 5 cents to 25 dollars, the average daily range of temperature, vocal range, a limited range of ideas.* **2a** the distance a gun can shoot or a projectile, laser, radio, or other apparatus can operate: *to be within range of the enemy. The useful range of these hand-held radio's is about three miles.* **b** the distance from a gun, launching pad, radio transmitter, or other place or device, of an object aimed at or used: *to set the sights of a howitzer for a range of 1,000 yards. That camera lens is set for a range of three feet to infinity.* **3** the greatest distance an aircraft, rocket, or the like, can travel on a single load of fuel. **4** a place to practice shooting: *a missile range.* **5** land for grazing. **6** the act of wandering or moving about. **7** a row or line of mountains: *the Green Mountain range of the Appalachian system. Mount Rainier is in the Cascade Range.* **8** a row, line, or series: *The library has ranges of books in perfect order.* **9** a line of direction: *The two barns are in direct range with the house.* **10** a rank, class, or order: *The cohesion of the nation was greatest in the lowest ranges* (William Stubbs). **11** the district in which certain plants or animals live or naturally occur: *the reindeer, who is even less Arctic in his range than the musk ox* (Elisha K. Kane). **12** a stove for cooking: *Gas and electric ranges have replaced the coal and wood range.* **13** *Mathematics.* **a** the set of all the values a given function may take on. **b** = domain. **14** *Statistics.* the difference between the smallest and the greatest values which a variable bears in frequency distribution: *The range of this variation is unusually small.* **15a** *U.S.* a row of townships, each six miles square, between two meridians six miles apart. **b** *Canadian.* a subdivision of a township; concession: *A real ghost roams about township 14, range 15* (Neepawa, Manitoba, Star). **16** *Surveying.* a line extended so as to intersect a transit line. **17** the part of an animal hide near the tail. [probably < verb]
—*v.i.* **1** to extend between certain limits: *prices ranging from $5 to $10.* **2** to wander; rove; roam: *to range through the woods. Our talk ranged over all that had happened on our vacation.* **3** to run in a line; extend: *a boundary ranging from east to west.* **4** to be found; occur: *a plant ranging from Canada to Mexico.* **5** (of a gun, radio, laser, or other device) to have a particular range. **6** to find the distance or direction of something. **7** to take up or have a position in a line or other arrangement. **8** to search an area: *The eye ranged over an immense extent of wilderness* (Washington Irving).
—*v.t.* **1** to wander over: *Buffalo once ranged these plains.* **2** to put in a row or rows: *Range the books by size.* **3** to put in groups or classes; classify. **4** to put in a line on someone's side: *Loyal citizens ranged themselves with the king.* **5** to make straight or even: *to range lines of type.* **6a** to find the proper elevation for (a gun). **b** to give the proper elevation to (a gun). **7** to direct (a telescope) upon an object; train.
—*adj.* of or on land for grazing: *a range pony, range cattle.*
[< Old French *ranger* to array < *rang;* see etym. under **rank**[1]]
—*Syn. n.* **1 Range, scope, compass** mean the extent of what something can do or take in. **Range** emphasizes the extent (and variety) that can be covered or included by something in operation or action, such as the mind, the eye, a machine, or a force: *The car was out of my range of vision.* **Scope** emphasizes the limits beyond which the understanding, view, application, or the like, cannot extend: *Some technical terms are outside the scope of this dictionary.* **Compass** also emphasizes limits, but implies more definite ones that are likely to be permanent: *Supernatural phenomena are beyond the compass of reason or science.*

from **rank**[1]:

[< Old French *rang,* earlier *reng* < Germanic (compare Old High German *hring* circle, ring). Compare etym. under **ranch**.]

1. Select the synonym(s) of *range.*

_____ a. occur   _____ c. derivative

_____ b. retraction   _____ d. extent

2. Which of the numbered dictionary definitions of *range* as a noun best fits the word's use in the reading selection? _____

3. The etymology of *range* shows that the word comes from the Old French *ranger* (to array) and from the Old High German *hring* (circle or ring). Use this information and your background knowledge to match the following:

_____ a. rank   aa. a row or line, usually soldiers, placed side by side

_____ b. derange   bb. sheet of ice for skating

_____ c. rink   cc. to disturb the order of arrangement of; throw into confusion

_____ d. ringhals   dd. to put in the proper, or any desired, order

_____ e. arrange   ee. South African species of cobra having a narrow hood and ring of color around the neck

CHAPTER EIGHT

4. Write a sentence correctly using *range*. (Be sure to include context clues to show you understand the meaning of the word.)

_____

_____

5. If the cost of a two-seater sports car varies from $15,000 to $25,000, what would be the *range* in price for this car? What is the *range* of your abilities in your college classes? How would you describe this *range*?

_____

_____

Theorem[1]

the|o|rem (thē′ər əm, thir′əm), *n.* **1** *Mathematics.* **a** a statement that is to be proved or that has been proved. *Example:* In an isosceles triangle the angles opposite the equal sides are equal. **b** a rule or statement of relations that can be expressed by an equation or formula: *Geometrical theorems grew out of empirical methods* (Herbert Spencer). **2** any statement or rule that can be proved to be true. **3** a kind of picture produced by painting through one or more colored stencils, made especially in the 1800's. [< Latin *theōrēma* < Greek *theōrēma, -atos* < *theōreîn* to consider; see etym. under **theory**]

from **theory:**

[< Late Latin *theōria* < Greek *theōríā* a looking at, thing looked at < *theōreîn* to consider, look at < *theōrós* spectator < *théā* a sight + *horán* see]

1. The etymology of *theorem* shows that the word comes from the Latin *theorema* and the Greek *theorema* (to consider) as well as from the Greek *theoros* (spectator). (Also see *theory*.) Use this information and your background knowledge to match the following:

_____ a. intuition

aa. planned or worked out in the mind; not from experience

_____ b. theater

bb. act of looking at, or thinking about, something for a long time

_____ c. spectacle

cc. place where plays or motion pictures are shown

_____ d. contemplation

dd. immediate perception or understanding of truths, facts, or events without reasoning

_____ e. theoretical

ee. thing to look at; sight

2. What are some characteristics of a *theorem*?

_____ a. expressed by equation or formula   _____ c. has been proved

_____ b. cannot be proved   _____ d. rule or statement

3. Which of the numbered dictionary definitions of *theorem* best fits the word's use in the reading selection? _____

4. What is the fundamental *theorem* of calculus as discussed in the reading selection?

_____

_____

SCIENCES: MATHEMATICS

5. Write a sentence correctly using *theorem*. (Be sure to include context clues to show you understand the meaning of the word.)

_____

_____

Variable[6]

var|i|a|ble (văr′ē ə bəl), *adj., n.* —*adj.* **1** apt to change; changeable; uncertain: *variable winds. The weather is more variable in New York than it is in California.* **SYN:** unsteady, unstable, fluctuating, wavering, mutable. **2** likely to shift from one opinion or course of action to another; inconsistent: *a variable frame of mind.* **SYN:** fickle. **3** that can be varied, changed, or modified: *Adjustable curtain rods are of variable length.* **SYN:** alterable. **4** *Biology.* deviating, as from the normal or recognized species, variety, or structure. **5** likely to increase or decrease in size, number, amount, or degree; not remaining the same or uniform: *a constant or variable ratio. The so-called variable costs—prices for story rights, producer, director,* scriptwriter, and stars—are, if you want a good product, the least amenable to trimming (Sunday Times). —*n.* **1** a thing or quality that varies: *Temperature and rainfall are variables.* **SYN:** inconstant. **2** *Mathematics.* **a** a quantity that can assume any of the values in a given set of values. **b** a symbol representing this quantity. **3** a shifting wind. **4** = variable star. **the variables**, the region between the northeast and the southeast trade winds: *The meeting of the two opposite currents [of wind] here produces the intermediate space called the ... variables* (Arthur Young). —**var′i|a|ble|ness**, *n.*

1. Select the synonym(s) of *variable*.

   _____ a. actual number   _____ c. symbol

   _____ b. constant   _____ d. inconstant

2. Which of the numbered dictionary definitions of *variable* (as a noun) best fits the word's use in the reading selection? _____

3. In which of the following sentences can *variable* be correctly placed in the blank?

   _____ a. A _____ is a symbol that is used to represent a quantity.

   _____ b. A _____ is a rule of correspondence between two sets.

   _____ c. To prove the theorem, we need a preliminary theorem called a _____.

   _____ d. X is a _____ in the following equation: $x = 13 - y$.

4. Write a sentence correctly using *variable*. (Be sure to include context clues to show you understand the meaning of the word.)

_____

_____

5. Write an equation using the *variables* x and y. Show it to your instructor or one of your classmates for verification.

_____

_____

ANSWERS TO CHAPTER 8 EXERCISES

Composite: **1.** d (synonym) **2.** cc, ee, dd, aa, bb **3.** a, c, d
Congruent: **1.** a, b **2.** 1 **3.** b
Derivative: **1.** c, d **2.** 4ab **3.** a, b, c, d
Domain: **1.** b, d **2.** cc, ee, dd, bb, aa **3.** 6
Exponent: **1.** b, c **2.** 4 **3.** a, b, d
Factor: **1.** a, c, d **2.** 2 **3.** bb, ee, aa, cc, dd
Function: **1.** a, d **2.** 3a **3.** ee, dd, cc, aa, bb
Hypotenuse: **1.** c **2.** ee, dd, bb, cc, aa **3.** b
Integral: **1.** d (field of study) **2.** 2a **3.** a, c
Inverse: **1.** b **2.** ee, dd, aa, bb, cc **3.** 3a
Postulate: **1.** a, d **2.** b, c **3.** b, d
Prime: **1.** 4 **2.** a, c **3.** dd, ee, bb, aa, cc
Range: **1.** a, d **2.** 13a **3.** aa, cc, bb, ee, dd
Theorem: **1.** dd, cc, ee, bb, aa **2.** a, c, d **3.** 1b
Variable: **1.** c, d **2.** 2 **3.** a, d

If you missed any of the items in the exercises, return to the exercise and to the dictionary definitions to see where you went wrong. Remember: If you get something right, you only affirm that you knew it. If you get something wrong and understand why, *you have learned something.*

MATHEMATICS POSTTEST

Fill in the blanks with the words from this list.

composite   factor   postulate
congruent   function   prime
derivative   hypotenuse   range
domain   integral   theorem
exponent   inverse   variable

1. A(n) _____ is a fundamental principle or necessary condition.

2. The number 13 is an example of a(n) _____ number.

3. A(n) _____ is the instantaneous rate of change of a function with respect to its variable.

4. *X* is an example of a(n) _____.

5. *Combination* and *compound* are synonyms of _____.

6. The _____ between 50 and 75 is 25.

7. The _____ of multiplication is division.

8. The number 5 is a(n) _____ in 3^5.

9. A(n) _____ is the set of all numbers that can be assigned to *x* in an equation with two variables.

10. The number 3 is a(n) _____ of 9.

11. A(n) _____ is the result of an integration in calculus.

12. A statement that can be proved or that has been proved is a(n) _____ .

13. *Harmonious* and *accordant* are synonyms of _____ .

14. A(n) _____ is a quantity whose value depends on the value given to one or more related quantities.

15. The Pythagorean theorem shows a relationship between the sides of the right triangle and the _____ .

Answers to this posttest are in the Instructor's Manual.

If you missed any of the words, you may need to return to the exercises and to the dictionary entries to see why your concepts for some words are incomplete.

CHAPTER NINE

SOCIAL SCIENCES: POLITICAL SCIENCE

OVERVIEW

Political science studies the principles, organization, and conduct of citizens and their governments. This field of study is important because an educated person is also a citizen and must know about the nature of government and the political system in which he or she lives.

Political science has six subfields: American politics, public administration, political philosophy, public law, comparative government, and international relations.

Students who major in political science may be interested in careers in government service, public administration, U.S. foreign service agencies, or international corporations or organizations. They may pursue careers in law, public relations, journalism, or teaching and research.

Introductory textbooks in political science are usually expository, that is, they explain broad concepts or generalizations. There may be many examples and illustrations in the form of charts, diagrams, or tables. Some textbooks may be organized in a chronological framework around a historical context. Since political science is concerned with people and their governments throughout history, essential dates and names of people and places are also important to recognize.

The vocabulary in political science consists mainly of general vocabulary terms that can also have a specialized meaning within the context of political science. Examples of such words are regime, pluralism, legitimacy, *and so on. You may add other terms you discover in your studies related to political science on the forms in Appendix D.*

117

VOCABULARY SELF-EVALUATION

The following words will be introduced in this reading selection. Place a check mark (√) in front of any that you know thoroughly and use in your speech or writing. Place a question mark (?) in front of any that you recognize but do not use yourself.

_____ cataclysm	_____ indictment	_____ promulgate
_____ coalition	_____ methodology	_____ regime
_____ deploy	_____ normative	_____ scope
_____ despotism	_____ paramount	_____ sedition
_____ empirical	_____ pluralism	_____ sovereignty

FUNDAMENTALS OF POLITICAL SCIENCE

Central to any discussion of political science is a recognition of the relationship between public support, which demonstrates legitimacy,* and public power, which implies authority. Additionally, it is necessary to understand the focus of political study, and the ways in which it differs from other social science investigations.

Political science is generally considered the systematic study of individual or group interactions with the governmental structures to which they are bound. The primary objective of political science research is the exploration of political systems and institutions and their impact as they relate to the functioning of daily life in a given society. In this pursuit, political inquiry† is unique among the social sciences. By using the scientific method, which includes observation and measurement techniques, practitioners of political science seek to identify uniformities in political behavior and assess institutional policies in such areas as the role of the judicial system, relations between executive and legislative power, the basis and maintenance of national sovereignty,[1] and the nature of political freedom and social justice.

The roots of modern political science are found in the earliest sources of Western thought, particularly in the works of Aristotle, who is regarded by many as the founder of the discipline. Political science in the United States, as a distinct field of study, traces its origins to the 1880s, during which time the first School of Govern-

---

* Legitimacy is conformity to recognized rules, legal standards, and customs that gives a government the power to rule.

† Inquiry is the formal search for information about a topic, that is, investigation or research.

ment was established at Columbia University. Through the years, the scope[2] and method of political inquiry has undergone several periods of redefinition. However, the preoccupation with the nature of political activity, which promulgates[3] or defines the distribution of power in a social context, has remained of paramount[4] importance.

Within the structure of political science are several subfields that deal with specific areas of political life. Among these are (1) political theory, which attempts to form more precise methodologies[5] for the study of the discipline as a whole; (2) international relations, the goal being the ongoing analysis of nation-state interactions and the foreign policies of individual governments as they pertain to avoiding or encouraging global cataclysm,[6] and (3) political philosophy, which deals with the development of normative[7] forms of analysis and prescriptive solutions to political instability. Further, political philosophy engages in examinations of regime[8] maintenance through public support, the lack of which may lead to acts of defiance and sedition.[9] It should be noted that these areas of concentration, along with others within the field, share the same fundamental cornerstones of empirical[10] analysis and verifiable observation as the basis for inquiry.

In 1953 American political scientist David Easton perhaps best defined the objective of the discipline when he described politics as "the authoritative allocation of values." If we accept that by the term *values* Easton was referring to the public resources of society, then the study of politics is really about what another theorist, Harold Lasswell, called "who gets what, when, and how."

Students interested in contemporary political science should be aware that the study of political life encompasses all aspects of those activities that involve the formulation and execution of public policy. These include economic, legal, and philosophical issues, among others. It is therefore an investigation that can be approached through perspectives ranging from very broad to extremely narrow.

Since the dawn of social organization, mankind has found the need to deploy[11] public power in order to ensure the survival and enhance the quality of human life. The formalization of political science as an academic inquiry has been the result of a desire to alter those forces that affect the pattern of daily life in a civilized society. Whether it has been the simplicity of rule by despotism[12] or the awkward complexity of constitutional pluralism,[13] humankind's quest for control has continued toward the development of fair and efficient political systems.

Objective study of political activity requires strict attention to the scientific approach and verification techniques. Nonetheless, it has been suggested that political science is also an attempt to understand institutionalized patterns of human relationships that, to a great degree, determine both man's individual and collective destiny. Due to a natural lack of precision involved in any study of human behavior, it is not always possible to draw absolute conclusions from the collection of empirical data. Thus, it is essential that researchers consider motivations of groups and coalitions[14] as well as attempting to determine their effect on the public policy debate. Put another way, the political whys are always as important as the whats.

In a world constantly involved in the social-evolutionary process, one of the challenges for future political scientists will be to refrain from simply offering well-researched indictments[15] of political realities. Instead, the discipline should serve as a source of political alternatives in the ongoing search for social order. As a result, political science can become one of the organizational tools by which society could develop a more promising tomorrow. ◆

POLITICAL SCIENCE PRETEST

Select words from this list and write them in the blanks to complete the sentences.

cataclysm	indictment	promulgate
coalition	methodology	regime
deploy	normative	scope
despotism	paramount	sedition
empirical	pluralism	sovereignty

1. A voluntary combination of parties is a(n) _____.
2. If you spread something far and wide, you _____ it.
3. The distance something can reach is called its _____.
4. To distribute something for future use is to _____ it.
5. _____ is the term used for a system of methods and procedures.
6. The relative absence of assimilation in a society is _____.
7. Any sudden, violent change is a(n) _____.
8. Action causing rebellion against the government is known as _____.
9. _____ may be defined as absolute power or control.
10. Something based on practical experience is _____.
11. Freedom from outside control is _____.
12. A formal written accusation is a(n) _____.
13. Something chief in importance is _____.
14. Any prevailing political system is a(n) _____.
15. Something setting up a standard is _____.

Answers to this pretest are in Appendix E.

Unless your instructor tells you to do otherwise, complete the exercises for each word you missed on the pretest. The words, with their meanings and exercises, are in alphabetical order. The superscript numbers indicate where the words appeared in the reading selection so that you can refer to them when necessary. There are several types of exercises, but for each word you will be asked to write a sentence using context clues. (See Chapter 3 if you need information about how to create context clues.) You are also asked to perform some activity that will help you make your concept of the word personal. *Complete this activity thoughtfully, for creating a personalized concept of the word will help you remember it in the future.*

Answers to all the exercises are at the end of the exercise segment.

POLITICAL SCIENCE EXERCISES

Cataclysm[6]

cat|a|clysm (kat′ə kliz əm), *n.* **1** a great flood, earthquake, or any sudden, violent change in the earth. **SYN:** calamity. **2** *Figurative.* any violent change or upheaval: *Atomic warfare between nations would be a cataclysm for all mankind. ... a day that has been designated by historians of the Wall Street cataclysm of that year as Black Thursday* (New York Times). [< Latin *cataclysmos* < Greek *kataklysmós* flood, ultimately < *kata-* down + *klýzein* wash]

1. In which of the following sentences can *cataclysm* correctly be placed in the blank?
   _____ a. Scientists say that some day California will have an earthquake that will be a _____ .
   _____ b. Run for the hills, the dam is broken! It's a _____ !
   _____ c. That wasn't a test we had in History, it was a _____ .
   _____ d. As they hiked through the hills, the men discovered a _____ .

2. Which of the following words describe a *cataclysm*?
   _____ a. sudden   _____ e. fast
   _____ b. calm   _____ f. violent
   _____ c. mild   _____ g. gradual
   _____ d. change   _____ h. slow

3. Which of the numbered dictionary definitions of *cataclysm* best fits the word's use in the reading selection? _____

4. Write a sentence correctly using *cataclysm*. (Be sure to include context clues to show you understand the meaning of the word.)

   _____

   _____

5. Name a *cataclysm* (literal or figurative) that you would find very disturbing.

   _____

   _____

Coalition[14]

co|a|li|tion (kō′ə lish′ən), *n.* **1** a union into one mass or body. **SYN:** fusion. **2a** voluntary union or combination, as of parties or principles. **SYN:** league. **b** a temporary alliance, especially of statesmen or political parties, for some special purpose. In wartime several countries may form a coalition against a common enemy. *All the great coalitions, beginning with the Hellenic coalition against Persia in the fifth century B.C., have de-* pended heavily on external pressure for their cohesion (Harper's). **SYN:** league. [< Late Latin *coalitiō, -ōnis* < Latin *coalēscere* coalesce]

1. Check any appropriate response to the following statement:
   "A *coalition* of Democrats and Republicans worked on the new tax law."
   _____ a. They never can agree on anything, can they?
   _____ b. Yes. Sometimes they do work together.
   _____ c. Which group was the winner?
   _____ d. That union will be temporary.

2. Select the synonym(s) of *coalition*.
   _____ a. league   _____ e. union
   _____ b. combination   _____ f. segment
   _____ c. support   _____ g. part
   _____ d. alliance   _____ h. fusion

3. Which of the numbered and lettered dictionary definitions of *coalition* best fits the word's use in the reading selection? _____

4. Have you ever been part of a *coalition*? (Think about sports, or school politics, or a social group.) Explain.

   _____

   _____

5. Write a sentence correctly using *coalition*. (Be sure to include context clues to show you understand the meaning of the word.)

   _____

   _____

Deploy[11]

de|ploy (di ploi′), *v., n.* — *v.t.* **1** to spread out (troops, military units, or other forces) from a column into a long battle line. **2** to distribute (forces) in convenient positions for future use: *A fleet of ships were deployed over the area in which the astronauts were expected to land.* **3** *Figurative: ... an English poet deploying all the forces of his genius* (Matthew Arnold).
— *v.i.* **1** (of troops or other forces) to spread out into a long battle line from a column. **2** *Figurative: The seat was even equipped with an inflatable dinghy which deploys automatically if the astronaut lands in the water* (Science News Letter).
— *n.* the action of deploying; deployment.
[< French *déployer* < Old French *desployer* < *des-* un- (< Latin *dis-*) + *ployer* fold < Latin *plicāre*. See related etym. at **display**.]

1. If you *deploy* something, you
   _____ a. collect it.   _____ d. display it.
   _____ b. spread it.   _____ e. find fault with it.
   _____ c. increase it.   _____ f. distribute it.

2. In which of the following sentences is *deploy* used correctly?
   _____ a. A good general will deploy his troops after careful planning.
   _____ b. Does the expedition plan to deploy supplies for the return trip?
   _____ c. I deploy you, don't go into that haunted house.
   _____ d. If you deploy teenagers, you can pay minimum wage.

3. Which of the numbered dictionary definitions of *deploy* best fits the word's use in the reading selection? _____

4. Write a sentence correctly using *deploy*. (Be sure to include context clues to show you understand the meaning of the word.)

_____

_____

5. Can you think of an instance in your life when you might have had to *deploy* something? What about the need to *deploy* your money supply as you go through school or to *deploy* your energy in order to complete all the necessary work?

_____

_____

Despotism[12]

des|pot|ism (des′pə tiz əm), *n.* **1** government by a monarch having unlimited power. **2** tyranny or oppression. **3** *Figurative.* absolute power or control: *Such is the despotism of the imagination over uncultivated minds* (Macaulay).
des|pot (des′pət, -pot), *n.* **1** a monarch having unlimited power; absolute ruler: *In ancient times many rulers were despots.* **2** a person who does just as he likes; one who exercises tyrannical power; tyrant or oppressor. **3** a title meaning "master" or "lord," used in Byzantine times to refer to an emperor, or a ruler of one of certain local Byzantine states. **4a** a bishop or patriarch in the Greek Church. **b** a noble, prince, or military leader in Italian cities in the 1300's and 1400's. [< Middle French *despot,* learned borrowing from Medieval Greek *despótēs* absolute ruler, master < Greek, master (of the household)]

1. Which of the following would be an example of *despotism*?
   - _____ a. a father who makes all the decisions in the family without considering wishes of the other family members
   - _____ b. a government headed by a president elected by the people
   - _____ c. a business manager who takes advice from his coworkers
   - _____ d. a government headed by a leader who has complete power

2. If the government of your country were a *despotism*, you might
   - _____ a. be able to change things with your vote.
   - _____ b. feel angry because you were controlled so completely.
   - _____ c. move away.
   - _____ d. persuade the ruler to give up some power.

3. Which of the following words describes *despotism*?
   - _____ a. absolute   _____ d. strict
   - _____ b. tyrannical   _____ e. moderate
   - _____ c. oppressive   _____ f. unlimited

4. Have you ever had to deal with *despotism*, if not in a governmental situation, perhaps in a family or school situation, or in a relationship with another person?

_____

_____

5. Write a sentence correctly using *despotism*. (Be sure to include context clues to show you understand the meaning of the word.)

_____

_____

Empirical[10]

em|pir|i|cal (em pir′ə kəl), *adj.* **1** based on experiment and observation: *Chemistry is largely an empirical science.* **2** based entirely on practical experience, without regard to science or theory: *an empirical knowledge of medicine.* —**em|pir′i-cal|ly,** *adv.*

1. In which of the following sentences can *empirical* correctly be placed in the blank?
   _____ a. Queen Victoria was probably the most _____ monarch of the nineteenth century.
   _____ b. Carefully collected _____ data can add to the base of knowledge in almost any field of study.
   _____ c. It is also important to record accurately any _____ data.
   _____ d. Many people rely on _____ evidence when making a decision.

2. If information is based on *empirical* data, it may be based
   _____ a. on experiment.   _____ c. on guesswork.
   _____ b. on experience.   _____ d. on observation.

3. Which of the numbered dictionary definitions of *empirical* best fits the word's use in the reading selection? _____

4. Write a sentence correctly using *empirical*. (Be sure to include context clues to show you understand the meaning of the word.)

_____

_____

5. What is some of the *empirical* evidence you have gathered to create your ideas about friendship?

_____

_____

Indictment[15]

in|dict|ment (in dīt′mənt), *n.* **1** a formal written accusation, especially on the recommendation of a grand jury: *an indictment for murder. When an indictment does come down, the accused individuals will have an opportunity at trial to defend their innocence* (New York Times). *I do not know the method of drawing up an indictment against a whole people* (Edmund Burke). **2** an in-dicting or being indicted; accusation: *Mr. Bond has written . . . a perfectly stunning indictment of the welfare state* (New Yorker).
in|dict (in dīt′), *v.t.* **1** to charge with an offense or crime; accuse: *Let anyone who will, indict him on the charge of loving base gains* (Benjamin Jowett). **2** (of a grand jury) to find evidence against (an accused person) to be enough so that a trial

is necessary: *The jury indicted all eleven men named by the FBI* (Newsweek). [alteration of Middle English *endyten* < Anglo-French *enditer* to charge, accuse, Old French, to indite, dictate < Latin *in-* in + *dictāre* declare, dictate, express in writing (frequentative) < *dīcere* say, speak]

(Note: In the pronunciation of this word, the "c" is silent, and the second "i" is long.)

1. Which of the following would be an *indictment*?
    _____ a. a letter thanking a party hostess for a good time
    _____ b. a form accusing someone of murder
    _____ c. a note telling someone about plans for a trip
    _____ d. a letter telling someone of the terrible things that person has done

2. Check any appropriate response to the following statement: "The politician's speech yesterday was an *indictment* of our current tax laws."
    _____ a. I agree with him. They are the best we have ever had.
    _____ b. He likes them because he helped pass the tax bill.
    _____ c. He thinks they are terrible, doesn't he?
    _____ d. He certainly is outspoken in his dislike of them.

3. Which of the numbered dictionary definitions of *indictment* best fits the word's use in the reading selection? _____

4. If you could issue an *indictment* against any one person or thing in your life, who or what would it be?

    _____

    _____

5. Write a sentence correctly using *indictment*. (Be sure to include context clues to show you understand the meaning of the word.)

    _____

    _____

Methodology[5]

meth|od|ol|o|gy (meth′ə dol′ə jē), *n., pl.* **-gies.**
1 the system of methods or procedures used in any field: *the methodology of the modern historian.* **2** a branch of logic dealing with the application of its principles in any field of knowledge. **3** the methods of teaching; the branch of education dealing with the means and ways of instruction. [< New Latin *methodologia* < Greek *méthodos* method + *-logiā* science, system, treatment < *légein* speak]

1. In which of the following sentences can *methodology* correctly be placed in the blank?
    _____ a. In the academic world, each field has its own accepted
    _____ .

   _____ b. Before John can get his teaching credential, he must take a
              course in _____ .

   _____ c. Jane's _____ for weight loss includes diet and
              exercise.

   _____ d. A branch of logic that analyzes principles that should guide
              inquiry is _____ .

2. Complete the verbal analogy.
   woman : women :: *methodology* : _____
   a. methodologys   c. methodologist
   b. noun   d. methodologies

3. Which of the numbered dictionary definitions of *methodology* best fits
   the word's use in the reading selection? _____

4. Write a sentence correctly using *methodology*. (Be sure to include context
   clues to show you understand the meaning of the word.)

   _____

   _____

5. What do you think some of the differences in *methodology* are in chemistry and political science?

   _____

   _____

Normative[7]

nor|ma|tive (nôr′mə tiv), *adj.* **1** establishing or
setting up a norm or standard: *The normative
judgments themselves are more clearly anchored
in fact than in most other books dealing with this
difficult topic* (Harold P. Green). **2** based on
standards of usage: *normative grammar.* —**nor′-
ma|tive|ly,** *adv.* —**nor′ma|tive|ness,** *n.*
norm (nôrm), *n.* **1** a standard for a certain group,
type, model, or pattern: *to determine the norm
for a test.* **2** an average; mean: *sales above the
norm for the year. In arithmetic this class is
above the norm for the eighth grade.* [< Latin
nōrma rule, pattern]

1. Check any appropriate response to the following statement:
   "In our *normative* study, we found a wide variety of behaviors."
   _____ a. Were you able to come to any conclusions?
   _____ b. People are really crazy, aren't they?
   _____ c. Such studies are a waste of time.
   _____ d. Are other researchers conducting similar studies?

2. Complete the verbal analogy.
   difficult : difficulty :: *normative* : _____
   a. normativeness   c. normal
   b. normativness   d. normalty

3. Which of the numbered dictionary definitions of *normative* best fits the word's use in the reading selection? _____

4. If you were part of a *normative* study of testing behavior, would you be close to or away from the central behavior? That is, are you like or unlike other people you know when you are taking a test?

_____

_____

5. Write a sentence correctly using *normative*. (Be sure to include context clues to show you understand the meaning of the word.)

_____

_____

Paramount[4]

par|a|mount (par′ə mount), *adj., n.* — *adj.* chief in importance; above others; supreme: *Truth is of paramount importance. ... to make Britain the paramount power in India* (Macaulay). **SYN:** See syn. under **dominant**.
— *n.* an overlord; supreme ruler.
[< Anglo-French *paramont* above < *par-* by + *amont* up < Latin *ad montem* to the mountain]
— **par′a|mount|ly**, *adv.*

from **dominant:**

— *Syn. adj.* **1 Dominant, predominant, paramount** mean uppermost. **Dominant** means rul-ing, and therefore having the most influence, power, or authority: *Efficiency is the dominant idea in many businesses.* **Predominant** means before others in influence, power, or authority, and therefore principal or superior: *Love of liberty is predominant in struggles for independence.* **Paramount** means first in importance, authority, or rank, and therefore supreme: *It is of paramount importance that we finish the work on time.*

1. In which of the following sentences is *paramount* used correctly?
   _____ a. John's paramount interest is in collecting stamps.
   _____ b. He paramounts them in a special stamp album.
   _____ c. Our paramount object on the hike was to see a yellow-bellied sapsucker.
   _____ d. After weeks of dieting, food was the paramount thought in Mary's mind.

2. If something is *paramount*, it may be
   _____ a. important to everyone.
   _____ b. important to no one.
   _____ c. important to only one person.
   _____ d. animal, vegetable, or mineral.

3. Complete the verbal analogy.
   subordinate : down :: *paramount* : _____
   a. highest   d. up
   b. primary   e. chief
   c. ruler

4. Write a sentence correctly using *paramount*. (Be sure to include context clues to show you understand the meaning of the word.)

_____

_____

5. What person is of *paramount* importance in your life?

_____

_____

Pluralism[13]

plu|ral|ism (plŭr′ə liz əm), *n.* **1** the character, condition, or an instance of being plural. **2** *Sociology.* **a** a condition in which ethnic and other minority groups are able to maintain their identities in a society without conflicting with the dominant culture; the relative absence of assimilation in a society. **b** belief in or advocacy of such a condition. **3** the theory or belief, incorporated in or essential to various systems of philosophy, that reality has its essence or ultimate being in several or many principles or substances. **4** *Ecclesiastical.* the system or practice by which one person holds two or more offices, especially benefices, at the same time.
plu|ral (plŭr′əl), *adj., n.* **—adj. 1** more than one: plural citizenship. **2** *Grammar.* **a** more than one in number: *"Boy" is singular; "boys" is plural.* **b** showing more than one in number: *the plural ending "-s," the plural form "fishes."* **3** having to do with or involving a plurality of persons or things; being one of such a plurality: *Better have none than plural faith* (Shakespeare).
—n. *Grammar.* **1** a form of a word to show it means more than one. *Books* is the plural of *book; men* is the plural of *man; are* is the plural of *is; we* is the plural of *I; these* is the plural of *this.* **2** a word or class of words used to show more than one. *Abbr:* pl.
[< Latin *plūrālis* < *plūs, plūris* more, comparative of *multus* much]

1. In which of the following sentences can *pluralism* correctly be placed in the blank?
   _____ a. _____ permitted the man to hold two church offices.
   _____ b. The emphasis on preserving tribal customs in Alaska is an example of _____ .
   _____ c. I don't like to live alone; I believe in _____ .
   _____ d. Do you believe everyone in a society should be much the same, or do you believe in _____ ?

2. *Pluralism* may exist
   _____ a. in any religious group.
   _____ b. in a philosophical belief.
   _____ c. in a society.
   _____ d. when any two people are together.

3. Which of the numbered and lettered dictionary definitions of *pluralism* best fits the word's use in the reading selection? _____

4. Our society permits *pluralism*, so you may identify with, and exhibit the practices of, an ethnic or minority group if you wish. With what group do you identify? How do you show your identification? (For example, do you celebrate special holidays? Wear special clothes? Eat special foods? Repeat stories, sing songs, say special prayers?)

_____

_____

5. Write a sentence correctly using *pluralism*. (Be sure to include context clues to show you understand the meaning of the word.)

_____

_____

Promulgate[3]

pro|mul|gate (prō mul′gāt; *especially British* prom′əl gāt), *v.t.*, **-gat|ed, -gat|ing. 1** to announce officially; proclaim formally: *The king promulgated a decree. The constitution probably will soon be promulgated and elections are promised within a year* (Newsweek). **2** to spread far and wide: *Schools try to promulgate knowledge and good habits.* [< Latin *prōmulgāre*] **—promul′ga|tor,** *n.*

1. If you *promulgate* something, you
   _____ a. propose it.   _____ d. create it.
   _____ b. announce it.   _____ e. proclaim it.
   _____ c. spread it.   _____ f. recall it.

2. Check any appropriate response to the following statement:
   "If you *promulgate* the rules of the fraternity two weeks before the party, we will all have a better time."
   _____ a. Good idea. You can't follow them if you don't know them!
   _____ b. I agree. Let's get rid of those dumb rules.
   _____ c. Last year we tacked them on the bulletin board.
   _____ d. Who needs rules?

3. Which of the numbered dictionary definitions of *promulgate* best fits the word's use in the reading selection? _____

4. Write a sentence correctly using *promulgate*. (Be sure to include context clues to show you understand the meaning of the word.)

_____

_____

5. If you could *promulgate* one idea to the entire world, what would it be?

_____

_____

Regime[8]

re|gime or **ré|gime** (ri zhēm′, rā-), *n.* **1** the system of government or rule; prevailing system: *Under the old regime women could not vote. The Russians may mean what they say when they describe their present régime as a transitory stage* (Bulletin of Atomic Scientists). **2** any prevailing political or social system. **3** the period or length of a regime. **4** *Informal.* a system of living; regimen: *The baby's regime includes two naps a day.* [< French *régime,* learned borrowing from Latin *regimen.* See etym. of doublet **regimen.**]

reg|i|men. (rej′ə men, -mən), *n.* **1** a set of rules or habits of diet, exercise, or manner of living intended to improve health, reduce weight, cultivate the mind, or otherwise make something better or achieve some goal. **2** the act of governing; government; rule. **3** *Grammar.* the influence of one word in determining the case or mood of another; government. [< Latin *regimen, -inis* < *regere* to rule, straighten. See etym. of doublet **regime.**]

SOCIAL SCIENCES: POLITICAL SCIENCE

(Note: Read the pronunciation guide carefully!)

1. In which of the following sentences can *regime* correctly be placed in the blank?
   - _____ a. I try to follow a healthful _____ of diet and exercise.
   - _____ b. If you _____ your life carefully, you can be happy and healthy.
   - _____ c. The purpose of the revolution is to overthrow the current _____.
   - _____ d. That author belongs to the old _____; no one reads him today.

2. Which of the following might be called a *regime*?
   - _____ a. a city government
   - _____ b. a textbook
   - _____ c. a group of friends
   - _____ d. an established system
   - _____ e. a school administration
   - _____ f. a national government

3. Which of the numbered dictionary definitions of *regime* best fits the word's use in the reading selection? _____

4. List four elements of a *regime* that may result in better grades for you.

   _____

   _____

5. Write a sentence correctly using *regime*. (Be sure to include context clues to show you understand the meaning of the word.)

   _____

   _____

Scope[2]

scope[1] (skōp), *n.* **1a** the distance the mind can reach; extent of view: *Very hard words are not within the scope of a child's understanding.* **SYN:** compass. See syn. under **range. b** the area over which any activity operates or is effective; range of application: *This subject is not within the scope of our investigation. Beyond the scope of all speculation* (Edmund Burke). **SYN:** compass. See syn. under **range. 2** room to range; space; opportunity: *Football gives scope for courage and quick thinking. I gave full scope to my imagination* (Laurence Sterne). **3** the range or length of flight of an arrow or other missile. **4a** extent; length; sweep: *The yacht's gig was towing easily at the end of a long scope of line* (Joseph Conrad). **b** the length of cable at which a ship rides when at anchor. **5** *Archaic.* an aim; purpose; ultimate object. [< Italian *scopo*, learned borrowing from Late Latin *scopus* < Greek *skopós* aim, object < *skopeîn* behold, consider]

1. Check any appropriate response to the following statement:
   "The *scope* of Margaret Mead's interests led her beyond what had previously been thought of as the field of anthropology."
   - _____ a. She should have investigated more things.
   - _____ b. She made the field broader, didn't she?
   - _____ c. So many things were of interest to her.
   - _____ d. A narrow person in a narrow field.

2. Select the synonym(s) of *scope*.

_____ a. range   _____ d. sweep
_____ b. extent   _____ e. compass
_____ c. length   _____ f. object

3. Which of the numbered and lettered dictionary definitions of *scope* best fits the word's use in the reading selection? _____

4. Write a sentence correctly using *scope*. (Be sure to include context clues to show you understand the meaning of the word.)

_____

_____

5. What is the *scope* of your interest in athletics? List the sports you care about. Is the *scope* of your interest broad or narrow?

_____

_____

Sedition[9]

se|di|tion (si dish′ən), *n.* **1** speech or action causing discontent or rebellion against the government; incitement to discontent or rebellion: *Sedition against the Federal Government, the Court held, is a field in which Congress alone has jurisdiction to enact laws* (Wall Street Journal). **2** *Archaic.* a revolt; rebellion. [< Old French *sedicion*, learned borrowing from Latin *seditiō, -ōnis* < *sē-* apart + *īre* to go]

1. Which of the following would be an example of *sedition*?

_____ a. attempting the violent overthrow of an existing government
_____ b. making others so angry that they join you in trying to destroy the city government
_____ c. speaking out against current laws
_____ d. a political cartoon criticizing the president

2. Check any appropriate response to the following statement: "*Sedition* is hard to define in a democracy."

_____ a. I agree, because we value freedom of speech.
_____ b. We want people to speak out, but they must not become dangerous.
_____ c. Yes. It is easier to define it in a totalitarian society.
_____ d. Sedition is any speech against the government and that's that!

3. If you were involved in *sedition*, you might

_____ a. go to prison.
_____ b. make friends with the ruling government.
_____ c. believe very strongly in your cause.
_____ d. be willing to take great risks.

SOCIAL SCIENCES: POLITICAL SCIENCE

4. Some political groups believe our present form of government should be overthrown and replaced with another form of government. What actions could they undertake that *would not* be *sedition*?

_____

_____

What actions *would* be called *sedition*?

_____

_____

5. Write a sentence correctly using *sedition*. (Be sure to use context clues to show you understand the meaning of the word.)

_____

_____

Sovereignty[1]

sov|er|eign|ty (sov'rən tē, suv'-), *n., pl.* **-ties.** **1** supreme power or authority; supremacy: *the sovereignty of the sea. The United States of America is a sovereign nation, but the 50 states which compose it do not have full sovereignty* (Payson S. Wild). **2** freedom from outside control; independence in exercising power or authority: *Countries that are satellites lack full sovereignty. Our [national] sovereignty is not something to be hoarded, but something to be used* (Wendell Willkie). **3** a state, territory, community, or other political area, that is independent or sovereign. **4** the rank, power, or jurisdiction of a sovereign; royal authority or dominion.
sov|er|eign (sov'rən, suv'-), *n., adj.* —*n.* **1** the supreme ruler; king or queen; monarch. Queen Victoria was the sovereign of Great Britain from 1837 to 1901. *It was not for me to bandy civilities with my sovereign* (Samuel Johnson). **2** a person, group, or nation having supreme control or dominion; ruler; governor; lord; master: *sover-eign of the seas.* **3** a British gold coin, worth one pound or formerly 20 shillings.
—*adj.* **1** having the rank or power of a sovereign: *a sovereign prince. Here lies our sovereign lord the king* (John Wilmot). **2** greatest in rank, authority, or power: *a sovereign court, sovereign jurisdiction.* **3** independent of the control of another government or governments: *a sovereign state. When the thirteen colonies won the Revolutionary War, America became a sovereign nation.* **4a** above all others; supreme; greatest: *Character is of sovereign importance. The knowledge of Truth . . . is the sovereign good of human nature* (Francis Bacon). SYN: chief, paramount. **b** greatest in degree; utmost; extreme: *. . . a sovereign contempt for everyone* (Henry James). **5** excellent or powerful: *There is no sovereign cure for colds.* **6** of, belonging to, or characteristic of a sovereign or sovereignty: *sovereign power.* [< Old French *soverain* < Vulgar Latin *superānus* < Latin *super* over] —**sov'er|eign|ly,** *adv.*

1. Which of the following would have *sovereignty?*
   _____ a. Henry VIII of England in the sixteenth century
   _____ b. the president of a democracy
   _____ c. Switzerland
   _____ d. the state of New York

2. If a government has *sovereignty,*
   _____ a. it is independent of outside control.
   _____ b. it has authority over all its citizens.
   _____ c. other governments may control some of its actions.
   _____ d. it can enter into agreements with other nations.

3. Which of the numbered dictionary definitions of *sovereignty* best fits the word's use in the reading selection? _____

4. Write a sentence correctly using *sovereignty*. (Be sure to include context clues to show you understand the meaning of the word.)

_____

_____

5. The state in which you live does not have *sovereignty*. Name something that your state does not completely control but that is controlled by the federal government. (One example is the maximum speed permitted on highways.)

_____

_____

ANSWERS TO CHAPTER 9 EXERCISES

Cataclysm: **1.** a, b   **2.** a, d, e, f   **3.** 2
Coalition: **1.** b, d   **2.** a, b, d, e, h   **3.** 2b
Deploy: **1.** b, f   **2.** a, b   **3.** 3
Despotism: **1.** a, d   **2.** b, c   **3.** a, b, c, d, f
Empirical: **1.** b, c, d   **2.** a, b, d   **3.** 1
Indictment: **1.** b, d   **2.** c, d   **3.** 2
Methodology: **1.** a, b, d   **2.** d (plural)   **3.** 1
Normative: **1.** a, d   **2.** a (noun form)   **3.** 1
Paramount: **1.** a, c, d   **2.** a, c, d   **3.** d (analogy)
Pluralism: **1.** a, b, d   **2.** b, c   **3.** 2a
Promulgate: **1.** b, c, e   **2.** a, c   **3.** 2
Regime: **1.** a, c, d   **2.** a, d, e, f   **3.** 1
Scope: **1.** b, c   **2.** a, b, c, d, e   **3.** 1b
Sedition: **1.** a, b   **2.** a, b, c   **3.** a, c, d
Sovereignty: **1.** a, c   **2.** a, b, d   **3.** 1

If you missed any of the items in the exercises, return to the exercise and to the dictionary definition to see where you went wrong. Remember: If you get something right, you only affirm that you knew it. If you get something wrong and understand why, *you have learned something*.

POLITICAL SCIENCE POSTTEST

Fill in the blanks with the words from this list.

cataclysm	indictment	promulgate
coalition	methodology	regime
deploy	normative	scope
despotism	paramount	sedition
empirical	pluralism	sovereignty

1. _____ means "supreme authority."

2. A(n) _____ is a calamity.

3. To spread out (figuratively) is to _____ .

4. Another word for oppression is _____ .

5. A(n) _____ is an accusation.

6. *Regimen* is a synonym for _____ .

7. _____ is incitement to rebellion.

8. Something above others is _____ .

9. Another word for _____ is *league*.

10. _____ data come from observation and experiment.

11. The system by which a person may hold more than one office is called _____ .

12. _____ means "methods of teaching."

13. To _____ is to proclaim formally.

14. _____ means "based on standards of usage."

15. _____ is a synonym for *length*, or *sweep*.

Answers to this posttest are in the Instructor's Manual.

If you missed any of the words, you may need to return to the exercises and to the dictionary entries to see why your concepts for some words are incomplete.

C H A P T E R   T E N

SOCIAL SCIENCES: PSYCHOLOGY

OVERVIEW

Psychology is the study of the nature of humans as they interact with their environment. It is useful in understanding ourselves and others, either in daily social and business contacts or in a vocational or career area.

There are many different subfields in psychology, each representing a different emphasis in its application to human beings. These subfields include experimental psychology, humanistic psychology, social psychology, developmental psychology, and applied professional psychology. Experimental psychology is concerned with the understanding of our general life processes and interactions, such as thinking processes, sensory perceptions, motivation, and so on. The subfield of humanistic psychology includes an emphasis on the human personality, the study of the family, and clinical studies. Developmental psychology focuses on the various phases of human development from childhood through adulthood, and social psychology relates the study of psychology to general societal issues, including theories of culture, application to law, and death and dying. Lastly, the applied professional study of psychology is concerned with the preparation of trained and licensed counselors for work in industry, mental hospitals, clinics, law enforcement, and social welfare.

Introductory textbooks in psychology are usually expository, that is, they explain broad concepts or generalizations. The ideas may also be presented to show relationships between theories or principles as well as cause-and-effect interactions of observed phenomena. The text may be adversative in that it will show opposing viewpoints on the same theory. Many texts also include historical references and may be organized according to a chronological sequence.

The vocabulary in psychology is a combination of technical and general vocabulary. The general words are those we might use every day but that can also have a specific meaning in the context of psychology. Examples of such words are intelligence, readiness, *and* learning. *Many of the technical words such as* neurosis *and* psychosis *are scientific in nature and have Latin or Greek etymology.*

Be sure to read any charts or graphs in psychology textbooks, as they may reinforce the vocabulary presented in other parts of the text. Additional sources of vocabulary in the field of psychology come from other activities in which you apply psychological concepts or ideas. These include lab experiments, audiovisual presentations, field-work experiences, and guest speakers or lecturers. You may add other terms you discover in your studies related to psychology on the forms in Appendix D.

VOCABULARY SELF-EVALUATION

The following words will be introduced in this reading selection. Place a check mark (√) in front of any that you know thoroughly and use in your speech or writing. Place a question mark (?) in front of any that you recognize but do not use yourself.

_____ anxiety	_____ neurosis	_____ repression
_____ cognition	_____ paradigm	_____ stimulus
_____ hypothesis	_____ psychosis	_____ subjective
_____ innate	_____ psychotherapy	_____ theory
_____ introspection	_____ reliability	_____ validity

A PERSPECTIVE OF PSYCHOLOGY: PAST AND PRESENT

A BRIEF HISTORY OF PSYCHOLOGY

The field of psychology can be traced historically through four schools of influence. These schools are structuralism, behaviorism, Gestalt, and psychoanalysis. Each of these schools formulated theories[1] and from them, hypotheses,[2] that each set out to prove or disprove.

The earliest school, structuralism, was founded in 1879 when Wilhelm Wundt opened a psychological laboratory in

Leipzig, Germany. Wundt and his students believed that the main purpose of psychology was to describe and analyze conscious experience. The primary method used by this school was to have a subject respond to a stimulus[3] and report on the response to this stimulus in a process called introspection.[4] In this way a sensation such as "wetness" could be understood when the subject described the way it was experienced.

The school of behaviorism was introduced in 1913 by an American psychologist, John B. Watson. Behaviorism was developed as a reaction to structuralism, which was considered to be too subjective.[5] A more scientific approach, behaviorism called for the measurement of observable behavior. The method developed by the behaviorists was to present a known stimulus to the subject and to measure the response and the time required to make it. The purpose of this method was to determine the connection or association between the stimulus and the response. The hypothesis asserted that the stronger the association, the more permanent the behavior.

The school of Gestalt (meaning "pattern or form") psychology stated that behavior could not be broken down into parts but must be studied as a whole. This school, also developed as a reaction against structuralism, began in Germany about 1912. Max Wertheimer is considered to be its founder. Gestalt theory states that human beings and animals perceive organized patterns and not individual parts merely added together. This theory of behavior takes into account both past experience and present motivation, which greatly influence and modify perception and behavior.

An Austrian physician, Sigmund Freud, founded the fourth school, psychoanalysis, in the late 1800s and early 1900s. Psychoanalysis attempted to explain and treat emotional disturbances. Freud pointed out that many things going on in the mind are unconscious and that sometimes a person represses needs and desires that are unacceptable to himself and society. And, because of this repression,[6] mental disorders or physical disorders are formed. Serious mental disorders in which the patient loses touch with reality are called psychoses,[7] while less serious afflictions are called neuroses.[8] Treatment of both psychoses and neuroses may take place through a process called psychotherapy.[9]

Psychology has made many advances since it began as a science over one hundred years ago. It is probably safe to say that modern psychologists rarely belong to any one of the historical schools. Instead they may draw on this rich background of theory and experimentation, add more recently determined information to it, and develop their own more advanced theories that can be used to help explain, predict, control, or modify behavior.

THE STUDY OF LEARNING

Many psychologists today study learning theory as a special interest. Among the areas that may be considered are how learning takes place, how it can be measured, and how certain factors interfere with it.

Learning, according to many of those who study it, depends on certain innate[10] characteristics present in the organism as well as the influence of the environment on that organism. These two factors interact in humans to produce cognition.[11] While repeating an action over and over until it is automatic, until it becomes a habit, may be called "learning" in an animal, understanding is essential in humans. Just how understanding takes place is the focus of continuing study.

Other psychologists concern themselves with how learning can be measured. They try to find out how much a person knows or how much he or she has improved over a period of time. There are many tests available that serve this purpose, and most students have taken several of them by the time they reach college age. Those who create the tests take care to see that such tests have both reliability[12] and validity.[13] Without reliability we cannot depend on the test to give the same results each time it is given. And without validity we cannot be sure the test measures what it claims to measure. Tests that are designed to measure specific learning behavior and that meet special statistical requirements are called standardized tests.

However, even with dependable tests and capable students, test results can be unexpected. Studies of these unexpected results show that emotions such as anxiety[14] or anger can greatly alter performance on a test. In addition, certain personality factors may influence test scores. For example, a student who is willing to risk and who uses the smallest cues to assist him is likely to do better on objective tests.

As in many other fields of science, the work of one psychologist can serve as a basis for those who follow. In whatever that area of specialization, the psychologist's efforts may result in a paradigm[15] of knowledge that will help unlock the mysteries of human learning. ◆

PSYCHOLOGY PRETEST

Select words from this list and write them in the blanks to complete the sentences.

anxiety	neurosis	repression
cognition	paradigm	stimulus
hypothesis	psychosis	subjective
innate	psychotherapy	theory
introspection	reliability	validity

1. An inborn ability is a(n) _____ characteristic.

2. Something assumed because it seems likely to be a true explanation is a(n) _____ .

3. An explanation that has been tested and confirmed as a general principle is a(n) _____ .

4. Intense fear of flying would be a possible reason for seeking

   _____ .

5. Something you can depend on shows _____ .

6. Examining your own thoughts is _____ .

7. Another word for pattern is _____ .

8. Those ideas that belong to an individual and not to the external world could be considered _____ .

9. _____ is a way of excluding ideas from a person's consciousness.

10. _____ is an intellectual process by which knowledge is gained.

11. Insanity is an example of a(n) _____, as it represents a profound disorganization of the mind.

12. The _____ of something hot causes an individual to recoil and move away from the source of heat.

13. Someone who is filled with _____ may be afraid of those around him.

14. An extremely nervous person might be diagnosed as having a(n) _____ .

15. Testing for the truth of an idea is testing for its _____ .

Answers to this pretest are in Appendix E.

Unless your instructor tells you to do otherwise, complete the exercises for each word you missed on the pretest. The words, with their meanings and exercises, are in alphabetical order. The superscript numbers indicate where the words appeared in the reading selection so that you can refer to them when necessary. There are several types of exercises, but for each word you will be asked to write a sentence using context clues. (See Chapter 3 if you need information about how to create context clues.) You are also asked to perform some activity that will help you make your concept of the word personal. *Complete this activity thoughtfully, for creating a personalized concept of the word will help you remember it in the future.*

Answers to all the exercises are at the end of the exercise segment.

PSYCHOLOGY EXERCISES

Anxiety[14]

anx|i|e|ty (ang zī′ə tē), *n., pl.* **-ties**. **1** uneasy thoughts or fears about what may happen; troubled, worried, or uneasy feeling: *Mother felt anxiety when my baby brother was so sick. We all felt anxiety when the prairie fire came close to town. Anxiety is one of the major characteristics of our time* (Atlantic). SYN: concern, apprehension, dread, misgiving. **2** eager desire: *Her anxiety to succeed led her to work hard.* **3** *Psychiatry.* a state of fear and mental tension commonly occurring in mental disorders. [< Latin *anxietās* < *anxius* anxious < *angere* choke]

1. In which of the following sentences can *anxiety* correctly be substituted for the underlined word?
   _____ a. The mother is filled with <u>concern</u> for her baby's health.
   _____ b. George experiences <u>apprehension</u> when he has to give a speech.
   _____ c. Increased heart rate and respiration can indicate <u>dread</u>.
   _____ d. <u>Misgiving</u> at Christmastime can be very expensive.

2. Complete the verbal analogy.
give : take :: *anxiety* : _____
   a. nervousness
   b. desire   d. confidence
   c. panic   e. dread

3. Which of the numbered definitions in the dictionary entry for *anxiety* best fits its use in the reading selection? _____

4. Write a sentence correctly using *anxiety*. (Be sure you include context clues to show you understand the meaning of the word.)

_____

_____

5. Have you ever experienced *anxiety*? When was it? Before a test? Before a date?

_____

_____

Cognition[11]

cog|ni|tion (kog nish′ən), *n.* **1** the act of knowing; perception; awareness. SYN: sensation. **2** a thing known, perceived, or recognized. **3** (in Scottish law) official notice; cognizance: *The Council appointed a Committee to take cognition of the matter* (James Grant). **4** *Obsolete.* the act or faculty of coming to know; knowledge. [< Latin *cognitiō, -ōnis* < *cognōscere* recognize < *co-* (intensive) + *gnōscere* know]

(Note: This is an intellectual process by which knowledge is gained.)

1. Which of the following would be an example of *cognition*?
   _____ a. swimming
   _____ b. reading a book
   _____ c. studying for an exam
   _____ d. driving a car

2. The etymology of *cognition* shows that the word comes from the Latin *gnoscere* (to know). Use this information and your background knowledge to match the following:
   _____ a. recognize   aa. to let know
   _____ b. connoisseur   bb. to know again
   _____ c. notify   cc. one who knows things well; an expert
   _____ d. diagnosis   dd. well known because of something bad
   _____ e. notorious   ee. the process of finding out about a disease

3. Which of the numbered dictionary definitions of *cognition* best fits the word's use in the reading selection? _____

4. What act of *cognition* do you enjoy most? Studying alone? Reading in the library? Researching a paper? Other?

_____

_____

5. Write a sentence correctly using *cognition*. (Be sure to include context clues to show you understand the meaning of the word.)

_____

_____

Hypothesis[2]

hy|poth|e|sis (hī poth′ə sis, hi-), *n., pl.* **-ses.**
1 something assumed because it seems likely to be a true explanation; theory: *Let us act on the hypothesis that he is honest.* **syn**: See syn. under **theory. 2** a proposition assumed as a basis for reasoning; supposition. A theorem in geometry is made up of a hypothesis and a conclusion. **3** a mere assumption; guess: *Your reasoning ... seems plausible, but still it is only hypothesis* (Scott). [< New Latin *hypothesis* < Greek *hypóthesis* < *hypo-* under + *thésis* a placing < *tithénai* to place]

from **theory:**

— *Syn.* **1a, b.** Theory, hypothesis as terms in science mean a generalization reached by inference from observed particulars and proposed as an explanation of their cause, relations, or the like. **Theory** implies a larger body of tested evidence and a greater degree of probability: *The red shift in the spectra of galaxies supports the theory that the universe is continuously expanding.* **Hypothesis** designates a merely tentative explanation of the data, advanced or adopted provisionally, often as the basis of a theory or as a guide to further observation or experiment: *Archeological discoveries strengthened the hypothesis that Troy existed.*

1. In which of the following sentences can *hypothesis* correctly be placed in the blank?
   _____ a. In this case, our _____ is that *a* is the cause of *b*.
   _____ b. Something proved is _____ .
   _____ c. Your reasoning is good, but it is only _____ .
   _____ d. The _____ you have suggested can be worked out in our experiment.

2. Complete this verbal analogy.
   explain : tell :: *hypothesis* : _____
   a. imagination   c. conclusion
   b. supposition   d. condition

3. Which of the following might be said of *hypothesis*?
   _____ a. It requires further testing.
   _____ b. It may explain a few observations.
   _____ c. It attempts to explain.
   _____ d. It is known to be true.

4. Write a sentence correctly using *hypothesis*. (Be sure to include context clues to show you understand the meaning of the word.)

_____

_____

5. Do you have a *hypothesis* about what makes you happy? (You must experiment to find out if it is true; since it doesn't apply generally, it isn't a theory.)

_____

_____

Innate[10]

in|nate (i nāt′, in′āt), *adj.* **1** born in a person; natural: *A good artist has an innate talent for drawing. A good comedian has an innate wit.* **syn**: native, inborn, inbred. **2** existing naturally in anything; inherent. **3** *Philosophy.* (of ideas or principles) present in the mind or soul as originally constituted or created; not learned or otherwise acquired. [< Latin *innātus* < *in*- in + *nāscī* be born] — **in|nate′ly**, *adv.* — **in|nate′ness**, *n.*

1. In which of the following sentences is *innate* used correctly?
   _____ a. John has innate musical ability. Some day he will be famous.
   _____ b. Mother says my stubbornness is innate.
   _____ c. A hospital is an innate place to have a baby.
   _____ d. Mary's innate energy has resulted in many accomplishments.

2. The etymology of *innate* shows that the word comes from the Latin *nasci* (to be born). Use this information and your background knowledge to match the following:
   _____ a. natal   aa. a people occupying the same country
   _____ b. native   bb. like a child
   _____ c. nation   cc. born in a certain place or country
   _____ d. naive   dd. having to do with or dating from one's birth
   _____ e. renaissance   ee. a revival; new birth

3. Place an "s" before any synonym and an "a" before any antonym of *innate*.
   _____ a. inherent   _____ d. natural
   _____ b. inbred   _____ e. native
   _____ c. learned   _____ f. inborn

4. Write down at least two of your own *innate* characteristics.

_____

_____

5. Write a sentence correctly using *innate*. (Be sure to include context clues to show you understand the meaning of the word.)

_____

_____

Introspection[4]

in|tro|spec|tion (in´trə spek´shən), *n.* the examination of one's own thoughts and feelings: *Philosophical people are given to introspection. I was forced to make an introspection into mine own mind* (John Dryden).
in|tro|spec|tive (in´trə spek´tiv), *adj.* inclined to examine one's own thoughts and feelings; characterized by introspection: *an introspective essay.* —**in´tro|spec´tive|ly,** *adv.* —**in´tro|spec´-tive|ness,** *n.*
in|tro|spect (in´trə spekt´), *v.i.* to look within; be introspective. —*v.t.* to look into; examine. [< Latin *intrōspectus,* past participle of *intrōspicere* < *intrō-* into + *specere* to look]

1. In which of the following sentences can *introspection* be correctly placed in the blank?
   _____ a. After using _____, the police charged John with the crime.
   _____ b. Philosophers often practice _____.
   _____ c. Meditation can be a form of _____.
   _____ d. Through _____, I may be able to understand my own feelings.

2. The etymology of *introspection* shows that the word came from the Latin *specere* (to look) and *intro* (into). Use this information and your background knowledge to match the following:
   _____ a. aspect   aa. easily seen; clearly visible
   _____ b. conspicuous   bb. watchful on all sides; careful
   _____ c. expect   cc. a thing to look at; a sight
   _____ d. circumspect   dd. to look forward to
   _____ e. spectacle   ee. one view of a subject

3. Which of the following would be called *introspection*?
   _____ a. considering your reasons for doing something
   _____ b. deciding why you cry at a sad movie
   _____ c. recalling a dream and thinking about its meaning
   _____ d. telling a friend why you were late for a meeting

4. Write a sentence correctly using *introspection*. (Be sure to include context clues to show you understand the meaning of the word.)

   _____

   _____

5. Do you think that animals are *introspective*? Why?

   _____

   _____

SOCIAL SCIENCES: PSYCHOLOGY

Neurosis[8]

neu|ro|sis (nů rō′sis, nyů-), *n., pl.* **-ses** (-sēz).
1 any one of various mental or emotional disorders, characterized by depression, anxiety, abnormal fears, and compulsive behavior. A neurosis is less severe than a psychosis. *A neurosis is an emotional problem that is solved in an irrational manner* (Marguerite Clark). **2** any action of nerve cells. [earlier, a functional disease < New Latin *neurosis* < Greek *neûron* nerve, sinew + *-ōsis* -osis]

1. In which of the following sentences can *neurosis* correctly be placed in the blank?
    _____ a. Betty reacts with unreasonable fear to elevator rides. We think she has a _____ .
    _____ b. Jack's _____ makes him perform compulsive acts, such as washing his hands all the time.
    _____ c. Her anxiety is so severe that the doctor's diagnosis is _____ .
    _____ d. It surely must be a _____ that makes Jim afraid of dynamite.

2. If you have a *neurosis*,
    _____ a. you are really crazy.
    _____ b. you can function well most of the time.
    _____ c. you might be very depressed.
    _____ d. you will improve if you take vitamins.

3. Complete this verbal analogy.
    warm : hot :: *neurosis* : _____
    a. emotional   c. anxiety
    b. psychosis   d. therapy

4. Do you know of anyone who displays signs of *neurosis*?

    _____

    _____

5. Write a sentence correctly using *neurosis*. (Be sure to use context clues to show that you understand the meaning of the word.)

    _____

    _____

Paradigm[15]

par|a|digm (par′ə dim, -dīm), *n.* **1** a pattern; example: *Sir John is impeccable, a paradigm of the gentleman soldier* (Harper's). **2** *Grammar.* **a** an example, such as of a noun, verb, or pronoun, in all its inflections. **b** the set of inflectional forms for a word or class of words: *The final step in morphology is the establishment of paradigms, which can be viewed as sets of grammatical suffixes* (Harold B. Allen). [< Latin *paradigma* < Greek *parádeigma, -matos* pattern, ultimately < *para-* side by side + *deiknýnai* to show, point out]

1. In which of the following sentences is *paradigm* used correctly?
    _____ a. Sam found a paradigm on the sidewalk.
    _____ b. Captain James is the paradigm of the gentleman officer.
    _____ c. Some people regard science as the paradigm of knowledge.
    _____ d. The student's task was to write out the paradigm of an irregular verb.

2. Select the synonym(s) of *paradigm*.
    _____ a. example   _____ d. model
    _____ b. description   _____ e. pattern
    _____ c. perfection   _____ f. reprint

3. If you create a *paradigm*,
    _____ a. others are likely to copy it.
    _____ b. you are certain to win the lottery.
    _____ c. you may be recognized as an expert in your field.
    _____ d. it may set out all the forms of a noun or verb.

4. Write a sentence correctly using *paradigm*. (Be sure to use context clues to show you understand the meaning of the word.)

    _____

    _____

5. Who, in your opinion, is an outstanding *paradigm* of a professional athlete?

    _____

    _____

Psychosis[7]

psy|cho|sis (sī kō′sis), *n., pl.* **-ses** (-sēz). **1** any severe form of mental disturbance or disease which may also be associated with physical disease, and which produces deep and far-reaching disruption of normal behavior and social functioning: *Alcoholism may be a symptom of ... psychosis, or may bring to notice an already existing psychosis* (Strecker, Ebaugh, and Ewalt). **2** = insanity. [< New Latin *psychosis* < Greek *psȳchē* soul, mind + New Latin *-osis* -osis]

1. Which of the following can be said of a *psychosis*?
    _____ a. It is serious.
    _____ b. It is a disease.
    _____ c. One shouldn't worry about it.
    _____ d. Treatment is needed.

SOCIAL SCIENCES: PSYCHOLOGY

2. Check any appropriate response to the following statement:
   "The patient was hospitalized because of his *psychosis*."
   _____ a. "Overwork," the doctor said, and sent him to the hospital.
   _____ b. Bob was hospitalized for surgery.
   _____ c. Joe was not feeling well, so the doctor suggested some tests.
   _____ d. Dick's mental state is so serious that he must be hospitalized.

3. Which of the following conditions might indicate *psychosis*?
   _____ a. trying to make everyone happy
   _____ b. running for public office
   _____ c. believing one is Napoleon
   _____ d. laughing at inappropriate times

4. Can you think of someone recently in the news who shows signs of *psychosis*?

   _____

   _____

5. Write a sentence correctly using *psychosis*. (Be sure to include context clues to show you understand the meaning of the word.)

   _____

   _____

Psychotherapy[9]

psy|cho|ther|a|py (sī'kō ther'ə pē), *n.* the treatment of mental or emotional disorders by psychological means, especially those involving intercommunication, as by psychoanalysis.
psy|cho|a|nal|y|sis (sī'kō ə nal'ə sis), *n.* **1a** the examination of a person's mind to discover the unconscious desires, fears, anxieties, or motivating forces which produce certain mental and emotional disorders: *Psychoanalysis aims at and achieves nothing more than the discovery of the unconscious in mental life* (Sigmund Freud). **b** a method of psychotherapy based on such examination; analysis of mind or personality. **2** the theory originated and first developed by Freud.

1. In which of the following sentences is *psychotherapy* used correctly?
   _____ a. Hypnosis may be used in psychotherapy.
   _____ b. Through psychotherapy, Amy was able to ease her nervous disorders.
   _____ c. Psychotherapy can be avoided by using vitamin therapy.
   _____ d. Psychotherapy may involve telling about one's problems.

2. Check any appropriate response to the following statement:
   "Dr. Morse has taken special training in *psychotherapy*."
   _____ a. He can treat mental disorders using special techniques.
   _____ b. Dr. Morse is a brilliant surgeon.
   _____ c. I understand he prescribes diet and exercise as a cure.
   _____ d. He can cure you in two sessions.

3. The etymology of *psycho* is found at *psychosis* and shows that *psycho* comes from the Greek *psyche* (mind, spirit, soul). Use this information and your background knowledge to match the following:

_____ a. psychology   aa. examination of the mind

_____ b. psychoanalysis   bb. chart of a person's mental makeup

_____ c. psychogram   cc. measurement of mental facts and relations

_____ d. psychometrics   dd. science of the mind

_____ e. psychosurgery   ee. brain surgery

4. Write a sentence correctly using *psychotherapy*. (Be sure to include context clues to show you understand the meaning of the word.)

_____

_____

5. What kinds of illness do you think *psychotherapy* might cure?

_____

_____

Reliability[12]

re|li|a|bil|i|ty (ri lī'ə bil'ə tē), *n.* the quality or state of being reliable; trustworthiness; dependability: *An employee has perfect reliability if he always does his work responsibly.*

(Note: *Specifically,* the extent to which an experiment, test, or measuring procedure yields the same results on repeated trials.)

1. Which of the following would be an example of *reliability*?

_____ a. Mr. Jones arrives at work every weekday at exactly 9:00 A.M.

_____ b. Harry wakes up every morning at 7:30 A.M.

_____ c. Mary manages the money for her club, with never a loss.

_____ d. Two forms of a standardized test can be given with similar results.

2. Match the sentences in number 1 with the synonyms below that best fit the sentence meaning.

_____ a.   aa. trustworthiness

_____ b.   bb. dependability

_____ c.   cc. repeated results

_____ d.   dd. not used correctly

3. Check any appropriate response to the following statement:
"The *reliability* of the Nelson Denny vocabulary test makes it a useful instrument for college students."

_____ a. The test is created for college-age students.

_____ b. We can depend on the results even if we give the test twice.

_____ c. Results of the test are easily obtained from the tables given.

_____ d. Vocabulary tests are not fair to foreign students.

4. On a scale of 1 to 10, with 10 high, judge the *reliability* of your car.

_____

_____

5. Write a sentence correctly using *reliability*. (Be sure to include context clues to show you understand the meaning of the word.)

_____

_____

Repression[6]

re|pres|sion (ri presh′ən), *n.* **1** the act of repressing: *The repression of a laugh made him choke. Fourteen months of military repression ... plainly had failed* (Newsweek). **2** the condition of being repressed: *Repression by her strict parents only made her behave worse.* SYN: constraint. **3** *Psychoanalysis.* a defense mechanism by which unacceptable or painful impulses, emotions, or memories are put out of the conscious mind, their energy or effect remaining (according to Freudian theory) in the unconscious, where it influences personality and behavior.

re|press (ri pres′), *v.t.* **1** to prevent from acting; check: *She repressed an impulse to cough. To save his life he could not repress a chuckle* (Booth Tarkington). SYN: curb, restrain. **2** to keep down; put down; suppress: *The dictator repressed the revolt.* **3** *Psychoanalysis.* to make the object of repression; force (a painful or undesirable memory or impulse) from the conscious mind into the unconscious mind. [< Latin *repressus*, past participle of *reprimere* < *re-* back + *premere* to press] —**re|press′er,** *n.* —**re|press′i|ble,** *adj.*

1. In which of the following sentences is *repression* used correctly?

_____ a. Mary said she didn't notice the man, but he certainly made a repression on me.

_____ b. After a year of military repression, the dictator was overthrown.

_____ c. Repression of his childhood anger made Tom an unhappy adult.

_____ d. Bank and business failures led to an economic repression.

2. Select the correct definition for *repression* as it is used in the following sentence:

"John seems to have put painful memories into his unconscious mind. This *repression* may show itself in his behavior."

_____ a. hiding away

_____ b. constraint

_____ c. forcing out of conscious mind

_____ d. restraining by force

3. Which of the numbered dictionary definitions of *repression* best fits the word's use in the reading selection? _____

4. Write a sentence correctly using *repression*. (Be sure to include context clues to show you understand the meaning of the word.)

_____

_____

5. We are usually not aware of the things we repress, but one result of *repression* may be guilt. Is there anything you feel guilty about? What might you have repressed to cause this feeling?

_____

_____

Stimulus[3]

stim|u|lus (stim′yə ləs), *n., pl.* **-li** (-lī). **1** something that stirs to action or effort: *Ambition is a great stimulus. We need some imaginative stimulus ... to carry us year after year ... through the routine work which is so large a part of our life* (Walter Pater). SYN: incentive, spur. **2** something that excites the body or some part of the body to a specific activity or function; something that produces a response, such as the transmit- ting of an impulse along a nerve, the movement of a muscle, or a changed state of consciousness, in an organism: *The doctor used mild electric shocks as a stimulus to keep the patient's heart beating. The stimulus of a loud sound, carried by nerves to the brain, made the baby cry.* **3** *Botany.* a sting, such as a stinging hair on a nettle. [< Latin *stimulus* (originally) a goad]

1. In which of the following sentences is *stimulus* used correctly?
   _____ a. The stimulus of the bright light made her eyes blink.
   _____ b. Being poor can be a stimulus to hard work.
   _____ c. He used a stimulus when he planted corn in the garden.
   _____ d. Hunger was the stimulus that drove her to the refrigerator.

2. Which of the following might be said of a *stimulus*?
   _____ a. It may come from an external or internal source.
   _____ b. Whatever it may be, it is not likely to work.
   _____ c. To a dog, it might be a cat.
   _____ d. Psychology is the only science that uses this word.

3. Which of the numbered dictionary definitions of *stimulus* best fits the word's use in the reading selection? _____

4. What is the *stimulus* that causes you to wake up in the morning?

_____

_____

5. Write a sentence correctly using *stimulus*. (Be sure to include context clues to show you understand the meaning of the word.)

_____

_____

Subjective[5]

sub|jec|tive (səb jek′tiv), *adj.* **1** existing in the mind; belonging to the person thinking rather than to the object thought of. Ideas and opinions are subjective; facts are objective. **2** about the thoughts and feelings, as of the speaker, writer, or painter; personal. Lyric poetry is subjective, expressing the feelings of the poet; narrative poetry is generally objective, telling a story. **3** *Grammar.* being or serving as the subject of a sentence; nominative. **4** *Psychology.* **a** originating within or dependent on the mind of the individual rather than an external object. **b** = introspective. **5** *Philosophy.* **a** of or relating to reality as perceived by the mind, as distinct from reality as independent of the mind. **b** influenced by an individual's state of mind: *a subjective perception or apprehension.* **c** having to do with the substance of anything, as opposed to its qualities and attributes. **6** *Medicine.* (of symptoms) discoverable by the patient only. **7** *Obsolete.* of or having to do with someone who is subject to rule or control. —**sub|jec′tive|ly,** *adv.* —**sub|jec′tive-ness,** *n.*

SOCIAL SCIENCES: PSYCHOLOGY

1. Check any appropriate response to the following statement:
   "Joe makes *subjective* judgments."
   _____ a. He considers other's opinions
   _____ b. He depends on written presentations.
   _____ c. He weighs evidence carefully.
   _____ d. He uses his personal feelings and opinions.

2. Complete this verbal analogy.
   likely : probable :: *subjective* : _____
   a. careful   d. personal
   b. thoughtful   e. possible
   c. objective

3. Which of the numbered dictionary definitions of *subjective* best fits the word's use in the reading selection? _____

4. Write a sentence correctly using *subjective*. (Be sure to include context clues to show you understand the meaning of the word.)

   _____

   _____

5. Most people judge music and art *subjectively*. When might it be wrong to do so?

   _____

   _____

Theory[1]

the|o|ry (thē′ər ē, thir′ē), *n., pl.* **-ries. 1a** an explanation; explanation based on thought; explanation based on observation and reasoning, especially one that has been tested and confirmed as a general principle explaining a large number of related facts: *the theory of evolution. Einstein's theory of relativity explains the motion of moving objects. According to one scientific theory of life, the more complicated animals developed from the simpler ones.* **b** a hypothesis proposed as an explanation; conjecture: *Whether I am right in the theory or not . . . the fact is as I state it* (Edmund Burke). **2** the principles or methods of a science or art rather than its practice: *the theory of music, the theory of modern warfare.* **3a** an idea or opinion about something: *I think the fire was started by a careless smoker. What is your theory?* **b** thought or fancy as opposed to fact or practice: *He is right only as to theory, because the facts contradict him.* **4** Mathematics. a set of theorems which constitute a connected, systematic view of some branch of mathematics: *the theory of probabilities.* **5** *Obsolete.* mental view; contemplation.
in theory, according to theory; theoretically: *In theory the plan should have worked.*
[< Late Latin *theōria* < Greek *theōriā* a looking at, thing looked at < *theōreîn* to consider, look at < *theōrós* spectator < *théā* a sight + *horân* see]
— **Syn. 1a, b. Theory, hypothesis** as terms in science mean a generalization reached by inference from observed particulars and proposed as an explanation of their cause, relations, or the like. **Theory** implies a larger body of tested evidence and a greater degree of probability: *The red shift in the spectra of galaxies supports the theory that the universe is continuously expanding.* **Hypothesis** designates a merely tentative explanation of the data, advanced or adopted provisionally, often as the basis of a theory or as a guide to further observation or experiment: *Archeological discoveries strengthened the hypothesis that Troy existed.*

1. In which of the following sentences is *theory* used correctly?
   _____ a. Einstein was famous for his theory of relativity.
   _____ b. Mary used the theory of fudge making to cook that candy.
   _____ c. Freshman students at the music school must study music theory.
   _____ d. Harry had a theory about how the fire started.

2. Which of the following might correctly be called a *theory*?
   _____ a. the theory of gravity
   _____ b. the theory of probabilities
   _____ c. the theory of relativity
   _____ d. the theory of heights

3. Which of the numbered dictionary definitions of *theory* best fits the word's use in the reading selection? _____

4. Have you ever discussed *theories* of life and love with a friend? Who was the friend? Did you reach any conclusions?

   _____

   _____

5. Write a sentence correctly using *theory*. (Be sure to include context clues to show you understand the meaning of the word.)

   _____

   _____

Validity[13]

va|lid|i|ty (və lid′ə tē), *n., pl.* **-ties. 1** truth or soundness: *the validity of an argument, the validity of an excuse.* SYN: authenticity. **2** legal soundness or force; being legally binding: *the validity of a contract.* SYN: legality. **3** effectiveness: *He had ... too high an opinion of the validity of regular troops* (Benjamin Franklin). SYN: efficacy.

from **valid:**

[< Latin *validus* strong < *valēre* be strong]

(Note: *Specifically,* validity refers to the extent to which the results of an evaluation procedure serve the particular uses for which they were intended. That is, if the purpose of a test is to measure computation skill the valid test will do that with some degree of success.)

1. In which of the following sentences is *validity* used correctly?
   _____ a. I admire John's validity; he is an honest man.
   _____ b. I believe your argument; it has validity.
   _____ c. The court has given validity to common-law marriages.
   _____ d. Our test produces the desired effect, so we say it has validity.

2. Select the synonym(s) of *validity*.

_____ a. ineffectiveness   _____ d. effectiveness
_____ b. authenticity   _____ e. illegality
_____ c. legality   _____ f. efficacy

3. Which of the numbered dictionary definitions of *validity* best fits the word's use in the reading selection? _____

4. Write a sentence correctly using *validity*. (Be sure to include context clues to show you understand the meaning of the word.)

_____

_____

5. Think of the last time you were late for an appointment. Did your excuse have *validity*?

_____

_____

ANSWERS TO CHAPTER 10 EXERCISES

Anxiety: **1.** a, b, c   **2.** d (antonym)   **3.** 1
Cognition: **1.** b, c   **2.** bb, cc, aa, ee, dd   **3.** 1
Hypothesis: **1.** a, c, d   **2.** b (synonym)   **3.** a, b, c
Innate: **1.** a, b, d   **2.** dd, cc, aa, bb, ee   **3.** s, s, a, s, s, s
Introspection: **1.** b, c, d   **2.** ee, aa, dd, bb, cc   **3.** a, b, c
Neurosis: **1.** a, b, c   **2.** b, c   **3.** b (degree)
Paradigm: **1.** b, c, d   **2.** a, d, e   **3.** a, c, d
Psychosis: **1.** a, b, d   **2.** d   **3.** c
Psychotherapy: **1.** a, b, d   **2.** a   **3.** dd, aa, bb, cc, ee
Reliability: **1.** a, c, d   **2.** bb, dd, aa, cc   **3.** b
Repression: **1.** b, c   **2.** c   **3.** 3
Stimulus: **1.** a, b, d   **2.** a, c   **3.** 2
Subjective: **1.** d   **2.** d (synonym)   **3.** 4
Theory: **1.** a, c, d   **2.** a, b, c   **3.** 1a
Validity: **1.** b, c, d   **2.** b, c, d   **3.** 1

If you missed any of the items in the exercises, return to the exercise and to the dictionary definition to see where you went wrong. Remember: If you get something right, you only affirm that you knew it. If you get something wrong and understand why, *you have learned something.*

PSYCHOLOGY POSTTEST

Fill in the blanks with the words from this list.

anxiety	neurosis	repression
cognition	paradigm	stimulus
hypothesis	psychosis	subjective
innate	psychotherapy	theory
introspection	reliability	validity

1. The opposite of objective is _____ .

2. _____ is the process of looking within.

3. A noun or verb set out in all its inflectional forms is a(n) _____ .

4. When a test measures what it claims to measure, we say it has _____ .

5. _____ is a defense mechanism by which unpleasant thoughts are put out of the mind.

6. An assertion that must be tested to find out if it is true is a(n) _____ .

7. A mild nervous disorder is a(n) _____ .

8. One treatment of such a mental disorder is _____ .

9. Einstein is responsible for the _____ of relativity.

10. The _____ of failing two exams made Jane hire a tutor.

11. A(n) _____ is a deep, far-reaching behavior disorder.

12. A troubled, uneasy feeling might be called _____ .

13. If a test gives the same results on repeated trials, it is said to have _____ .

14. Something not learned, but natural, is _____ .

15. _____ is the act of knowing.

Answers to this posttest are in the Instructor's Manual.

If you missed any of the words, you may need to return to the exercises and to the dictionary entries to see why your concepts for some words are incomplete.

CHAPTER ELEVEN

SOCIAL SCIENCES: ECONOMICS

◆

OVERVIEW

*Economics employs systematic analysis to study the way in which societies are orga-
nized to produce the goods and services that are the underpinnings of their communi-
ties. Issues studied in economics include inflation, shortages, unemployment, price
setting, regulation, foreign trade, determination of wages, government policies, and
growth and income distribution.*

*Some areas of concentration within economics are international trade and develop-
ment; economic history and comparative systems; labor and manpower economics;
econometrics and systems; public finance and planning; land, resource, and urban
economics; industrial organization; transportation and public utilities; economics
and social welfare; and economic projecting and planning.*

*A degree in economics can prepare students for employment in national and multina-
tional corporations, financial institutions, unions, and at all levels of government
and agribusiness. It can also serve as preparation for advanced studies in economics,
business, law, and public administration. Some activities of an economist are statistical forecasting, cost analysis, marketing research, evaluation of social programs, and
strategic pricing.*

*Economics textbooks are structured in a variety of ways. They can be expository, with
presentations of broad concepts and generalizations. They may include real-world
examples and problems linked with the theory and ideas in the text. There may be
supplemental material, such as graphs, tables, and biographical data of leaders in the
field. Finally, some textbooks include a form of argumentation and discussion of the
pros and cons of various issues.*

The vocabulary in economics is a combination of general and specialized terminology. There are general vocabulary words, such as price, efficiency, *and* trust, *that also have a specialized meaning within the context of economics. There are also specialized terms such as* cartel *and* mercantilism, *as well as compound nouns, such as* capital transaction, income effect, *and* export subsidies, *that reflect concepts unique to the study of economics. You may add other terms you discover in your studies related to economics on the forms in Appendix D.*

VOCABULARY SELF-EVALUATION

The following words will be introduced in this reading selection. Place a check mark (√) in front of any that you know thoroughly and use in your speech or writing. Place a question mark (?) in front of any that you recognize but do not use yourself.

_____ aggregate	_____ expenditure	_____ oligopoly
_____ capitalism	_____ externality	_____ recession
_____ cartel	_____ fiscal	_____ revenue
_____ consumption	_____ inflationary	_____ sector
_____ entrepreneur	_____ monopoly	_____ tariff

MICROECONOMICS AND MACROECONOMICS

Economics is the science of how people produce goods and services and how they distribute and use them. The study of economics is divided into two basic categories: microeconomics and macroeconomics. Microeconomics is concerned with the economic decisions made by individual people or firms, while macroeconomics deals with the economy as a whole.

The economy itself is also divided into two parts: the private sector[1] and the public sector. The private sector is concerned mostly with microeconomic issues, while the public sector, the government, is concerned with macroeconomic issues. An individual firm uses microeconomic principles to make decisions based on its own self-interest. A firm must make decisions on what to produce, how to produce it, and how much to produce in order to maximize its operating profit. These decisions are affected by the market in which the firm operates. Free competition produces competitive markets. Examples of markets other than a perfect competition market include monopoly,[2] oligopoly,[3] and cartel.[4]

Many firms would like to become a monopoly. A monopoly is desirable because this structure allows the monopolist, the single seller of a good or item with no close substitute, to have a great influence on the price of the good produced. An oligopoly is a market condition where a few large companies produce a similar product and thus dominate the market. Oligopolies and monopolies tend to exist where research and development costs are high. The U.S. automobile industry is an example of an oligopoly. While monopolies are generally not allowed to exist in the United States, there are a few natural monopolies. Most utilities, those that perform a public service such as the gas and electric companies, are natural monopolies regulated by the government. Artificial monopolies are those that result from deliberate efforts to eliminate any competition.

Another market condition not permitted to exist in the United States is the cartel. A cartel exists when several firms divide the market among themselves and then restrict output in order to maintain high prices. OPEC (Organization of Petroleum Exporting Countries) is the best known example of a cartel. Many Middle Eastern countries have joined together to restrict the output of oil and set a high price for each barrel, thus controlling the market worldwide and creating an immense profit for themselves.

The public sector, on the other hand, focuses on macroeconomics to deal with the aggregate,[5] or total, economy. Although the main motivation of capitalism[6] is self-interest, ideally those in the public sector are not seeking personal gain from their positions. The government in a capitalist economy seeks to maintain a stable economy while discouraging those activities that are harmful to the economy or society as a whole. The public sector accomplishes this through both public finance policies and regulation.

Although the economy is dynamic and constantly changing, the public sector tries to maintain as stable an economy as possible. A volatile economy plagued by the unemployment and idle factories caused by a recession[7] or the increasing price levels of inflationary[8] periods does not stimulate new business activity. The government seeks to avoid these and other problems associated with various business cycles through the use of fiscal[9] policy. Fiscal policy involves the government's use of its spending and taxing powers to influence the economy. One form of taxation is the tariff,[10] or fee, on imported goods for the purpose of generating additional monies, or in some cases, to discourage the importation of certain goods that may be inhibiting the sale and/ or production of U.S.-made goods.

The public sector also uses regulation to maintain the economy. In order for the country's entrepreneurs,[11] or independent businessmen, to undertake new business activity, a competitive environment must be maintained. This is the reason for the public sector's prohibition and regulation of most monopolies and cartels.

Many economic issues also have a social side. Some business activities can produce an externality,[12] which is the side effect of economic production. Pollution caused by a manufacturing process is an example of a negative externality. It is also an indirect cost of production. The government may decide to use the fiscal instrument of taxation if the natural resources used in the production of the good are not fully reflected in its selling price. Placing a tax on the good increases its price so as to reflect the true cost of production. Because of the law of supply and demand, the price increase will usually result in decreased consumption,[13] or use, of the good. This taxation process, then, could be used to correct for a negative externality such as pollution.

For example, Company X produces aluminum widgets in a major U.S. city. Aluminum is heavily used in the manufacturing process and causes an enormous air pollution problem. Because of this problem, the government decides to place a tax on the widget in order to provide funds for dealing with the air pollution in the city. The tax on the widget will make it more expensive and will reduce consumer demand. With a reduction in demand will come a reduction in production along with decreased pollution. The money from the tax, or the revenue[14] collected, may be spent by the government, then, on further research into industrial air pollution problems. This expenditure[15] of funds collected through the taxation of a good/product with a negative externality (air pollution) would be another component of the public sector's fiscal policy.

Finally, even though the issues may be varied and complex, understanding the dimensions and dynamics of economics is vital to the future growth and development of our country. ◆

ECONOMICS PRETEST

Select words from this list and write them in the blanks to complete the sentences.

aggregate	expenditure	oligopoly
capitalism	externality	recession
cartel	fiscal	revenue
consumption	inflationary	sector
entrepreneur	monopoly	tariff

1. Any clearly defined section or division of the economy can also be characterized as a(n) _____ .

2. A(n) _____ is the exclusive control of a commodity or service.

3. The condition in the market in which few producers supply a commodity and can influence its price is known as a(n) _____ .

4. The total amount or the sum of those things in a large group, such as consumer demands, is a(n) _____ .

5. A(n) _____ is a list of duties that a government charges on imports and exports.

6. A policy designed to handle public finance issues is known as a(n) _____ policy.

7. A period of temporary business reduction less extreme than a depression and that influences the total economy is called a(n) _____ .

8. A sudden increase in prices resulting from too great expansion in paper money or bank credit defines a(n) _____ period.

9. Something on the outside that is a result of economic activity is called a(n) _____ .

10. The economic system within the United States is known as _____ .

11. A(n) _____ is one who owns and manages his own business.

12. _____ is defined as the amount used up, such as in the use of a resource.

13. A source of income for the government such as through taxes is called _____ .

14. Using up or paying out of money, time, or effort is a(n) _____ .

15. A(n) _____ is a large group of business firms that agree to operate as a monopoly.

Answers to this pretest are in Appendix E.

Unless your instructor tells you to do otherwise, complete the exercises for each word that you missed on the pretest. The words, with their meanings and exercises, are in alphabetical order. The superscript numbers indicate where the words appeared in the reading selection so that you can refer to them when necessary. There are several types of exercises, but for each word you will be asked to write a sentence using context clues. (See Chapter 3 if you need information about how to create context clues.) You are also asked to perform some activity that will help you make your concept of the word personal. *Complete this activity thoughtfully, for creating a personalized concept of the word will help you remember it in the future.*

Answers to all the exercises are at the end of the exercise segment.

ECONOMICS EXERCISES

Aggregate[5]

ag|gre|gate (*n., adj.* ag′rə git, -gāt; *v.* ag′rə gāt), *n., adj., v.,* **-gat|ed, -gat|ing**. —*n.* **1** total amount; sum: *The aggregate of all the gifts was over $100.* **2** a mass of separate things joined together; combined mass; collection: *A lump of sugar is an aggregate of sugar crystals.* **3** any material, such as sand or gravel, that is mixed with water and cement to make concrete. **4** *Geology.* rock composed of several different mineral constituents capable of being separated by mechanical means: *Granite is a type of aggregate.* —*adj.* **1a** total. **b** gathered together in one mass or group. **syn:** combined, collective. **2** *Botany.* consisting of many florets arranged in a dense mass: *an aggregate flower.* **3** *Geology.* composed of different mineral fragments united into one rock by heat, as granite.

—*v.t.* **1** to amount to; come to; total: *The money collected will aggregate $1,000.* **2** to gather together in a mass or whole; collect; unite: *Granite is made of small particles aggregated together.* **syn:** mass. —*v.i.* to come together in a mass; accumulate. **in the aggregate,** taken together; considered as a whole; collectively: *The payments on our house amount in the aggregate to a big sum of money. Our judgment of a man's character is derived from observing a number of successive acts, forming in the aggregate his general course of conduct* (George C. Lewis). [< Latin *aggregātus,* past participle of *aggregāre* add to, ultimately < *ad-* to + *grex, gregis* flock] —**ag′gre|gate′ly,** *adv.* —**ag′gre|gate′ness,** *n.* —**ag′gre|ga′tor,** *n.*

1. In which of the following sentences can *aggregate* be correctly placed in the blank?
   _____ a. An individual can purchase an _____ for his collection.
   _____ b. The _____ was lost when the company moved to another location.
   _____ c. Households can influence the level of _____ demand by the amount that they consume or use.
   _____ d. The _____ of all the donations to the charity for abused children was $1,000.

2. Select the synonym(s) of *aggregate*.
   _____ a. individual   _____ c. collective
   _____ b. total   _____ d. solitary

3. The etymology of *aggregate* shows that the word comes from the Latin *aggregare* (to + flock). Use this information and your background knowledge to match the following:
   _____ a. congregate   aa. to separate from others; set apart; isolate
   _____ b. egregious   bb. to come together into a crowd or mass; assemble
   _____ c. gregarious   cc. group or division in classification; class
   _____ d. segregate   dd. fond of being with others
   _____ e. category   ee. very great; outrageous; flagrant

4. One of the concerns of economists is the study of *aggregates*, or totals, in the entire nation. Some of these *aggregates* include total production, national income, and total employment. What might be some of the other *aggregates* you might study if you were an economist?

   _____

   _____

5. Write a sentence correctly using *aggregate*. (Be sure to include context clues to show you understand the meaning of the word.)

   _____

   _____

Capitalism[6]

cap|i|tal|ism (kap′ə tə liz′əm), *n.* **1** an economic system in which private individuals or groups of individuals own land, factories, and other means of production. They compete with one another, using the hired labor of other persons, to produce goods and services for profit: *The characteristic feature of modern capitalism is mass* production of goods destined for consumption by the masses (Newsweek). **2** the concentration of wealth with its power and influence in the hands of a few. **3** a system which favors the existence of capitalists or the concentration of wealth in the hands of a few.

SOCIAL SCIENCES: ECONOMICS

1. In which of the following sentences is *capitalism* used correctly?
   _____ a. Capitalism is an economic system in which the means of production are owned and operated by individual owners, or capitalists.
   _____ b. Capitalism is a form of political dictatorship, since the state owns all production and property.
   _____ c. The United States is an example of capitalism, since there is private ownership of capital and freedom of choice for people to buy what they please and to work where they wish.
   _____ d. The first economic stage in modern civilization was capitalism in which the means of production were controlled by the landed aristocracy.

2. Complete the verbal analogy.
   communism : Russia :: *capitalism* : _____
   a. China   c. Yugoslavia
   b. USA   d. Cuba

3. Select the characteristics of *capitalism*.
   _____ a. government control
   _____ b. private ownership
   _____ c. production of goods and services for profit
   _____ d. competition

4. Write a sentence correctly using *capitalism*. (Be sure to include context clues to show you understand the meaning of the word.)

   _____

   _____

5. We live in the economic system of *capitalism*. In your opinion, what are some of the positive aspects of *capitalism*? What are some of the negative aspects?

   _____

   _____

Cartel[4]

car|tel (kär tel′, kär′təl), *n.* **1** a large group of business firms that agree to operate as a monopoly, especially to regulate prices and production: *The methodical Swiss, who think that there is a place for everything, staunchly believe that the place for industry is in cartels* (Time). **SYN:** syndicate, combine. **2** a written agreement between countries at war for the exchange of prisoners or some other purpose. **3a** a written challenge to a duel. **b** a letter of defiance. **4** Also, **Cartel.** (in France and Belgium) a political group with a common cause or object; a bloc. **5** *Rare.* a paper or card bearing writing or printing. [< Middle French *cartel* < Italian *cartello* little card < *carta* card < Latin *charta*]

1. What is an example of an international *cartel* famous for influencing gasoline prices?

    _____ a. Shell Oil   _____ c. ARCO

    _____ b. Russian-American   _____ d. OPEC

2. What are some characteristics of a *cartel*?

    _____ a. two or three businesses

    _____ b. a large group of businesses

    _____ c. an agreement

    _____ d. regulation of prices and production

3. In which of the following sentences is *cartel* used correctly?

    _____ a. The oil cartel regulated prices throughout the world.

    _____ b. A cartel is illegal in the United States, since it does not allow for open competition.

    _____ c. One cartel merged with another to form a duopoly.

    _____ d. A cartel needs to advertise to help it compete with other companies.

4. How do *cartel* and monopoly relate to each other? Do we have recognized *cartels* in the United States?

    _____

    _____

5. Write a sentence correctly using *cartel*. (Be sure to include context clues to show you understand the meaning of the word.)

    _____

    _____

Consumption[13]

con|sump|tion (kən sump′shən), *n.* **1** the act of consuming; using up; use: *We took along some food for our consumption on the trip. The science of economics deals with the production, distribution and consumption of wealth.* **2** the amount used up: *Our consumption of fuel oil increases in cold weather.* **3** a disease that destroys part of the body, especially the lungs; tuberculosis. [< Latin *cōnsumptiō, -ōnis* < *cōnsūmere;* see etym. under **consume**]

from **consume:**

[< Latin *cōnsūmere* < *com-* (intensive) + *sūmere* take up]

1. Select the synonym(s) of *consumption*.

    _____ a. fiscal   _____ c. expense

    _____ b. inflation   _____ d. using up

2. Complete the verbal analogy.
   capitalism : communism :: *consumption* : _____
   a. saving   c. working
   b. spending   d. exercising

3. The etymology of *consumption* shows that the word comes from the Latin *consumere* (to take up). Use this information and your background knowledge to match the following.

   _____ a. resume   aa. to take for granted without proving; suppose

   _____ b. sumptuous   bb. to begin again; go on

   _____ c. presume   cc. costly; magnificent; rich

   _____ d. subsume   dd. having to do with the spending of money; regulating expenses, especially to control extravagance or waste

   _____ e. sumptuary   ee. to bring (an idea, term, principle, proposition, or the like) under another

4. Write a sentence correctly using *consumption*. (Be sure to include context clues to show you understand the meaning of the word.)

   _____

   _____

5. Not all purchased goods are intended for *consumption*. What are some goods that you have purchased that you did not intend for *consumption*?

   _____

   _____

Entrepreneur[11]

en|tre|pre|neur (än'trə prə nėr'), *n.* a person who organizes and manages a business or industrial undertaking. An entrepreneur takes the risk of not making a profit and gets the profit when there is one: *In the uppermost executive echelons of TV, there is not one recognized major theatrical entrepreneur* (New York Times). [< Old French *entrepreneur* < *entreprendre* undertake; see etym. under **enterprise**]

from **enterprise:**

[< Old French *entreprise*, feminine past participle of *entreprendre* undertake < *entre-* between (< Latin *inter-*) + *prendre* take < Latin *prehendere*]

1. In which of the following sentences is *entrepreneur* used correctly?

   _____ a. Henry Ford was a famous entrepreneur who started the Ford Motor Company.

   _____ b. The entrepreneur went to work at the government office in the suburbs.

   _____ c. An entrepreneur usually is not very independent and prefers to be a follower.

_____ d. There may be more than one entrepreneur in a company who is very creative and takes risks in developing new products.

2. Who of the following might likely be an *entrepreneur?*
_____ a. a government employee
_____ b. a city worker
_____ c. a man who owns a travel agency
_____ d. a woman in real estate sales

3. The etymology of *entrepreneur* shows that the word comes from the Old French *enterprendre* (to undertake). Use this information and your background knowledge to match the following.
_____ a. reprehend aa. open to attack; assailable; vulnerable
_____ b. comprise bb. to arrest; seize
_____ c. apprehend cc. to be made up of; consist of; include
_____ d. prehensile dd. to reprove or blame; rebuke
_____ e. pregnable ee. adapted for seizing, grasping, or holding on

4. Would you like to be an *entrepreneur?* Why or why not? What business would you operate or own as an *entrepreneur?*

_____

_____

5. Write a sentence correctly using *entrepreneur.* (Be sure to use context clues to show you understand the meaning of the word.)

_____

_____

Expenditure[15]

ex|pend|i|ture (ek spen′də chŭr, -chər), *n.* **1** the act or process of spending; a using up or paying out: *A large piece of work requires the expenditure of money, time, and effort.* **2** the amount of money, time, or effort, spent; expense: *Her expenditures for Christmas presents were $25 and several hours of work.*

1. Select the synonym(s) of *expenditure.*
_____ a. savings   _____ c. payment
_____ b. earnings   _____ d. outlay

2. Which of the following have *expenditures?*
_____ a. consumers   _____ c. businesses
_____ b. governments _____ d. resources

SOCIAL SCIENCES: ECONOMICS

3. In which of the following sentences is *expenditure* used correctly?

_____ a. One expenditure within the large metropolitan city is that for welfare assistance.

_____ b. The annual expenditure includes a new entrepreneur for the company.

_____ c. The budget process tries to balance some revenue or income for each expenditure.

_____ d. New taxes were needed because of the unexpected expenditure for emergency aid to the flood-stricken area of the state.

4. Write a sentence using *expenditure*. (Be sure to include context clues to show you understand the meaning of the word.)

_____

_____

5. What is the biggest *expenditure* for you as a student? Why?

_____

_____

Externality[12]

ex|ter|nal|i|ty (eks′tĕr nal′ə tē), *n., pl.* **-ties. 1** the quality or condition of being external. **2** an external thing.

ex|ter|nal (ek stĕr′nəl), *adj., n.* **—adj. 1** on the outside; outer: *An ear of corn has an external husk.* **SYN:** outward, exterior. **2** entirely outside; coming from without: *the external air.* **3** to be used only on the outside of the body: *Liniment and rubbing alcohol are external remedies.* **4** having existence outside one's mind. **5** *Figurative.* easily seen but not essential; superficial: *Going to church is an external act of worship. His art criticism had external brilliance but no substance.* **6** having to do with international affairs; foreign: *War affects a nation's external trade.* **7** *Zoology,* *Anatomy.* situated toward or on the outer surface; remote from the median line or center. **8** *British.* (of a student) having studied elsewhere than in the university where he is examined: *Once a year he returned to London to sit for his exams as an external student after pirating the appropriate learning from half a dozen different universities* (Manchester Guardian). **—n.** an outer surface or part; outside. **externals,** clothing, manners, or other outward acts or appearances: *He judges people by mere externals rather than by their character.* [< Latin *externus* outside (< *exterus* outside < *ex* out of) + English *-al¹*] **—ex|ter′nal|ly,** *adv.*

1. What are some of the characteristics of an *externality*? (Review the reading selection if necessary.)

_____ a. related to economic production

_____ b. side effect

_____ c. positive or negative

_____ d. related to an entrepreneur

2. The etymology of *externality* (see *external*) shows that the word comes from the Latin *externus* (outside). Use this information and your background knowledge to match the following:

_____ a. extremity   aa. an outer surface or part; outward appearance

_____ b. exotic   bb. the very end; farthest possible place; last part or point

_____ c. exodus   cc. a going out; departure

CHAPTER ELEVEN

_____ d. exorbitant dd. from a foreign country; not native

_____ e. exterior ee. exceeding what is customary, proper, or reasonable; very expensive

3. What are some examples of negative *externalities* in the economy?

_____ a. air pollution

_____ b. water pollution

_____ c. increase in employment

_____ d. destruction of resources

4. *Externalities* are the side effects, both positive and negative, of economic production. The reading selection discusses some *negative externalities*. What do you think are some of the *positive externalities* of economic production?

_____

_____

5. Write a sentence correctly using *externality*. (Be sure to include context clues to show you understand the meaning of the word.)

_____

_____

Fiscal[9]

fis|cal (fis′kəl), *adj., n.* —*adj.* **1** = financial. **SYN:** See syn. under **financial**. **2** having to do with public finance: *Important changes were made in the government's fiscal policy.*
—*n.* a public prosecutor in some countries: *cited before the fiscal of the empire* (Sarah Austin).
[< Latin *fiscālis* < *fiscus* purse; see etym. under **fisc**] —**fis′cal|ly**, *adv.*

1. Select the synonym(s) of *fiscal*.

_____ a. physical _____ c. monetary

_____ b. aggregate _____ d. financial

2. Which of the numbered dictionary definitions of *fiscal* best fits the word's use in the reading selection? _____

3. In which of the following sentences can *fiscal* be correctly placed in the blank?

_____ a. The _____ statements presented the plans for the holiday meeting.

_____ b. The national _____ policy deals with military situations only.

_____ c. The budget for _____ 1981 was based on receipts estimated to be $600 billion.

_____ d. The government can choose to pursue a _____ policy to stimulate or reduce demand for goods and services.

SOCIAL SCIENCES: ECONOMICS

4. Write a sentence correctly using *fiscal*. (Be sure to include context clues to show you understand the meaning of the word.)

_____

_____

5. The government has a *fiscal* policy by which our leaders make decisions that will affect the economy related to spending money and raising taxes. Do you have your own personal *fiscal* policy? If so, what is it?

_____

_____

Inflationary[8]

in|fla|tion|ar|y (in flā′shə ner′ē), *adj.* of or having to do with inflation; tending to inflate: *the inflationary effect of government spending.*
in|fla|tion (in flā′shən), *n.* **1** the act of swelling (as with air, gas, pride, or satisfaction). **2** a swollen state; too great expansion. **3** an increase of the currency of a country by issuing much paper money. **4** a sharp and sudden rise in prices resulting from a too great expansion in paper money or bank credit: *Inflation spirals inexorably on* (Atlantic).

1. Complete the verbal analogy.
   recessionary : decline :: *inflationary* : _____
   a. moderation   c. status quo
   b. increase   d. decline

2. What happens during an *inflationary* cycle?
   _____ a. a sharp and sudden increase in prices
   _____ b. a sharp and sudden decrease in prices
   _____ c. a reduction in money or credit
   _____ d. too great an expansion in money and credit

3. Select the synonym(s) of *inflationary*.
   _____ a. lessening   _____ c. decreasing
   _____ b. expanding   _____ d. swelling

4. Why should we be concerned about *inflationary* spirals or increases in our economy? How might *inflationary* spirals affect your earning and spending abilities?

_____

_____

5. Write a sentence correctly using *inflationary*. (Be sure to include context clues to show you understand the meaning of the word.)

_____

_____

Monopoly[2]

mo|nop|o|ly (mə nop′ə lē), *n., pl.* **-lies.** **1** the exclusive control of a commodity or service: *In most communities, the telephone company has a monopoly. You have, in this Kingdom, an advantage in lead, that amounts to a monopoly* (Edmund Burke). **2** such a control granted by a government: *An inventor has a monopoly on his invention for a certain number of years. Raleigh held a monopoly of cards, Essex a monopoly of sweet wines* (Macaulay). **3** control that is not exclusive but which enables the person or company to fix prices. **4** a commercial product or service that is exclusively controlled or nearly so. **5** a person or company that has a monopoly on some commodity or service: *The pilots' association was now the compactest monopoly in the world* (Mark Twain). **6** the exclusive possession or control of something intangible: *a monopoly of a person's time. No one person has a monopoly of virtue. Neither side has a monopoly of right or wrong* (Edward A. Freeman). [< Latin *monopōlium* < Greek *monopṓlion* < *mónos* single + *pōleîn* to sell]

1. In which of the following sentences can *monopoly* be correctly placed in the blank?

    _____ a. A _____ represents a division or segment of the population.

    _____ b. Some of the shortcomings of a _____ include misallocation of resources and restriction of new technology.

    _____ c. An example of a natural _____ is a public utility, such as a gas or electric company, that is regulated by the government.

    _____ d. A _____ is the practice in international trade of setting lower prices in distant markets than in the home country.

2. Select the characteristics of a *monopoly*.

    _____ a. a unique good or service

    _____ b. many companies

    _____ c. a single seller

    _____ d. exclusive control

3. What are some possible problems with the structure of a *monopoly*?

    _____ a. increased competition

    _____ b. concentration of power

    _____ c. reduction in prices

    _____ d. price controls

4. Write a sentence correctly using *monopoly*. (Be sure to include context clues to show you understand the meaning of the word.)

    _____

    _____

5. How does the definition of *monopoly* relate to the board game Monopoly, which is divided into real estate segments? If you have not played the game, what type of *monopoly* affects your daily living or your community and how (gas company, water company, etc.)?

    _____

    _____

SOCIAL SCIENCES: ECONOMICS

Oligopoly[3]

ol|i|gop|o|ly (ol′ə gop′ə lē), *n., pl.* **-lies.** a condition in a market in which so few producers supply a commodity or service that each of them can influence its price, with or without an agreement between them: *Ultimately, it is the oligopolies and not the State that set the economic priorities of our society* (Manchester Guardian). [< *oligo-* + *-poly*, as in *monopoly*]

1. What would be an example of an *oligopoly*?
   _____ a. the steel industry
   _____ b. a local small liquor store
   _____ c. an automobile company
   _____ d. an independent garage owner

2. Select the characteristics of an *oligopoly*.
   _____ a. many producers
   _____ b. a condition in the market
   _____ c. influences prices
   _____ d. few producers

3. In which of the following sentences is *oligopoly* correctly used?
   _____ a. An oligopoly carries out its production in a large scale and has a nationwide sales network.
   _____ b. The local oligopoly is run by a small businessman who started the company by himself.
   _____ c. An example of an oligopoly is the steel industry, since a few large firms control industry output.
   _____ d. A telephone or a gas company is an example of an oligopoly.

4. How do monopoly and *oligopoly* relate to each other? Do they have any common characteristics?

   _____

   _____

5. Write a sentence correctly using *oligopoly*. (Be sure to include context clues to show you understand the meaning of the word.)

   _____

   _____

Recession[7]

re|ces|sion[1] (ri sesh′ən), *n.* **1** the action or fact of going backward; moving backward. **2** the action or fact of sloping backward. **3** withdrawal, as of the minister and choir after the service in some churches. **4** a period of temporary business reduction, shorter and less extreme than a depression: *When the country entered the 1949 recession, many analysts again warned business to batten down the hatches* (Newsweek). [< Latin *recessiō, -ōnis* < *recēdere*; see etym. under **recede**]

from **recede:**

[< Latin *recēdere* < *re-* back + *cēdere* to go]

1. Select the characteristics of *recession*.
   _____ a. more extreme than a depression
   _____ b. temporary business reduction
   _____ c. less extreme than a depression
   _____ d. long-term business reduction

2. Which of the numbered dictionary definitions of *recession* best fits the word's use in the reading selection? _____

3. The etymology of *recession* shows that the word comes from the Latin *recedere* (back + to go). Use this information and your background knowledge to match the following:

   _____ a. secede   aa. to go before or in front of; precede in time or place

   _____ b. abscess   bb. a granting, yielding

   _____ c. predecessor   cc. collection of pus in the tissues of some part of the body

   _____ d. antecede   dd. to withdraw formally from an organization

   _____ e. concession   ee. a person holding a position of office before another

4. Write a sentence correctly using *recession*. (Be sure to include context clues to show you understand the meaning of the word.)

   _____

   _____

5. What do you think are some of the consequences of a *recession* for individual businesses? For the nation as a whole? Have you ever been affected by a *recession*?

   _____

   _____

Revenue[14]

rev|e|nue (rev′ə nü, -nyü), *n.* **1** money coming in; income: *The government got much revenue from taxes last year.* **2** a particular item of income. **3** a source of income. **4** the government department that collects taxes: *the Internal Revenue Service.* [< Middle French *revenue* < Old French, a return, feminine past participle of *revenir* come back < Latin *revenīre* < *re-* back + *venīre* come]

1. Select the synonym(s) of *revenue*.
   _____ a. earnings   _____ c. income
   _____ b. debit   _____ d. assets

2. The etymology of *revenue* shows that the word comes from the Latin *revenire* (back + to come). Use this information and your background knowledge to match the following:

_____ a. circumvent

_____ b. parvenu

_____ c. intervention

_____ d. supervene

_____ e. convention

aa. to come as something additional or interrupting

bb. meeting arranged for some particular purpose; gathering; assembly

cc. person who has risen above his class, especially one who has risen through the acquisition of wealth or political power

dd. to get the better of or defeat by trickery

ee. interfering in any affair so as to affect its course or issue

3. *Revenue* is the income that the government receives from a variety of sources. What are some of these sources?

_____ a. gasoline taxes   _____ c. cartels

_____ b. tariffs   _____ d. income taxes

4. What is the primary source of your *revenue*? Is the amount of *revenue* that you will receive an important criterion in a career decision? Why or why not?

_____

_____

5. Write a sentence correctly using *revenue*. (Be sure to include context clues to show you understand the meaning of the word.)

_____

_____

Sector[1]

sec|tor (sek′tər), *n., v. —n.* **1** the part of a circle, ellipse, or the like, between two radii and the included arc. **2** a clearly defined military area which a given military unit protects or covers with fire; part of a front held by a unit. **3** any clearly defined section or division; segment: *the consumer-oriented sector of the economy* (Atlantic). *Direct mail is the fastest growing sector in the advertis-ing industry* (London Times). **SYN:** zone, quarter. **4** an instrument consisting of two rulers connected by a joint, used in measuring or drawing angles. *—v.t.* to divide into sectors; provide with sectors. [< Late Latin *sector, -ōris* (in Latin, a cutter) < *secāre* to cut]

1. Select the synonym(s) of *sector*.

_____ a. division   _____ c. entirety

_____ b. section   _____ d. segment

2. Which of the numbered dictionary definitions of *sector* best fits the word's use in the reading selection? _____

3. The etymology of *sector* shows that the word comes from the Late Latin *secare* (to cut). Use this information and your background knowledge to match the following:

_____	a. sectile	aa.	to cut apart (animal, plant, organ, or tissue) in order to examine or study the structure
_____	b. segment	bb.	that can be cut smoothly by a knife but cannot withstand pulverization
_____	c. dissect	cc.	cross-section of the vegetation of an area, usually that part growing along a long narrow strip
_____	d. intersect	dd.	piece or part cut off, marked off, or broken off; division; section
_____	e. transect	ee.	to cut or divide by passing through or crossing; cross

4. Write a sentence correctly using *sector*. (Be sure to include context clues to show you understand the meaning of the word.)

_____

_____

5. Which *sector* of the economy do you find more interesting, public or private? Why?

_____

_____

Tariff[10]

tar|iff (tar′if), *n., v.* —*n.* **1** a list of duties or taxes that a government charges on imports or exports. **2** the system of duties or taxes on imports and exports. **3** any duty or tax in such a list or system: *There is a very high tariff on imported jewelry. Heavy revenue duties ... have the same effect as protective tariffs in obstructing free trade* (Time). **4** the table of prices in a hotel, restaurant, or similar establishment: *The tariff at the Grant Hotel ranges from $10 to $25 a day for a single room.* **5** any scale of prices; book of rates; schedule: *a revised tariff for passenger travel.* **6** *Obsolete.* an arithmetical table, especially one used to save calculating discounts; ready reckoner. —*v.t.* **1** to put a tariff on. **2** to set a value or price for, according to a tariff. **3** to list the tariff or tariffs on. [< Italian *tariffa* schedule of customs rates < Arabic *ta′rīf* information, notification]

1. Which of the numbered dictionary definitions of *tariff* best fits the word's use in the reading selection? _____

2. Why would the government impose a *tariff*?
   _____ a. to generate additional money
   _____ b. to reduce government revenue
   _____ c. to encourage importation
   _____ d. to discourage importation of certain goods

3. Select the synonym(s) of *tariff*.
   _____ a. credit   _____ c. tax
   _____ b. duty   _____ d. cartel

4. What foreign items have you purchased that have included a *tariff* on them that you are aware of (car, jewelry, motorcycle, cigars, toys)?

_____

_____

5. Write a sentence correctly using *tariff*. (Be sure to include context clues to show you understand the meaning of the word.)

_____

_____

ANSWERS TO CHAPTER 11 EXERCISES

Aggregate: 1. c, d 2. b, c 3. bb, ee, dd, aa, cc
Capitalism: 1. a, c 2. b (example) 3. b, c, d
Cartel: 1. d 2. b, c, d 3. a, b
Consumption: 1. d 2. a (antonym) 3. bb, cc, aa, ee, dd
Entrepreneur: 1. a, d 2. c, d 3. dd, cc, bb, ee, aa
Expenditure: 1. c, d 2. a, b, c 3. a, c, d
Externality: 1. a, b, c 2. bb, dd, cc, ee, aa 3. a, b, d
Fiscal: 1. c, d 2. 2 3. c, d
Inflationary: 1. b (characteristic) 2. a, d 3. b, d
Monopoly: 1. b, c 2. a, c, d 3. b, d
Oligopoly: 1. a, c 2. b, c, d 3. a, c
Recession: 1. b, c 2. 4 3. dd, cc, ee, aa, bb
Revenue: 1. a, c 2. dd, cc, ee, aa, bb 3. a, b, d
Sector: 1. a, b, d 2. 3 3. bb, dd, aa, ee, cc
Tariff: 1. *n.* 3 2. a, d 3. b, c

If you missed any of the items in the exercises, return to the exercise and to the dictionary definition to see where you went wrong. Remember: If you get something right, you only affirm that you knew it. If you get something wrong and understand why, *you have learned something*.

ECONOMICS POSTTEST

Fill in the blanks with the words from this list.

aggregate	expenditure	oligopoly
capitalism	externality	recession
cartel	fiscal	revenue
consumption	inflationary	sector
entrepreneur	monopoly	tariff

1. A tax, or duty, on imports is a type of _____ .

2. An expense is a(n) _____ .

3. OPEC is an example of a(n) _____ .

4. _____ is the side effect of economic production.

5. Competition among private individuals or groups is also known as _____ .

6. *Use* is a synonym for _____ .

7. A synonym for _____ is *financial*.

8. Another word for *total amount* is _____ .

9. A market condition of few producers influencing the price of a commodity or service is called a(n) _____ .

10. A(n) _____ is a temporary business reduction.

11. Tending to increase or rise in prices describes a(n) _____ cycle.

12. An independent businessman could also be called a(n) _____ .

13. A(n) _____ is a segment or division.

14. *Income* is another word for _____ .

15. Exclusive control or exclusive possession is a characteristic of a(n) _____ .

Answers to this posttest are in the Instructor's Manual.

If you missed any of the words, you may need to return to the exercises and to the dictionary entries to see why your concepts for some words are incomplete.

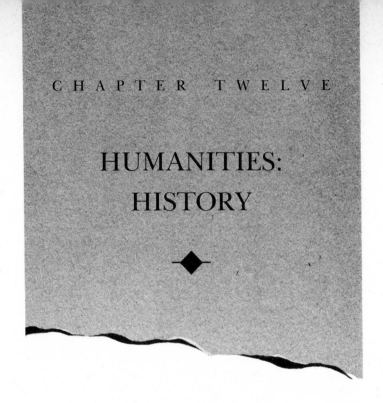

CHAPTER TWELVE

HUMANITIES: HISTORY

◆

OVERVIEW

History is the study of the past of our society and how it impacts the present. It is concerned with trends, movements, and the growth of ideas. The study of history can enhance the quality of life for an individual through analysis of the history of other civilizations and cultures.

Major fields of study, or subdisciplines, within history include ancient and medieval history, the history of Europe, Africa, Near East, India and Southeast Asia, East Asia, Latin America, the United States, and Western and world civilization. There are also special fields of study, such as the history of science, history of religion, Russian history, and so forth.

Training in history prepares students for a wide range of career opportunities, including work in business, public relations, advertising, journalism, law, government, police and police-related agencies, and teaching of either history or social science.

Introductory textbooks in history can be structured in a variety of formats, including expository, descriptive, chronological, narrative, or cause and effect. Various time periods and political and social events provide the framework for many textbooks. Others approach the study of history through the cause-and-effect structure, with detailed analysis of events and their consequences.

The vocabulary in the field of history consists primarily of general vocabulary terms that can also have a specialized meaning within the context of history. Examples of such words are agrarian, precedent, *and* schism. *There are also many terms that have come from individuals (eponyms) and become synonymous with an era, event, or practice of government.* Machiavellian, Napoleonic, *and* Hamiltonian, *are such terms. Finally, specialized vocabulary is coined to represent the unique characteristics of certain eras, or time periods, such as* enlightenment, progressivism, *and* reformation. *You may add other terms you discover in your studies related to history on the forms in Appendix D.*

VOCABULARY SELF-EVALUATION

The following words will be introduced in this reading selection. Place a check mark (√) in front of any that you know thoroughly and use in your speech or writing. Place a question mark (?) in front of any that you recognize but do not use yourself.

_____ agrarian	_____ facet	_____ polemic
_____ analogous	_____ metamorphosis	_____ precedent
_____ antipathy	_____ nascent	_____ precept
_____ cursory	_____ nonpareil	_____ quintessential
_____ draconian	_____ palpable	_____ schism

HOW HISTORIANS DIFFER: TWO VIEWS OF A PERIOD IN U.S. HISTORY

Historians do not all have the same view of the events in their field of study. It is not uncommon for scholars to look at the same occurrences, interpret them differently, and arrive at widely differing conclusions. One example of such a difference of opinion concerns the period of American history immediately following the American Revolution and ending nearly a century later following the Civil War. Two groups of historiographers (those who study and write about history) reached decidedly different conclusions about this period in history.

One group of writers, the traditionalists, ally themselves with the thinking of the French statesman Alexis de Tocqueville and his view of the "democratic renaissance." He saw this period in American history as the quintessential[1] rebirth of the central European "free" man in a new setting. This group of historiographers seeks old-world precedents[2] for interpreting the American experience, and attempts to establish relationships of historical and sociological significance that have a common origin, source, or cause. Certainly this type of historical analysis is widely used, since almost any period of ancient history in itself provides the interested observer with unlimited examples and experiences analogous[3] to more current happenings.

In sharp contrast to this traditional philosophy, the first generation of exceptionalist historians (also called romanticists), such as George Bancroft and Washington Irving, saw each separate facet[4] of the federal republic's birth and growing pains as a unique and exceptional occurrence. These historians were quick to put forward the opinion that the success of the American Revolution, the geographical and economic expansion, and the industrial development of the new nation were events nonpareil[5] in the pre-American era.

Even a cursory[6] examination of some of the historical events that occurred during this period will provide palpable[7] evidence to support either or both schools of historical analysis. While a traditional historian of the period would have little trouble linking philosophies of populism* and progressivism† with the social and class struggles in Europe, exceptionalists Theodore Roosevelt and Frederick Jackson Turner directly related agrarian[8] expansion, class antipathy[9] resulting from rapidly increasing industrialization, and subordination of the American Indians to the American scene and to the "great frontier" in particular. It has been argued that it was, in fact, the circumstance of the endless frontier that provided both the inspiration and motivation for the exceptionalist school of historical writing. It is interesting to note that Russian historical observers writing on the American "segment of the world class struggle" were consistently traditional in their point of view. They saw nothing unique or exceptional—perhaps because they had an even greater frontier of their own.

Historical opinion and writing often have roots in the events and theology of Judaism and Christianity. It is from such origins that traditional scholars Cotton and Increase Mather drew their comparison between Old Testament prophesy and early American history. Although this example concerns a period of history earlier than the national period we are discussing, the "Mather influence" continues to irritate a whole new generation of exceptionalist historians. In their frustration, some writers stop just short of suggesting draconian[10] measures to discredit the Matherian school of historical analysis. Writers B. E. Andrews and John DeBow want no part of reminiscence or recollection of things past to explain or justify the American metamorphosis,[11] no recalling of Old Testament or Old World precepts[12] to illustrate their concepts of American historical reality. The exceptionalist historian seeks no ties between feudal barons of the Middle Ages and the ex–plantation owners of the post–Civil War period, or between vassals and sharecroppers.

This division of historians who have studied the same recorded historical evidence into two schools of thought, and the schism[13] produced thereby, provides the nascent[14] student of history with an abundance of both thought-provoking and controversial material. Such polemic[15] writing surely must encourage beginning historians in their own reading, observations, and conclusions. ◆

---

* Populism refers to the beliefs of the People's Party, formed in 1891. The Populists advocated government control of the railroads, limitation of private ownership of land, an increase in currency, and an income tax.

† Progressivism refers to the Progressive Party. The first was formed in 1912 and advocated direct primaries, the initiative, the referendum, the recall, and woman suffrage. Progressive Parties were also formed in 1924 and 1948.

HISTORY PRETEST

Select words from this list and write them in the blanks to complete the sentences.

agrarian	facet	polemic
analogous	metamorphosis	precedent
antipathy	nascent	precept
cursory	nonpareil	quintessential
draconian	palpable	schism

1. Things comparable are _____ .

2. Something superficial is _____ .

3. _____ means "just beginning to develop."

4. Something obvious is _____ .

5. A(n) _____ serves as an example.

6. _____ means "agricultural."

7. A breach is a(n) _____ .

8. A(n) _____ is a teaching.

9. _____ means "without equal."

10. A(n) _____ is a feeling against something.

11. *Harsh* is a synonym for _____ .

12. _____ means "controversial."

13. A change of substance is _____ .

14. _____ means "of the purest kind."

15. A distinct part of something is a(n) _____ .

Answers to this pretest are in Appendix E.

Unless your instructor tells you to do otherwise, complete the exercises for each word you missed on the pretest. The words, with their meanings and exercises, are in alphabetical order. The superscript numbers indicate where the words appeared in the reading selection so that you can refer to them when necessary. There are several types of exercises, but for each word you will be asked to write a sentence using context clues. (See Chapter 3 if you need information about how to create context clues.) You are also asked to perform some activity that will help you make your concept of the word personal. *Complete this activity thoughtfully, for creating a personalized concept of the word will help you remember it in the future.*

Answers to all the exercises are at the end of the exercise segment.

HISTORY EXERCISES

Agrarian[8]

a·grar·i·an (ə grãr′ē ən), *adj., n.* — *adj.* **1a** having to do with farming land, its use, or its ownership. **b** for the support and advancement of farmers and farming: *an agrarian movement.* **2** agricultural. **3** growing wild in the fields, as certain plants. — *n.* a person who favors a new or more equitable division of rural land.
[< Latin *agrārius* (< *ager, agrī* field)]

1. In which of the following sentences can *agrarian* correctly be placed in the blank?

   _____ a. My friend Tom farms sixty acres, so I call him an

   _____ .

   _____ b. Government _____ policies have harmed many farmers.

   _____ c. Certain _____ plants cause damage to those plants intentionally grown.

   _____ d. _____ practices in colonial America, particularly the continuous planting of cotton and tobacco, greatly depleted the soil.

2. If you are interested in things *agrarian*, you might

   _____ a. go to medical school.
   _____ b. raise hundreds of acres of wheat.
   _____ c. join with other farmers to influence government policy.
   _____ d. sell your farm to a land developer.

3. Which of the numbered and lettered dictionary definitions of *agrarian* best fits the word's use in the reading selection? _____

4. Write a sentence correctly using *agrarian*. (Be sure to include context clues to show you understand the meaning of the word.)

   _____

   _____

5. Can any country survive without a successful *agrarian* population? Do we have such a population in this country?

   _____

   _____

Analogous[3]

a·nal·o·gous (ə nal′ə gəs), *adj.* **1** alike in some way; similar in the quality or feature that is being thought of, or in circumstances or uses; comparable (to): *The human heart is analogous to a* pump. *Who can say that the anatomy of modern despotism is significantly analogous to the anatomy of despotism in the declining Roman Empire?* (Bulletin of Atomic Scientists). **SYN:**

corresponding, like. **2** *Biology.* corresponding in function, but not in structure and origin: *The wing of a fly is analogous to the wing of a bird.* [< Latin *analogus* (with English *-ous*) < Greek *análogos* proportionate < *aná lógon* according to due ratio] — a|nal′o|gous|ly, *adv.* — a|nal′o|gous-ness, *n.*

1. Match the following statement with a similar statement below: "The historiographer showed that Hitler and Napoleon were *analogous.*"
   _____ a. The historian made a study of invading armies.
   _____ b. The writer saw differences between Germany and France.
   _____ c. Some historians are interested in powerful rulers.
   _____ d. The writer set out similarities between the German and the French leaders.

2. Select any adjective that describes something *analogous.*
   _____ a. corresponding   _____ d. dissimilar
   _____ b. inconsistent   _____ e. resembling
   _____ c. comparable   _____ f. similar

3. Which of the following might be *analogous,* and how are they alike?
   _____ a. a bird's wing and an airplane's wing

   Alike in _____.

   _____ b. a window and a light bulb

   Alike in _____.

   _____ c. love and hate

   Alike in _____.

   _____ d. television and live theater

   Alike in _____.

4. If you could make your life *analogous* to the life of any public figure, whom would you choose?

   _____

   _____

5. Write a sentence correctly using *analogous.* (Be sure to include context clues to show you understand the meaning of the word.)

   _____

   _____

Antipathy[9]

an|tip|a|thy (an tip′ə thē), *n., pl.* **-thies. 1** a strong or fixed dislike; a feeling against; aversion: *She felt an antipathy to snakes.* SYN: repugnance, abhorrence, disgust. **2** something or someone that arouses such a feeling; an object of aversion or dislike: *The Scots and nonconformists were antipathies of Dr. Johnson.* **3** *Obsolete.* contrariety of feeling, disposition, or nature. [< Latin *antipathīa* < Greek *antipátheia* < *anti-* against + *páthos* feeling]

1. Check any appropriate response to the following statement:
"George is developing an *antipathy* to his country's form of government."
   _____ a. It must mean he is a happy citizen.
   _____ b. He should try to move away.
   _____ c. Oh, everyone has family problems.
   _____ d. If enough others feel that way, there may be a change.

2. Place an "s" by any synonym and an "a" by any antonym of *antipathy*.
   _____ a. repugnance   _____ d. disgust
   _____ b. affection   _____ e. aversion
   _____ c. fondness   _____ f. abhorrence

3. Which of the numbered dictionary definitions of *antipathy* best fits the word's use in the reading selection? _____

4. Write a sentence correctly using *antipathy*. (Be sure to include context clues to show you understand the meaning of the word.)

   _____

   _____

5. For what or whom do you have an *antipathy*?

   _____

   _____

Cursory[6]

cur|so|ry (kėr'sər ē), *adj.* without attention to details; hasty and superficial: *He gave the lesson a cursory glance, expecting to study it later. Even a cursory reading of the letter showed many errors.* SYN: rapid, hurried. [< Latin *cursōrius* of a race < *currere* run] —**cur'so|ri|ly**, *adv.* —**cur'so|ri|ness**, *n.*

1. Place an "s" by any synonym and an "a" by any antonym of *cursory*.
   _____ a. careful   _____ d. superficial
   _____ b. thorough   _____ e. hurried
   _____ c. painstaking   _____ f. swearing

2. In which of the following sentences is *cursory* used correctly?
   _____ a. This is too important to be treated in a cursory manner.
   _____ b. He gave her a cursory look and went on down the street.
   _____ c. Her cursory attitude made her continually late.
   _____ d. Although his studies were cursory, he still passed the examination.

3. The etymology of *cursory* shows that it comes from the Latin *currere* (to run). Use this information and your background knowledge to match the following:

_____	a. concur	aa. to have or express the same opinion
_____	b. current	bb. a steady and smooth movement, as of water
_____	c. cursive	cc. covering a wide field of subjects; rambling
_____	d. cursor	dd. to happen again repeatedly
_____	e. discursive	ee. a flashing moving pointer on a computer screen
_____	f. recur	ff. written with flowing strokes

4. What is the most recent thing you read in a *cursory* fashion?

   _____

   _____

5. Write a sentence correctly using *cursory*. (Be sure to include context clues to show you understand the meaning of the word.)

   _____

   _____

Draconian[10]

Dra|co|ni|an (drə kō′nē ən), *adj.* **1** of or having to do with Draco, a legislator of Athens in the 600's B.C., or his severe code of laws. **2** severe; cruel; harsh.

(Note: There is not yet agreement whether this word is completely naturalized. Some writers and dictionaries use a capital D, while others do not. A capital letter indicates that the word still refers primarily to the person or place that inspired it (in this case, the Athenian legislator), while a lowercase letter indicates the word has been used widely enough to have taken on a more general meaning, in this instance the meanings "severe," "cruel," and "harsh.")

1. Match the following statement with a similar statement below:
   "Some believe war preferable to a *draconian* peace."
   _____ a. Peace promotes a happy society.
   _____ b. Only the strong can endure a harsh peace.
   _____ c. Wars are fought by those who believe might makes right.
   _____ d. Some prefer to fight in open battle rather than live in a peaceful but cruel society.

2. Place an "s" by any synonym and an "a" by any antonym of *draconian*.
   _____ a. lenient   _____ d. stringent
   _____ b. stern   _____ e. mild
   _____ c. rigid   _____ f. merciful

3. Complete the verbal analogy.

   open : closed :: *draconian* : _____

   a. indulgent   c. intemperate

   b. inflexible   d. impartial

4. Write a sentence correctly using *draconian*. (Be sure to include context clues to show you understand the meaning of the word.)

   _____

   _____

5. Do you believe the death penalty is a *draconian* law?

   _____

   _____

Facet[4]

✱fac|et (fas′it), *n., v.,* **-et|ed, -et|ing** or (*especially British*) **-et|ted, -et|ting.** — *n.* **1** any one of the small, polished, flat surfaces of a cut gem. **2** anything like the facet of a gem. See the picture above on the following page. **3** *Figurative.* any one of several sides or views; a distinct part; phase; aspect: *a facet of the mind, a facet of a problem. Selfishness was a facet of his character that we seldom saw.* **4** *Zoology.* one of the individual external visual units of a compound eye: *The eyes of certain insects have facets.* **5** *Architecture.* the vertical band or strip between the flutes of a column. **6** *Anatomy.* a small, smooth, flat surface, especially on a bone.

— *v.t.* **1** to cut facets on: *Next, we visited the rooms in which the diamonds were faceted* (New Yorker). **2** *Geology.* to grind off flat surfaces on (ridges, stones, or the like).

— *v.i. Geology.* to be ground off by glacial action, winds, or water.

[< French *facette* (diminutive) < Old French *face;* see etym. under **face**]

✱**facet**
definition 1

facets

1. In which of the following sentences is *facet(s)* used correctly?

   _____ a. The facet of Jim's personality I like best is his honesty.

   _____ b. In biology, we are studying the facets of a fly's eye.

   _____ c. My job is to facet stones for jewelry.

   _____ d. Bob damaged the facet of his ulna when he broke his arm.

2. Check any appropriate response to the following statement: "That *facet* of the problem is easily understood."

   _____ a. We will have to work hard to figure this out.

   _____ b. That is an easy phase.

   _____ c. But some other aspects are difficult.

   _____ d. Each distinct part should be considered carefully.

3. Which of the numbered dictionary definitions of *facet* best fits the word's use in the reading selection? _____

4. What *facet* of your education is the most interesting?

   _____

   _____

5. Write a sentence correctly using *facet*. (Be sure to include context clues to show you understand the meaning of the word.)

_____

_____

Metamorphosis[11]

met|a|mor|pho|sis (met′ə môr′fə sis), *n., pl.* **-ses** (-sēz). **1** a change of form, structure, or substance. **2** *Figurative.* a noticeable or complete change in appearance, character, circumstances, or condition: *His visage . . . changed as from a mask to a face. . . . I know not that I have ever seen in any other human face an equal metamorphosis* (Charlotte Brontë). **3** a change in form, shape, or substance by or as if by witchcraft; transformation: *Metamorphosis is a favorite game in fairy tales: princes into swans, ogres into dragons, mice into horses, and a pumpkin into a coach.* **4** the changed form resulting from any such change. **5** a marked change in the form, and usually the habits, of an animal in its development after the embryonic stage. Tadpoles become frogs by metamorphosis; they lose their tails and grow legs. *It is the process of losing the larval organs and gaining the missing adult organs which is called metamorphosis* (A. Franklin Shull). ~~See picture below.~~ **6** the structural or functional modification of a plant organ or structure during the course of its development. **7** *Physiology.* metabolism. [< Latin *metamorphōsis* < Greek *metamórphōsis*, ultimately < *metá* (change) over + *morphē* form]

1. Check any appropriate response to the following statement:
   "The old house has undergone *a metamorphosis* since Bill and Mary bought it."
   _____ a. Why did they tear it down?!
   _____ b. That must cost a great deal of money.
   _____ c. Do you approve of the changes they made?
   _____ d. I hope they preserved its character.

2. Which of the following might undergo a *metamorphosis*?
   _____ a. a woman   _____ d. a plant
   _____ b. a man   _____ e. an insect
   _____ c. an animal   _____ f. a frog

3. Which of the numbered dictionary definitions of *metamorphosis* best fits the word's use in the reading selection? _____

4. Write a sentence correctly using *metamorphosis*. (Be sure to include context clues to show you understand the meaning of the word.)

_____

_____

5. Mentally picture yourself after undergoing *metamorphosis*. What or whom do you look like?

_____

_____

Nascent[14]

nas|cent (nas'ənt, nā'sənt), *adj.* **1** in the process of coming into existence; just beginning to exist, grow, or develop: *a nascent sense of right and wrong.* SYN: incipient, inchoate. **2** *Chemistry.* **a** having to do with the state or condition of an element at the instant it is set free from a combination. **b** (of an element) being in a free or uncombined state. [< Latin *nāscēns, -entis,* present participle of *nāscī* be born] **—nas'cent|ly,** *adv.*

1. Match the following statement with a similar statement below:
   "A study of the population revealed *nascent* revolutionary tendencies."
   _____ a. A study of the people showed history was repeating itself.
   _____ b. Information gathered offered evidence of the beginnings of a revolution.
   _____ c. Facts demonstrated a revolution had occurred.
   _____ d. A study has been made of the beginnings of the nation.

2. The etymology of *nascent* shows that the word comes from the Latin *nasci* (to be born). Use this information and your background knowledge to match the following:
   _____ a. cognate   aa. a song pertaining to the birthday of Christ
   _____ b. natal   bb. a newborn child
   _____ c. neonate   cc. having a common ancestor; related by blood
   _____ d. noël   dd. pertaining to the time or place of one's birth

3. Which of the following describes something *nascent*?
   _____ a. beginning   _____ d. incipient
   _____ b. completed   _____ e. initial
   _____ c. ultimate   _____ f. commencing

4. What segment of your knowledge base is *nascent*? Traveling abroad? Making investments? Learning a profession?

   _____

   _____

5. Write a sentence correctly using *nascent*. (Be sure to include context clues to show you understand the meaning of the word.)

   _____

   _____

Nonpareil[5]

non|pa|reil (non'pə rel'), *adj., n.* **—** *adj.* having no equal; peerless: *The literary salons have had a major part in making Paris the city nonpareil, for centuries the undisputed cultural centre of the world* (Canadian Forum).
— *n.* **1** a person or thing having no equal: *Though you were crown'd The nonpareil of beauty* (Shakespeare). **2** a beautifully colored finch of the southern United States; painted bunting. **3** a kind of apple. **4** *Printing.* **a** a size of type; 6-point. **b** a slug 6 points high used between lines. **5** a small chocolate drop covered with tiny white pellets of sugar.
[< Middle French *nonpareil* < *non-* not (< Latin) + *pareil* equal < Vulgar Latin *pāriculus* (diminutive) < Latin *pār, paris* equal]

CHAPTER TWELVE

1. In which of the following sentences can *nonpareil* correctly be placed in the blank?

   _____ a. My sister Ann is a _____ housekeeper and cook.

   _____ b. The art critic praised the _____ beauty of the Mona Lisa.

   _____ c. The violinist, Itzhak Perlman, is a virtuoso and a _____ .

   _____ d. The candidate does not belong to any political party, so he is said to be _____ .

2. Complete the verbal analogy.

   clean : spotless :: *nonpareil* : _____

   a. careless
   b. helpless
   c. restless
   d. matchless

3. The etymology of *nonpareil* indicates the word comes from the Latin *par, paris* (equal). Use this information and your background knowledge to match the following:

   _____ a. compare   aa. equality, as in amount or value

   _____ b. pair   bb. to bet an original wager and its winnings on a subsequent event

   _____ c. parity   cc. a person who has equal standing with another

   _____ d. parlay   dd. two equal or similar items

   _____ e. peer   ee. to represent as similar or equal

4. Write a sentence correctly using *nonpareil*. (Be sure to include context clues to show you understand the meaning of the word.)

   _____

   _____

5. Who do you think is the female singer *nonpareil* today?

   _____

   _____

Palpable[7]

pal|pa|ble (pal′pə bəl), *adj.* **1** readily seen or heard and recognized; obvious: *a palpable error. For shore it was, and high ... and palpable to view* (Byron). **syn:** perceptible, plain, evident, manifest. **2** that can be touched or felt; tangible: *A hit, a very palpable hit* (Shakespeare). **3** *Medicine.* perceptible by palpation. [< Late Latin *palpābilis* < Latin *palpāre* to feel, stroke, pat] **— pal′pa|ble|ness,** *n.* **— pal′pa|bly,** *adv.*

1. Check any appropriate response to the following statement:
   "One of John's characteristics is a *palpable* honesty."
   _____ a. It is the facet of his personality I like best.
   _____ b. I've never trusted him.
   _____ c. That may be why children and dogs like him.
   _____ d. People like that should be in jail!

2. Place an "s" by any synonym and an "a" by any antonym of *palpable*.
   _____ a. evident   _____ f. noticeable
   _____ b. apparent   _____ g. unseen
   _____ c. concealed   _____ h. distinct
   _____ d. perceptible   _____ i. obvious
   _____ e. invisible

3. Which of the numbered dictionary definitions of *palpable* best fits the word's use in the reading selection? _____

4. What is your most *palpable* physical characteristic?

   _____

   _____

5. Write a sentence correctly using *palpable*. (Be sure to include context clues to show you understand the meaning of the word.)

   _____

   _____

Polemic[15]

po|lem|ic (pə lem′ik), *n., adj.* —*n.* **1** a disputing discussion; argument; controversy: *Writing polemics against a czar in a candlelit cellar could be dangerous* (Newsweek). **2** a person who takes part in a controversy or argument.
—*adj.* of controversy or disagreement; of dispute: *My father's little library consisted chiefly of books in polemic divinity* (Benjamin Franklin). **SYN:** controversial.
[< Greek *polemikós* belligerent < *pólemos* war]
—**po|lem′i|cal|ly,** *adv.*

1. A *polemic* is likely to be
   _____ a. harmonious.   _____ d. peaceable.
   _____ b. an argument.   _____ e. neutral.
   _____ c. a debate.   _____ f. a disagreement.

2. In which of the following sentences can *polemic* correctly be placed in the blank?
   _____ a. I don't find the book interesting; it is too full of
       _____s.
   _____ b. Olson's writing is _____ and not always fair to his opponents.

_____ c. Their discussion was calm, and neither resorted to
_____s.

_____ d. If you practice _____s in the United States, you
will be sent to jail.

3. Complete the verbal analogy.
happy : sad :: *polemic* : _____
a. argumentative   c. belligerent
b. amiable   d. interminable

4. In what area of your life are you likely to engage in a *polemic*? Why do you feel so strongly?

_____

_____

5. Write a sentence correctly using *polemic*. (Be sure to include context clues to show you understand the meaning of the word.)

_____

_____

Precedent²

prec|e|dent (*n*. pres′ə dənt; *adj*. pri sē′dənt, pres′ə-), *n.*, *adj.* — *n.* **1** an action that may serve as an example or reason for a later action: *Last year's school picnic set a precedent for having one this year. There was no precedent for Roosevelt's election to a third term as President.* **2** *Law.* a judicial decision, case, or proceeding that serves as a guide or pattern in future similar or analogous situations: *A decision of a court often serves as a precedent in another court. Precedent to a court is what past performances are to sports and the theater* (Wall Street Journal). [< adjective]
— *adj.* = preceding. [< Latin *praecēdēns, -entis,*
present participle of *praecēdere* precede] — **pre-ced′ent|ly**, *adv.*
pre|cede (prē sēd′), *v.*, **-ced|ed, -ced|ing.** — *v.t.* **1** to go or come before in order, place, or time: *A precedes B in the alphabet. A band preceded the soldiers in the parade. She preceded me into the room. Mr. Eisenhower preceded Mr. Kennedy as President.* **2** to be higher than in rank or importance: *A major precedes a captain. A knight precedes a pawn in the game of chess.* **3** to introduce by something preliminary; preface. — *v.i.* to go or come before in rank, order, place, or time. [< Latin *praecēdere* < *prae-* before + *cēdere* to go. Compare etym. under **precession**.]

1. Check any appropriate response to the following statement:
"The governor set a *precedent* by taking the question directly to the people."
_____ a. That's a crime, and he should be run out of office.
_____ b. Other governors will do the same thing.
_____ c. It should have been done before, I think.
_____ d. He's interested in the opinions of the people.

2. The etymology of *precedent* (see *precede*) indicates that the word comes from the Latin *cedere* (to go, or to yield). Use this information and your background knowledge to match the following:
_____ a. ancestor   aa. to go forward or onward
_____ b. decease   bb. a forefather
_____ c. exceed   cc. to move back or away
_____ d. proceed   dd. to die
_____ e. recede   ee. to go beyond the limits of

3. Which of the numbered dictionary definitions of *precedent* best fits the word's use in the reading selection? _____

4. Write a sentence correctly using *precedent*. (Be sure to include context clues to show you understand the meaning of the word.)

_____

_____

5. Often we are unaware that an activity is setting a *precedent* until later action uses it as an example. What activities have you observed that have set a *precedent*?

_____

_____

Precept[12]

pre|cept (prē′sept), *n.* **1** a rule of action or behavior; maxim: *"If at first you don't succeed, try, try again" is a familiar precept. His high-school science course covered many of the basic precepts of modern physics.* **SYN:** teaching, adage, axiom, direction. **2** *Law.* a writ; warrant; a written order issued pursuant to law. [< Anglo-French *precep,* and *precept,* learned borrowing from Latin *praeceptum* (originally) neuter past participle of *praecipere* to order, advise, anticipate < *prae-* before + *capere* to take]

1. In which of the following sentences is *precept(s)* used correctly?
   _____ a. Robert says he obeys the Ten Commandments not as precepts of divine law but as practical rules of conduct.
   _____ b. I believe one should raise a child by precept and example.
   _____ c. Has the precept been delivered to the court?
   _____ d. She finds it hard to live by outdated precepts.

2. Match the following statement with a similar statement below:
   "My grandmother serves *precepts* with her cookies."
   _____ a. Families usually follow certain rules of behavior.
   _____ b. Grandmother believes she should feed our minds and our bodies.
   _____ c. Learn the rules of behavior before you go out in public.
   _____ d. Communication between generations is important.

3. Which of the numbered dictionary definitions of *precept* best fits the word's use in the reading selection? _____

4. One *precept* that has been around for years is "Don't look a gift horse in the mouth." What does it mean? Is there any *precept* that your family uses to guide behavior?

_____

_____

5. Write a sentence correctly using *precept*. (Be sure to include context clues to show you understand the meaning of the word.)

_____

_____

Quintessential[1]

quin|tes|sen|tial (kwin'tə sen'shəl), *adj.* having the nature of a quintessence; of the purest or most perfect kind: *Costain has created what amounts to a quintessential recapture of the English novel, from Smollett to Dickens* (Wall Street Journal). *They don't pay sufficient attention to the quintessential requirement: that it be easy for the reader to find what he is looking for* (Atlantic).
quin|tes|sence (kwin tes'əns), *n.* **1** the purest form of some quality; pure essence. **SYN:** pith.

2 the most perfect example of something: *Her costume was the quintessence of good taste and style.* **3** (in medieval philosophy) the ether of Aristotle, a fifth element (added to earth, water, fire, and air) permeating all things and forming the substance of the heavenly bodies. [< Middle French *quinte essence*, learned borrowing from Medieval Latin *quinta essentia* fifth essence, translation of Greek *pémptē ousiā* Aristotle's "fifth substance"]

1. In which of the following sentences can *quintessential* correctly be placed in the blank?
    _____ a. Sam is the _____ bore, as far as I am concerned.
    _____ b. Many believe Paris to be the _____ city of the world.
    _____ c. When I travel, I take only the _____s.
    _____ d. According to my teacher, the _____ characteristic of music is melody.

2. If John is the *quintessential* stage actor,
    _____ a. he performs best in the movies.
    _____ b. he probably has won many awards.
    _____ c. he has yet to be discovered.
    _____ d. others study his acting methods.

3. Complete the verbal analogy.
    ease : without discomfort :: *quintessential* : _____
    a. an example   c. only example
    b. best example   d. natural example

4. Write a sentence correctly using *quintessential*. (Be sure to include context clues to show you understand the meaning of the word.)

_____

_____

5. In your opinion, who is the *quintessential* male singer today?

_____

_____

Schism[13]

schism (siz'əm, skiz'-), *n.* **1** a division into hostile
groups: ... *the possibility of a serious schism in
the ranks of one of the two big British parties*
(Wall Street Journal). **2** a discord or breach between persons or things. **3a** the division, either of
the whole Church or of some portion of it, into
separate and hostile organizations, because of
some difference of opinion about religion. **b** the
offense of causing or trying to cause such a
schism. **c** a sect or group formed by a schism
within a church. [< Latin *schisma* < Greek
schisma, -atos < *schizein* to split]

1. In which of the following sentences is *schism* correctly used?
   _____ a. A schism in the earth causes an earthquake.
   _____ b. There is a difference of opinion in the church, but we hope it will not produce a schism.
   _____ c. Any schism in a political party weakens it.
   _____ d. There seems to be a widening schism between the rich and the poor in many countries.

2. Place an "s" by any synonym and an "a" by any antonym of *schism*.
   _____ a. division   _____ d. healing
   _____ b. union   _____ e. unanimity
   _____ c. rupture   _____ f. split

3. Which of the numbered and lettered dictionary definitions of *schism* best fits the word's use in the reading selection? _____

4. What might cause a *schism* in a family?

   _____

   _____

5. Write a sentence correctly using *schism*. (Be sure to include context clues to show you understand the meaning of the word.)

   _____

   _____

ANSWERS TO CHAPTER 12 EXERCISES

Agrarian: **1.** b, c, d   **2.** b, c   **3.** 1a
Analogous: **1.** d   **2.** a, c, e, f   **3.** a (function), b (function and composition), c (intense emotion), d (function or purpose)
Antipathy: **1.** b, d   **2.** s, a, a, s, s, s   **3.** 1
Cursory: **1.** a, a, a, s, s, —   **2.** a, b, d   **3.** aa, bb, ff, ee, cc, dd
Draconian: **1.** d   **2.** a, s, s, s, a, a   **3.** a (antonym)
Facet: **1.** a, b, c, d   **2.** b, c, d   **3.** *n.* 3
Metamorphosis: **1.** b, c, d   **2.** a, b, c, d, e   **3.** 2
Nascent: **1.** b   **2.** cc, dd, bb, aa   **3.** a, d, e, f
Nonpareil: **1.** a, b, c   **2.** d (synonym)   **3.** ee, dd, aa, bb, cc

Palpable: 1. a, c **2.** s, s, a, s, a, s, a, s, s **3.** 1
Polemic: 1. b, c, f **2.** a, b, c **3.** b (antonym)
Precedent: 1. a, c, d **2.** bb, dd, ee, aa, cc **3.** *n.* 1
Precept: 1. a, b, c, d **2.** b **3.** 1
Quintessential: 1. a, b, d **2.** b, d **3.** b (definition)
Schism: 1. b, c, d **2.** s, a, s, a, a, s **3.** 2

If you missed any of the items in the exercises, return to the exercise and to the dictionary definition to see where you went wrong. Remember: If you get something right, you only affirm that you knew it. If you get something wrong and understand why, *you have learned something.*

HISTORY POSTTEST

Fill in the blanks with the words from this list.

agrarian   facet   polemic
analogous   metamorphosis   precedent
antipathy   nascent   precept
cursory   nonpareil   quintessential
draconian   palpable   schism

1. A(n) _____ is a small, polished flat surface.

2. A synonym of _____ is *incipient.*

3. A small chocolate drop with white sugar pellets is a(n) _____.

4. _____ means "aversion."

5. A disputing discussion is a(n) _____.

6. A(n) _____ serves as a pattern.

7. The perfect example of something is _____.

8. A(n) _____ is a division into hostile groups.

9. One who favors equitable division of rural land is a(n) _____.

10. Something similar is _____.

11. _____ refers to a severe code of laws.

12. *Hasty* is a synonym of _____.

13. _____ is a marked change.

14. In law, a(n) _____ is a warrant.

15. _____ means "tangible."

Answers to this posttest are in the Instructor's Manual.
    If you missed any of the words, you may need to return to the exercises and to the dictionary entries to see why your concepts for some words are incomplete.

CHAPTER THIRTEEN

HUMANITIES: ENGLISH

◆

OVERVIEW

English is a broadly based field that studies composition, language, and literature. It is versatile, helping develop lifelong skills related to writing, reading, and thinking. English has a broad application for a variety of careers, including business, communications, media, theater, teaching, law, and data processing, as well as providing a foundation for advanced graduate and professional study.

Composition courses help strengthen a student's ability to express ideas and feelings effectively in writing. They also help students understand the significance and complexity of the writing process. Courses are offered in such areas as basic writing, creative writing, functional composition for the vocationally oriented student, research methods and term paper writing, and technical writing related to the technical language of science and industry.

Language or linguistics courses taught in the English department focus on the study of the nature of language, its comparison with other symbol systems, and of language in the context of culture.

The study of literature ranges from the various types and periods (historical), to specific authors (biographical), to special groups in society. There are courses in the nature of literature and its forms (poem, play, novel, short story, film, biography) and how literature works to portray fundamental human concerns. World literature courses can range from antiquity to the modern era. British and American authors such as Shakespeare and Hemingway are studied, as well as the literature of specific groups in society, including women, children, Afro-Americans, Hispanic Americans, and so forth.

Introductory texts in English usually are expository; that is, they explain broad concepts or generalizations. Some provide narration or a story with a plot, characters, and settings. Many texts include historical references and present information in chronological sequence or time order. Some texts include anthologies with many articles or essays written by different authors.

The vocabulary in English is a combination of general and technical terms. The general words are those we might use every day but that can also have a specific meaning in the context of English, such as symbol, conflict, *or* critique. *Many of the technical words, such as* sonnet *or* fiction, *have Latin and Old or Middle English etymology. You may add other terms you discover in your studies related to English on the forms in Appendix D.*

VOCABULARY SELF-EVALUATION

The following words will be introduced in this reading selection. Place a check mark (√) in front of any that you know thoroughly and use in your speech or writing. Place a question mark (?) in front of any that you recognize but do not use yourself.

_____ delineate	_____ epitome	_____ patron
_____ denouement	_____ ligature	_____ personify
_____ deus ex machina	_____ montage	_____ profound
_____ eloquent	_____ motif	_____ repartee
_____ epithet	_____ narrative	_____ soliloquy

SHAKESPEARE AND HIS WRITING

William Shakespeare is regarded by many critics as the greatest writer in the history of the English language. His numerous tragedies and comedies contain such a wide variety of themes that they create a montage[1] of life. In his comedies he used improbable devices like mistaken identities and the transformation of humans into animals, yet he produced delightful works that pleased his audiences then and still please us today. He used the device of the fool as a ligature[2] between acts, as a transition between subplots, and in the denouement[3] of the play. *Twelfth Night* is typical of his use of the buffoon in this manner. Although the fool's appearance is somewhat a deus ex machina,[4] his final repartee[5] creates a convincing example of the wise fool* motif.[6]

Unlike many of the seventeenth-century dramatists who came after him, Shakespeare was able to delineate[7] believable characters. These characters were so forcefully portrayed that they became famous for the qualities they displayed, and their names are now inseparable from those qualities. Romeo, for example, represents the epitome[8] of male lovers. Shylock is the symbol of a moneygrubber, and Puck personifies[9] a mischievous spirit.

Shakespeare's eloquent[10] use of the English language produced elaborate dialogues between his characters, and his famous soliloquies[11] are among the most outstanding examples of English language use. This splendid use of the language is displayed not only in his plays but also in his narrative[12] poems and in his sonnets.† His narrative poems, dedicated to a noble patron,[13] were extremely popular, and as a result of their publication, Shakespeare prospered financially.

Although Shakespeare used traditional verse forms in his sonnets, his extraordinary use of the language produced glowing songs devoted to love, such as Sonnet 18, which begins "Shall I compare thee to a summer's day?" and profound[14] refrains depicting troubled man, as seen in Sonnet 55: "Like as the waves make towards the pebbled shore / So do our minutes hasten to their end."

While the works of many writers are unappreciated until after their creators are dead, William Shakespeare's works were received enthusiastically during his lifetime. He borrowed openly from works well known at that time and from English history, so he was not an original storyteller, but his talent and skill with the language have made modern readers give him the epithet,[15] "Shakespeare the Genius."

---

* "Wise fool" is a figure of speech called an oxymoron. It contradicts itself. Other examples are John Milton's "visible darkness" and Byron's "when love is 'kindly cruel.' " (Also consider "rolling stop" and "poor little rich girl.")

† A sonnet is a fourteen-line poem usually grouped as eight lines (an octave) and six lines (a sestet).

ENGLISH PRETEST

Select words from this list and write them in the blanks to complete the sentences.

delineate	epitome	patron
denouement	ligature	personify
deus ex machina	montage	profound
eloquent	motif	repartee
epithet	narrative	soliloquy

1. Something that comes just in time to solve a problem is a(n) _____.

2. If we represent a thing as a person, we _____ it.

3. An idea repeated in a work of art or literature is called a(n) _____.

4. Anything used to tie or bind can be called a(n) _____.

5. One who supports something is its _____ .

6. The solution of a plot is a(n) _____ .

7. To _____ means to trace the outline of something.

8. A fluent speaker uses _____ expression.

9. Witty replies are called _____ .

10. A combination of images is a(n) _____ .

11. A(n) _____ tells a story.

12. Something going far deeper than understood is _____ .

13. Talking to oneself is called a(n) _____ .

14. A person who is typical of something can be called a(n)

_____ .

15. A word or phrase used in place of a person's name is a(n)

_____ .

Answers to this pretest are in Appendix E.

Unless your instructor tells you to do otherwise, complete the exercises for each word you missed on the pretest. The words, with their meanings and exercises, are in alphabetical order. The superscript numbers indicate where the words appeared in the essay so that you can refer to them when necessary. There are several types of exercises, but for each word you will be asked to write a sentence using context clues. (See Chapter 3 if you need information about how to create context clues.) You are also asked to perform some activity that will help you make your concept of the word personal. *Complete this activity thoughtfully, for creating a personalized concept of the word will help you remember it in the future.*

Answers to all the exercises are at the end of the exercise segment.

ENGLISH EXERCISES

Delineate[7]

de|lin|e|ate (di lin′ē āt), *v.t.*, -at|ed, -at|ing. **1** to trace the outline of: *The map delineated clearly the boundary between Mexico and Texas.* **2** to draw; sketch. **3** *Figurative.* to describe in words; portray: *He delineated his plan in a thorough report.* **SYN**: depict, picture. [< Latin *dēlīneāre* (with English *-ate*[1]) < *dē-* + *līnea* line]

1. In which of the following sentences is *delineate* used correctly?
   _____ a. Sometimes Sue is not able to delineate between right and wrong.
   _____ b. In this test the student must delineate each of the states and name each capital.

_____ c. The artist was able to delineate the suspect's face as the witness described it.

_____ d. It is the writer's ability to delineate characters that makes her novels sell so well.

2. If you *delineate* something, you might

_____ a. sing it.   _____ d. throw it.

_____ b. write it.   _____ e. play it.

_____ c. draw it.   _____ f. sketch it.

3. Which of the numbered dictionary definitions of *delineate* best fits the word's use in the reading selection? _____

4. Write a sentence correctly using *delineate*. (Be sure to include context clues to show you understand the meaning of the word.)

_____

_____

5. *Delineate* the figure of a person here.

Denouement[3]

de|noue|ment or **dé|noue|ment** (dā´nü mäN´), *n.* **1a** the solution of a plot in a story, play, situation, or the like: *The particulars of the dénouement you shall know in due season* (Tobias Smollett). *It's all fairly conventional and unsubtle, with an anticlimactic dénouement; but the Cornish setting is attractive* (New York Times). **b** the passage in the story, play, or other literary work, in which this takes place. **2** outcome; end: *He also, no doubt, wanted to go himself as a fitting denouement to his career* (Atlantic). [< French *dénouement* < *dénouer* untie < *dé-* (< Latin *dis-*) out + *nouer* < Latin *nōdāre* to tie < *nōdus* knot]

(Note: Watch out for the pronunciation of this word. It is still very French. Do you see that it literally says "to tie out (untie) the knot"?)

1. If you understand the *denouement* of a movie,

_____ a. you can't figure out what happened.

_____ b. you understand the plot.

_____ c. you are puzzled about what the story means.

_____ d. the director's development of the plot is clear.

2. Select the synonym(s) of *denouement*.

_____ a. puzzle   _____ c. outcome

_____ b. clarification   _____ d. solution

3. The *denouement* of a play would come

_____ a. in the first act.   _____ c. in the second act.

_____ b. in the last act.   _____ d. in every act.

4. Which movie or TV program that you have seen recently had a plot with a satisfying *denouement*? How about one with an unsatisfying *denouement*?

_____

_____

5. Write a sentence correctly using the word *denouement*. (Be sure to include context clues to show you understand the meaning of the word.)

_____

_____

Deus ex machina[4]

de|us ex ma|chi|na (dē′əs eks mak′ə nə), *Latin.* **1** a person, god, or event that comes just in time to solve a difficulty in a story, play, or other literary or dramatic work, especially when the coming is contrived or artificial: *There is ... Ferral, a French representative of big business, whom Malraux uses as the novel's deus ex machina* (New Yorker). (*Figurative.*) *Mr. Galbraith re-* jects the notion that somewhere in Wall Street there was a deus ex machina who somehow engineered the boom and bust (New York Times). **2** (literally) a god from a machine (referring to a mechanical device used in the ancient Greek and Roman theater by which actors who played the parts of gods were lowered from above the stage to end or resolve the dramatic action).

(Note: Read the pronunciation of this phrase very carefully!)

1. Which of the following is an example of *deus ex machina*?
   _____ a. A poor man solves his problems by suddenly inheriting one million dollars.
   _____ b. A poor man gets a job, works hard, and is a success.
   _____ c. The enemy drops dead of a heart attack just before he can shoot the hero.
   _____ d. Prince Charming arrives in time to take a dateless girl to the prom.

2. If a modern playwright uses a *deus ex machina*, he is likely to
   _____ a. get bad reviews from the critics.
   _____ b. get good reviews from the critics.
   _____ c. be called unrealistic.
   _____ d. be called realistic.

3. Complete this verbal analogy.
   happiness : rare :: *deus ex machina* : _____
   a. realistic   c. sadness
   b. unnatural   d. natural

4. Write a sentence correctly using *deus ex machina*. (Be sure to include context clues to show you understand the meaning of the word.)

_____

_____

5. Create and describe a *deus ex machina* for your present life situation.

_____

_____

Eloquent[10]

el|o|quent (el'e kwent), *adj.* 1 having the power of expressing one's feeling or thoughts with grace and force; having eloquence: *an eloquent speaker. The curse of this country is eloquent men* (Ralph Waldo Emerson). **syn:** voluble, fluent, glib. 2 very expressive: (*Figurative.*) *eloquent eyes.* [< Latin *ēloquēns, -entis,* present participle of *ēloquī < ex-* out + *loquī* speak] — **el'o-quent|ly,** *adv.*

1. Which professionals might find it necessary to be *eloquent*?
   _____ a. a scientist _____ d. a politician
   _____ b. an artist _____ e. a lawyer
   _____ c. a minister _____ f. a teacher

2. In which of the following sentences can *eloquent* correctly be placed in the blank?
   _____ a. John's talk was so _____ , we were moved to tears.
   _____ b. The speaker who confuses his audience probably is _____ .
   _____ c. An actress who is _____ will likely be offered many parts.
   _____ d. I believe he is guilty, but his lawyer's _____ speech saved him.

3. Select the synonym(s) of *eloquent*.
   _____ a. expressive _____ d. meaningful
   _____ b. informative _____ e. fluent
   _____ c. forceful _____ f. factual

4. Identify someone who is *eloquent*. Is it a minister? An actor or actress? A politician?

_____

_____

5. Write a sentence correctly using *eloquent*. (Be sure to include context clues to show you understand the meaning of the word.)

_____

_____

CHAPTER THIRTEEN

Epithet[15]

ep|i|thet (ep′ə thet), *n.* **1** a descriptive expression; a word or phrase expressing some quality or attribute. In "crafty Ulysses," "Richard the Lion-Hearted," and "Honest Abe," the epithets are "crafty," "Lion-Hearted," and "Honest." *Such epithets like pepper, Give zest to what you write* (Lewis Carroll). **2** a word or phrase (sometimes insulting or contemptuous) used in place of a person's name. **3** that part of the scientific name of an animal or plant which denotes a species, variety, or other division of a genus. *Example:* In *Canis familiaris* (the dog), *familiaris* is the specific epithet. In *Prunus persica* (the peach), *persica* is the specific epithet. **4** *Obsolete.* a phrase or expression. [< Latin *epitheton* < Greek *epitheton* < *epi-* on, in addition + *tithénai* to place]

1. Which of the following sentences use(s) an *epithet*?
   _____ a. He won't be Clark Kent anymore, but instead will be *Dirty Harry*.
   _____ b. Good grief! She dresses like a *bag lady*!
   _____ c. A crowd of *three thousand* attended the concert.
   _____ d. Winston Churchill coined the phrase *iron curtain* in 1946.

2. If someone created an *epithet* for you, you might
   _____ a. punch him in the nose.
   _____ b. try to sell it at the swap meet.
   _____ c. be pleased to be thought of in such a manner.
   _____ d. give one back to him.

3. Which of the numbered dictionary definitions of *epithet* best fits the word's use in the reading selection? _____

4. Write a sentence correctly using *epithet*. (Be sure to include context clues to show you understand the meaning of the word.)

   _____

   _____

5. Think of an *epithet* for your best friend that reflects his or her best quality. Write it here.

   _____

   _____

Epitome[8]

e|pit|o|me (i pit′ə mē), *n.* **1** a condensed account; summary. An epitome contains only the most important points of a book, essay, article, or other literary work. *In general nothing is less attractive than an epitome* (Macaulay). **syn:** compendium. **2** *Figurative.* a person or thing that is typical or representative of something: *Solomon is often spoken of as the epitome of wisdom.* [She] *is rated the epitome of fashion elegance* (Eugenia Sheppard). *The rubber plant and the antimacassar were the epitome of good taste* (New York Times Magazine). **syn:** embodiment. **in epitome,** in a diminutive form; in miniature: *The characteristics and pursuits of various ages and races of men are always existing in epitome in every neighborhood* (Thoreau). [< Latin *epitomē* < Greek *epitomē* < *epitémnein* cut short < *epi-* into + *témnein* cut] **e|pit|o|mize** (i pit′ə mīz), *v.t.,* **-mized, -miz|ing.** **1** to make a summary of: *to epitomize a long report.* **syn:** abridge, condense. **2** *Figurative.* to be typical or representative of: *Galahad and Lancelot epitomize the knighthood of ancient Britain. Helen Keller epitomizes the human ability to overcome handicaps. John Finley epitomized the sensible attitude for oldsters to take by his witty motto, "Nothing succeeds like successors"* (Harper's). **3** to contain in a brief form: *His problems epitomize the problems of the entire neighborhood.* **syn:** concentrate. — **e|pit′o|miz′er,** *n.*

(Note: This word doesn't follow the usual pronunciation rules.)

1. Which of the following is a characteristic of an *epitome*?

    _____ a. It is one example of something.

    _____ b. It is a typical representative.

    _____ c. It contains unimportant details.

    _____ d. It is a summary.

2. Check any appropriate response to the following statement:
    "I think Elizabeth Taylor is the *epitome* of a fashionably dressed movie star."

    _____ a. I don't agree, but you have a right to think so.

    _____ b. Yes, she is awful, isn't she?

    _____ c. Yes, she is. It must cost a fortune.

    _____ d. Mr. Blackwell has put her on the permanent "best dressed" list.

3. Which of the numbered dictionary definitions of *epitome* best fits the word's use in the reading selection? _____

4. What song do you believe *epitomizes* modern rock music?

    _____

    _____

5. Write a sentence correctly using *epitome*. (Be sure to include context clues to show you understand the meaning of the word.)

    _____

    _____

Ligature²

❋lig|a|ture (lig′ə chủr, -chər), *n., v.,* **-tured, -tur|ing.**
— *n.* **1** anything used to bind or tie up, such as a band, bandage, or cord; tie. **2** a thread, wire, or string, used by surgeons to tie up a bleeding artery or vein or to remove a tumor by strangulation, etc. **3** the act of binding or tying up.
4 *Music.* **a** a slur or a group of notes connected by a slur, showing a succession of notes sung to one syllable or in one breath, or played with one stroke of the bow. **b** = tie. **c** (in some medieval music) one of various compound note forms designed to indicate groups of two or more tones which were to be sung to a single syllable.

5a two or three letters joined in printing to form one character. **b** a mark connecting two letters.
— *v.t.* to bind, tie up, or connect with a ligature.
[< Late Latin *ligātūra* < Latin *ligāre* bind]

❋ligature
definitions 4a, 5a

music

ff ffi ffl fi fl
printing

1. In which of the following sentences can *ligature* correctly be placed in the blank?

    _____ a. The _____ was old and worn, so we replaced it with a plastic tie.

    _____ b. Between mother and child, the _____ is strong.

    _____ c. In first-aid class, we were taught how to make a _____ out of cloth.

    _____ d. If you don't want to invest in the stock market, I suggest that you buy _____s.

2. Which of the following is an example of a *ligature*?
_____ a. a group of notes to be played as a slur
_____ b. a series of pictures shown together
_____ c. type combining two or more letters
_____ d. a cord used to tie off a blood vessel

3. Which of the numbered and lettered dictionary definitions of *ligature* best fits the word's use in the reading selection? _____

4. Write a sentence correctly using *ligature*. (Be sure to include context clues to show you understand the meaning of the word.)

_____

_____

5. Do you ever wear a *ligature*? On what part of your body?

_____

_____

Montage[1]

mon|tage (mon täzh′), *n.*, *v.*, **-taged, -tag|ing.**
—*n.* **1** the combination of several distinct pictures to make a composite picture. Montage is frequently used in photography. **2** a composite picture so made: *These dramatic photographs . . . were only montages* (Newsweek). **3** in motion pictures and television: **a** the use of a rapid succession of pictures, especially to suggest a train of thought. **b** the use of a combination of images on the screen at once, often revolving or otherwise moving around or toward a focal point. **c** a part of a motion picture using either of these devices. **4** *Radio.* a rapid sequence of separate or blended voices and sound effects which suggest varying states of mind. **5** any combining or blending of different elements: *His latest novel is a montage of biography, history, and fiction.*
—*v.t.* to make (pictures, scenes, voices, or other images, sounds, or elements) into a montage: *to montage a theatrical set.*
[< French *montage* a mounting < Old French *monter* to mount[1]]

(Note: Be careful about pronouncing this word. It still shows its French background.)

1. Which of the following could be called a *montage*?
_____ a. one large picture made up of several smaller pictures
_____ b. a rapid presentation of short scenes, all on the same theme
_____ c. a picture of a house painted on a wall
_____ d. several framed paintings hanging on a wall

2. If you create a *montage*,
_____ a. you may combine many sounds.
_____ b. it may be made up of many pictures.
_____ c. it may be made up of many designs.
_____ d. you must use a movie camera.

3. Which of the numbered and lettered dictionary definitions of *montage* best fits the word's use in the reading selection? _____

4. Imagine a *montage* representing your present life. What pictures would be included?

_____

_____

5. Write a sentence correctly using *montage*. (Be sure to include context clues to show you understand the meaning of the word.)

_____

_____

Motif[6]

mo|tif (mō tēf′), *n.* **1** a subject for development or treatment in art, literature, or music; principal idea or feature; motive; theme: *This opera contains a love motif.* **2** a distinctive figure in a design, painting, or decoration. **3** *Music.* motive. [< French *motif* < Middle French, adjective < Late Latin *mōtīvus* moving. See etym. of doublet **motive.**]

1. A *motif* might appear in the work of which of the following?

_____ a. a playwright   _____ d. a writer

_____ b. an architect   _____ e. a designer

_____ c. a composer   _____ f. a poet

2. A *motif* in a play would probably be

_____ a. apparent to the audience.

_____ b. hidden from view.

_____ c. important to the playwright.

_____ d. something repeated.

3. Which of the numbered dictionary definitions of *motif* best fits the word's use in the reading selection? _____

4. Write a sentence correctly using *motif*. (Be sure to include context clues to show you understand the meaning of the word.)

_____

_____

5. What is the *motif* of your favorite song? Of your favorite type of music?

_____

_____

Narrative[12]

nar|ra|tive (nar′ə tiv), *n., adj.* —*n.* **1** a story or account; tale: *pages of narrative broken by occasional descriptive passages. His trip through Asia made an interesting narrative.* SYN: anecdote. **2** the practice or act of telling stories; narration: *The path of narrative with care pursue, Still mak-* *ing probability your clue* (William Cowper). —*adj.* **1** that narrates or recounts: *"Hiawatha" and "Evangeline" are narrative poems.* **2** of or having the character of narration: *narrative conversation.* —**nar′ra|tive|ly,** *adv.* SYN: *n.* **1 Narrative, narration** mean something told as a story or account. **Narrative** applies chiefly to what is told, emphasizing the events or experiences told like a story: *His experiences in the Near East made an interesting narrative.* **Narration** applies chiefly to the act of telling or to the way in which the story or account is put together and presented: *His narration of his trip was interesting.*

nar|rate (na rāt′, nar′āt), *v.,* **-rat|ed, -rat|ing.**
— *v.t.* to tell the story of; relate: *In narrating interesting facts, his comments . . . often fatigue by their plenitude* (Anna Seward). SYN: repeat, recount. See syn. under **describe.**
— *v.i.* to tell events or stories: *Most men . . . speak only to narrate* (Thomas Carlyle).
[< Latin *nārrāre* relate (with English *-ate¹*)]

1. Which of the following might be a *narrative?*
   _____ a. a story _____ d. fiction
   _____ b. poetry _____ e. a dance
   _____ c. a history _____ f. a painting

2. Check any appropriate response to the following statement:
   "I've been asked to speak the *narrative* for a film on Alaska."
   _____ a. Will you tell a story about the land or the people?
   _____ b. They want you to say just a few words.
   _____ c. So you will play the background music.
   _____ d. That should be an interesting tale.

3. Complete the verbal analogy.
   summary : short :: *narrative* : _____
   a. story   c. long
   b. short   d. tells

4. What was the subject of a recent *narrative* you gave? Was it about a trip you took? A movie you saw? A party you attended?

   _____

   _____

5. Write a sentence correctly using *narrative.* (Be sure to include context clues to show you understand the meaning of the word.)

   _____

   _____

Patron[13]

pa|tron¹ (pā′trən), *n., adj.* —*n.* **1** a person who buys regularly at a given store or goes regularly to a certain hotel or restaurant: *The enormous demand for military boots was rendering it . . . difficult for him to give to old patrons that . . . attention which he would desire to give* (Arnold Bennett). **2** a person who gives his approval and support to some person, art, cause, or undertaking: *a patron of artists; a renowned patron of learning* (Jonathan Swift). *Books . . . ought to have no patrons but truth and reason* (Francis Bacon). SYN: sponsor, benefactor. **3** a guardian saint; patron saint: *St. Crispin, the patron of shoemakers.* **4** (in ancient Rome) an influential man who took certain persons under his protection, or a master who had freed a slave but retained some claims upon him. **5** a person who holds the right to present a clergyman to a benefice. **6** *Obsolete.* a founder of a religious order.
—*adj.* guarding; protecting: *a patron saint.*
[< Old French *patroun,* learned borrowing from Latin *patrōnus* patron advocate, protector; person to be respected < *pater, patris* father. See etym. of doublets **padrone, patroon¹, pattern.**]

1. Which of the following acts would show that a person was a *patron?*
   _____ a. visiting the same store frequently
   _____ b. sending $1,000 to the new performing arts center
   _____ c. attending a free movie
   _____ d. providing housing for a young artist

2. The etymology of *patron* shows that the word comes from the Latin *pater* (father). Use this information and your background knowledge to match the following:

_____ a. patriarch   aa. father; used as a title of address for a priest in some countries; also, a military chaplain

_____ b. patriot   bb. pertaining to the characteristics of a father; fatherly

_____ c. patrimony   cc. the paternal leader of a family or tribe

_____ d. padre   dd. a person who loves, supports, and defends his homeland

_____ e. paternal   ee. an inheritance from a father or other ancestor

_____ f. expatriate   ff. to leave one's homeland to reside in another country

3. Which of the numbered and lettered dictionary definitions of *patron* best fits the word's use in the reading selection? _____

4. Write a sentence correctly using *patron*. (Be sure to include context clues to show you understand the meaning of the word.)

_____

_____

5. If you were very wealthy, for what causes would you be a *patron*?

_____

_____

Personify[9]

per|son|i|fy (pər son′ə fī), *v.t.,* **-fied, -fy|ing. 1** to be a type of; embody: *Satan personifies evil.* **SYN:** exemplify. **2** to regard or represent as a person. We often personify the sun and moon, referring to the sun as *he* and the moon as *she*. We personify time and nature when we refer to *Father Time* and *Mother Nature*. *Greek philosophy has a tendency to personify ideas* (Benjamin Jowett). [probably patterned on French *personnifier* < *personne* person + *-fier* -fy] —**per|son′i|fi′er,** *n.*

1. In which of the following sentences is *personify* used correctly?

_____ a. Sam saved a man from drowning; I think he personifies bravery.

_____ b. We personify justice as a blindfolded woman to show it is impartial.

_____ c. Mary personified her date as "a real dog."

_____ d. Harry, on the other hand, personified Mary as "some tomato."

2. If we *personify* something, we
_____ a. make an unnecessary reference.
_____ b. give it the qualities of a person.
_____ c. refer to a person as a general example.
_____ d. must be aware of special qualities.

3. Complete the verbal analogy.
personification : noun :: *personify* : _____
a. adjective   d. adverb
b. noun   e. conjunction
c. verb

4. Complete this sentence: My best friend *personifies* the characteristic of

_____

_____

5. Write a sentence correctly using *personify*. (Be sure to include context clues to show you understand the meaning of the word.)

_____

_____

Profound[14]

pro|found (prə found′), *adj., n.* —*adj.* **1** very deep: *a profound sigh, a profound sleep.* **2** felt strongly; very great: *profound despair; profound sympathy.* **3** going far deeper than what is easily understood; having or showing great knowledge or understanding: *a profound book, a profound thinker, a profound thought. Could this conflict of attachments be resolved by a profounder understanding of the principle of loyalty?* (Atlantic). **SYN:** abstruse, recondite. **4** carried far down; going far down; low: *a profound bow.*
—*n.* **1** the deep; the sea; the ocean. **2** an immeasurable abyss, as of space or time. [Middle English *profound* < Old French *parfond,* and *profond,* learned borrowing from Latin *profundus* < *prō-* forth + *fundus* bottom] — **pro|found′ly**, *adv.* — **pro|found′ness**, *n.*

1. In which of the following sentences can *profound* correctly be placed in the blank?
_____ a. After hearing of her grandfather's death, Mary gave a _____ sigh.
_____ b. Martin's _____ knowledge of astronomy led him to the discovery of a new star.
_____ c. His _____ comments made us realize he didn't know what he was talking about.
_____ d. Instead, we think his ignorance is _____ .

2. Place an "s" beside any synonym and an "a" beside any antonym of *profound*.
_____ a. deep   _____ d. not understood
_____ b. complete   _____ e. shallow
_____ c. far reaching   _____ f. superficial

3. Which of the numbered dictionary definitions of *profound* best fits the word's use in the reading selection? _____

4. Write a sentence correctly using *profound*. (Be sure to include context clues to show you understand the meaning of the word.)

_____

_____

5. Is there anyone for whom you have *profound* respect? Who is it?

_____

_____

Repartee[5]

rep|ar|tee (rep′ər tē′), *n.* **1** a witty reply or replies: *Droll allusions, good stories, and smart repartees ... fell thick as hail* (Charles J. Lever). SYN: sally, retort. **2** talk characterized by clever and witty replies: *accomplished in repartee.* **3** cleverness and wit in making replies: *framing comments ... that would be sure to sting and yet leave no opening for repartee* (H. G. Wells). [< French *repartie* < *repartir* to reply, set out again, ultimately < Latin *re-* back, again + *pars, partis* a part, portion, share]

(Note: This word does not follow the usual pronunciation rules.)

1. A person who is skilled in *repartee*
   _____ a. can think of a quick reply.
   _____ b. usually is thought of as clever.
   _____ c. probably dislikes talking.
   _____ d. likes an exchange of words.

2. Check any appropriate response to the following statement: "I love to listen to Jim's *repartee*."
   _____ a. I do, too. It puts me right to sleep.
   _____ b. He is as clever as Bob Hope.
   _____ c. I think he should be host on the "Tonight" show.
   _____ d. It helps me understand the history lesson.

3. Which of the following adjectives describes *repartee*?
   _____ a. quick   _____ c. clever
   _____ b. witty   _____ d. intelligent

4. Name a television personality who is known for his or her *repartee*.

_____

_____

5. Write a sentence correctly using *repartee*. (Be sure to include context clues to show you understand the meaning of the word.)

_____

_____

Soliloquy[11]

so|lil|o|quy (sə lil'ə kwē), *n., pl.* **-quies. 1** a talking to oneself. **2** a speech made by an actor to himself, especially when alone on the stage. It reveals his thoughts and feelings to the audience, but not to the other characters in the play. **3** a similar speech by a character in a book, poem, or other literary work. [< Late Latin *sō-liloquium* (introduced by Saint Augustine) < Latin *sōlus* alone + *loquī* speak]

1. Which of the following could correctly be called a *soliloquy*?
   _____ a. a dramatist revealing a character's feelings to the audience
   _____ b. the president's state-of-the-union address
   _____ c. Lincoln's Gettysburg Address
   _____ d. talking to your reflection in the mirror

2. In which of the following sentences can *soliloquy* correctly be placed in the blank?
   _____ a. A poem in which a person speaks his ideas could be called a _____ .
   _____ b. In the quiet room, the only thing to be heard was Susan's _____ .
   _____ c. Listening carefully, John could hear the _____ between Jim and Mary.
   _____ d. Shakespeare uses Hamlet's _____ to set out the character's thoughts.

3. Which of the numbered dictionary definitions of *soliloquy* best fits the word's use in the reading selection? _____

4. Write a sentence correctly using *soliloquy*. (Be sure to include context clues to show you understand the meaning of the word.)

   _____

   _____

5. In what situation might you *hear* a *soliloquy*? When might you *give* one?

   _____

   _____

ANSWERS TO CHAPTER 13 EXERCISES

Delineate: 1. b, c, d   **2.** b, c, f   **3.** 3
Denouement: 1. b, d   **2.** b, c, d   **3.** b
Deus ex machina: 1. a, c, d   **2.** a, c   **3.** b (characteristic)
Eloquent: 1. c, d, e, f   **2.** a, c, d   **3.** a, c, e
Epithet: 1. a, b, d   **2.** a, c, d   **3.** 1
Epitome: 1. b, d   **2.** a, c, d   **3.** 2
Ligature: 1. a, c   **2.** a, c, d   **3.** 1

Montage: **1.** a, b   **2.** a, b, c   **3.** 5
Motif: **1.** a, b, c, d, e, f   **2.** a, c, d   **3.** 1
Narrative: **1.** a, b, c, d   **2.** a, d   **3.** c (characteristic)
Patron: **1.** a, b, d   **2.** cc, dd, ee, aa, bb, ff   **3.** 2
Personify: **1.** a, b   **2.** b, d   **3.** c (part of speech)
Profound: **1.** a, b, d   **2.** s, s, s, s, a, a   **3.** 2
Repartee: **1.** a, b, d   **2.** b, c   **3.** a, b, c
Soliloquy: **1.** a, d   **2.** a, b, d   **3.** 2

If you missed any of the items in the exercises, return to the exercise and to the dictionary definition to see where you went wrong. Remember: If you get something right, you only affirm that you knew it. If you get something wrong and understand why, *you have learned something.*

ENGLISH POSTTEST

Fill in the blanks with the words from this list.

delineate	epitome	patron
denouement	ligature	personify
deus ex machina	montage	profound
eloquent	motif	repartee
epithet	narrative	soliloquy

1. A(n) _____ is a contrived solution.

2. To embody is to _____ .

3. A(n) _____ is a distinctive feature in a design.

4. A bandage is an example of a(n) _____ .

5. A(n) _____ is a benefactor.

6. *Outcome* is a synonym for _____ .

7. To draw is to _____ .

8. To be very expressive is to be _____ .

9. _____ is clever talk.

10. Another word for _____ is *composite.*

11. An anecdote is a(n) _____ .

12. _____ means "very deep."

13. A special type of actor's speech is a(n) _____ .

14. A(n) _____ represents a general class.

15. "Jack-the-giant-killer" is John's _____ .

Answers to this posttest are in the Instructor's Manual.

If you missed any of the words, you may need to return to the exercises and to the dictionary entries to see why your concepts for some words are incomplete.

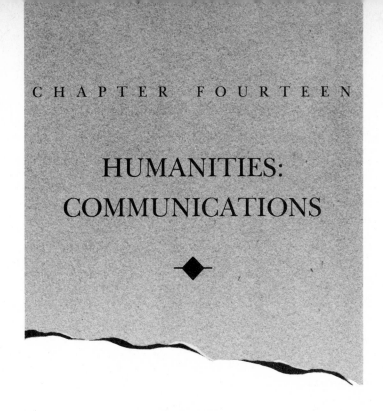

CHAPTER FOURTEEN

HUMANITIES: COMMUNICATIONS

◆

OVERVIEW

Communication studies are concerned with the nature of human communication, the symbol systems by which it functions, the context or environment in which it occurs, its media, its ethics, and its effects. The field offers training in skills generally believed to be necessary for success in public or private life.

Communications curriculum can include coursework in mass communication, interpersonal communication, intercultural communication, organizational communication, and oral communication. Some programs include opportunities for participation in intercollegiate forensics as well as practical experience with on-campus production labs for film, audio, graphics, journalism (school newspaper), and television.

Career opportunities for those with communications backgrounds include advertising, journalism, news, photocommunications, public relations, radio, television, and film. Because of the importance of effective communication in all aspects of our society, other career opportunities include work in management, personnel training, sales, education, and law.

Introductory communications textbooks are usually expository and descriptive in that they explain broad principles, concepts, or generalizations as well as statements of ideas, problems, or situations. There may be charts, diagrams, and photographs to visually represent concepts or exercises, games, case problems, and speeches as practical applications of concepts and theories presented in the text. Some textbooks are instructional and present step-by-step information related to the production aspects of the various specializations or fields within communication.

The majority of vocabulary for this field consists of general terms, such as stimuli *and* persuasion, *that also have specialized meanings in the context of communications. There are also technical terms related to the production aspects of media, including* masthead *and* by-line, *or to oral communication, including* oculesics *and* hypernasality. *Those programs offering forensics within the communication program (if they do not have a separate speech communications department) would use specific terminology related to argument analysis with* generalizations *and* fallacies *of various types. You may add terms you discover in your studies related to communications on the forms in Appendix D.*

VOCABULARY SELF-EVALUATION

The following words will be introduced in this reading selection. Place a check mark (√) in front of any that you know thoroughly and use in your speech or writing. Place a question mark (?) in front of any that you recognize but do not use yourself.

_____ admonitory	_____ diversified	_____ parsimony
_____ augment	_____ diversion	_____ pragmatic
_____ covert	_____ libel	_____ slander
_____ defamation	_____ ostensibly	_____ vast
_____ demographic	_____ overt	_____ vicarious

THE BUSINESS OF MASS COMMUNICATION

The old saying that "love makes the world go round" is romantic but inaccurate. Actually, communication makes the world go round, for if it were not for the giving and receiving of messages, the world would likely be in confusion. These messages can be carried out on the interpersonal level (you and a friend, for example) or on the machine-assisted interpersonal level (you and your friend using the telephone or you and the automatic bank teller) or by means of mass communications (you playing a tape or listening to the radio, going to a movie, reading a magazine, and so forth). Most of us have enough experience with the first two types of communication to understand the processes involved, but the field of mass communication is complex and requires some explanation.

The business of mass communication is vast[1] and in some ways diversified.[2] It includes the forms of communication called "sight media" (newspapers and magazines), those called "sound media" (radio and sound recording), and those called "sight and sound media" (films and television). But in many ways these different media are alike. Each employs one or more machines in order to transmit public messages to a large, scattered, heterogeneous audience. Each is in fact a business, which is controlled by a complex, formal organization in which control of expenditures, management of employees, and coordination of activities are all overseen by various levels of authority. Each business is, in fact, a bureaucracy.

Another way the media businesses are alike is that each is guarded by many gatekeepers* who have control over what material eventually reaches the public. Anyone who wants to have his material published or produced will find that there is overt[3] rejection all along the line: from clerks who return unsolicited material, from editors who declare it unfit, and from receptionists who refuse to admit the author to the inner office, to name but a few of the gatekeepers!

Two other ways the different media businesses are alike have to do with money. All media businesses require a great deal of money to operate, and they exist to make a profit. Millions of dollars may be needed to publish a weekly news magazine, and no amount of parsimony[4] will significantly reduce the expense. Radio and television stations require many thousands of dollars to operate, while producing a film may cost many millions. The pragmatic[5] manager prepares for this expense by recruiting backers to supply funds, and in many cases the manager must augment[6] those funds by selling ad-

vertising. (The cost of the advertising, of course, is passed on to the consumer of the product being advertised.) Unless the business has enough money to cover all its costs and can generate enough to have a profit, it will not last long. To produce that money, publications and productions must appeal to readers and viewers so that direct sales (purchase of materials and tickets for attendance) and advertising revenues keep coming in. Demographic[7] data can provide information about intended audiences and are often consulted, for competition is keen in the business of mass communications.

THE FUNCTIONS OF MASS COMMUNICATORS

The different mass communicators function alike in several ways. First, they provide information. Correspondents working for newspapers, news magazines, and radio and television stations gather and turn in information from around the globe. Their employers then report the information to their audiences. Mass communicators also serve an admonitory[8] function. Warnings may vary from facts about weather fronts approaching an area, to programs on contagious diseases, to page spreads on the dangers of smoking.

A second function is that of interpretation of information. Frequently, this is straightforward and is labeled "opinion." But covert[9] views of the management may appear in the news reports, and even an ostensibly[10] factual report may be full of interpretation and opinion. For example, a public figure supported by the communication medium (singular of *media*) may be given favored treatment: Only ap-

---

* A gatekeeper is any person or group who has control over what material will reach the public.

propriate statements will be made public; only appealing pictures will be shown. On the other hand, for a candidate the medium does not support, management may report segments of statements so that a negative impression is given, or unflattering photos or film shots will be shown. However, care will always be taken that no defamation[11] of character takes place. Printing or speaking material that is openly false and unjust is illegal. Our laws protect all of us, including public figures, against libel[12] and slander.[13]

A third function served by mass communicators is the transmission of social values. For instance, photos, films, and stories of happy, helpful mothers serve to remind us of the value of motherhood in our society. Currently, whether it should be so or not, we are reminded of the importance of being thin. This function is usually carried out intentionally, but sometimes the work produced by reporters, writers, photographers, and filmmakers is influenced by acculturation.[†]

A final function provided by mass communicators is that of entertainment. For many of us, newspapers, magazines, radio, television, and films provide the only diversions[14] we have in our lives. We do not play games or musical instruments or enjoy lengthy conversations. We do not participate in life but observe it through the actions of others, and we thus obtain vicarious[15] pleasure through the media.

And so we see that mass communicators give us information, tell us what to think of it, tell us what social values to embrace and what practices to avoid, and provide us with amusement for our spare time. Communications surround us and do, indeed, make our world go round. ◆

[†] Acculturation, in this case, is the tendency of media professionals to accept the ideas, attitudes, and opinions of the group that they cover or with whom they have a great deal of contact.

COMMUNICATIONS PRETEST

Select words from this list and write them in the blanks to complete the sentences.

admonitory   diversified   parsimony
augment   diversion   pragmatic
covert   libel   slander
defamation   ostensibly   vast
demographic   overt   vicarious

1. Something kept from sight is _____.

2. _____ information gives statistics of populations.

3. Something _____ warns against a fault or oversight.

4. _____ means "of immense extent."

5. Extreme economy is _____.

6. Something apparent is _____.

7. To make greater in size is to _____ .

8. Relief from work or care is _____ .

9. _____ means "concerned with practical results."

10. A written, damaging statement is _____ .

11. Work done for others is _____ work.

12. _____ means "as openly stated or shown."

13. An attack on the good name of someone is _____ .

14. Something _____ is in various forms.

15. To speak falsely is to _____ .

Answers to this pretest are in Appendix E.

Unless your instructor tells you to do otherwise, complete the exercises for each word you missed on the pretest. The words, with their meanings and exercises, are in alphabetical order. The superscript numbers indicate where the words appeared in the reading selection so that you can refer to them when necessary. There are several types of exercises, but for each word you will be asked to write a sentence using context clues. (See Chapter 3 if you need information about how to create context clues.) You are also asked to perform some activity that will help you make your concept of the word personal. *Complete this activity thoughtfully, for creating a personalized concept of the word will help you remember it in the future.*

Answers to all the exercises are at the end of the exercise segment.

COMMUNICATIONS EXERCISES

Admonitory[8]

ad|mon|i|to|ry (ad mon′ə tôr′ē, -tōr′-), *adj.* containing admonition; admonishing; warning: *The librarian raised an admonitory finger for silence.*
ad|mo|ni|tion (ad′mə nish′ən), *n.* **1** an admonishing; gentle reproof or warning: *He received an admonition from his teacher for not doing his homework. Now all these things ... are written for our admonition (I Corinthians 10:11).* **2** counsel; recommendation: *The doctor's admonition was to work out a stiff knee.* [< Old French *amonition,* learned borrowing from Latin *admonitiō, -ōnis* < *admonēre* advise < *ad-* to + *monēre* advise, warn]

1. Something *admonitory* is intended to be
_____ a. good advice. _____ d. a reproof.
_____ b. a promise. _____ e. a direct order.
_____ c. cautioning. _____ f. helpful.

2. Which of the following might serve an *admonitory* function?

_____ a. a counselor   _____ f. a film

_____ b. a parent   _____ g. a TV program

_____ c. a child   _____ h. an employer

_____ d. a teacher   _____ i. an advertisement

_____ e. a book

3. In which of the following sentences is *admonitory* used correctly?

_____ a. John's parents sent him an admonitory letter.

_____ b. At the Academy Awards, each winner gave an admonitory speech.

_____ c. Have you seen the admonitory videotape on smoking produced by the American Cancer Society?

_____ d. A computer spelling-checker serves an admonitory function.

4. Write a sentence correctly using *admonitory*. (Be sure to include context clues to show you understand the meaning of the word.)

_____

_____

5. What is the most recent *admonitory* information you have received?

_____

_____

Augment[6]

aug|ment (*v.* ôg ment′; *n.* ôg′ment), *v., n.* —*v.t.* **1** to make greater in size, number, amount, or degree; enlarge: *The king augmented his power by taking over rights that had belonged to the nobles.* **syn:** amplify, swell. See syn. under **increase. 2** to add an augment to. —*v.i.* to become greater; increase; grow; swell: *The sound of traffic augments during the morning rush hour.*

—*n.* **1** a prefix or lengthened vowel marking the past tenses of verbs in Greek and Sanskrit. **2** *Obsolete.* increase; augmentation. [< Late Latin *augmentāre* < Latin *augmentum* an increase < *augēre* to increase] —**aug|ment′a-ble,** *adj.* —**aug|ment′er, aug|men′tor,** *n.*

1. In which of the following sentences can *augment* correctly be placed in the blank?

_____ a. Authorities fear the rain will _____ the river and cause a flood.

_____ b. If they permit jets to land at this airport, the noise level will _____ greatly.

_____ c. The gambler planned to _____ his bank roll by going to Las Vegas.

_____ d. A few hours spent at the shopping mall will probably _____ your bank account.

2. Select the synonym(s) of *augment*.

_____ a. enlarge   _____ d. amplify

_____ b. lessen   _____ e. increase

_____ c. expand   _____ f. decrease

3. Complete the verbal analogy.

happy : sad :: *augment* : _____

a. enlarge   d. extend

b. intense   e. more

c. diminish

4. What have you done recently to *augment* your bank account?

_____

_____

5. Write a sentence correctly using *augment*. (Be sure to include context clues to show you understand the meaning of the word.)

_____

_____

Covert[9]

co|vert (*adj.* 1, *n.* 3 kō′vərt, kuv′ərt; *adj.* 2,3; *n.* 1, 2 kuv′ərt, kō′vərt), *adj., n.* —*adj.* **1** kept from sight; secret; hidden; disguised: *The children cast covert glances at the box of candy they were told not to touch.* SYN: concealed. See syn. under **secret.** **2** *Law.* married and under the authority or protection of her husband. **3** *Rare.* covered; sheltered.
—*n.* **1a** a hiding place; shelter. **b** a thicket in which wild animals or birds hide. **2** a covering. **3** = covert cloth.
coverts, the smaller and weaker feathers of a bird that cover the bases of the larger feathers of the wing and tail; tectrices: *The coverts of the wings are of a deep blackish green* (Goldsmith). [< Old French *covert,* past participle of *covrir;* see etym. under **cover**] —**co′vert|ly,** *adv.* —**co′vert|ness,** *n.*

from **secret:**

— *Syn. adj.* **1 Secret, covert, clandestine** mean done, made, or carried on without the knowledge of others. **Secret** is the general word and applies to concealment of any kind and for any purpose: *They have a secret business agreement.* **Covert,** a more formal word, suggests partial concealment, and applies to anything kept under cover, disguised, or not openly revealed: *A hint is a covert suggestion.* **Clandestine,** also formal, suggests concealment for an unlawful or improper purpose: *He feared someone would learn of his clandestine trips.*

1. Place an "s" by any synonym and an "a" by any antonym of *covert.*

_____ a. secret   _____ d. concealed

_____ b. obvious   _____ e. disguised

_____ c. hidden   _____ f. overt

2. Check any appropriate response to the following statement: "John made *covert* remarks to Bill about Mary's behavior."

_____ a. John always speaks right up.

_____ b. Why is he being so secretive?

_____ c. John is a gossip, I think.

_____ d. At least he is open about it.

3. Which of the numbered and lettered dictionary definitions of *covert* best fits the word's use in the reading selection? _____

4. Write a sentence correctly using *covert*. (Be sure to include context clues to show you understand the meaning of the word.)

_____

_____

5. Have you ever participated in any *covert* activity? (Something you did not want your friends or parents to know about, perhaps.) What was it?

_____

_____

Defamation[11]

def|a|ma|tion (def′ə mā′shən, dē′fə-), *n.* the act of defaming or condition of being defamed; slander or libel: *It contrives to mention accusingly or suspiciously a far larger number of scholars and public figures than any earlier exercise in defamation* (Harper's).
de|fame (di fām′), *v.t.,* **-famed, -fam|ing. 1** to attack the good name of; harm the reputation of; speak evil of; slander or libel: *Men in public life*

are sometimes defamed by opponents. Other ventures have tried to defame respectable people by use of the ... principle of guilt by association (Harper's). **SYN:** calumniate, vilify, malign. **2** *Archaic.* to disgrace. **3** *Obsolete.* to accuse. [< Old French *diffamer,* and Medieval Latin *defamare,* both < Latin *diffāmāre* damage by rumor, spread rumor < *dis-* abroad + *fāma* rumor]

1. *Defamation* of one's character might
   _____ a. be carried out by a friend.
   _____ b. be the act of an opponent.
   _____ c. lead to a lawsuit.
   _____ d. make one happy.

2. Complete the verbal analogy.
   demonstration : demonstrate :: *defamation* : _____
   a. defame   c. defamate
   b. defamatory d. defamer

3. Check any appropriate response to the following statement:
   "Alice's *defamation* of Sue was heard by many people at the party."
   _____ a. That may damage Sue's reputation.
   _____ b. Alice and Sue are such good friends.
   _____ c. What an unkind thing to do!
   _____ d. Oh, that doesn't matter.

4. If it is true that "sticks and stones may break my bones, but names will never hurt me," what is so bad about *defamation*?

_____

_____

5. Write a sentence correctly using *defamation*. (Be sure to include context clues to show you understand the meaning of the word.)

_____

_____

Demographic[7]

dem|o|graph|ic (dem′ə graf′ik), *adj.* of or having to do with demography: *Migration offers little by way of a solution of the world's demographic problem* (Wall Street Journal). —**dem′o|graph′i-cal|ly,** *adv.*

de|mog|ra|phy (di mog′rə fē), *n.* the science dealing with statistics of human populations, including size, distribution, diseases, births and deaths: *The analysis of fluctuations of animal populations has importance for human demography* (F. S. Bodenheimer). [< Greek *dêmos* people + English *-graphy*]

1. In which of the following sentences can *demographic* correctly be placed in the blank?
   _____ a. The latest _____ data tell the size of the U.S. population.
   _____ b. If you want to know how many people had measles last year, you can consult the _____ tables.
   _____ c. _____ data show the number of live births in each state.
   _____ d. You can find out which state has the most people by reading _____ information.

2. Which of the following is a characteristic of *demographic* data?
   _____ a. scientific   _____ d. useful
   _____ b. guesswork   _____ e. factual
   _____ c. careful   _____ f. careless

3. Complete the verbal analogy.
   <u>submarine</u> : under :: *demographic* : _____
   a. data   d. people
   b. over   e. facts
   c. science

4. Write a sentence correctly using *demographic*. (Be sure to include context clues to show you understand the meaning of the word.)

   _____

   _____

5. What kind of *demographic* data might you use in an attempt to get a job?

   _____

   _____

Diversified[2]

di|ver|si|fied (də vėr′sə fīd, dī-), *adj.* in various forms; varied; diverse: *diversified producers, diversified investments.*

di|verse (də vėrs′, dī-), *adj.* **1** different; completely unlike: *A great many diverse opinions were expressed at the meeting. But O the truth, the truth! the many eyes That look on it! the diverse things they see* (George Meredith). **2** varied: *A person of diverse interests can talk on many subjects.* SYN: multiform, diversified. [variant of *divers*; the *-e* added on analogy of *converse, reverse*] —**di|verse′ly,** *adv.* —**di|verse′ness,** *n.*

1. In which of the following sentences is *diversified* used correctly?

_____ a. The diversified scenery of California ranges from mountains to desert to seacoast.

_____ b. Music by Beethoven and Elton John formed the diversified program.

_____ c. My stock broker recommends a diversified investment portfolio.

_____ d. John wore a diversified suit to the interview.

2. Which of the following might be *diversified*?

_____ a. the crops a farmer raises

_____ b. the parts played by an actor during his career

_____ c. the courses one must take in college

_____ d. the books in a library

3. Complete the verbal analogy.

eat : verb :: *diversified* : _____

a. noun   c. adjective

b. adverb   d. conjunction

4. What *diversified* activities do you carry out at home? At your job? At school?

_____

_____

5. Write a sentence correctly using *diversified*. (Be sure to include context clues to show you understand the meaning of the word.)

_____

_____

Diversion[14]

di|ver|sion (də vėr′zhən, dī-), *n.* **1** the act or process of diverting; turning aside: *A magician's talk creates a diversion of attention so that people do not see how he does his tricks. High tariffs often cause a diversion of trade from one country to another.* **SYN:** deviation. **2** a relief from work or care; amusement; entertainment; pastime: *Watching television is a popular diversion. Golf is my father's favorite diversion.* **SYN:** sport, recreation. **3** an attack or feint intended to distract an opponent's attention from the point of main attack. **SYN:** distraction. [< Late Latin *dīversiō, -ōnis* < Latin *dīvertere*; see etym. under **divert**]

di|vert (də vėrt′, dī-), *v.t.* **1** to turn aside: *A ditch diverted water from the stream into the fields.* **2** to amuse; entertain: *We were diverted by the clown's tricks. Listening to music diverted him after a hard day's work. I diverted myself with talking to my parrot* (Daniel Defoe). **3** to distract: *A juggler or magician diverts attention from one hand by making feints with the other. The siren of the fire engine diverted the audience's attention from the play.* **4** *Figurative.* to embezzle; steal: *The dishonest treasurer diverted funds from the club's treasury.* — *v.i.* to turn aside from a course: *They ordered the pilot of the routine domestic flight to divert to North Korea* (Manchester Guardian Weekly). [< Old French *divertir,* learned borrowing from Latin *dīvertere* < *dis-* aside, apart + *vertere* turn]

1. In which of the following sentences can *diversion* correctly be placed in the blank?

_____ a. Harold created a _____ while Maude stole the diamond ring.

_____ b. Jimmy knows the multiplication tables but still has trouble with long _____ .

_____ c. The military plan calls for the _____ to be carried out by Sergeant Miller's platoon.

_____ d. My favorite _____ is bowling.

2. Check any appropriate response to the following statement:
"The treasurer has been charged with *diversion* of club funds."

_____ a. Now we won't be able to pay our bills.

_____ b. I'm glad we voted him into office.

_____ c. Do we have insurance to cover that?

_____ d. Will we have a party to celebrate?

3. Which of the numbered dictionary definitions of *diversion* best fits the word's use in the reading selection? _____

4. Write a sentence correctly using *diversion*. (Be sure to include context clues to show you understand the meaning of the word.)

_____

_____

5. What is your favorite *diversion*? (Definition 2.)

_____

_____

Libel[12]

li|bel (līʹbəl), *n., v.,* **-beled, -bel|ing** or (*especially British*) **-belled, -bel|ling.** —*n.* **1** a written or published statement, picture, etc., that is likely to harm the reputation of the person about whom it is made; false or damaging statement. SYN: calumny. **2** the act or crime of writing or publishing such a statement, picture, etc. **3** any false or damaging statement or implication about a person: *His conversation is a perpetual libel on all his acquaintance* (Richard Brinsley Sheridan). SYN: slander, vilification. **4** (in admiralty, ecclesiastical, and Scottish law) a formal written declaration of the allegations of a plaintiff and the grounds for his suit. —*v.t.* **1** to write or publish a libel about, such as a statement or picture. **2** to make false or damaging statements about. SYN: malign. **3** to institute suit against by means of a libel, as in an admiralty court.
[Middle English *libel* a formal written statement, little book < Old French *libel,* or *libelle,* learned borrowing from Latin *libellus* (diminutive) < *liber* book]
▶See **slander** for usage note.

from **slander:**

▶ **Slander** and **libel** are sharply distinguished from each other in modern United States law. *Slander* applies only to what is spoken; *libel* applies only to what is written or printed.

1. Check any appropriate response to the following statement:
"I understand that Jim's disagreement with Bill has become *libel*."

_____ a. A friendly argument won't hurt anything.

_____ b. Another instance where the lawyers will make some money!

_____ c. I'm sorry it has gone so far.

_____ d. Which one put it in writing, Jim or Bill?

2. Complete the verbal analogy.
   clown : funny :: *libel* : _____
   a. slander   c. unhappy
   b. small   d. false

3. Which of the numbered dictionary definitions of *libel* best fits the word's use in the reading selection? _____

4. The next time you read a news story about a crime, read carefully and note the care taken by the reporting service (newspaper or magazine) to keep from committing *libel*. List two recent crime news stories where the term *allege*, which means "to state as a fact without proof," is used. Why is the term used?

   _____

   _____

5. Write a sentence correctly using *libel*. (Be sure to include context clues to show you understand the meaning of the word.)

   _____

   _____

Ostensibly[10]

os|ten|si|bly (os ten′sə blē), *adv.* on the face of it; as openly stated or shown; apparently: *Though ostensibly studying his history, he was really drawing pictures behind the big book.*
os|ten|si|ble (os ten′sə bəl), *adj.* according to appearances; declared as genuine; apparent; pretended; professed: *Her ostensible purpose was to borrow sugar, but she really wanted to see her neighbor's new furniture.* SYN: seeming. [< French *ostensible* < Latin *ostēnsus*, past participle of *ostendere* to show < *ob-* toward + *tendere* stretch]

1. In which of the following sentences can *ostensibly* correctly be placed in the blank?
   _____ a. Mark was dismissed from his job, _____ for reasons of economy.
   _____ b. Jim flies to Mexico in his private plane every month _____ to bring back Mexican works of art.
   _____ c. Ruth works at the mission two days a week and _____ helps the poor.
   _____ d. Every day Peggy visits the store where John works, _____ to see if any new items are in stock.

2. If you do something *ostensibly*,
   _____ a. you are honest and open.
   _____ b. you are hiding something.
   _____ c. you may have good reason to do so.
   _____ d. someone may catch you at it.

3. Complete the verbal analogy.
   ghostly : adjective :: *ostensibly* : _____
   a. adjective   d. adverb
   b. verb   e. conjunction
   c. noun

4. Write a sentence correctly using *ostensibly*. (Be sure to include context clues to show you understand the meaning of the word.)

   _____

   _____

5. Have you ever carried out an activity *ostensibly* for one reason but actually for another reason? What was it?

   _____

   _____

Overt[3]

o|vert (ō′vėrt, ō vėrt′), *adj.* **1** open or public; evident; not hidden: *Hitting someone is an overt act. I know only his overt reasons for refusing; he may have others.* SYN: plain, manifest, apparent. **2** *Heraldry,* (of a bearing) having an open figure; outspread, as the wings of a bird in flight. [< Old French *overt* < Vulgar Latin *ōpertus,* alteration of Latin *apertus,* past participle of *aperīre* open] — **o′vert|ly,** *adv.* — **o′vert|ness,** *n.*

1. In which of the following sentences is *overt* used correctly?
   _____ a. Robbing a bank is an overt act against society.
   _____ b. Peter says he is happy, but his overt behavior makes us wonder.
   _____ c. A swap meet or flea market is held in an overt place.
   _____ d. "Body language" is overt.

2. Place an "s" by any synonym and an "a" by any antonym of *overt*.
   _____ a. open   _____ d. hidden
   _____ b. public   _____ e. evident
   _____ c. manifest   _____ f. apparent

3. Complete the verbal analogy.
   weary : tired :: *overt* : _____
   a. plane   c. show
   b. plain   d. secret

4. In what *overt* way do you like to celebrate your birthday?

   _____

   _____

5. Write a sentence correctly using *overt*. (Be sure to include context clues to show you understand the meaning of the word.)

_____

_____

Parsimony[4]

par|si|mo|ny (pär′sə mō′nē), *n.* **1** extreme economy; stinginess: *There is no need to dwell on the other limitations of his character, his jealousy, his parsimony* (Atlantic). **SYN:** niggardliness. **2** sparingness in the use or expenditure of means: (*Figurative.*) *This is the grand overriding law of the parsimony of nature: every action within a system is executed with the least possible expenditure of energy* (Scientific American). [< Latin *parsimōnia*, ultimately < *parcere* spare]

1. If you practice *parsimony*, you might
   _____ a. have lots of money in the bank.
   _____ b. do so because you are poor.
   _____ c. annoy your friends.
   _____ d. spend too much money

2. In which of the following sentences can *parsimony* correctly be placed in the blank?
   _____ a. Mr. Smith's _____ led him to give much money to charity.
   _____ b. George learned _____ from his mother, who was thrifty.
   _____ c. _____ is important to Tom; he likes to spend money.
   _____ d. _____ in early life can result in comfortable retirement.

3. Which of the numbered dictionary definitions of *parsimony* best fits the word's use in the reading selection? _____

4. Write a sentence correctly using *parsimony*. (Be sure to include context clues to show you understand the meaning of the word.)

_____

_____

5. In what area of your life would you be *least* likely to practice *parsimony*?

_____

_____

Pragmatic[5]

prag|mat|ic (prag mat′ik), *adj., n.* — *adj.* **1** concerned with practical results or values; viewing things in a matter-of-fact way. **2** of or having to do with pragmatism: *a pragmatic philosophy.* **3** having to do with the affairs of a state or community. **4** busy; active. **5** meddlesome; interfering.

SYN: officious. **6** conceited; opinionated. **7** matter-of-fact: *Their pragmatic ... approach increasingly fits the apolitical mood of the workers* (Economist). **8** treating the facts of history systematically, with special reference to their causes and effects.
— *n.* **1** = pragmatic sanction. **2** = busybody. **3** a conceited person.

[< Latin *prāgmaticus* < Greek *prāgmatikós* efficient, one skilled in business or civil affairs < *prâgma, -atos* civil business; deed, act < *prâs-sein* to do, act. Compare etym. under **practical.**] — **prag|mat′i|cal|ly,** *adv.* — **prag|mat′i|cal|ness,** *n.*

1. In which of the following sentences can *pragmatic* correctly be placed in the blank?
   _____ a. I'm not interested in philosophy; I'm far too _____.
   _____ b. John's _____ approach to the problem helped him find a solution.
   _____ c. However, Betty finds his _____ outlook on life very annoying.
   _____ d. My dog's death was a _____ experience for me.

2. If a person is *pragmatic,*
   _____ a. he deals with facts.
   _____ b. she is practical and active.
   _____ c. he is contemplative and deeply thoughtful.
   _____ d. she is a meddlesome busybody.

3. Which of the numbered dictionary definitions of *pragmatic* best fits the word's use in the reading selection? _____

4. In what areas of life are you most *pragmatic* (definition *adj.* 1)? Housework? Schoolwork? Your job? Love life?

   _____

   _____

5. Write a sentence correctly using *pragmatic.* (Be sure to include context clues to show you understand the meaning of the word.)

   _____

   _____

Slander[13]

slan|der (slan′dər, slän′-), *n., v.* — *n.* **1a** a false report meant to do harm to the good name and reputation of another: *Do not listen to slander.* **SYN:** defamation, calumny. **b** *Law.* a spoken statement tending to damage a person's reputation. **2** the spreading of false reports about persons: *The mayor sued the television station for slander when it accused him of dishonest use of city funds. The worthiest people are the most injured by slander* (Jonathan Swift).

— *v.t.* to talk falsely about. **SYN:** defame, calumniate. — *v.i.* to speak or spread slander.
[< Anglo-French *esclandre* scandal, adapted from Latin *scandalum.* See etym. of doublet **scandal.**] — **slan′der|er,** *n.*
▶ **Slander** and **libel** are sharply distinguished from each other in modern United States law. *Slander* applies only to what is spoken; *libel* applies only to what is written or printed.

1. Which of the following describes *slander*?
   _____ a. false   _____ d. damaging
   _____ b. defaming   _____ e. harmful
   _____ c. violent   _____ f. spoken

2. Check any appropriate response to the following statement:
"John's *slander* of Mr. Williams took place on July 4th."

   _____ a. That's a pleasant way to spend a holiday.

   _____ b. Those who heard it were surprised and shocked.

   _____ c. Yes, I know; I read it.

   _____ d. I suppose this means a lawsuit.

3. Which of the numbered and lettered dictionary definitions of *slander* best fits the word's use in the reading selection? _____

4. Write a sentence correctly using *slander*. (Be sure to include context clues to show you understand the meaning of the word.)

   _____

   _____

5. What comment could you make about a political figure that would be *slander*?

   _____

   _____

Vast[1]

vast (vast, väst), *adj., n.* —*adj.* 1 of great area; of immense extent; extensive: *Texas and Alaska cover vast territories.* SYN: immense, tremendous, colossal. 2 of large dimensions; of very great size; huge; massive: *vast forms that move fantastically* (Edgar Allan Poe). SYN: immense, tremendous, colossal. 3 very great in amount, quantity, or number: *A billion dollars is a vast amount of money. It is a building with a vast col-*lection of chambers and galleries. SYN: immense, tremendous, colossal. 4 *Figurative.* unusually large or comprehensive in grasp or aims: *the vast and various affairs of government.*
—*n.* 1 an immense space: *her return to the unconscious vast* (Eden Philpotts). 2 *Dialect.* a very great number or amount: *They had heard a vast of words* (Robert Louis Stevenson).
[< Latin *vastus* immense, empty] —**vast'ness**, *n.*

1. Place an "s" by any synonym and an "a" by any antonym of *vast*.

   _____ a. tremendous   _____ d. limited

   _____ b. colossal   _____ e. miniature

   _____ c. immense   _____ f. extensive

2. In which of the following sentences can *vast* correctly be placed in the blank?

   _____ a. Jack has a _____ knowledge of botany.

   _____ b. Siberia has _____ areas where no people live.

   _____ c. The Eiffel Tower in Paris is a _____ monument to engineering skill.

   _____ d. The trout is a _____ fish.

3. Which of the numbered dictionary definitions of *vast* best fits the word's use in the reading selection? _____

4. Have you ever been in a structure that could be described as *vast*? Where were you?

   _____

   _____

5. Write a sentence correctly using *vast*. (Be sure to include context clues to show you understand the meaning of the word.)

_____

_____

Vicarious[15]

vi|car|i|ous (vī kãr′ē əs, vi-), *adj.* **1** done or suffered for others: *vicarious work, vicarious punishment.* **2** felt by sharing in the experience of another: *The invalid received vicarious pleasure from reading travel stories.* **3** taking the place of another; doing the work of another: *a vicarious agent.* **4** delegated: *vicarious authority.* **5** based upon the substitution of one person for another: *this vicarious structure of society, based upon what others do for us.* **6** *Physiology.* denoting the performance by or through one organ of functions normally discharged by another, as for example in vicarious menstruation. [< Latin *vicārius* (with English *-ous*) substituted < *vicis* a turn, change, substitution. See etym. of doublet **vicar**.] —**vi|car′i|ous|ly**, *adv.* —**vi|car′i|ous|ness**, *n.*

(Note: In several of its definitions, *vicarious* has to do with substitute activity where one person or thing acts in place of another. But in one definition (number 2 in the entry here) *vicarious* activity is carried out as a substitution. That is, the person who has the *vicarious* experience is not acting at all but is living through the actions of another person.)

1. In which of the following sentences is *vicarious* used correctly?
   _____ a. In earlier times a rich man who was supposed to serve in the military might pay someone to be his vicarious agent.
   _____ b. I can't attend the board meeting; please attend for me in a vicarious capacity.
   _____ c. Christians believe that Christ's vicarious sacrifice removes the sin of those who are His followers.
   _____ d. Mr. Smith was not able to go to medical school, but he receives vicarious satisfaction from the fact that his son is a doctor.

2. Check any appropriate response to the following statement:
   "I had a *vicarious* experience when I watched your color slides of Alaska yesterday."
   _____ a. I'm sorry they didn't mean anything to you.
   _____ b. Why don't you take the trip next year?
   _____ c. It was fun to share my trip with you.
   _____ d. It's the next best thing to actually traveling, isn't it?

3. Which of the numbered dictionary definitions of *vicarious* best fits the word's use in the reading selection? _____

4. Write a sentence correctly using *vicarious*. (Be sure to include context clues to show you understand the meaning of the word.)

_____

_____

5. What *vicarious* (definition 2) experiences do you enjoy most? Watching sports events? Romantic movies? Adventure films?

_____

_____

ANSWERS TO CHAPTER 14 EXERCISES

Admonitory: **1.** a, c, d, f **2.** a, b, c, d, e, f, g, h, i **3.** a, c, d
Augment: **1.** a, b, c **2.** a, c, d, e **3.** c (antonym)
Covert: **1.** s, a, s, s, s, a **2.** b, c **3.** *adj.* 1
Defamation: **1.** b, c **2.** a (noun/verb) **3.** a, c
Demographic: **1.** a, b, c, d **2.** a, c, d, e **3.** d (root meaning)
Diversified: **1.** a, b, c **2.** a, b, c, d **3.** c (part of speech)
Diversion: **1.** a, c, d **2.** a, c **3.** 2
Libel: **1.** b, c, d **2.** d (characteristic) **3.** 1
Ostensibly: **1.** a, b, d **2.** b, c, d **3.** d (part of speech)
Overt: **1.** a, b, d **2.** s, s, s, a, s, s **3.** b (synonym)
Parsimony: **1.** a, b, c **2.** b, d **3.** 1
Pragmatic: **1.** a, b, c **2.** a, b, d **3.** *adj.* 1
Slander: **1.** a, b, d, e, f **2.** b, d **3.** 1a
Vast: **1.** s, s, s, a, a, s **2.** a, b, c **3.** *adj.* 2
Vicarious: **1.** a, b, c, d **2.** b, c, d **3.** 2

If you missed any of the items in the exercises, return to the exercise and to the dictionary definition to see where you went wrong. Remember: If you get something right, you only affirm that you knew it. If you get something wrong and understand why, *you have learned something.*

COMMUNICATIONS POSTTEST

Fill in the blanks with the words from this list.

admonitory	diversified	parsimony
augment	diversion	pragmatic
covert	libel	slander
defamation	ostensibly	vast
demographic	overt	vicarious

1. Printed vilification is _____.

2. _____ means "manifest."

3. *Colossal* is a synonym for _____.

4. _____ means "delegated."

5. Number of births would come from _____ data.

6. _____ is harming someone's reputation.

7. _____ means "warning."

8. Something _____ is concealed.

9. To enlarge is to _____.

10. _____ means "varied."

11. *Niggardliness* is another word for _____.

12. _____ means "matter-of-fact."

13. Spoken calumny is _____.

14. A word meaning "turning aside" is _____.

15. *Apparently* is a synonym for _____.

Answers to this posttest are in the Instructor's Manual.

If you missed any of the words, you may need to return to the exercises and to the dictionary entries to see why your concepts for some words are incomplete.

CHAPTER FIFTEEN

HUMANITIES: ART

♦

OVERVIEW

Art is the product of human activity that appeals primarily to the imagination. To some it is an attempt to find that which is fundamental, enduring, and essential in the universe. The field of art studies these various products, and training in the arts provides cultural and personal development.

There is a variety of subfields within art, including art history (theory and appreciation); studio work, such as design, drawing, sculpture, painting, print making, photography, ceramics, textile, and so on; and teaching preparation in drawing, painting, and crafts.

Art programs prepare students for careers as art scholars, creative artists, or art teachers. Some of the numerous job opportunities include work as a curator or administrator of a museum or gallery, art reviewer, researcher and consultant for theater designers and museums, tour leader or guide, art reference librarian, free-lance artist, arts and crafts teacher, advertising or billboard designer, cartoonist or illustrator, and industrial or fashion designer.

Introductory textbooks in the field are usually expository, that is, they explain broad concepts or generalizations. Art history textbooks are usually chronological and are organized according to the order of significant historical events in history or specified time periods or eras. They also contain numerous photographs and sketches.

The vocabulary in the art field consists mainly of specific terminology that defines procedures or techniques, such as calligraphy, collage, *or* fresco. *Other words represent historical trends or movements in art, such as* baroque, realism, *or* romanticism. *You may add other terms you discover in your studies related to art on the forms in Appendix D.*

VOCABULARY SELF-EVALUATION

The following words will be introduced in this reading selection. Place a check mark (√) in front of any that you know thoroughly and use in your speech or writing. Place a question mark (?) in front of any that you recognize but do not use yourself.

_____ aesthetic	_____ gradation	_____ perception
_____ asymmetry	_____ hue	_____ realist
_____ baroque	_____ impressionism	_____ romanticism
_____ cubism	_____ monochromatic	_____ surrealism
_____ distortion	_____ palette	_____ symbolism

ART AND SOCIETY

The definition of art, to many, is the creation of objects by an artist who intended the work to have an aesthetic,[1] or pleasing, appeal to people. An artist can use color to generate emotions in the viewer. He can make choices in his palette[2] of colors that will alter the mood of a piece dramatically. A monochromatic[3] color scheme that uses only gradations,[4] or degrees in lightness or darkness, of one color creates quite a different feeling for the viewer than a piece of art with many colors and levels of intensity.

In the creation of a work of art, the tools available to an artist go beyond the limits of paint, canvas, and brush. An artist can make a visible suggestion of something invisible through the use of symbolism,[5] using images to represent something else. For example, the images of two elderly people could represent the complex emotions of loneliness and isolation. An artist can also use distortion[6] or exaggeration of the shape of images as well as asymmetry,[7] with uneven or irregular proportions to convey a unique meaning or feeling. For example, the distortion of the human face, with one eye represented larger than the other, often shocks the viewer's sense of reality. On the other hand, the artist who is a realist[8] and who is concerned with representing things as they really are, uses proportion and symmetry, or balance, to portray the beauty of images as one sees them in nature. Thus, an artist's perception[9] and insight into reality or his or her own personal experiences can be presented using a variety of techniques.

Art throughout the centuries often mirrors the ideals and values of the society it depicts. In the seventeenth century in Europe, the richly ornamental baroque[10] art characterized the wealth and self-indulgence of that time. Some of the famous baroque artists, whose work was rich in movement and symbolism, were Gianlorenzo Bernini, Peter Paul Rubens, and Rembrandt van Rijn. Romanticism[11] in the idealizing society of the nineteenth century sought to appeal to human emotions through the depiction of faultless people and places painted in hauntingly beautiful hues,[12] or colors. Romantic masters who utilized strong contrasting colors in their work include Eugene Delacroix, whose paintings were very melodramatic, and Paul Gaugin, whose work, done while living in Tahiti, represents the exotic and dangerous.

During the late nineteenth century, impressionism[13] developed in and around Paris and represented in many ways a melding with a societal interest in the sciences. The impressionists used a multitude of distinct and unfused brush strokes in their paintings to represent the effects of light and color on landscapes and cities. Some of the impressionists pursued optical research through the medium of paint. Some of the artists who utilized this technique were Claude Monet, Georges Seurat, and Edgar Degas.

Finally, the twentieth century, known for its departure from traditional societal standards and politics, produced two interesting movements in art. One was cubism,[14] which represented a tendency to test different and contradictory ways of representing objects and space. This important movement, which emphasized lines and geometric shapes, was central to much of the modern art of the entire twentieth century. Two famous artists known as founders of this movement were Georges Braque and Pablo Picasso.

Surrealism[15] also began in the early twentieth century and became known as a political movement as well. Surrealism was concerned with a "super reality," one found through dreams and fantasies that were emphasized in the research and literature of modern psychology of that time. Surrealists were anarchists who were against proper social behavior and all forms of government and were allied for a time with communism. Surrealists such as Salvador Dali produced modern and shocking art, with nightmarish effects achieved through the distortion of shapes and images.

Art, as we have seen, is varied and complex and often reflects the changes and growth in the social recognition and acceptance of reality. Finally, art is an intensely personal experience for both the artist and the viewer and one that frequently defies interpretation as well as analysis. ◆

ART PRETEST

Select words from this list and write them in the blanks to complete the sentences.

aesthetic	gradation	perception
asymmetry	hue	realist

baroque   impressionism   romanticism
cubism   monochromatic   surrealism
distortion   palette   symbolism

1. _____ refers to the name of primary colors such as red, yellow, and blue.

2. Everyone seems to have _____ needs, that is, we are interested in beauty wherever it may be found.

3. A(n) _____ is one who attempts to reproduce every visual detail to create the illusion of reality.

4. Artists of the _____ period in the sixteenth and seventeenth centuries experimented with contrasting light and dark patterns to create a dramatic effect.

5. _____ embraced the use of dreamlike and hallucinatory images from the subconscious.

6. A twentieth-century art movement that used a geometric format was _____.

7. A(n) _____ color scheme is one in which only one color or shades of color are used throughout.

8. _____ means "twisting, stretching, deforming, or enlarging the shape and size of things."

9. A different type of _____ can occur each time a piece of art is viewed.

10. Artists often use _____ in their work, using colors, design elements, or figures to represent something else.

11. _____, or a lack of balance or harmony, is used by artists to create interest and curiosity on the part of the viewer.

12. Many artists work from a(n) _____, which they use to lay out and mix their colors.

13. An interest in emotions, the exotic, and the dangerous is a feature of _____.

14. _____, or degrees, of color or hue can be used to create a stimulating visual effect.

15. The style of _____ requires that a viewer see the work from a distance because of the use of brush strokes or dots of color to create an image.

Answers to this pretest are in Appendix E.

Unless your instructor tells you to do otherwise, complete the exercises for each word you missed on the pretest. The words, with their meanings and exercises, are in alphabetical order. The superscript numbers indicate where the words appeared in the reading selection so that you can refer to them when necessary. There are several types of exercises, but for each word you will be asked to write a sentence using context clues. (See Chapter 3 if you need information about how to create context clues.) You are also asked to perform some activity that will help you make your concept of the word personal. *Complete this activity thoughtfully, for creating a personalized concept of the word will help you remember it in the future.*

Answers to all the exercises are at the end of the exercise segment.

ART EXERCISES

Aesthetic[1]

aes|thet|ic (es thet′ik; *especially British* ēs-thet′ik), *adj., n.* —*adj.* **1** having to do with the beautiful, as distinguished from the useful, scientific, or moral; based on or determined by beauty rather than by practical or moral considerations: *The committee laid stress on aesthetic elements, such as architecture and design* (Claude M. Berkeley). **2** (of persons) having or showing an appreciation of beauty in nature and art. **3** (of things) showing good taste; artistic; pleasing: *an aesthetic wallpaper. The ruins have a romantic or an impersonal, aesthetic appeal to all people, but to the Greeks they are a living force* (Atlantic). —*n.* **1** an aesthetic philosophy or point of view: *Once again, Balanchine tamed an alien movement to his own distinctive personal aesthetic* (Doris Hering). **2** an aesthete. Also, **esthetic**. [< Greek *aisthētikós* sensitive; see etym. under **aesthetics**] —**aes|thet′i|cal|ly**, *adv.*

1. Complete the verbal analogy.
   practical : useful :: *aesthetic* : _____
   a. scientific   c. instrumental
   b. moral   d. beautiful

2. Which of the numbered dictionary definitions of *aesthetic* best fits the word's use in the reading selection? _____

3. Who might be the *most* interested in an *aesthetic* environment?
   _____ a. a historian   _____ c. a philosopher
   _____ b. an artist   _____ d. a chemist

4. Do you have more of an *aesthetic* or a practical orientation to life? Explain.

   _____

   _____

5. Write a sentence correctly using *aesthetic*. (Be sure to include context clues to show you understand the meaning of the word.)

   _____

   _____

Asymmetry[7]

a|sym|me|try (ā sim′ə trē, a-), *n.* lack of symmetry. [< Greek *asymmetriā* < *asýmmetros* < *a-* not + *sýmmetros* having symmetry]
sym|me|try (sim′ə trē), *n., pl.* **-tries. 1** a regular, balanced form, or arrangement on opposite sides of a line or plane, or around a center or axis: *Its asymmetry was deliberate, for the Japanese believe that symmetry stunts the imagination* (Atlantic). **2** pleasing proportions between the parts of a whole; well-balanced arrangement of parts; harmony: *A swollen cheek spoiled the symmetry of his handsome face. In a scale passage ... you*

have symmetry of timing—whether the notes follow each other at even intervals or not (Time). **3** *Botany*. agreement in number of parts among the cycles of organs that compose a flower. [<

Latin *symmetria* < Greek *symmetriā* < *sýmmetros* symmetrical < *syn-* together + *métron* a measure]

1. In which of the following sentences is *asymmetry* used correctly?
   _____ a. Balance by contrast is a type of asymmetry and includes oppositions between color and shape.
   _____ b. An example of asymmetry is the equal balance of shapes and figures.
   _____ c. When a painter chooses asymmetry, she does so because she wants to create harmony and balance.
   _____ d. Asymmetry is both complex and interesting and can create psychological interest for the viewer.

2. Select the synonym(s) of *asymmetry*.
   _____ a. harmony   _____ c. correlation
   _____ b. disproportion   _____ d. imbalance

3. Complete the verbal analogy.
   monochromatic : polychromatic :: *asymmetry* : _____
   a. symmetry   c. balance
   b. polystyrene   d. proportion

4. Write a sentence correctly using *asymmetry*. (Be sure to include context clues to show you understand the meaning of the word.)

   _____

   _____

5. How are distortion and *asymmetry* related? How does *asymmetry* in a work of art affect you?

   _____

   _____

Baroque[10]

ba|roque (bə rōk′, -rok′), *adj., n.* —*adj.* **1a** having to do with a style of art and architecture characterized by the use of curved forms and lavish ornamentation. Baroque architecture prevailed in Europe from about 1550 to the late 1700's. **b** having to do with a style of music characterized by complex rhythms and melodic ornamentation: *baroque opera.* **c** = rococo. **2** tastelessly odd; fantastic; grotesque: *baroque development of ladies' fashion.* **3** irregular in shape: *baroque pearls.*
—*n.* **1** the baroque style. **2** architecture or other work in this style.
[< French *baroque* < Portuguese *barroco* a rough pearl] —**ba|roque′ly,** *adv.*

1. Check any appropriate response to the following statement:
   "The *baroque* style is very appealing to many people."
   _____ a. Many people desire order and linearity in a style of decoration.
   _____ b. Many people like decorations that are very elaborate.
   _____ c. Intricate designs with scrolls and curves in a detailed pattern are preferred by some.
   _____ d. That style is important to those who like simplicity in design.

2. Select the characteristics of *baroque*.

_____ a. reserved   _____ c. ornate

_____ b. flamboyant   _____ d. elaborate

3. Complete the verbal analogy.

surrealism : Salvador Dali :: *baroque* : _____

a. Eugene Delacroix   c. Claude Monet

b. Pablo Picasso   d. Peter Paul Rubens

4. What elements in the *baroque* style do you like? Would you ever decorate in a *baroque* decor? Why or why not?

_____

_____

5. Write a sentence correctly using *baroque*. (Be sure to include context clues to show you understand the meaning of the word.)

_____

_____

Cubism[14]

cub|ism (kyü′biz əm), *n.* a style of painting, drawing, and sculpture, developed in the early 1900's, in which objects are represented by cubes and other geometrical forms rather than by realistic details: *Picasso ... said that ... "Cubism is no different from any other school of painting ... it is an art dealing primarily with forms"* (New Yorker).

1. Complete the verbal analogy.

impressionism : nineteenth century :: *cubism* : _____

a. seventeenth century   c. nineteenth century

b. twentieth century   d. eighteenth century

2. Check any appropriate response to the following statement:

"*Cubism* seems to be more popular than romanticism in contemporary art."

_____ a. Feelings and emotions are important elements appreciated in modern works of art.

_____ b. The exotic and dangerous represented in art is attractive and saleable.

_____ c. There is an interest in a geometrical reduction of natural forms.

_____ d. Some people have an aesthetic need for simplicity in design and shape.

3. Select the characteristics of *cubism*.

_____ a. emotions   _____ c. phantasms

_____ b. simple geometrical forms   _____ d. cubes

4. Write a sentence correctly using *cubism*. (Be sure to include context clues to show you understand the meaning of the word.)

_____

_____

5. Do you prefer the style of *cubism* in art? What geometrical forms would you like to decorate with—square, rectangle, circle, triangle?

_____

_____

Distortion[6]

dis|tor|tion (dis tôr′shən), *n.* **1** a distorting; twisting out of shape: (*Figurative*) *Exaggeration is a distortion of the truth.* **2** the fact or condition of being distorted: *The sick man's face was in complete distortion.* **3** anything distorted: *His story of the fishing trip was full of distortions.* **4** a distorted form or image. **5** *Electronics.* the inaccurate reproduction of a signal by modification of the wave form during amplification or transmission: *Distortion tends to run somewhat higher [on a cassette tape] than on other media, especially at high frequencies* (Charles Lincoln).

dis|tort (dis tôrt′), *v.t.* **1** to pull or twist out of shape; make crooked or ugly; change the normal appearance of: *Rage distorted his face, making it very ugly.* **syn:** contort. **2** *Figurative.* to change from the truth; give a twist or turn to (the mind, thoughts, views): *The driver distorted the facts of the accident to escape blame. The medium of television can strikingly if unintentionally distort events out of true focus* (C. L. Sulzberger). **syn:** misrepresent, falsify. [< Latin *distortus,* past participle of *distorquēre* < *dis-* (intensive) + *torquēre* twist] — **dis|tort′er,** *n.* — **dis|tort′ing|ly,** *adv.*

1. Select the synonym(s) of *distortion*.
   - _____ a. contortion   _____ c. deviation
   - _____ b. symmetry   _____ d. linearity

2. The etymology of *distortion* (from *distort*) shows that the word comes from the Latin *distortus* (to twist). Use this information and your background knowledge to match the following:
   - _____ a. tortuous   aa. causing very great pain
   - _____ b. extort   bb. a force causing rotation or torsion
   - _____ c. torment   cc. to obtain (money, promise, or other commitment) by threats, force, fraud, or wrong use of authority
   - _____ d. torque   dd. to reply quickly or sharply
   - _____ e. retort   ee. full of, involving, or causing torture

3. Complete the verbal analogy
   symbolism : representation :: *distortion* : _____
   a. symmetry   c. illumination
   b. aesthetics   d. exaggeration

4. How can symbolism and *distortion* be related? Provide some examples either from your background knowledge or from a creative viewpoint.

_____

_____

5. Write a sentence correctly using *distortion*. (Be sure to include context clues to show you understand the meaning of the word.)

_____

_____

Gradation[4]

gra|da|tion (grā dā′shən), *n*. **1a** a change by steps or stages; gradual change: *Our acts show gradation between right and wrong. She sometimes contemplated a little sorrowfully the gradation from her former simplicity to her present sophistication.* **b** the fact or condition of including or being arranged in a series of degrees: *a variety of forms exhibiting gradation.* **2** Often, **gradations.** one of the steps, stages, or degrees in a series: *There are many gradations between poverty and wealth. The rainbow shows gradations of color besides the six main colors.* **3** the act or process of grading. **4** = ablaut. **5** *Geology.* the process by which the surface of the earth is leveled off, or the bed of a stream is brought to equilibrium, through the action of wind, ice, water, etc. **6** *Obsolete.* an advancing, step by step; gradual progress. [< Latin *gradātiō, -ōnis* < *gradus, -ūs* step, degree; see etym. under **grade**]

from **grade:**

[< Middle French *grade*, learned borrowing from Latin *gradus, -ūs* step, degree, related to *gradī* to walk, go]

1. Select the synonym(s) of *gradation*.

_____ a. quantity   _____ c. shading

_____ b. degree   _____ d. slope

2. The etymology of *gradation* shows that the word comes from the Latin *gradatio* (step or degree). Use this information and your background knowledge to match the following:

_____ a. retrogress   aa. to break a law or command; to sin against

_____ b. digress   bb. act of going in or entering

_____ c. transgress   cc. to move backward; go back, especially to an earlier or less advanced condition

_____ d. ingress   dd. to turn aside from the main subject in talking or writing

_____ e. egress   ee. going out

3. Which of the numbered dictionary definitions of *gradation* best fits the word's use in the reading selection? _____

4. Write a sentence correctly using *gradation*. (Be sure to include context clues to show you understand the meaning of the word.)

_____

_____

5. Describe the *gradation* in color apparent in a rainbow.

_____

_____

Hue[12]

hue[1] (hyü), *n*. **1** that property of color by which it can be distinguished from gray of equal brightness as red, yellow, blue, and other regions of the spectrum; color: *silks of many hues. The girls' dresses showed most of the hues of the rainbow.* **SYN:** See syn. under **color**. **2** a variety of a color; shade or tint: *She finally found silk of the particular pinkish hue that she sought.* **3** *Figurative.* aspect or type: *politicians of every hue.* **4** *Archaic.* color of the skin; complexion: *the* ashen hue of age (Scott). **5** *Obsolete.* form; appearance: *the native hue of resolution* (Shakespeare). [Old English *hīw*] —**hue′less**, *adj.*

1. Select the synonym(s) of *hue*.

    _____ a. color   _____ c. gradation
    _____ b. shade   _____ d. quantity

2. Check any appropriate response to the following statement:
    "I prefer a room decorated in many hues."

    _____ a. A variety of ornate designs would be appealing.
    _____ b. I would like a room decorated in the primary colors of red, yellow, and blue.
    _____ c. Various colors from the palette of the desert would match the furnishings.
    _____ d. This room needs more furnishings.

3. Complete the verbal analogy.
    distortion : shock :: *hue* : _____
    a. gradation   c. emotions and feelings
    b. baroque   d. monochromatic

4. If you were going to paint a room, what range of *hues* would you select? What could you compare them to—rainbow, desert, spring day?

    _____

    _____

5. Write a sentence correctly using *hue*. (Be sure to include context clues to show you understand the meaning of the word.)

    _____

    _____

Impressionism[13]

im|pres|sion|ism (im presh′ə niz əm), *n.* **1** a style of painting that gives the impression made by the subject on the artist without much attention to details. Impressionism was developed by French painters of the late 1800's. **2** a style of literature characterized by the creation of general impressions and moods rather than realistic detail. **3** a style of music characterized by the use of unusual and rich harmonies, tonal qualities, and other effects, to suggest the composer's impressions, as of a scene or an emotion.

1. Complete the verbal analogy.
    romanticism : Paul Gaugin :: *impressionism* : _____
    a. Eugene Delacroix   c. Paul Klee
    b. Claude Monet   d. Pablo Picasso

2. Select the characteristics of *impressionism*.

_____ a. sensory   _____ c. fantastic
_____ b. detailed   _____ d. ornate

3. In which of the following sentences can *impressionism* correctly be placed in the blank?

_____ a. _____ is a nineteenth-century movement in painting that was concerned with the effect of light on landscapes and objects.

_____ b. The term _____ is used to refer to the study of ancient Greek and Roman art begun in the fourteenth century.

_____ c. _____ was a style associated with complex works of painting and sculpture that were rich in movement and symbolism.

_____ d. Claude Monet, Georges Seurat, and Edgar Degas are French artists aligned with the movement called _____.

4. Write a sentence correctly using *impressionism*. (Be sure to include context clues to show you understand the meaning of the word.)

_____

_____

5. Compare romanticism and *impressionism*. Which do you prefer and why?

_____

_____

Monochromatic[3]

mon|o|chro|mat|ic (mon′ə krō mat′ik), *adj.*
1 having or showing one color only. **2** (of light) consisting of one wave length: *The use of monochromatic light ... does not improve the acuity of the eye to more than a very small extent* (Science News). **3** producing such light. —**mon′- o|chro|mat′i|cal|ly**, *adv.*

1. What might be an antonym of *monochromatic*?

_____ a. polychromy   _____ c. monochroic
_____ b. polychromatic _____ d. multichromatic

2. Which of the following are examples of a *monochromatic* color scheme?

_____ a. white walls and drapes
_____ b. black walls and white drapes
_____ c. pink walls and drapes
_____ d. pink walls and white drapes

3. In which of the following sentences is *monochromatic* used correctly?

_____ a. Using a "warm" color such as yellow with a "cool" color such as blue would create a *monochromatic* effect.

_____ b. Too much white added to ultramarine blue can result in a monochromatic color.

_____ c. A monochromatic color scheme can sometimes create for the viewer a high level of intensity not usually found in polychromatic schemes.

_____ d. Old black-and-white televisions provide a monochromatic viewing screen.

4. If you were to paint one room in your apartment or house in a *monochromatic* scheme, what would it be and why?

_____

_____

5. Write a sentence correctly using *monochromatic*. (Be sure to include context clues to show you understand the meaning of the word.)

_____

_____

Palette[2]

pal|ette (pal′it), *n.* **1** a thin board, usually oval or oblong with a thumb hole at one end, used by an artist to lay and mix his colors on. **2** a set of colors on this board. **3** the selection of colors used by a particular artist: *to use a wide palette.* **4** Also, **pallette.** a small rounded plate protecting the armpit on a suit of armor. [< French *palette* < Old French (diminutive) < *pale* shovel, oar blade < Latin *pāla* spade, shoulder blade]

1. Which of the numbered dictionary definitions of *palette* best fits the word's use in the reading selection? _____

2. In which of the following sentences is *palette* used correctly?
   _____ a. A tattered palette was worn by the elderly gentleman.
   _____ b. The artist used a wide palette in painting the mural.
   _____ c. A mixture of acrylics and oils was dabbed on the palette.
   _____ d. Instead of a palette the artist chose a female model as his subject.

3. What other equipment besides a *palette* might an artist need?
   _____ a. a canvas   _____ c. a hose
   _____ b. brushes   _____ d. a trowel

4. Write a sentence correctly using *palette*. (Be sure to include context clues to show you understand the meaning of the word.)

_____

_____

5. If you were an artist, what colors would you have on your *palette*? Why would you choose those colors?

_____

_____

Perception[9]

per|cep|tion (pər sep′shən), *n.* **1** the act of perceiving: *His perception of the change came in a flash.* **SYN**: insight, apprehension, discernment, comprehension. **2** the power of perceiving: *a keen perception. Defect in manners is usually the defect of fine perceptions* (Emerson). **3** understanding that is the result of perceiving; percept: *He had a clear perception of what was wrong, and soon fixed it.* **4** *Psychology.* the study of the complex process by which patterns of environmental energies become known as objects, events, people, and other aspects of the world. [< Latin *perceptiō, -ōnis* < *percipere* perceive]
per|ceive (pər sēv′), *v.,* **-ceived, -ceiv|ing.** — *v.t.*
1 to be aware of through the senses; see, hear, taste, smell, or feel: *Did you perceive the colors of that bird? We perceived a little girl coming toward us* (Frederick Marryat). **SYN**: See syn. under **see. 2** to take in with the mind; observe: *I soon perceived that I could not make him change his mind. I plainly perceive some objections remain* (Edmund Burke). **SYN**: understand, comprehend. See syn. under **see.**
— *v.i.* to grasp or take in something with the senses or mind.
[< Old North French *perceivre* < Latin *percipere* < *per-* thoroughly + *capere* to grasp] — **perceiv′er**, *n.*

1. In which of the following sentences is *perception* used correctly?
   _____ a. Asymmetry creates a balance of things that are out of perception.
   _____ b. Realists hope to paint a perception of life as it really is.
   _____ c. Some color systems are related to the physiology of perception rather than to aesthetics.
   _____ d. In impressionist paintings, one's perception of the work is distorted by standing too close to the work.

2. The etymology of *perception* shows that the word comes from the Latin *capere* (to grasp). Use this information and your background knowledge to match the following:
   _____ a. intercept
   _____ b. precept
   _____ c. capacious
   _____ d. inception
   _____ e. susceptible

   aa. easily influenced by feelings or emotions; very sensitive
   bb. beginning or originating; commencement
   cc. rule of action or behavior; maxim
   dd. able to hold much; large and roomy
   ee. to take or seize on the way from one place to another

3. Select the synonym(s) of *perception*.
   _____ a. experience   _____ c. insight
   _____ b. intelligence   _____ d. recognition

4. Has your initial *perception* of a person ever been altered or changed once you really got to know him or her? Explain.

_____

_____

5. Write a sentence correctly using *perception*. (Be sure to include context clues to show you understand the meaning of the word.)

_____

_____

Realist[8]

re|al|ist (rē′ə list), *n., adj.* —*n.* **1** a person interested in what is real and practical rather than what is imaginary or theoretical: *The multitude of protectionists do not dream. They are hard, if mistaken, realists* (Spectator). **2** a writer or artist who represents things as they are in real life. **3** a person who believes in realism.
—*adj.* realistic: *a dramatic and realist attempt to reveal ultimate degradation* (Punch).

1. Select the characteristics of a *realist*.
   _____ a. literal truth   _____ c. distorted
   _____ b. romantic   _____ d. practical

2. Which of the numbered dictionary definitions of *realist* best fits the word's use in the reading selection? _____

3. Check any appropriate reply to the following statement:
   "This painting demonstrates the style of a *realist*."
   _____ a. It portrays the life and harsh realities of peasants and workers.
   _____ b. The use of symbolism creates a romantic effect.
   _____ c. This painting is very emotional and poetic.
   _____ d. The painter portrays real aspects of the world in everyday terms.

4. Write a sentence correctly using *realist*. (Be sure to include context clues to show you understand the meaning of the word.)

_____

_____

5. If you were a painter and wanted to be known as a *realist*, what would you paint and why?

_____

_____

Romanticism[11]

ro|man|ti|cism (rō man′tə siz əm), *n.* **1** the romantic tendency in literature and art; a style of literature, art, and music, especially widespread in the 1800's. Romanticism allows freedom of form and stresses strong feeling, imagination, love of nature, and often the unusual and supernatural. **2** romantic spirit or tendency: *You hope she has remained the same, that you may renew that piece of romanticism that has got into your head* (W. Black).

1. Select the characteristics of *romanticism*.
   _____ a. impractical _____ c. individualistic
   _____ b. emotional _____ d. reasonable

2. In which of the following sentences is *romanticism* used correctly?
   _____ a. A prominent feature of romanticism is an attitude of emotional candor.
   _____ b. Many paintings of the era of romanticism constitute a puzzle with many geometric shapes.
   _____ c. The exotic and dangerous were common themes for some of the artists of romanticism.
   _____ d. Dreams and hallucinations are reflected in the artwork of romanticism.

3. Complete the verbal analogy.
   surrealism : fantastic :: *romanticism* : _____
   a. decorative c. unconscious
   b. practical d. imaginative

4. If you were an artist during the era of *romanticism*, what would you paint and why?

   _____

   _____

5. Write a sentence correctly using *romanticism*. (Be sure to include context clues to show you understand the meaning of the word.)

   _____

   _____

Surrealism[15]

sur|re|al|ism (sə rē′ə liz əm), *n.* a modern movement in painting, sculpture, literature, motion pictures, and other forms of art, that tries to show what takes place in dreams and in the subconscious mind. Surrealism is characterized by unexpected arrangements and distortions of images. *Dadaism, the school of determinedly impromptu expression, was giving way to the more rigidly formulated doctrines of surrealism* (New Yorker). [< French *surréalisme* < *sur-* beyond, sur-[1] + *réalisme* realism]

1. Select the characteristics of *surrealism*.
   _____ a. emotion _____ c. unreality
   _____ b. conscious _____ d. subconscious

2. In which of the following sentences is *surrealism* used correctly?
   _____ a. Surrealism is an artistic strategy utilizing images from dreams and hallucinations.
   _____ b. A movement named surrealism directed attention to the life and harsh realities of peasants and workers.
   _____ c. Surrealism was a broad movement that emphasized the value of emotion over reason.

_____ d. The movement of surrealism was indebted to the psychologist Sigmund Freud, who was interested in the meaning of dreams.

3. Complete the verbal analogy.
   realist : literal truth :: *surrealism* : _____
   a. symmetrical balance   c. sensuous surfaces
   b. fantastic illusion   d. common perspectives

4. Write a sentence correctly using *surrealism*. (Be sure to include context clues to show you understand the meaning of the word.)

   _____

   _____

5. What is appealing to you about the movement called *surrealism*? Do you like fantastic images and forms? Are you interested in dreams and the subconscious?

   _____

   _____

Symbolism[5]

sym|bol|ism (sim′bə liz əm), *n.* **1** the use of symbols; representation by symbols. **2** a system of symbols; organized set or pattern of symbols: *The cross, the crown, the lamb, and the lily are parts of Christian symbolism. Symbolisms developed in the church to add impressiveness to the setting and liturgy* (Matthew Luckiesh). **3** symbolic meaning or character: *Symbolism, then, is a second and independent factor in dream-distortion, existing side by side with the censorship* (Sigmund Freud). **4** (in literature or art) the principles or practice of a symbolist or the symbolists: *Their sculpture and architecture glow with color … and full-dimensional symbolism* (Time).

1. Select the synonym(s) of *symbolism*.
   _____ a. representation   _____ c. characterization
   _____ b. distortion   _____ d. falsification

2. In which of the following sentences can *symbolism* be correctly placed in the blank?
   _____ a. _____ was evident in the perfect replication of the important leaders of the Roman empire in their portrait paintings.
   _____ b. Expressionist work is famous for its _____ of the harshness and anonymity of city life.
   _____ c. Gaugin used _____ to show his discontent with the spiritual ills of Western civilization.
   _____ d. Realists used _____ to accurately record the visible world.

3. Select some of the better examples of *symbolism*.
   _____ a. an abstract clock representing the passage of time
   _____ b. fruit and fish on a platter
   _____ c. faceless people without emotion
   _____ d. a cat chasing a dog

4. React to the following statement: Paintings with *symbolism* are more dramatic and meaningful than other types of paintings. (Discuss your level of agreement or disagreement.)

_____

_____

5. Write a sentence correctly using *symbolism*. (Be sure to include context clues to show you understand the meaning of the word.)

_____

_____

ANSWERS TO CHAPTER 15 EXERCISES

Aesthetic: **1.** d (characteristic) **2.** 3 **3.** b, c
Asymmetry: **1.** a, d **2.** b, d **3.** a (antonym)
Baroque: **1.** b, c **2.** b, c, d **3.** d (artist/example)
Cubism: **1.** b (time period) **2.** c, d **3.** b, d
Distortion: **1.** a **2.** ee, cc, aa, bb, dd **3.** d (definition)
Gradation: **1.** b, c **2.** cc, dd, aa, bb, ee **3.** 2
Hue: **1.** a, b, c **2.** b, c **3.** c (purpose of use)
Impressionism: **1.** c (artist/example) **2.** a, b **3.** a, d
Monochromatic: **1.** b **2.** a, c **3.** c, d
Palette: **1.** 3 **2.** b, c **3.** a, b
Perception: **1.** c, d **2.** ee, cc, dd, bb, aa **3.** c, d
Realist: **1.** a, d **2.** 2 **3.** a, d
Romanticism: **1.** b, c **2.** a, c **3.** d (characteristic)
Surrealism: **1.** c, d **2.** a, d **3.** b (characteristic)
Symbolism: **1.** a, c **2.** b, c **3.** b, c

If you missed any of the items in the exercises, return to the exercise and to the dictionary definitions to see where you went wrong. Remember: If you get something right, you only affirm that you knew it. If you get something wrong and understand why, *you have learned something.*

ART POSTTEST

Fill in the blanks with the words from this list.

aesthetic	gradation	perception
asymmetry	hue	realist
baroque	impressionism	romanticism
cubism	monochromatic	surrealism
distortion	palette	symbolism

1. A person interested in what is real and practical is a(n)

_____ .

2. _____ allows freedom of form and stresses strong feeling and imagination.

3. _____ is a modern movement that tries to show what takes place in dreams and in the subconscious mind.

4. A style of art characterized by the use of curved forms and lavish ornamentation is called _____.

5. _____ is a style of art in which objects are represented by cubes and other geometrical forms.

6. A(n) _____ is a variety of color, shade, or tint.

7. One of the steps, stages, or degrees in a series is a(n) _____.

8. _____ means "having to do with the beautiful."

9. An artist uses a(n) _____ to mix his colors.

10. A color scheme showing one color is called _____.

11. _____ in art is characterized by representations of things for the thing itself.

12. _____ is a style of art that gives a general feeling or perception of a subject without much attention to details.

13. Twisting something out of shape is known as _____.

14. *Insight, apprehension, discernment,* and *comprehension* are synonyms of _____.

15. Lacking a well-balanced arrangement of parts or harmony is called _____.

Answers to this posttest are in the Instructor's Manual.

If you missed any of the words, you may need to return to the exercises and to the dictionary entries to see why your concepts for some words are incomplete.

BUSINESS: BUSINESS ADMINISTRATION

◆

OVERVIEW

The field of business administration is concerned with the social, economic, and behavioral environment in which we live and which underlies the effective adminis-tration of contemporary businesses at both the national and international levels. Coursework in business helps prepare students to be professional managers of today's and tomorrow's business organizations and for lifelong careers in commerce, finance, and industry in both the public and not-for-profit sectors.

There are numerous areas within business administration, including accounting, finance, general business, computer accounting, resource administration, interna-tional business, management, marketing, production and operations management, real estate, and small business and entrepreneurship.

Employment opportunities for business administration majors include careers in a variety of organizations, including public accounting firms, banks, savings and loans, and other financial institutions. Additional employment opportunities are with commercial and high-technology industries, aerospace, transportation, communica-tions, computer information systems, and the foreign trade sector. Finally, those entrepreneurs who want to own their own businesses will benefit from a degree in business administration.

Introductory textbooks in business administration are usually expository and descrip-tive in nature. They present broad concepts and generalizations as well as statements of situations, ideas, or problems. Many texts also include case studies and career and business profiles as realistic examples of the concepts and ideas of business administra-tion.

The vocabulary in business administration is a combination of general and specialized terminology. There are general terms, such as incentive *and* pecuniary, *that also have a specialized meaning within the context of business administration. Specialized vocabulary in the form of compound nouns (*business cycle, gross national product, venture capital*) have also been developed to represent unique concepts or theoretical constructs. You may add other terms you discover in your studies related to business administration on the forms in Appendix D.*

VOCABULARY SELF-EVALUATION

The following words will be introduced in this reading selection. Place a check mark (√) in front of any that you know thoroughly and use in your speech or writing. Place a question mark (?) in front of any that you recognize but do not use yourself.

_____ adversary	_____ fiat	_____ pecuniary
_____ axiom	_____ incentive	_____ proliferation
_____ contingency	_____ innovative	_____ ramification
_____ ensconced	_____ lucrative	_____ redress
_____ entitlement	_____ minutiae	_____ remuneration

MANAGEMENT STYLE
AND ITS EVOLUTION

The oldest method of management theory is the autocratic* system. This system was not invented by industry; it was a natural continuation of age-old relationships. Those in power ruled by fiat;[1] they gave orders, and their subjects obeyed or suffered the consequences. With the advent of the Industrial Age, the ruled became the factory workers, and a new class of ruler emerged: the factory owner-manager. Ensconced[2] in his position as owner, the manager decided what should be produced, how it should be produced, and what the worker would be paid. Few objected. It was not necessarily an efficient method of getting things done, but

---

* Autocratic means "having absolute power or authority; ruling without checks or limitations."

in those days competition was weak, raw materials were cheap and plentiful, and labor worked for what the owner was willing to pay. The accepted axiom[3] was "the boss knows what is best for business."

With the passage of time, both employers and employees recognized the inefficiency of the factory system. In 1912 Frederick Winslow Taylor developed what came to be called "scientific management." Taylor's time and motion studies measured the minutiae[4] of the workplace in order to increase the efficiency of both men and machines. Unfortunately, efficiency seemed to call for fitting the worker to the needs of the machine. Employee opinions were not sought because it did not occur to the employer that the employee might know a better, more efficient way to get the job done. The employer believed that the harder the employee worked, the more lucrative[5] the business would be. Changes were made for the sake of "efficiency" and only incidentally for the convenience of the worker. The employee could not yet expect attention to his problems or the right to seek redress[6] for wrongs.

About twenty-five years later, Elton Mayo's work at the Western Electric plant in Chicago produced further information about the worker's place in efficient production. Mayo's investigation showed the workplace to be essentially a social situation. The worker's view of work and willingness to be productive were closely linked to the worker's interactions with coworkers and supervisors and to perceptions of the company's attention to his or her welfare. When coworkers and supervisors did "a fair day's work," the worker performed better. When the company "cared about" the worker, he or she was more efficient. One ramification[7] of Mayo's study was the realization that the worker's *total* life affected job performance.

In the late 1940s Peter Drucker, sometimes called "the father of corporate society," reinforced the idea that the job should be designed to fit the worker psychologically as well as physically. Yet it was not until the 1970s that major companies started using incentives,[8] job enrichment programs, and other humanistic approaches to increase productivity through worker satisfaction. Researchers continued to expound the theory that workers are motivated by psychological rewards as well as the usually acknowledged pecuniary[9] rewards.

By 1970 competition was keen between highly developed countries. *Quality* and *cost* were now key words. The United States was finding out that some countries were outproducing us and that the quality of their goods and services was superior to ours.

At the end of World War II, Japanese industry was in ruins. Before the war, Japan had been known as the producer of cheap trinkets. Its new government made a decision to drop the emphasis on cheap products and concentrate on high-quality goods. But how was the desired level of quality to be achieved?

Japan turned to the United States for help. They wanted to know how we were able to produce goods with superior quality. Our response was that we had quality control inspectors on every assembly line. Every defective part of a product was removed from the line and added to the scrap pile. The Japanese, however, could not afford this system; they could not afford to throw away expensive raw materials.

To overcome this problem, the Japanese initiated an innovative[10] system called the "quality circle": Quality will automatically be built into all products when workers understand exactly what they are to do and why they are to do it and when they are able to control many of their own activities on the job. Compensation for a job well done would extend beyond the usual remuneration.[11] Salary might not be particularly high, but the feeling that the workplace was much like a family would give the worker a sense of being necessary and appreciated. Entitlements[12] might include payment of rent and utilities, meals while on the job, and group vacations. Management's attitude was "Let's listen carefully to what the workers have to say. After all, the person closest to the job usually knows the most about it." Such a notion could never have been imagined in the early days of business management!

Quality circles were formed in all areas of business and industry, manufacturing, banking, and even education. Now more than nine million Japanese workers are members of circles, each contributing to the quality of the product and the quality of working life. Not all circles are effective, but the quality of Japanese products has prompted U.S. businessmen to look at Japan's styles of management in order to adapt them to the American working environment.

Today, American management does not consider one particular management style to be best. Rather, managers look at each situation and modify their styles accordingly. This contingency[13] approach pays particular attention to the educational level of workers, to the task involved, and to the relationship of the supervisor-manager to the employee. Many testing instruments have been devised and administered to both employees and employers to find the preferred and most productive style of management. Such an approach keeps management and labor from being adversaries.[14] The newer approach is to work together as partners toward a common goal.

The success of Japanese business and industry has led to a proliferation[15] of the quality circle idea. Many leading American companies have adapted and integrated it into their organizational structure. Hewlett-Packard, Monsanto, Gaines Dog Food, and other companies are now strong advocates of a more participative system. And the commitment of some Japanese companies is very strong: When Honda, Nissan, and Toyota develop new plants in their worldwide markets, they spend as much money on the training of their workers as they do on equipping their plants. ◆

BUSINESS ADMINISTRATION PRETEST

Select words from this list and write them in the blanks to complete the sentences.

adversary   fiat   pecuniary
axiom   incentive   proliferation
contingency   innovative   ramification
ensconced   lucrative   redress
entitlement   minutiae   remuneration

1. Something one has a right to is a(n) _____.

2. Doing things a new way is _____.

3. _____ means "sheltered safely."

4. A spreading into parts is a(n) _____.

5. Something yielding gain is _____.

6. A person or group opposing is a(n) _____.

7. Something in the form of money is _____ .

8. An authoritative order is a(n) _____ .

9. Something incidental to something else is a(n) _____ .

10. To set right is to _____ .

11. A cause of action or effort is a(n) _____ .

12. Reproduction, as by cell division, is _____ .

13. A self-evident truth is a(n) _____ .

14. Another term for payment is _____ .

15. Trifling details are _____ .

Answers to this pretest are in Appendix E.

Unless your instructor tells you to do otherwise, complete the exercises for each word you missed on the pretest. The words, with their exercises, are in alphabetical order. The superscript numbers indicate where the words appeared in the reading selection so that you can refer to them when necessary. There are several types of exercises, but for each word you will be asked to write a sentence using context clues. (See Chapter 3 if you need information about how to create context clues.) You are also asked to perform some activity that will help you make your concept of the word personal. *Complete this activity thoughtfully, for creating a personalized concept of the word will help you remember it in the future.*

Answers to all the exercises are at the end of the exercise segment.

BUSINESS ADMINISTRATION EXERCISES

Adversary[14]

ad|ver|sar|y (ad′vər ser′ē), *n., pl.* **-sar|ies**, *adj.*
— *n.* **1** a person or group opposing or hostile to another person or group; enemy; antagonist: *The United States and Japan were adversaries in World War II.* SYN: foe. **2** a person or group on the other side in a contest; opponent: *Which school is our adversary in this week's football game?* SYN: rival, contestant.
— *adj.* antagonistic; adverse: *"The hearings,"* Senator Watkins said on the opening day, *"are not to be adversary in character"* (New Yorker).

the Adversary, Satan, as the enemy of mankind; the Devil: *Or shall the Adversary thus obtain his end?* (Milton).
[< Latin *adversārius* < *adversus;* see etym. under **adverse**]

from **adverse:**

[< Latin *adversus* turned against, past participle of *advertere* turn to < *ad-* to + *vertere* turn]

(Note: The term *adversarial* is sometimes used as the adjective form, instead of *adversary*.)

1. If you are an *adversary*, you
   _____ a. may cooperate with everyone.
   _____ b. may be angry.
   _____ c. may plan to get even.
   _____ d. are working against someone or something.

2. In which of the following sentences can *adversary* correctly be placed in the blank?

_____ a. An _____ relationship may involve a lawsuit.

_____ b. Another term for best friend is _____.

_____ c. Don't think of your teacher as an _____ but rather as an ally.

_____ d. A good football coach will know the plays used by each _____.

3. Place an "s" before any synonym and an "a" before any antonym of *adversary*.

_____ a. opponent   _____ f. supporter

_____ b. backer   _____ g. ally

_____ c. rival   _____ h. competitor

_____ d. foe   _____ i. opposer

_____ e. comrade

4. Write a sentence correctly using *adversary*. (Be sure to include context clues to show you understand the meaning of the word.)

_____

_____

5. Is there someone who is your *adversary*? How do you handle the situation? If you have no *adversary*, how do you maintain this situation?

_____

_____

Axiom[3]

ax|i|om (ak′sē əm), *n*. **1** a statement taken to be true without proof; self-evident truth: *It is an axiom that a whole is greater than any one of its parts. It is an axiom that if equals are added to equals the results will be equal.* **2** a well-established principle, rule, or law: *It is an axiom that medicine should be kept out of the reach of young children.* [< Latin *axiōma* < Greek *axiōma* < *áxios* worthy]

1. Check any appropriate response to the following statement: "A good parent guides a child by *axiom* and by example."

_____ a. The rules of behavior have to be set out clearly.

_____ b. I agree that punishment is what works best.

_____ c. Tell them what you expect and then show them.

_____ d. Children learn by hearing and by seeing.

2. Select the synonym(s) of *axiom*.

_____ a. statement   _____ d. proof

_____ b. law   _____ e. evidence

_____ c. principle   _____ f. rule

3. Which of the numbered dictionary definitions of *axiom* best fits the word's use in the reading selection? _____

4. Write down an *axiom* you heard when you were growing up. For example: "Beauty is skin deep," "Pretty is as pretty does," "If at first you don't succeed, try, try again."

_____

_____

5. Write a sentence correctly using *axiom*. (Be sure to include context clues to show you understand the meaning of the word.)

_____

_____

Contingency[13]

con|tin|gen|cy (kən tin′jən sē), *n., pl.* **-cies.** **1** a happening or event depending on something that is uncertain; possibility: *The explorer carried supplies for every contingency.* **2** an accidental happening; uncertain event; chance: *Football players seldom think of injury as a contingency while they are playing.* **3** uncertainty of occurrence; dependence on chance. **4** *Philosophy.* **a** the mode of existence, or of coming to pass, which does not involve necessity. **b** a happening by chance or free will. **5** something incidental to something else.

1. Check any appropriate response to the following statement: "John is a good manager and plans for every *contingency*."
   _____ a. He is in charge of every social gathering.
   _____ b. His business is likely to succeed.
   _____ c. He tries to prepare for the unexpected.
   _____ d. Life can be full of surprises.

2. Complete the verbal analogy.
   delight : please :: *contingency* : _____
   a. plans   c. event
   b. dependent   d. possibility

3. Which of the numbered and lettered dictionary definitions of *contingency* best fits the word's use in the reading selection? _____

4. Write a sentence correctly using *contingency*. (Be sure to include context clues to show you understand the meaning of the word.)

_____

_____

5. What *contingencies* have you considered in planning your formal schooling? A change in the job market? An increase in costs and fees? A change of interests?

_____

_____

Ensconced[2]

en|sconce (en skons′), *v.t.,* **-sconced, -sconc-ing. 1** to shelter safely; hide: *The soldiers were ensconced in strongly fortified trenches. We were ensconced in the cellar during the tornado.* **2** to settle comfortably and firmly: *The cat ensconced itself in the armchair.* [< *en-*[1] + *sconce*[3] fortification, probably < Dutch *schans*]

1. Which of the following might be *ensconced*?
   - _____ a. a large stand of trees
   - _____ b. the president of a company
   - _____ c. a flock of birds
   - _____ d. several children

2. If you were *ensconced*, you might be
   - _____ a. situated.   _____ d. placed.
   - _____ b. established.   _____ e. settled.
   - _____ c. stationed.   _____ f. installed.

3. Which of the numbered dictionary definitions of *ensconced* best fits the word's use in the reading selection? _____

4. Who is *ensconced* as the boss of your family? Of your love relationship?

_____

_____

5. Write a sentence correctly using *ensconced*. (Be sure to include context clues to show you understand the meaning of the word.)

_____

_____

Entitlement[12]

en|ti|tle|ment (en tī′təl mənt), *n.* something to which one is entitled; a privilege: *A careful campaign ... must be developed to enable older people fully to understand their entitlements under the new law* (New York Times).
en|ti|tle (en tī′təl), *v.t.,* **-tled, -tling. 1** to give a claim or right (to); provide with a reason to ask or get something: *The one who wins is entitled to first prize. A ticket will entitle you to admission.*
SYN: empower, qualify, enable. **2** to give the title of; name: *The author entitled his book "Treasure Island." The Queen of England is also entitled "Defender of the Faith."* SYN: denominate, designate. **3** to give or call by an honorary title. Also, **intitle.** [< Old French *entituler,* learned borrowing from Late Latin *intitulāre* < Latin *in-* in + *titulus* title, inscription, claim]

1. Check any appropriate response to the following statement:
"My new job has no *entitlements*."
   _____ a. I would purchase some health insurance, if I were you.
   _____ b. It sounds like the ideal job!
   _____ c. That's probably okay if they pay you enough.
   _____ d. That may be all right for you, but I prefer a few extras.

2. An *entitlement* is
   _____ a. something you buy.
   _____ b. something you earn.
   _____ c. something you give to your employer.
   _____ d. something in addition to regular pay.

3. Complete the verbal analogy:
   entitle : v.t. :: *entitlement* : _____
   a. claim   d. v.i.
   b. n.   e. adj.
   c. privilege

4. If you owned a business, what *entitlements* would you offer your employees? What would be your purpose in offering those *entitlements*?

   _____

   _____

5. Write a sentence correctly using *entitlement*. (Be sure to include context clues to show you understand the meaning of the word.)

   _____

   _____

Fiat[1]

fi|at (fī′ət, -at), *n., v.* —*n.* **1** an authoritative order or command; decree: *to determine by the fiat of the king alone the course of national policy* (William Stubbs). **2** an authoritative sanction; authorization.
—*v.t.* **1** to attach a fiat to; sanction. **2** to declare by a fiat.
[< Latin *fīat* let it be done < *fierī*, passive of *facere* do]

1. Which of the following might issue a *fiat*?
   _____ a. the president of a democracy
   _____ b. a president-for-life
   _____ c. the owner of a business
   _____ d. a medical doctor

2. Check any appropriate response to the following statement:
"My father rules our family by *fiat*."
   _____ a. That seems fair enough.
   _____ b. I wouldn't like that at all!

_____ c. It's nice when everyone has a say in family policy.

_____ d. How soon do you plan to move out?

3. Which of the numbered dictionary definitions of *fiat* best fits the word's use in the reading selection? _____

4. Write a sentence correctly using *fiat*. (Be sure to include context clues to show you understand the meaning of the word.)

_____

_____

5. If you could issue a *fiat* that would be obeyed in your family or in your school, what would it be?

_____

_____

Incentive[8]

in|cen|tive (in sen′tiv), *n., adj.* — *n.* a thing that urges a person on; a cause of action or effort; motive; stimulus: *The fun of playing the game was a greater incentive than the prize. This accentuated the world shortage, and added incentive to soaring prices for the metal* (Wall Street Journal). **SYN:** spur, incitement, provocation. See syn. under **motive**.
— *adj.* arousing to feeling or action; inciting; encouraging. **SYN:** exciting, provocative.
[< Latin *incēntīvum*, noun use of neuter adjective (in Late Latin, inciting) < *incinere* strike up; blow into (a flute) < *in-* in, into + *canere* to sing]

1. In which of the following sentences can *incentive* correctly be placed in the blank?

_____ a. His father's promise of a bicycle was the _____ Joe needed to work harder in school.

_____ b. Our company has a system of _____ pay.

_____ c. It is a good idea to _____ a child for good behavior.

_____ d. The _____ offered was a cookie now, nothing later.

2. Which of the following might be an *incentive*?

_____ a. extra pay   _____ d. vacation time

_____ b. a candy bar   _____ e. a half-price sale

_____ c. an A in a class   _____ f. failing a class

3. Select the synonym(s) of *incentive*.

_____ a. spur   _____ d. incitement

_____ b. payment   _____ e. exciting

_____ c. provocation   _____ f. provocative

4. School is hard work. What is the major *incentive* that keeps you attending classes?

_____

_____

5. Write a sentence correctly using *incentive*. (Be sure to include context clues to show you understand the meaning of the word.)

_____

_____

Innovative[10]

in|no|va|tive (in′ə vā′tiv), *adj.* tending to innovate; characterized by innovation: *Inventors are innovative people.* — **in′no|va′tive|ness,** *n.*
in|no|vate (in′ə vāt), *v.,* -vat|ed, -vat|ing. — *v.i.* to make changes; bring in something new or new ways of doing things: *It is difficult to innovate when people prefer the old, familiar way of doing things. It were good ... that men in their innovations would follow the example of time itself, which indeed innovateth greatly, but quietly* (Francis Bacon).
— *v.t.* to introduce (something); bring in for the first time: *The scientist innovated new ways of research. Every moment alters what is done, And innovates some act till then unknown* (John Dryden).
[< Latin *innovāre* (with English -*ate*[1]) < *in-* (intensive) + *novus* new] — **in′no|va′tor,** *n.*
in|no|va|tion (in′ə vā′shən), *n.* **1** a change made in the established way of doing things: *The new principal made many innovations. The scheme of a Colony revenue by British authority appeared therefore to the Americans in the light of a great innovation* (Edmund Burke). **syn:** novelty. **2** the act of making changes; bringing in new things or new ways of doing things: *Many people are opposed to innovation. Innovation is for showoffs and pioneers alike* (New Yorker).

1. Check any appropriate response to the following statement:
   "I think Kim is a truly *innovative* person."
   _____ a. Yes, I agree. Same old thing all the time: boring, boring.
   _____ b. She thinks of new and different ways to do things.
   _____ c. I like the changes she makes.
   _____ d. Kim and I prefer the old, familiar way of doing things.

2. Something *innovative* may be
   _____ a. a change.   _____ d. familiar.
   _____ b. a novelty.   _____ e. opposed.
   _____ c. different.   _____ f. new.

3. Complete the verbal analogy.
   national : nation :: *innovative* : _____
   a. innovativeness   c. innovating
   b. innovated   d. innovational

4. Write a sentence correctly using *innovative*. (Be sure to include context clues to show you understand the meaning of the word.)

_____

_____

5. What popular musician do you think is *innovative*?

_____

_____

Lucrative[5]

lu|cra|tive (lü′krə tiv), *adj.* bringing in money;
yielding gain or profit; profitable: *a lucrative
profession, a lucrative investment.* SYN: gainful,
remunerative. [< Latin *lucrātīvus* < *lūcrārī* to
gain < *lucrum* gain] **—lu′cra|tive|ly,** *adv.* **—lu′-
cra|tive|ness,** *n.*

1. If you had a *lucrative* business, you might
   _____ a. plan carefully and work hard.
   _____ b. be able to retire at an early age.
   _____ c. have to sell at a loss.
   _____ d. find it easy to get investors.

2. If something is *lucrative*, it
   _____ a. is remunerative.   _____ d. is gainful.
   _____ b. produces wealth.   _____ e. is profitable.
   _____ c. is expensive.   _____ f. pays well.

3. Complete the verbal analogy.
   lucrative : lucrativeness :: _____ : _____
   a. noun : verb   c. adjective : adverb
   b. adjective : noun   d. noun : adjective

4. What do you think is the most *lucrative* business in the world? Does it
   have any disadvantages?

   _____

   _____

5. Write a sentence correctly using *lucrative*. (Be sure to include context
   clues to show you understand the meaning of the word.)

   _____

   _____

Minutiae[4]

mi|nu|ti|ae (mi nü′shē ē, -nyü′-), *n.pl.* very small
matters; trifling details: *scientific minutiae. They
waited ... for the exchange of pass-words, the
delivery of keys, and all the slow minutiae attend-
ant upon the movements of a garrison in a well-
guarded fortress* (Scott). [< Latin *minūtiae* trifles,
plural of *minūtia* smallness < *minūtus;* see etym.
under **minute²**]

mi|nu|ti|a (mi nü′shē ə, -nyü′-), *n.* singular of
minutiae.

from **minute:²**

[< Latin *minūtus* made small,
past participle of *minuere* diminish < *minus* less;
see etym. under **minus.** See etym. of doublet
menu.]

(Note: Read the pronunciation of this word carefully. It is usually used in
the plural.)

1. Match the following statement with a similar statement below:
   "The editor was overconcerned with *minutiae*."
   _____ a. He watched the passage of time very closely.
   _____ b. He made very sure that no one earned a bonus.
   _____ c. He worried about minor details too much.
   _____ d. He fired anyone who was a clock watcher.

BUSINESS: BUSINESS ADMINISTRATION

2. Complete the verbal analogy.

facts : fact :: *minutiae* : _____

a. minute   c. minutiae

b. minutia   d. minutus

3. Check any appropriate response to the following statement:

"Martin is concerned with the *minutiae* of life."

_____ a. Why does he focus on trifling matters?

_____ b. He is wise to take a broad view of life, I think.

_____ c. Small details drive me crazy.

_____ d. He would probably make a good scientist.

4. Write a sentence correctly using *minutiae*. (Be sure to include context clues to show you understand the meaning of the word.)

_____

_____

5. Is there a part of your life in which *minutiae* are important? The upkeep of your car? Your wardrobe? Your hair? Your love life?

_____

_____

Pecuniary[9]

pe|cu|ni|ar|y (pi kyü′nē er′ē), *adj.* **1** of or having to do with money: *I pass my whole life, miss, in turning an immense pecuniary mangle* (Dickens). **2** in the form of money: *pecuniary assistance, a pecuniary gift.* [< Latin *pecūniārius* < *pecūnia* money < *pecū* money; cattle] — **pe|cu′ni|ar′i|ly**, *adv.*

(Note: The etymology is interesting. Why would the Latin word *pecu* mean both "money" and "cattle"?)

1. In which of the following sentences is *pecuniary* correctly used?

_____ a. Last year's pecuniary loss caused the company to lower its dividend.

_____ b. Bill took the job for pecuniary motives only.

_____ c. He shouldn't be surprised then, if his only reward is pecuniary.

_____ d. Mary's haircut is really pecuniary; it makes her look like a turkey.

2. Check any appropriate response to the following statement:

"Sara has little interest in *pecuniary* gain."

_____ a. She is more interested in spiritual matters.

_____ b. She gives her time and effort for little pay.

_____ c. Do you suppose she inherited money from her family?

_____ d. The world doesn't need people like that!

3. Complete the verbal analogy.
   customary : adjective :: *pecuniary* : _____
   a. noun   c. adverb
   b. verb   d. adjective

4. With what project would you like *pecuniary* assistance? A new car? A better wardrobe? School expenses?

   _____

   _____

5. Write a sentence correctly using *pecuniary*. (Be sure to include context clues to show you understand the meaning of the word.)

   _____

   _____

Proliferation[15]

pro|lif|er|a|tion (prō lif′ə rā′shən), *n.* **1** reproduction, as by budding or cell division. **2** a spreading; propagation: *The draft of the test ban treaty contained an expression of desire to prevent the proliferation of nuclear weapons* (Seymour Topping). [< French *prolifération* < *prolifère* < Medieval Latin *prolifer;* see etym. under **proliferous**] **pro|lif|er|ate** (prō lif′ə rāt), *v.i., v.t.,* **-at|ed, -at|ing.** **1** to grow or produce by multiplication of parts, as in budding or cell division. **2** to multiply; spread; propagate: *These conferences proliferate like measles spots* (Harper's). [back formation < proliferation]

from **proliferous:**

   [< Medieval Latin *prolifer* < Latin *prōlēs* offspring (see etym. under **proletarian**) + *-fer* bearing + English *-ous*]

1. Check any appropriate response to the following statement:
   "In the past twenty years, there has been a great *proliferation* of fast-food outlets."
   _____ a. There are so many different kinds of them now.
   _____ b. I wish I had invested in them several years ago.
   _____ c. It's too bad they haven't caught on.
   _____ d. You can find them everywhere, it seems.

2. *Proliferation* might occur in which of the following areas?
   _____ a. in a disease
   _____ b. in a plant
   _____ c. in business practices
   _____ d. in television programming

3. Complete the verbal analogy.
   separation : division :: *proliferation* : _____
   a. multiplication   c. subtraction
   b. addition   d. growth

4. Write a sentence correctly using *proliferation*. (Be sure to include context clues to show you understand the meaning of the word.)

   _____

   _____

5. If you could prevent the *proliferation* of one thing, what would it be?

_____

_____

Ramification[7]

ram|i|fi|ca|tion (ram′ə fə kā′shən), *n.* **1** a dividing or spreading out into branches or parts. **2** the manner or result of branching; offshoot; branch; part; subdivision; consequence.
ram|i|fy (ram′ə fī), *v.*, **-fied, -fy|ing.** —*v.i.* to divide or spread out into parts resembling branches: *Quartz veins ramify through the rock in all directions* (F. Kingdon-Ward).
—*v.t.* to cause to branch out.
[< French, Old French *ramifier* < Medieval Latin *ramificari* < Latin *rāmus* branch + *facere* make]

1. In which of the following sentences can *ramification* correctly be placed in the blank?
   _____ a. Mary has no interest at all in any _____ of party politics.
   _____ b. When we read the etymology of a word, we can explore the fine shades of meaning and all their _____s.
   _____ c. The _____s of the cypress tree create an unusual silhouette.
   _____ d. After the _____, all the parts are unified into one whole.

2. A *ramification* is
   _____ a. a dividing.   _____ d. a subdivision.
   _____ b. a branch.   _____ e. a part.
   _____ c. an offshoot.   _____ f. a consequence.

3. Complete the verbal analogy.
   <u>non</u>sense : no :: *ramification* : _____
   a. tree   c. make
   b. branch   d. part

4. What *ramifications* do you hope for as a result of attending college?

_____

_____

5. Write a sentence correctly using *ramification*. (Be sure to include context clues to show you understand the meaning of the word.)

_____

_____

Redress[6]

re|dress (*v.* ri dres′; *n.* rē′dres, ri dres′), *v., n.*
—*v.t.* **1** to set right; repair; remedy: *King Arthur tried to redress wrongs in his kingdom.* **2** to ad-   just evenly again: *I called the New World into existence to redress the balance of the Old* (George Canning).

—*n.* **1** the act or process of setting right; relief; reparation: *Anyone who has been injured unfairly deserves redress. My griefs ... finding no redress, ferment and rage* (Milton). **SYN:** restitution. **2** the means of a remedy: *There was no redress against the lawless violence to which they were* *perpetually exposed* (John L. Motley). [< Middle French *redresser* < *re-* again + Old French *dresser* to straighten, arrange. Compare etym. under **dress**, verb.] —**re|dress'er, re|dres'- sor,** *n.*

(Note: *Redress* involves righting a wrong, usually without goodwill resulting.)

1. In which of the following sentences can *redress* correctly be placed in the blank?
   _____ a. Fired from his job, Mr. Olson is seeking _____ in the courts.
   _____ b. Can we _____ social wrongs through legislation?
   _____ c. The Constitution says we can petition the government for _____ of grievances.
   _____ d. You can _____ for a month, but it won't help.

2. Check any appropriate response to the following statement:
   "The company says it intends to *redress* our grievances."
   _____ a. I'll believe it when I see it.
   _____ b. They are trying to make things better.
   _____ c. They must be doing that because all the workers are happy.
   _____ d. That survey must have made worker dissatisfaction clear to management.

3. Which of the numbered dictionary definitions of *redress* best fits the word's use in the reading selection? _____

4. Write a sentence correctly using *redress*. (Be sure to include context clues to show you understand the meaning of the word.)

   _____

   _____

5. Have you ever had to *redress* a wrong? What did it involve? Your family? A friend? Your job? Have you had to seek *redress* for yourself?

   _____

   _____

Remuneration[11]

re|mu|ner|a|tion (ri myü'nə rā'shən), *n.* reward; pay; payment: *Remuneration to employes for the quarter was down $3 million* (Wall Street Journal).
re|mu|ner|ate (ri myü'nə rāt), *v.t.,* **-at|ed, -at|ing.** to pay, as for work, services, or trouble; reward: *The boy who returned the lost jewels was remunerated. The harvest will remunerate the laborers for their toil.* **SYN:** recompense. See syn. under **pay.** [< Latin *remūnerāre* (with English *-ate¹*) < *re-* back + *mūnerāre* to give < *mūnus, -eris* gift]

1. Check any appropriate response to the following statement:
   "My *remuneration* for this job is very small."
   _____ a. I'm glad it's no trouble.
   _____ b. Do you do it because you think it is a contribution to society?
   _____ c. You might as well be a volunteer.
   _____ d. You don't need a station wagon; a small car will do.

2. You might receive *remuneration* for which of the following?
   _____ a. working as a regular employee
   _____ b. serving as a consultant
   _____ c. winning a lottery
   _____ d. selling a business

3. Complete the verbal analogy.
   remuneration : remunerate :: _____ : _____
   a. v.t. : n.   c. adj. : n.
   b. n. : v.t.   d. adj. : adv.

4. Some say a young person should not receive *remuneration* for jobs done around the home. Do you agree? Did/do you receive such *remuneration*?

   _____

   _____

5. Write a sentence correctly using *remuneration*. (Be sure to include context clues to show you understand the meaning of the word.)

   _____

   _____

ANSWERS TO CHAPTER 16 EXERCISES

Adversary: **1.** b, c, d   **2.** a, c, d   **3.** s, a, s, s, a, a, a, s, s
Axiom: **1.** a, c, d   **2.** b, c, f   **3.** 1
Contingency: **1.** b, c, d   **2.** d (synonym)   **3.** 5
Ensconced: **1.** b, d   **2.** a, b, c, d, e, f   **3.** 2
Entitlement: **1.** a, c, d   **2.** b, d   **3.** b (part of speech, abbrev.)
Fiat: **1.** b, c, d   **2.** b, d   **3.** *n.* 1
Incentive: **1.** a, b, d   **2.** a, b, c, d, e, f   **3.** a, c, d, e, f
Innovative: **1.** b, c   **2.** a, b, c, e, f   **3.** a (adjective : noun)
Lucrative: **1.** a, b, d   **2.** a, b, d, e, f   **3.** b (parts of speech)
Minutiae: **1.** c   **2.** b (singular)   **3.** a, c, d
Pecuniary: **1.** a, b, c   **2.** a, b, c   **3.** d (part of speech)
Proliferation: **1.** a, b, d   **2.** a, b, c, d   **3.** a (synonym)
Ramification: **1.** a, b, c   **2.** a, b, c, d, e, f   **3.** b (meaning of combining form)
Redress: **1.** a, b, c   **2.** a, b, d   **3.** *n.* 1
Remuneration: **1.** b, c   **2.** a, b   **3.** b (parts of speech, abbrevs.)

If you missed any of the items in the exercises, return to the exercise and to the dictionary definition to see where you went wrong. Remember: If you get something right, you only affirm that you knew it. If you get something wrong and understand why, *you have learned something.*

BUSINESS ADMINISTRATION POSTTEST

Fill in the blanks with the words from this list.

adversary	fiat	pecuniary
axiom	incentive	proliferation
contingency	innovative	ramification
ensconced	lucrative	redress
entitlement	minutiae	remuneration

1. A(n) _____ is a decree.

2. _____ are very small matters.

3. An uncertain event is a(n) _____ .

4. A(n) _____ is an enemy.

5. _____ means "gainful."

6. Something _____ is sheltered safely.

7. A(n) _____ is a motive or stimulus.

8. _____ means "having to do with money."

9. A consequence is also called a(n) _____ .

10. _____ means "payment."

11. A(n) _____ is a well-established rule.

12. Something characterized by change is _____ .

13. _____ means "propagation."

14. *Restitution* is a synonym for _____ .

15. A(n) _____ is a privilege.

Answers to this posttest are in the Instructor's Manual.

If you missed any of the words, you may need to return to the exercises and to the dictionary entries to see why your concepts for some words are incomplete.

CHAPTER SEVENTEEN

BUSINESS: ACCOUNTING

◆

OVERVIEW

Accounting is the art, practice, or system of keeping, analyzing, and interpreting business accounts. Accounting enables companies and governmental agencies to summarize and report in an understandable fashion a large number of transactions.

Accounting is usually an option or concentration within the business administration degree program. An Associate of Arts or Associate in Science degree can also be earned in accounting. Courses in accounting include financial and managerial accounting, income taxation, cost accounting, auditing, governmental and not-for-profit accounting, and controllership.

Career options for students with accounting degrees include professional employment in public, private, or governmental accounting. Specific employment opportunities include work as a certified public accountant (CPA), tax specialist, auditor, or controller.

The introductory textbooks in the field are a combination of expository and process analysis in format. They explain broad concepts or generalizations as well as state-ments of situations, ideas, or problems with explanations or examples. They also include step-by-step processes for completing accounting tasks. Charts, graphs, and tables help to visually represent concepts.

The vocabulary in accounting consists mainly of general vocabulary terms that also have a specialized meaning within the context of accounting, such as cost, audit, credit, *and* earnings. *You may add other terms you discover from your studies related to accounting on the forms in Appendix D.*

VOCABULARY SELF-EVALUATION

The following words will be introduced in this reading selection. Place a check mark (√) in front of any that you know thoroughly and use in your speech and writing. Place a question mark (?) in front of any that you recognize but do not use yourself.

_____ amortize	_____ depreciation	_____ ledger
_____ assets	_____ disclosure	_____ liabilities
_____ audit	_____ dividends	_____ requisition
_____ credit	_____ equity	_____ transaction
_____ debit	_____ intangible	_____ voucher

AN ACCOUNTING SYSTEM
FOR A NEW BUSINESS

Starting a new business requires developing an accounting system to keep track of the financial activities for both management and tax purposes.

The basic unit of an accounting system is the ledger[1] account. A ledger account should be kept for every aspect of the business. It is a double-entry two-sided system. The left side is the debit[2] side and the right side is the credit[3] side, and these can be abbreviated as dr. and cr.

The various aspects of the business will fall into one of three major categories: assets,[4] liabilities,[5] and owner's equity.[6] Assets are resources owned by the business that are expected to benefit future operations. Cash on hand, machinery, and accounts receivable are examples of asset accounts. Liabilities are the company's debts. These are the obligations that the business must pay in money or services at some time in the future. These can include accounts payable to creditors,

short-term notes payable for money borrowed, and salaries owed employees. Asset accounts normally have debit balances, and liability accounts have credit balances.

The last category is owner's equity, which is the value of cash or other assets invested by the owner in the company as well as proceeds from the profitable operation of the company. The owner's equity includes revenue and expenses and is equal to assets minus liabilities. An owner's equity account normally has a credit balance. For publicly held corporations, this category is called "stockholder's equity." The owner of a privately held company may withdraw his equity from the company at any time. On the other hand, the owners of a public company, the stockholders, remove a portion of their equity in the company through the distribution of dividends,[7] or shares of the profit of the company.

If a company borrows money to buy machinery, this transaction[8] will require that two ledger account entries be made. A ledger account for the asset of plant equipment would be increased by placing the amount paid for the machinery in the left, or debit, side of the account. This would be offset by an entry on the right, or credit, side of the ledger account for notes payable (liability). This double-entry system allows the accounts to always be in balance.

Assets such as machinery decline in economic potential due to wear, age, and deterioration over time. Depreciation[9] is the spreading of the cost of such a tangible asset over its useful life. The cost of intangible,[10] or immaterial, assets such as trademarks may also be spread over their lifetime, or amortized.[11] Amortization is the conversion of an intangible asset to an expense. The reason for spreading the cost of these assets over their lifetimes is because they help generate revenue, or income, for that entire period. To assign all the cost of the asset to one accounting period overstates expenses for that period and then understates them for the rest of the asset's life.

Of all the accounts, the cash account (paper money, coins, checks, money orders, and bank deposits) is one of the most difficult to adequately control. One cash-control procedure is the voucher[12] system, which requires written authorizations, records, and other procedures. For example, when a member of a company or business needs supplies, he or she completes a requisition[13] form that lists the supplies and their costs. This will result in both a purchase order (PO) being generated by the purchasing department and an invoice by the outside firm supplying the goods. The purpose of the voucher is to ensure that the purchase is authorized and that both the purchase order and invoice have the same amount listed before a check is written in payment for the goods or supplies.

Once an accounting system has been established, a certified public accountant (CPA) should periodically audit,[14] or examine, the records to ensure that generally accepted accounting principles and procedures are being followed and that no fraud has occurred. Public corporations are required to make a public disclosure[15] of their financial statements to aid potential investors, stockholders, creditors, financial analysts, and others interested in the company.

Finally, accounting is basically an information system. Procedures for systematically recording and evaluating daily business activities help manage the financial information of a company. ◆

ACCOUNTING PRETEST

Select words from this list and write them in the blanks to complete the sentences.

amortize	depreciation	ledger
assets	disclosure	liabilities
audit	dividends	requisition
credit	equity	transaction
debit	intangible	voucher

1. A complete record of all assets, liabilities, and proprietorship items are kept in a(n) _____ .

2. A(n) _____ is the left-hand side of an account.

3. The amount that a business or property is worth beyond what is owed is called its _____ .

4. The _____ are entries on a balance sheet that express the value of the resources of a person, business, or organization.

5. A(n) _____ is money earned as a profit by a company and divided among the owners or stockholders.

6. A business with more _____ , or debts, than assets has a good chance of failing.

7. A piece of business or the carrying on of any kind of business is called a(n) _____ .

8. The right-hand side of an account in the ledger account is called a(n) _____ .

9. A(n) _____ is a lessening, or lowering, in price, value, or estimation and can be spread over time.

10. A(n) _____ asset is something that cannot be touched or felt, such as honesty or goodwill.

11. Choosing to make monthly payments on a house shows that you have decided to _____ your debt.

12. Written evidence of payment, such as a cancelled check, is called a(n) _____ .

13. A demand made for something, especially a formal written demand, is called a(n) _____ .

14. The company policy requires an annual _____ , or systematic examination, of business accounts.

15. A written statement of the company's financial position is an act of public _____ .

Answers to this pretest are in Appendix E.

Unless your instructor tells you to do otherwise, complete the exercises for each word that you missed on the pretest. The words, with their meanings and exercises, are in alphabetical order. The superscript numbers indicate where the words appeared in the reading selection so that you can refer to them when necessary. There are several types of exercises, but for each word you will be asked to write a sentence using context clues. (See Chapter 3 if you need information about how to create context clues.) You are also asked to perform some activity that will help you make your concept of the word personal. *Complete this activity thoughtfully, for creating a personalized concept of the word will help you remember it in the future.*

Answers to all the exercises are at the end of the exercise segment.

ACCOUNTING EXERCISES

Amortize[11]

am|or|tize (am'ər tīz, ə môr'-), *v.t.,* **-tized, -tiz|ing.**
1 to set money aside regularly in a special fund
to accumulate at interest, for future paying or
settling of (a debt or other liability). **2** *Law.* to
convey (property) to a body, especially an ec-
clesiastical body, which does not have the right
to sell or give it away, as in mortmain. [< Old
French *amortiss-,* stem of *amortir* deaden < *a-* to
+ *mort* death < Latin *mors, mortis*] — **am'or|tiz'a-
ble,** *adj.* — **am'or|ti|za'tion,** *n.* — **a|mor'tize-
ment,** *n.*

1. When you *amortize* a debt, you
   _____ a. pay it all at once.
   _____ b. continue to add to it.
   _____ c. write it off through payments over a certain period of time.
   _____ d. make payments every ten years.

2. The etymology of *amortize* shows that the word comes from the Old
   French *amortiss* (to + death). Use this information and your background knowledge to match the following:
   _____ a. mortify   aa. building or room where dead bodies
                                   are kept until burial or cremation

   _____ b. mortgage   bb. after death

   _____ c. mortal   cc. to give a lender a claim to one's prop-
                                   erty in case a debt is not paid when due

   _____ d. postmortem   dd. sure to die sometime

   _____ e. mortuary   ee. to wound (a person's feelings); to make
                                   a person feel humbled and ashamed;
                                   humiliate

3. Complete the verbal analogy.
   depreciate : value :: *amortize* : _____
   a. asset   c. credit
   b. debt   d. debit

4. Have you ever *amortized* a debt (credit cards, car loan, house mortgage,
   and so forth)? How did such a process affect your monthly budget?

   _____

   _____

5. Write a sentence correctly using *amortize.* (Be sure to include context
   clues to show you understand the meaning of the word.)

   _____

   _____

Assets[4]

as|sets (as′ets), *n.pl.* **1** things of value; all items of value owned by a person or business and constituting the resources of the person or business. Real estate, cash, securities, inventories, patents, and good will are assets. *His assets include a house, a car, stocks, bonds, and jewelry.* (Figurative.) *Honesty is one of the judge's most valuable assets.* **2** property that can be used to pay debts. **3** *Accounting.* the entries on a balance sheet that express in terms of money the value of the tangible things or intangible rights which constitute the resources of a person, business, or organization, as of a given date. [< Old French *asez* enough < Latin *ad satis* sufficiently (misunderstood as a plural noun "sufficient things")]

1. Complete the verbal analogy.
   debit : owed :: *assets* : _____
   - a. produced
   - b. claimed
   - c. owned
   - d. loaned

2. In which of the following sentences can *assets* be correctly placed in the blank?
   - _____ a. _____ are the economic resources of a business, such as land, buildings, and equipment.
   - _____ b. Businesses can have "liquid" _____ , which include cash, receivables, and supplies.
   - _____ c. He had many _____ and therefore had to amortize a debt.
   - _____ d. The businessman needed to locate his _____ , which were left on the answering machine.

3. The etymology of *assets* shows that the word comes from the Latin *ad satis* (sufficiently). Use this information and your background knowledge to match the following:
   - _____ a. satiety
   - _____ b. saturate
   - _____ c. satire
   - _____ d. satiate
   - _____ e. satisfy

   - aa. to feed fully; satisfy fully
   - bb. to give enough to (a person); meet or fulfill (as desires, hopes, or demands)
   - cc. to soak thoroughly; fill up
   - dd. the use of mockery, irony, or wit to attack or ridicule something
   - ee. the feeling of having had too much; disgust or weariness caused by excess

4. Write a sentence correctly using *assets*. (Be sure to include context clues to show you understand the meaning of the word.)

   _____

   _____

5. What tangible *assets* (money, clothes, motorcycle, car, house, and so forth) do you have? What intangible *assets* (honesty, fairness) do you possess?

   _____

   _____

Audit[14]

au|dit (ô′dit), *v., n.* —*v.t.* **1** to examine and check (business accounts) systematically and officially. **2** to attend (a class or course) as a listener without receiving academic credit. **3** make an energy audit of: *"Honeywell," he says, "would audit a building, identify conservation possibilities, install the equipment, and monitor its operation* (Christian Science Monitor). —*v.i.* to examine the correctness of a business account: *Auditing is the Government's chief tax enforcement weapon* (Wall Street Journal). [< noun]

—*n.* **1** a systematic and official examination and check of business accounts. **2** a statement of an account that has been examined and checked officially. **3** = energy audit: *Audits to determine the needs of various offices are being initiated* (Tuscaloosa News). **4** *Archaic.* **a** a hearing. **b** a judicial hearing of complaints.
[< Latin *audītus* a hearing < *audīre* hear]

1. Select the synonym(s) of *audit*.
   _____ a. transaction   _____ c. acceptance
   _____ b. examination   _____ d. inspection

2. Complete the verbal analogy.
   amortize : debt :: *audit* : _____
   a. ledger
   b. dividends
   c. assets
   d. financial records

3. The etymology of *audit* shows that the word comes from the Latin *audire* (to hear). Use this information and your background knowledge to match the following:

   _____ a. audiovisual   aa. a hearing to test the ability or suitability of a musician, actor, or other performer

   _____ b. audible   bb. attentive listening to speech sounds and patterns, as opposed to simple hearing

   _____ c. auding   cc. an instrument for measuring keenness and range of hearing

   _____ d. audiometer   dd. having to do with or involving the transmission or reception of both sounds and images

   _____ e. audition   ee. can be heard; loud enough to be heard

4. Why do you think it is important to conduct an *audit* of a company or business?

   _____

   _____

5. Write a sentence correctly using *audit*. (Be sure to include context clues to show you understand the meaning of the word.)

   _____

   _____

Credit³

cred|it (kred′it), *n., v.* —*n.* **1a** belief in the truth of something; faith; trust: *I know he is sure of his facts and put credit in what he says.* **b** personal influence or authority based on the confidence of others or on one's own reputation: *Buckingham ... resolved to employ all his credit to prevent the marriage* (David Hume). **c** credibility; trustworthiness: *His revelations destroy their credit by running into detail* (Emerson). **2a** trust in a person's ability and intention to pay: *This store will extend credit to you by opening a charge account in your name.* **b** one's reputation in money matters: *If you pay your bills on time, your credit will be good.* **3a** money in a person's bank account: *When I deposit this check, I will have a credit of fifty dollars in my savings account.* **b** the balance in a person's favor in an account: *His bookseller's statement shows a credit of $5.* **4** *Bookkeeping.* **a** the entry of money paid on account. **b** the right-hand side of an account where such entries are made. **c** the sum entered, or the total shown, on this side. **5** delayed payment; time allowed for delayed payment: *The store allowed us six months' credit on our purchase.* **6** favorable reputation; good name: *The mayor was a man of credit in the community.* SYN: repute, standing, honor. **7** praise, honor, recognition: *The person who does the work should get the credit. He claims no credit for the scheme.* SYN: commendation, esteem, appreciation. **8** a person or thing that brings honor or praise: *Benjamin Franklin's great scientific achievements were a credit to his young country. You are a credit to the school* (Dickens). **9a** an entry on a student's record showing that he has passed a course of study: *You must pass the examination to get credit for the course.* **b** a unit of work entered in this way: *He needs three credits to graduate.* **c** *British.* a mark between a mere pass and distinction, awarded in examinations. **10** Usually, **credits. a** an acknowledgment of the authorship or source of material used in a publication, work done on a dramatic show, radio or television program, or other artistic production: *The credits are often listed at the beginning of a motion picture.* **b** a listing of the producers, directors, actors, technicians, and others who have given their skills to a motion picture, radio or television show, or a play. *Abbr:* cr.
—*v.t.* **1** to have faith in; believe; trust: *I can credit all that you are telling me because I had a similar experience. I ... am content to credit my senses* (Samuel Johnson). **2a** to enter on the credit side of an account: *The bank credited fifty dollars to his savings account.* **b** to assign to as a credit: *The grocer was credited with the value of two hundred deposit bottles.* **3** to give credit in a bank account or other statement of account. **4** to put an entry on the record of (a student) showing that he has passed a course of study. **5** *Archaic.* to bring honor to. **6** *Obsolete.* to supply with goods on credit.

credit to, to ascribe to; attribute to: *The shortage of wheat was credited to lack of rain. Some excellent remarks were ... borrowed from and credited to Plato* (Oliver Wendell Holmes).
credit with, to think that one has; give recognition to: *You will have to credit him with some sense for not panicking during the fire.*
do credit to, to bring honor or praise to: *The winning team did credit to the school's reputation.*
give credit for, a to think that one has: *Give me credit for some brains.* **b** to give recognition to: *Give him credit for the idea.* [*They*] *give her credit for sincerity* (J. Wilson).
give credit to, to have faith in; believe; trust: *He gives no credit to kings or emperors* (James Mozley).
on credit, on a promise to pay later. When you buy anything and promise to pay for it later, you are getting it on credit. *He bought a new car on credit since he could not afford to make such a large purchase in cash.*
to one's credit, to bring honor to; be to the honor or praise of; worthy of approval: *It is to the students' credit that they hate war and social injustice* (Fred M. Hechinger).
[< Middle French *crédit* < Italian *credito,* learned borrowing from Latin *creditum* a loan < *crēdere* trust, entrust, lend (money)] —**cred′it|less,** *adj.*
▶ **Credit with, accredit with** mean to believe someone or something responsible for saying, doing, feeling, or causing something. **Credit** emphasizes the idea of believing, not always with enough reason or evidence: *You credit me with doing things I never thought of.* **Accredit** emphasizes the idea of accepting because of some proof: *We accredit Peary with having discovered the North Pole.*

1. The etymology of *credit* shows that the word comes from the Latin *credere* (to trust, entrust, or lend, as in money). Use this information and your background knowledge to match the following:

   _____ a. credo   aa. a base or wicked person; villain
   _____ b. credulous   bb. worthy of belief; believable; reliable
   _____ c. miscreant   cc. statement of belief; creed
   _____ d. credible   dd. too ready to believe; easily deceived
   _____ e. credence   ee. belief or credit; faith; trust

2. Select the synonym(s) of *credit.*

   _____ a. assets   _____ c. cash
   _____ b. abilities   _____ d. confidence

3. Which of the numbered and lettered dictionary definitions of *credit* best fits the word's use in the reading selection? _____

4. Write a sentence correctly using *credit*. (Be sure to include context clues to show you understand the meaning of the word.)

_____

_____

5. Have you ever applied for or received *credit*? For what? Do you have a *credit* card? What do you think of the large number of *credit* cards in our society today?

_____

_____

Debit[2]

deb|it (deb′it), *n., v. Bookkeeping.* —*n.* **1** an entry of something owed in an account. **2** the left-hand side of an account, where such entries are made. **3** the sum or total shown on this side. *Abbr:* dr.
—*v.t.* **1** to charge with or as a debt: *The bank debited his account $500.* **2** to enter on the debit side of an account.
[alteration of earlier *debte;* spelling influenced by Latin *dēbitum.* Compare etym. under **debt**.]

from **debt:**

[< Old French *dete,* or *debte* < Latin *dēbitum* (thing) owed, neuter past participle of *dēbēre* to owe; (originally) keep (something) from someone < *dē-* away + *habēre* have. Compare etym. under **debit**.]

1. Where is the location of a *debit* in an accounting system?
   _____ a. bottom   _____ c. left
   _____ b. right   _____ d. middle

2. The etymology of *debit* shows that the word comes from the Latin *debere* (to owe). Use this information and your background knowledge to match the following:
   _____ a. duty   aa. an act of civility or respect
   _____ b. debenture   bb. a person's right; what is owed to a person
   _____ c. endeavor   cc. a written acknowledgment of a debt
   _____ d. devoir(s)   dd. a thing that is right to do; what a person ought to do; obligation
   _____ e. due   ee. to try hard; make an effort; strive

3. Select the synonym(s) of *debit*.
   _____ a. notation   _____ c. asset
   _____ b. account   _____ d. entry

4. What is a recent *debit* that you had in either your savings or checking account?

_____

_____

5. Write a sentence correctly using *debit*. (Be sure to include context clues to show you understand the meaning of the word.)

_____

_____

Depreciation[9]

de|pre|ci|a|tion (di prē'shē ā'shən), *n.* **1a** a lessening or lowering in price, value, or estimation: *The depreciation of a car is greatest during its first year.* **b** such a loss figured as part of the cost of doing business: *Depreciation, of course, is a bookkeeping charge which reduces reported earnings but does not involve the expenditure of cash* (Wall Street Journal). **2** a reduction in the value of money: *Foreign currency depreciation is a result of economic depression in the country concerned.* **3** *Figurative.* a speaking slightingly (of); belittling; disparagement.

de|pre|ci|ate (di prē'shē āt), *v.,* **-at|ed, -at|ing.** — *v.t.* **1** to lessen the value or price of: *The government has the power to depreciate currency.* **2** *Figurative.* to speak slightingly of; belittle: *That lazy boy is always depreciating the value of exercise.* **SYN:** underrate, disparage. — *v.i.* to lessen in value: *The longer an automobile is driven the more it depreciates.* [< Latin *dēpretiāre* (with English *-ate¹*) < *dē-* down + *pretium* price] — **de|pre'ci|at'ing|ly,** *adv.*

1. Which of the following would qualify for *depreciation*?

_____ a. a computer   _____ c. a food supply

_____ b. a water bill   _____ d. a car

2. The etymology of *depreciation* (see *depreciate*) shows that the word comes from the Latin *depretiare* (down + price). Use this information and your background knowledge to match the following:

_____ a. premium   aa. to think highly of; recognize the worth or quality of

_____ b. precious   bb. a reward, especially given as an incentive to buy; prize

_____ c. appraise   cc. a nearly correct amount; close estimate

_____ d. approximation   dd. to estimate the value, amount, quality, or merit of; judge

_____ e. appreciate   ee. having great value; worth much; valuable; of great importance

3. Select the synonym(s) of *depreciation*.

_____ a. accelerate   _____ c. lessen

_____ b. decrease   _____ d. increase

4. Write a sentence correctly using *depreciation*. (Be sure to include context clues to show you understand the meaning of the word.)

_____

_____

5. How does *depreciation* affect a person's equity? What do you own that you could consider for *depreciation*?

_____

_____

Disclosure[15]

dis|clo|sure (dis klō'zhər), *n.* **1** the act of disclos-
ing: *disclosure of a secret. His reluctant disclosure of his whereabouts led to many misunder-
standings.* **2** a thing disclosed; revelation: *The
newspaper's disclosures shocked the public.*

dis|close (dis klōz'), *v.,* **-closed, -clos|ing,** *n.*
—*v.t.* **1** to open to view; uncover: *The lifting of
the curtain disclosed a beautiful painting.* **2** to
make known; reveal: *This letter discloses a secret.* sʏɴ: See syn. under **reveal**. **3** *Obsolete.* to
unfold; unfasten. —*n. Obsolete.* disclosure.

1. Select the synonym(s) of *disclosure*.

   _____ a. transaction   _____ c. acknowledgment

   _____ b. requisition   _____ d. revelation

2. In which of the following sentences can *disclosure* be correctly placed in the blank?

   _____ a. The student needed to obtain a _____ before he could register.

   _____ b. A summary of accounting principles a company follows should be part of its _____ .

   _____ c. The secretary needed a _____ from the president before she could order new supplies.

   _____ d. The annual report of a company, which includes its financial status, is a form of _____ .

3. Why do companies make public *disclosures*?

   _____ a. to discuss recent audits

   _____ b. to present employee job descriptions

   _____ c. to acknowledge new board members

   _____ d. to inform stockholders and others of the company's financial status

4. Have you ever read an annual report of a company that is the public *disclosure* of its financial status? How might this information affect you if you were a stockholder in the company?

   _____

   _____

5. Write a sentence correctly using *disclosure*. (Be sure to include context clues to show you understand the meaning of the word.)

   _____

   _____

Dividends[7]

div|i|dend (div'ə dend), *n.* **1** a number or quantity to be divided by another: *In 8 ÷ 2, 8 is the divi-
dend.* **2** money earned as profit by a company and divided among the owners or stockholders of the company. **3** a share of such money. **4** a re-
fund of part of the premiums paid to an insur-
ance company, given to a person holding a participating insurance policy out of the com-

pany's surplus earnings: *With our policy-holder dividends your total savings can be really surprising* (Newsweek). **5** *Law.* a sum of money divided among the creditors of a bankrupt estate. **6** *Especially British.* a bonus: *Soldiers are citi-* *zens of death's grey land, Drawing no dividend from time's tomorrows* (Siegfried Sassoon). [< Latin *dīvidendum* (thing) to be divided; neuter gerundive of *dīvidere;* see etym. under **divide**]

1. In which of the following sentences is *dividends* used correctly?

   _____ a. The insurance company filed its dividends of the insurance policy.

   _____ b. After the board of directors had given its approval, shareholders were sent their year-end dividends.

   _____ c. Sometimes shares of stock are given to stockholders in addition to cash dividends.

   _____ d. The dividends were considered a liability by the policyholder.

2. Who might receive *dividends?*

   _____ a. a stockholder   _____ c. a policyholder

   _____ b. a mortgage lender _____ d. a company owner

3. Which of the numbered dictionary definitions of *dividend* best fits the word's use in the reading selection? _____

4. Write a sentence correctly using *dividends*. (Be sure to include context clues to show you understand the meaning of the word.)

   _____

   _____

5. Is it a good idea to put *dividends* that you might receive into a savings account? Why or why not?

   _____

   _____

Equity[6]

eq|ui|ty (ek′wə tē), *n., pl.* **-ties. 1** fairness; justice: *The judge was noted for the equity of his decisions.* SYN: impartiality. **2** what is fair and just: *In all equity, he should pay for the damage he did.* SYN: justice, right. **3a** a system of rules and principles as to what is fair or just. Equity supplements common law and statute law in the United States and the Commonwealth by covering cases in which fairness and justice require a settlement not covered by the common law. In the United States, law and equity are usually administered by the same court. **b** a claim or right according to equity. **c** fairness in the adjustment of conflicting interests. **d** = equity of redemption. **4a** the amount that a property is worth beyond what is owed on it. **b** a share in the ownership of a business; stock: *Leading industrial equities were fairly firm on selective demand today, although the best prices were not always maintained* (New York Times). [< Old French *equite*, learned borrowing from Latin *aequitās* < *aequus* even, just]

1. Select the synonym(s) of *equity*.

   _____ a. liabilities   _____ c. debit

   _____ b. impartiality   _____ d. stock

2. Which of the numbered dictionary definitions of *equity* best fits the word's use in the reading selection? _____

3. In which of the following sentences can *equity* be correctly placed in the blank?

_____ a. The owner's _____ needed to be entered in the ledger account.

_____ b. The firm needed to calculate its debits, or _____.

_____ c. The difference between the assets and the liabilities of a company is called its _____ .

_____ d. The company had a large _____, which included money invested in the company and its net earnings that had not been withdrawn by the owner.

4. Do you have *equity* in any tangible property such as a car, house, boat, or other item? If not, what would you like to have some *equity* in and why?

_____

_____

5. Write a sentence correctly using *equity*. (Be sure to include context clues to show you understand the meaning of the word.)

_____

_____

Intangible[10]

in|tan|gi|ble (in tan′jə bəl), *adj., n. —adj.* **1** not capable of being touched or felt: *Sound and light are intangible.* **syn:** insubstantial, impalpable. **2** *Figurative.* not easily grasped by the mind; vague: *She had that intangible something called charm.* —*n.* something intangible, such as good will. —**in|tan′gi|ble|ness,** *n.* —**in|tan′gi|bly,** *adv.*

1. Complete the verbal analogy.
   tangible : physical :: *intangible* : _____
   a. palpable   c. substantial
   b. nonmaterial   d. touchable

2. Select the synonym(s) of *intangible*.
   _____ a. flexible   _____ c. insubstantial
   _____ b. intellectual   _____ d. impalpable

3. Is the following sentence a literal or figurative (symbolic) use of *intangible*? (See the dictionary entry.)
   "He had an *intangible* understanding of the nature of the problem."
   _____ a. literal
   _____ b. figurative

4. Write a sentence correctly using *intangible*. (Be sure to include context clues to show you understand the meaning of the word.)

_____

_____

5. What do you value that is *intangible* in your life (health, friendship, intelligence, and so forth)?

_____

_____

Ledger[1]

ledg|er (lej′ər), *n.*, *v.* — *n.* **1a** a book of accounts in which a business keeps a record of all money transactions. **b** the book of final entry in book-keeping and accounting, where a complete record of all assets, liabilities, and proprietorship items are kept. It shows the changes that occur in these items during the month as a result of business operations carried on, by means of debits and credits. **2** a flat stone slab covering a grave. **3** a horizontal member of a scaffold, attached to the uprights and supporting the putlogs. **4a** Also, **leger**. = ledger bait. **b** = ledger tackle. — *v.i.* to fish with a ledger. [probably Middle English *leggen* lay[1]. Compare Dutch *ligger, legger* ledger.]

1. In which of the following sentences is *ledger* used correctly?
   _____ a. The small company entered all the charges to and payments from customers in a single-entry ledger account.
   _____ b. The secretary left a phone message in the ledger.
   _____ c. The accounting cycle includes making debit and credit entries in a general ledger.
   _____ d. The business manager used the ledger to write a business letter.

2. A *ledger* is a record book of financial matters for a business. What are other types of record books?
   _____ a. an address book   _____ c. a phone book
   _____ b. a calendar   _____ d. a journal

3. Who would probably need to see a *ledger* for a company?
   _____ a. a customer   _____ c. a bookkeeper
   _____ b. an accountant   _____ d. a company president

4. Have you ever kept a *ledger* for your personal money transactions? Could you compare a ledger to a checkbook? Why or why not?

_____

_____

5. Write a sentence correctly using *ledger*. (Be sure to include context clues to show you understand the meaning of the word.)

_____

_____

Liabilities[5]

li|a|bil|i|ty (lī′ə bil′ə tē), *n., pl.* **-ties.** **1** the state of being susceptible: *liability to disease.* **syn:** susceptibility. **2** the state of being under obligation: *liability for a debt.* **3** something that is to one's disadvantage: *His poor handwriting is a liability in getting a job as a clerk.* **syn:** handicap, impediment. **liabilities,** the debts or other financial obligations of a business, for money, goods, or services received: *A business with more liabilities than assets is bound to fail.*

1. In which of the following sentences is *liabilities* used correctly?
   _____ a. The company's liabilities were larger than their assets, and they were in financial trouble.
   _____ b. His liabilities included his charming personality and his trustworthiness.
   _____ c. The company car, office building, and machinery that had been paid for composed the company's liabilities.
   _____ d. A company can have short-term and long-term liabilities that they must pay.

2. Select the synonym(s) of *liabilities*.
   _____ a. obligation   _____ c. selection
   _____ b. permission   _____ d. indebtedness

3. Which of the following are part of a company's *liabilities*?
   _____ a. credits   _____ c. assets
   _____ b. debts   _____ d. financial obligations

4. Write a sentence correctly using *liabilities*. (Be sure to include context clues to show you understand the meaning of the word.)

   _____

   _____

5. Do you have any large *liabilities*, or financial obligations? If not, what do you think are the most common *liabilities* for adults today?

   _____

   _____

Requisition[13]

req|ui|si|tion (rek'wə zish'ən), *n., v.* —*n.* **1** the act of requiring: *His requisition of the car prevented others from using it.* **2** a demand made, especially a formal written demand: *The requisition of supplies for troops included new shoes, uniforms, and blankets.* **3** the condition of being required for use or called into service: *The car was in constant requisition for errands.* **4** an essential condition; requirement. —*v.t.* **1** to demand or take by authority: *to requisition supplies, horses, or labor.* **SYN**: commandeer. **2** to make demands upon: *The hospital requisitioned the city for more funds.*

1. In which of the following sentences is *requisition* used correctly?
   _____ a. The requisition was included in the message on the phone machine.
   _____ b. A requisition was signed by the president before the office equipment could be ordered.

_____ c. The requisition for the additional software was lost in the mail.

_____ d. The company needed a requisition from the stockholders.

2. Which of the numbered dictionary definitions of *requisition* best fits the word's use in the reading selection? _____

3. Select the synonym(s) of *requisition*.

_____ a. transaction   _____ c. debit

_____ b. demand   _____ d. request

4. What types of items do you think a company would include on a *requisition* for office supplies?

_____

_____

5. Write a sentence correctly using *requisition*. (Be sure to include context clues to show you understand the meaning of the word.)

_____

_____

Transaction[8]

trans|ac|tion (tran zak′shən, -sak′-), *n.* **1** the carrying on of any kind of business: *The store manager attends to the transaction of important matters himself.* **2** a piece of business: *A record is kept of every transaction of the firm.* **SYN:** proceeding, deal, matter, affair. **3** *Psychology.* any event or situation that is determined by a person's perception or participation rather than by external factors.
transactions, a record of what was done at the meetings of a society, club, or other group: *What the club says has an audience far beyond Manchester, because its transactions are sent to li-* braries in this country and to American libraries, including Harvard, the Library of Congress, and the main library in New York (Manchester Guardian). *Abbr:* trans.
[< Latin *trānsāctiō, -ōnis* < *trānsigere;* see etym. under **transact**].

from **transact:**

[< Latin *trānsāctus,* past participle of *trānsigere* accomplish < *trāns-* through + *agere* to drive]

1. In which of the following sentences can *transaction* be correctly placed in the blank?

_____ a. Each business _____ is entered on the balance sheet.

_____ b. The ledger provides a financial record of each _____ of the company.

_____ c. The student needed a _____ to complete the assignment.

_____ d. The _____ allowed the engine to run more efficiently.

2. Which of the numbered dictionary definitions of *transaction* best fits the word's use in the reading selection? _____

3. The etymology of *transaction* (see *transact*) shows that the word comes

from the Latin *agere* (to drive). Use this information and your background knowledge to match the following:

_____ a. antagonize   aa. a person who takes a leading part; active supporter; champion

_____ b. stratagem   bb. a teacher of children; schoolmaster

_____ c. demagogue   cc. to make an enemy of; arouse dislike in

_____ d. protagonist   dd. a popular leader who stirs up the people by appealing to their emotions and prejudices

_____ e. pedagogue   ee. a scheme or trick for deceiving an enemy

4. Write a sentence correctly using *transaction*. (Be sure to include context clues to show you understand the meaning of the word.)

_____

_____

5. What method do you use to record your financial *transactions* (checkbook, savings account passbook, personal journal or diary)? If you do not now have some sort of recording system, what might you use in the future and why?

_____

_____

Voucher[12]

vouch|er[1] (vou′chər), *n.* **1** a person or thing that vouches for something. **2** a written evidence of payment; receipt. Canceled checks returned to a person from his bank are vouchers.
vouch (vouch), *v., n.* —*v.i.* **1** to be responsible; give a guarantee (for): *I can vouch for the truth of the story. The principal vouched for the boy's honesty.* **2** to give evidence or assurance of a fact (for): *The success of the campaign vouches for the candidate's popularity.*
—*v.t.* **1** to guarantee (as a statement or document) to be true or accurate; confirm; bear witness to; attest. **2** to support or uphold with evidence; back with proof. **3** to support or substantiate (as a claim or title) by vouchers. **4** to cite, quote, or appeal to (as authority, example, or a passage in a book) in support or justification as of a view. **5** *Law.* to call into court to give warranty of title. **6** to sponsor or recommend (a person or thing); support; back. **7** *Archaic.* to call to witness.
—*n. Obsolete.* an assertion, declaration, or attestation of truth or fact.
[Middle English *vouchen* < Anglo-French *voucher,* Old French *vochier* < Latin *vocāre* call]

1. What is an example of a *voucher*?

_____ a. a receipt   _____ c. a money order

_____ b. a bill   _____ d. a cancelled check

2. The etymology of *voucher* (see *vouch*) shows that the word comes from the Latin *vocare* (to call). Use this information and your background knowledge to match the following:

_____ a. evoke   aa. to make angry; vex

_____ b. vocation   bb. to take back; repeal; cancel; withdraw

_____ c. revoke   cc. a particular occupation, business, profession, or trade

_____ d. advocate   dd. to call forth; bring out

_____ e. provoke   ee. to speak or write in favor of; recommend publicly; support

3. Which of the numbered dictionary definitions of *voucher* best fits the word's use in the reading selection? _____

4. What is the most common type of *voucher* that you receive each month as a record of payments that you have made for purchases?

_____

_____

5. Write a sentence correctly using *voucher*. (Be sure to include context clues to show you understand the meaning of the word.)

_____

_____

ANSWERS TO CHAPTER 17 EXERCISES

Amortize: **1.** c   **2.** ee, cc, dd, bb, aa   **3.** b (example)
Assets: **1.** c (definition)   **2.** a, b   **3.** ee, cc, dd, aa, bb
Audit: **1.** b, d   **2.** d (example)   **3.** dd, ee, bb, cc, aa
Credit: **1.** cc, dd, aa, bb, ee   **2.** a, c, d   **3.** 4abc
Debit: **1.** c   **2.** dd, cc, ee, aa, bb   **3.** a, d
Depreciation: **1.** a, d   **2.** bb, ee, dd, cc, aa   **3.** b, c
Disclosure: **1.** c, d   **2.** b, d   **3.** d
Dividends: **1.** b, c   **2.** a, c, d   **3.** 2
Equity: **1.** b, d   **2.** 4a   **3.** a, c, d
Intangible: **1.** b (definition)   **2.** c, d   **3.** b
Ledger: **1.** a, c   **2.** a, b, d   **3.** b, c, d
Liabilities: **1.** a, d   **2.** a, d   **3.** b, d
Requisition: **1.** b, c   **2.** *n.* 2   **3.** b, d
Transaction: **1.** a, b   **2.** 2   **3.** cc, ee, dd, aa, bb
Voucher: **1.** a, d   **2.** dd, cc, bb, ee, aa   **3.** 2

If you missed any of the items in the exercises, return to the exercise and to the dictionary definitions to see where you went wrong. Remember: If you get something right, you only affirm that you knew it. If you get something wrong and understand why, *you have learned something*.

ACCOUNTING POSTTEST

Fill in the blanks with the words from this list.

| amortize | depreciation | ledger |
| assets | disclosure | liabilities |

audit   dividends   requisition
credit   equity   transaction
debit   intangible   voucher

1. _____ is another word for debts, or other financial obligations.

2. *Proceeding, deal, matter,* or *affair* are synonyms of _____ .

3. A loss figured as part of the cost of doing business is called a(n) _____ .

4. A(n) _____ is a book of business transactions and can be structured as single entry or double entry.

5. The amount that a property is worth beyond what is owed on it is called the _____ .

6. _____ refers to money earned as profit by a company and divided among the owners or stockholders.

7. *Insubstantial* is a synonym of _____ .

8. A receipt is a type of _____ .

9. _____ means "to set money aside regularly for future payment or settlement of a debt or other liability."

10. An act of uncovering, revelation, or opening to public view is a(n) _____ .

11. Money paid on an account or a delayed payment is known as a(n) _____ .

12. A(n) _____ is a demand or requirement, often written.

13. Resources that are owned and paid for are _____ .

14. An entry of an amount owed, or the left-hand side of an account, where such entries are made is called a(n) _____ .

15. An examination and check of business accounts is a(n) _____ .

Answers to this posttest are in the Instructor's Manual.

If you missed any of the words, you may need to return to the exercises and to the dictionary entries to see why your concepts for some words are incomplete.

BUSINESS: COMPUTER SCIENCE AND DATA PROCESSING

OVERVIEW

Computer science is the study of computers, including their design, programming, and operation. This field is concerned with the interaction of man and machine and with the application of computers in contemporary society.

Computer science programs usually include coursework in mathematics (geometry and calculus), statistics, computer languages, information structures, and computer logic design.

Students who receive degrees in computer science are prepared for a variety of careers in business, industry, and government. This includes work in the areas of systems analysis, systems programming, applications programming, data engineering, data communications, and software engineering.

The introductory textbooks in computer science are a combination of expository and instructional, or process analysis, in format. They present concepts and generalizations along with instructions and the analysis of a process, particularly in the areas of programming and computer languages.

The vocabulary in computer science is an interesting mixture of general and special-ized terms and acronyms. General terms that have a specialized meaning in computer science include boot, chip, disk, *and* memory. *Specialized terminology includes such words as* on-line, debug, *and* software. *There are many acronyms (words formed from the initial letters of a series of words) as terminology for operations, equipment, and procedures. These include RAM (random access memory), CPU (central processing unit), and BASIC (Beginners All-Purpose Symbolic Instruction*

Code). You may add other terms you discover from your studies related to computer science on the forms in Appendix D.

VOCABULARY SELF-EVALUATION

The following words will be introduced in this reading selection. Place a check mark (√) in front of any that you know thoroughly and use in your speech and writing. Place a question mark (?) in front of any that you recognize but do not use yourself.

_____ binary	_____ documentation	_____ nanosecond
_____ byte	_____ generation	_____ output
_____ chip	_____ input	_____ peripheral
_____ cursor	_____ interface	_____ programming
_____ disk	_____ modem	_____ terminal

COMPUTER LITERACY: SOME BASICS

Microcomputers have revolutionized the worlds of business, education, and industry and have influenced our lives in many important ways. Until recently, access to computers has been confined to engineers and programmers. With this new technology comes the need to be computer literate.

The present-day computer represents the most recent advance in more complicated operations with numbers that began almost five thousand years ago with the Chinese abacus as the world's first calculating machine. The history of computers can be chronicled as a generation,[1] with each new change evolving from the models of an earlier period. In 1835 the English inventor Charles Babbage formulated the first programmable computer with his "analytical engine," which had both a storage unit and an arithmetic unit. At the end of the nineteenth century, Hans Hollerith, an American statistician, devised the punch-card system to tabulate data from the 1880 census. In 1911 Hollerith founded a company to manufacture this system, which later became known as International Business Machines (IBM).

Some historians consider the first generation of computers to include the creation of the room-size Mark I (1939); the first fully automatic electromechanical digital computer (using vacuum tubes), the ENIAC (1946); and the first electronic IBM computer for the commercial market (1951). In the 1960s, classified as the second generation, the use of transis-

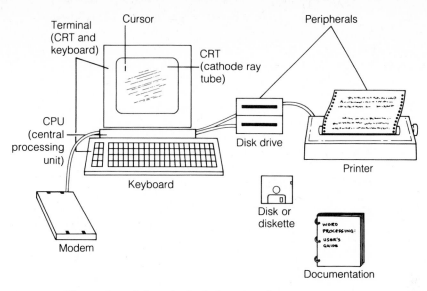

Illustration of the principal elements of a computer system

tors and time-sharing arrangements made computers more available and affordable to both business and education.

In the third generation of the 1970s, the advent of miniaturization, owing to the production of the silicon chip[2] that can accommodate thousands of electrical circuits in a small space, signaled the beginning of the microcomputer and minicomputer industry. In the fourth generation of the 1980s, these microcircuit computers operate in nanoseconds[3] (one-billionth of a second), which represents a thousand times the calculational speed of the second-generation computers. With this generation, the computer has become a personal and portable tool for the home as it had been for education and business. Over these generations, computers have become smaller, faster, and more affordable.

When you look at a computer, you usually see the physical part of the computer, or hardware, such as a keyboard (like a typewriter), a video display unit (like a television screen), and disk drives (like a box that holds small records). The keyboard and the video display unit are examples of a terminal,[4] which is an input/output device that communicates with the central processing unit (CPU) of the computer.

The video display unit is also called a CRT (cathode ray tube) on which is displayed data such as characters or graphics. A cursor[5] is the position indicator on the screen of the CRT and is usually a flashing or nonflashing square or rectangle. A disk drive, printer, or cassette tape recorder can be classified as peripherals[6] since they are equipment, usually hardware, that is external to the computer itself and connected to the computer with an interface. An interface[7] is a circuit that allows one type of electronic unit to communicate with another.

The computer's basic functions include input,[8] processing, memory, and output.[9] Input is the information fed into the computer for processing, usually from the keyboard, game paddle, light pen, mouse, or digitizer. Output is the information, or results, generated by a computer during the running of a program.

The smallest unit of information a computer circuit can recognize as input via an electrical signal is called a "bit." A bit represents a binary[10] digit, derived from the binary numbering system that makes use of 1s and 0s. (1 means that the electrical current is on; 0 means that the current is off.) In most microcomputers, eight bits make up one byte,[11] which is the sequence that represents a single character (letter, digit, or other symbol). All symbols that appear on a computer keyboard are called "characters" and are used to represent data.

Another function of the computer is processing. In the microcomputer all of the processing of data and bytes of instruction occurs in the CPU, with its arithmetic logic unit, control unit, and register. Each computer microprocessor has its own internal "language," or instructions, by which it functions. Machine language is the programming[12] language used by the microprocessor. Another programming language is BASIC, commonly used because many of its instructions are English words. Programs or segments of programs are also called software.

Memory is another function of the computer. The microprocessor has a limited capacity for retaining information and requires memory chips for additional information or storage. The amount of memory a computer has is expressed in kilobytes (K) as a multiple of 1,024 bytes. There are two main forms of memory: ROM and RAM. ROM is read-only memory programmed by the chip manufacturer and unalterable. RAM is random access memory and is the main type of memory used in a microcomputer. The computer can find one piece of information in RAM in about the same amount of time, no matter where it is stored.

Memory can be stored in a mass storage system outside the microprocessor on magnetic tape or on a computer disk.[13] A disk (hard or floppy) is made of magnetic-coated material and is shaped like a record. Disks are put into the disk drives to enter data into the computer for additional processing or memory. Most software programs are stored on disks.

The last important function of the computer is output, or the results generated by the computer after processing data. The most common output devices are the CRT (for a temporary display of information) and the line printer (for a hard, or permanent, copy of information). Other output devices include a voice synthesizer, which simulates human speech, and a music synthesizer, which produces musical sounds.

A computer can interact with other computers through a modem,[14] which is an input/output device that changes computer signals into tones that can be transmitted or received over telephone lines. With any piece of hardware or software comes documentation. Documentation[15] is the instruction manual and is especially important for use with sophisticated software application programs, and for the correct interfacing and functioning of peripherals.

Computers are an everyday part of modern life, and since the technology is constantly changing, being computer literate is an essential skill in today's society. ◆

COMPUTER SCIENCE PRETEST

Select words from this list and write them in the blanks to complete the sentences.

binary   documentation   nanosecond
byte   generation   output

chip   input   peripheral
cursor   interface   programming
disk   modem   terminal

1. A tiny piece of silicon imprinted or engraved with one or more micro-circuits or integrated circuits is a(n) _____.

2. Some of the fastest computers process information in _____s.

3. The information, or results, generated by a computer during the running of a program is called the _____.

4. A(n) _____ consists of a keyboard and a video display unit that are connected to the computer for communication and control processing.

5. The most common _____s used with microcomputers are disk drives, printers, and cassette tape recorders.

6. The sequence of eight bits that represents a single character is a(n) _____.

7. A(n) _____ connects the computer and the telephone line and allows for communication with other computers.

8. A(n) _____ is a position indicator on the screen that normally is a flashing or nonflashing square or rectangle.

9. BASIC is a widely used beginners' high-level _____ language.

10. Computers use _____ numbers consisting of 1s and 0s to store and manipulate information.

11. One of the cheapest forms of mass storage is the _____, which can be either hard or floppy.

12. Each piece of hardware and software comes with an instruction manual, or _____.

13. The first _____ of computers was noted for large size, slow processing time, and great expense.

14. The information given to the computer, usually from the keyboard, game paddle, or light pen, is known as _____.

15. A(n) _____ is used to connect two devices (computers and peripherals) that cannot be used directly together.

Answers to this pretest are in Appendix E.

Unless your instructor tells you to do otherwise, complete the exercises for each word that you missed on the pretest. The words, with their meanings and exercises, are in alphabetical order. The superscript numbers indicate where the words appeared in the reading selection so that you can refer to them when necessary. There are several types of exercises, but for each word you will be asked to write a sentence using context clues. (See Chapter 3 if you need information about how to create context clues.) You

are also asked to perform some activity that will help you make your concept of the word personal. *Complete this activity thoughtfully, for creating a personalized concept of the word will help you remember it in the future.*
Answers to all the exercises are at the end of the exercise segment.

COMPUTER SCIENCE EXERCISES

Binary[10]

bi|na|ry (bī′nər ē), *adj., n., pl.* **-ries.** —*adj.* consisting of two; involving two; dual: *a binary number, a binary choice such as yes or no.*
—*n.* **1** a set of two things; pair. **2** = binary star.
[< Late Latin *bīnārius* < Latin *bīnī* two at a time]

1. The etymology of *binary* shows that the word comes from the Latin *bini* (two at a time). Use this information and your background knowledge to match the following:

   _____ a. bicameral   aa. having two leaves
   _____ b. biennial   bb. criminal offense of marrying one person while still legally married to another
   _____ c. bifoliate   cc. having two points, as the crescent moon
   _____ d. bigamy   dd. composed of two houses, chambers, or branches
   _____ e. bicuspid   ee. lasting or living for two years

2. Complete the verbal analogy.
   triad : three :: *binary* : _____
   a. one   c. four
   b. two   d. five

3. In which of the following sentences is *binary* used correctly?
   _____ a. There is a separate binary system for each piece of hardware.
   _____ b. A binary requires three numbers to function.
   _____ c. "Bit" is a short way of saying "binary digit."
   _____ d. Computers use binary numbers to store and manipulate information.

4. Write a sentence correctly using *binary*. (Be sure to include context clues to show you understand the meaning of the word.)

   _____

   _____

5. Describe the *binary* system. Do you think that each computer uses the same *binary* code as its machine language? Why or why not?

   _____

   _____

Byte[11]

byte (bīt), *n.* a unit of eight bits in a computer memory. [< *b* (inar)*y* (digi)*t e*(ight)]

1. How many bits in a *byte*?

   _____ a. 2   _____ c. 6
   _____ b. 4   _____ d. 8

2. Fill in the missing parts to show the origin of the word *byte*.

   b( )y   ( )t   e( )

3. In what part of the computer would you find a *byte*?

   _____ a. the modem   _____ c. the memory
   _____ b. the monitor   _____ d. a peripheral

4. Why would it be advantageous to have a computer with kilo*bytes*?

   _____

   _____

5. Write a sentence correctly using *byte*. (Be sure to include context clues to show you understand the meaning of the word.)

   _____

   _____

Chip[2]

chip[1] (chip), *n., v.,* **chipped, chip|ping.** —*n.* **1** a small, thin piece cut from wood or broken from stone or pottery: *They used the chips of wood to start a fire.* SYN: fragment, flake. **2** the place where a small, thin piece has been cut or broken off: *This plate has a chip on the edge.* **3** a small, thin piece of food or candy. Potato chips are fried slices of potato. **4a** a round, flat piece used for counting or to represent money in games: *poker chips.* SYN: counter. **b** = bargaining chip: *The President could have used the need for grain as a chip in the ongoing SALT negotiations* (Maclean's). **5a** a strip of wood, palm leaf, or straw, used in making baskets or hats: *hats in chip.* **b** a basket or box made of very thin strips of wood: *Strawberries cost $1 a chip.* **6** a piece of dried dung, used for fuel in some regions: *The trappers made a fire of buffalo chips.* **7** a small piece cut off a diamond. **8** *Figurative.* **a** a worthless or trivial thing: *Basil did not care a chip* (Holme Lee). **b** a dried-up, parched, or tasteless substance: *meat burned to a chip.* **9** *Golf.* = chip shot. **10a** a tiny piece of silicon imprinted or engraved with one or more microcircuits. **b** = microcircuit. [< verb]

—*v.i.* **1** to cut or break off in small, thin pieces; become chipped: *This china chips easily. A poor grade of paint soon chips off.* SYN: flake. **2** to make a bet, especially in poker; chip in. **3** *Golf.* to make a chip shot. —*v.t.* **1** to separate (small pieces) by cutting or breaking: *He chipped off the old paint. They chipped several small pieces of stone from the walls* (Charles Kingsley). **2** to shape by cutting at the surface or edge with an ax or chisel, especially by removing small portions at a time: **a** to make by this method: *The Indians chipped flint arrowheads.* **b** to alter, especially to damage or disfigure, by breaking off pieces: *The vase had been chipped when it fell.* **3** to hew or chop with an ax, adz, or other tool: *The men were chipping and cutting wood.* **4** (of young birds) to break (the shell) when hatching: *Thou isle . . . that saw the unfledged eaglet chip his shell* (Byron). **5a** *Golf.* to hit (a ball) with a chip shot. **b** *Tennis and Soccer.* to slice or cut at (a ball); chop. **6** *British Slang.* to make fun of; jeer; chaff. **7** *Obsolete.* to pare (bread) by cutting the crust off.

1. What is the approximate size of a computer *chip*?

   _____ a. small   _____ c. large
   _____ b. medium   _____ d. minute

2. Which of the numbered and lettered dictionary definitions of *chip* best fits the word's use in the reading selection? _____

3. Check any appropriate response to the following statement:
"We need to increase the memory *chips* in our computer."

_____ a. We do not have enough counters to work the computer.

_____ b. The new software requires 512K, and we only have 64K.

_____ c. The computer has some parts missing.

_____ d. We need additional memory.

4. How did the development of the silicon *chip* revolutionize the computer industry?

_____

_____

5. Write a sentence correctly using *chip*. (Be sure to include context clues to show you understand the meaning of the word.)

_____

_____

Cursor[5]

cur|sor (kėr′sər), *n.* **1** the sliding glass of a slide rule or optical instrument, having a fine hairline on it, used to facilitate computing or sighting. **2** a flashing movable pointer on a computer display screen, indicating the position where a deletion, insertion, or other operation takes place. [< Latin *cursor* runner < *currere* run]

1. Which of the numbered dictionary definitions of *cursor* best fits the word's use in the reading selection? _____

2. The etymology of *cursor* shows that the word comes from the Latin *currere* (to run). Use this information and your background knowledge to match the following:

_____ a. courier   aa. formal and lengthy discussion of a subject, either written or spoken

_____ b. cursive   bb. turning or applying to a person or thing for aid

_____ c. discourse   cc. a messenger, especially one on urgent or official business

_____ d. precursor   dd. one that precedes and indicates or announces that someone or something is to come; forerunner

_____ e. recourse   ee. writing or printing in which the letters are joined together; flowing

3. In which of the following sentences is *cursor* used correctly?

_____ a. He looked at the cursor on the keyboard.

_____ b. The cursor is an output device that can be transferred to the line printer.

_____ c. The blinking cursor indicated the place to start typing a new letter using the word-processing program.

CHAPTER EIGHTEEN

_____ d. The arrow key controlled the direction of the cursor on the CRT.

4. Write a sentence correctly using *cursor*. (Be sure to include context clues to show you understand the meaning of the word.)

_____

_____

5. What is the purpose of the *cursor*? What type *cursors* have you seen or worked with?

_____

_____

Disk[13]

disk (disk), *n., v.* —*n.* **1** a thin, round, flat object shaped like a coin. **2** a round, flat surface, or a surface that seems so: *the sun's disk.* **3** a round, flat part in a plant or animal: *The yellow center of a daisy is a disk.* **4** *Anatomy, Zoology.* any one of various round, flat structures, especially the mass of fibrous cartilage lying between the bodies of adjacent vertebrae. **5** anything resembling a disk. **6** = phonograph record. **7** a floppy disk, hard disk, or similar magnetic disk for storing data: *Disks contain more recorded information now than ever before* (New York Times). **8** the puck used in ice hockey. **9** *Obsolete.* a discus. —*v.t.* to work (the soil) with a disk harrow. Also, **disc**. [< Latin *discus* < Greek *diskos* discus. See etym. of doublets **dais, desk, discus, dish.**] —**disk'like'**, *adj.*

1. In which of the following sentences is *disk* used correctly?
   _____ a. The software program contains only one floppy disk, with one side for the program and the other side for storage of data.
   _____ b. When you drop a disk, it's known as a slipped disk.
   _____ c. The disk did not boot correctly, and the program would not run, so we returned it to the manufacturer.
   _____ d. The latest development in the disk for use with a computer is the compact disk.

2. Complete the verbal analogy.
   interface : connection :: *disk* : _____
   a. input   c. peripheral
   b. output   d. storage

3. Which of the numbered dictionary definitions of *disk* best fits the word's use in the reading selection? _____

4. What is the purpose of a computer *disk*? What kind of information can be stored on a *disk*? If you've used a *disk* before, what was it or what could it do?

_____

_____

BUSINESS: COMPUTER SCIENCE AND DATA PROCESSING

5. Write a sentence correctly using *disk*. (Be sure to include context clues to show you understand the meaning of the word.)

_____

_____

Documentation[15]

doc|u|men|ta|tion (dok′yə men tā′shən), *n.* **1** the preparation and use of documentary evidence. **2** the documents used: *The noncritical air that pervades this book is somewhat compensated by the full documentation* (Edward D. Goldberger). **3** the collection, classification, processing, and transmission of information, especially through computers and other automatic equipment.

1. Check any appropriate response to the following statement: "The *documentation* for this software program is included in the package price."
   _____ a. The evidence is part of the program.
   _____ b. The manual for operating the program is enclosed with the software disk.
   _____ c. Instructions are necessary to run the software.
   _____ d. All the software we need is in the envelope.

2. Which of the numbered dictionary definitions of *documentation* best fits the word's use in the reading selection? _____

3. Select the synonym(s) of *documentation* as used in the reading selection.
   _____ a. directions   _____ c. memorandum
   _____ b. registration   _____ d. manual

4. Write a sentence correctly using *documentation*. (Be sure to include context clues to show you understand the meaning of the word.)

_____

_____

5. Could a software program be run without *documentation*? What is the function of *documentation*?

_____

_____

Generation[1]

gen|er|a|tion (jen′ə rā′shən), *n.* **1** all the people born in the same period of time. Your parents and their friends belong to one generation; you and your friends belong to the next generation. **2** about 20 or 30 years, or the time from the birth of one generation to the birth of the next generation: *The automobile was introduced in America during the generation before World War I.* **3** one step or degree in the descent of a family: *The picture showed four generations—great-grand-*mother, grandmother, mother, and baby. **4** a group of things produced within the same period of time, often on the model of an earlier product: *The new computers are ... much better priced in performance than the previous generation* (Wall Street Journal). **5** the production of offspring; procreation. **6** the act or process of producing; bringing into being; generating; production: *the generation of steam in a boiler. Steam and water power are used for the generation of electricity.*

7 *Biology.* a form or stage of a plant or animal, with reference to its method of reproduction: *the asexual generation of a fern.* **8** *Mathematics.* the formation of a line, surface, figure, or solid espe-cially by moving a point or line. **9** *Obsolete.* off-spring; descendants: *The book of the generation of Jesus Christ* (Matthew 1:1). **10** *Obsolete.* a class of persons; family; race.

1. Which of the numbered dictionary definitions of *generation* best fits the word's use in the reading selection? _____

2. Select the synonym(s) of *generation.*
   _____ a. production   _____ c. approximation
   _____ b. governance   _____ d. procreation

3. In which of the following sentences can *generation* be correctly placed in the blank?
   _____ a. Each _____ of computer has produced more ef-ficient and affordable technology.
   _____ b. Each _____ of the family gathered for a holiday picture.
   _____ c. The family searched for a new _____ of rela-tives.
   _____ d. Ice in a furnace produces a _____ of steam.

4. What do you predict will happen in the next *generation* of computers? What changes and/or innovations might we see? What would you like to see in future *generations* of computers?

   _____

   _____

5. Write a sentence correctly using *generation.* (Be sure to include context clues to show you understand the meaning of the word.)

   _____

   _____

Input[8]

in|put (in′pùt′), *n., v.,* **-put, -put|ting. —** *n.* **1** what is put in or taken in: *Get all the reluctant varia-bles under control and measure the ... intellec-tual and emotional input* (Saturday Review). **2** the power supplied to a machine. **3** coded informa-tion put into a computer. **4** the point of putting in or taking in something such as information or power. **5** *Scottish.* a contribution. — *v.t., v.i.* to put or be put into a computer or any system like that of a computer: *Part of the reason for the much faster rates at which data can be accepted by computers than by man is that data is carefully preprocessed before being input to a computer, whereas man has to extract information from the buzzing confusion of the real world* (Science Journal).

1. In which of the following sentences is *input* used correctly?
   _____ a. In order to input information, we need to redesign it.
   _____ b. He wanted to input information with the line printer.
   _____ c. James could input information on the mainframe computer from his office computer.
   _____ d. The keyboard is commonly used as an input device.

2. Which of the numbered dictionary definitions of *input* best fits the word's use in the reading selection? _____

3. Select the synonym(s) of *input*.
_____ a. intertwine _____ c. yield
_____ b. intake _____ d. enter

4. What are some *input* devices used with the computer? Which ones have you used? (See the reading selection if necessary.)

_____

_____

5. Write a sentence correctly using *input*. (Be sure to include context clues to show you understand the meaning of the word.)

_____

_____

Interface[7]

in|ter|face (in′tər fās′), *n., v.,* **-faced, -fac|ing.**
— *n.* **1** a surface lying between two bodies or spaces, and forming their common boundary. **2** a connection of two or more things brought together in an association, partnership, meeting, or other relationship: *"Interface" refers to anything that mediates between disparate items: machinery, people, thought. The equipment that makes the computer work visible to the user is often called an "interface," and the word is used highly metaphorically, as in "the interface be-* tween man and the computer, between the scientist and society" (Atlantic). *Responsibilities include master scheduling, customer interface* (New York Times).
— *v.i., v.t.* to match, harmonize, or work together smoothly: *This was to be a full-dress affair, including inflated space suits, which have to "interface"—a space-age verb meaning, roughly, to coordinate—with equipment in the cabin* (New Yorker).

1. Select the synonym(s) of *interface*.
_____ a. integrate _____ c. mediate
_____ b. detach _____ d. connect

2. In which of the following sentences can *interface* be correctly placed in the blank?
_____ a. A peripheral device requires an _____ in order to operate.
_____ b. The _____ controlled the software program.
_____ c. An _____ is needed between the computer and a disk drive.
_____ d. The CRT needed an _____ before it could control the line printer.

3. Which of the numbered dictionary definitions of *interface* best fits the word's use in the reading selection? _____

4. Write a sentence correctly using *interface*. (Be sure to include context clues to show you understand the meaning of the word.)

_____

_____

5. Explain the term *interface*. Does a disk drive need an *interface* to be hooked up to a computer? How is this done?

_____

_____

Modem[14]

mod|em (mod′əm, mō′dem), *n.* a device used in telecommunications to convert digital signals to analogue form and vice versa: *Modems ... adapt alphanumeric information (letters and numerals) for transmission over standard voice channels* (Scientific American). [blend of *mod(ulator)* and *dem(odulator)*]

1. A *modem* is a connection between the computer and the
   _____ a. interface.   _____ c. telephone line.
   _____ b. serial port.   _____ d. line printer.

2. Check any appropriate response to the following statement:
   "John purchased a *modem* for his new personal computer."
   _____ a. He wanted to be able to interact with the larger university computer while he was at home.
   _____ b. John wanted his computer to talk to his girlfriend.
   _____ c. He wanted to receive satellite signals on his computer.
   _____ d. He needed to collect data that his friend has on his own personal computer and be able to check the stock market prices each day.

3. Complete the verbal analogy.
   disk : storage :: *modem* : _____
   a. generation   c. interface
   b. conversion   d. production

4. Why would someone use a *modem*? What could be some of the benefits of having a *modem*? Have you ever seen or used a *modem*? Explain.

_____

_____

5. Write a sentence correctly using *modem*. (Be sure to include context clues to show you understand the meaning of the word.)

_____

_____

Nanosecond[3]

na|no|sec|ond (nā′nə sek′ənd, nan′ə-), *n.* a billionth of a second.

1. A *nanosecond* in processing time is a characteristic of what generation of computers?

   _____ a. first   _____ c. third

   _____ b. second   _____ d. fourth

2. What part of *nanosecond* means billionth?

   _____ a. sec

   _____ b. nano

   _____ c. second

3. In which of the following sentences is *nanosecond* used correctly?

   _____ a. The computer processes information in nanoseconds.

   _____ b. The nanoseconds help the computer work more efficiently.

   _____ c. There are a thousand nanoseconds in a second.

   _____ d. The fourth generation of computers complete simple calculations in a matter of a few nanoseconds.

4. Write a sentence correctly using *nanosecond*. (Be sure to include context clues to show you understand the meaning of the word.)

   _____

   _____

5. What else that you know operates or functions in *nanoseconds*? Brain? TV signals?

   _____

   _____

Output[9]

out|put (*n.* out′pút′; *v.* out′pút′, out pút′), *n., v.,* **-put, -put|ting.** —*n.* **1** the amount produced; product or yield: *the daily output of automobiles.* **2** the act of putting forth; production: *With a sudden output of effort he moved the rock.* **3** the power or energy produced as by a machine: *The power output of a transformer is necessarily less than the power input because of the unavoidable* loss in the form of heat (Sears and Zemansky). **4** information supplied by the storage unit of a computer. —*v.t.* to put out or deliver from the storage unit: *The computer, though it may hoard a large quantity of information, will output only a very small quantity: the replies to specific questions that are put to it* (Tom Margerison).

1. Complete the verbal analogy.

   input : insertion :: *output* : _____

   _____ a. connection   _____ c. interface

   _____ b. production   _____ d. admission

2. Check any appropriate response to the following statement:

   "We have not decided what *output* device to use with this data."

   _____ a. We could use the line printer for a hard, or permanent, copy.

   _____ b. The disk drive is not working properly.

   _____ c. The data has already been entered from a software program.

   _____ d. The CRT is appropriate with this data, as we only need a visual display.

3. Which of the numbered dictionary definitions of *output* best fits the word's use in the reading selection? _____

4. Why would one choose a line printer instead of a CRT as an *output* device? Which do you prefer?

_____

_____

5. Write a sentence correctly using *output*. (Be sure to include context clues to show you understand the meaning of the word.)

_____

_____

Peripheral[6]

pe|riph|er|al (pə rif′ər əl), *adj., n.* —*adj.* **1** having to do with, situated in, or forming an outside boundary: *More houses and parks were to be seen in the peripheral areas of the city.* **2a** of the surface or outer part of a body; external. **b** perceived or perceiving near the outer edges of the retina: *peripheral vision.* **3** of or having to do with the peripheral nervous system: *peripheral neurons.* **4** of or having to do with computer periph-erals: *It is likely that Poland will produce small central processors, tape readers, line printers and other components; East Germany will probably supply peripheral equipment* (Scientific American). —*n.* any part of the electromechanical equipment of a computer, such as magnetic tape, high-speed printers, keyboards, and display units. —**pe|riph′er|al|ly,** *adv.*

1. Which of the numbered dictionary definitions of *peripheral* best fits the word's use in the reading selection? _____

2. What is an example of a *peripheral*?
   _____ a. a keyboard   _____ c. a CRT
   _____ b. a disk drive   _____ d. hardware

3. In which of the following sentences can *peripheral* be correctly placed in the blank?
   _____ a. A disk drive is an example of a _____.
   _____ b. Software is primarily a _____ device.
   _____ c. A _____ requires an interface to be connected to the computer.
   _____ d. A _____ is used to help view the CRT.

4. Write a sentence correctly using *peripheral*. (Be sure to include context clues to show you understand the meaning of the word.)

_____

_____

5. List two *peripherals* that were discussed in the reading selection. Have you ever used a *peripheral*? If so, which one and how did it function?

_____

_____

Programming[12]

pro|gram|ming or **pro|gram|ing** (prō′gram ing,
-grə ming), *n.* **1** the planning and arranging of a
program or programs, especially for radio and
television. **2** the technique or process of preparing instructions for a computer or other automatic
machine.

from **program:**

[< Late Latin *programma* < Greek *prógramma*,
-atos proclamation < *prográphein* write publicly <
pro- forth + *gráphein* to write]

1. The etymology of *programming* (see *program*) shows that the word comes
   from the Greek *pro* (forth) and *graphein* (to write). Use this information
   and your background knowledge to match the following:

   _____ a. grammar   aa. a short poem expressing a single
                                   thought or observation with terseness
                                   and wit

   _____ b. epigram   bb. brief article, announcement, or notice
   _____ c. diagram   cc. system of rules implicit in a language
   _____ d. graphology   dd. to plan, sketch, or outline in order to
                                   explain or clarify something

   _____ e. paragraph   ee. study of handwriting as a means of ana-
                                   lyzing the character of the writer

2. Check any example of *programming* language.
   _____ a. BASIC   _____ c. CPU
   _____ b. machine language   _____ d. RAM

3. In which of the following sentences is *programming* used correctly?
   _____ a. BASIC is an easy programming language to learn.
   _____ b. Programming is a concentration of study within the major of
              computer science.
   _____ c. The hardware used a simple programming language.
   _____ d. The student needed to learn programming before she could
              add the peripheral to her computer.

4. How important is *programming* to the use of the computer? Would you
   like to be a programmer? If so, what type of programs would you like to
   develop?

   _____

   _____

5. Write a sentence correctly using *programming*. (Be sure to include context clues to show you understand the meaning of the word.)

   _____

   _____

Terminal[4]

ter|mi|nal (ter'mə nəl), *adj., n.* **—adj. 1a** at the end; forming the end part: *a terminal appendage.* **b** *Botany.* growing at the end of a branch or stem: *a terminal bud or flower.* **2** coming at the end: *a terminal examination.* **syn:** final, ultimate. **3** having to do with or completing a term: *a terminal payment.* **4a** at the end of a railroad line. **b** having to do with or for the handling of freight at a terminal. **5** marking a boundary, limit, or end: *a terminal pillar.* **6a** of or having to do with the end of life; approaching or resulting in death; fatal: *a terminal disease, terminal cancer.* **b** *Figurative: The government is suffering from terminal insanity (Harper's) . . . a three-thousand-room hotel development in Bali, "whose impact on that island will be terminal"* (New Yorker). **—n. 1** the end; end part. **syn:** extremity. **2a** either end of a railroad line, airline, bus line, or shipping route, at which are located sheds, hangars, garages, offices, and stations to handle freight and passengers; terminus. **b** a city or station at the end of a railroad, bus route, or the like. **3** a device for making an electrical connection: *the terminals of a battery.* **4a** a teletype machine. **b** a typewriter keyboard or other device connected to a computer for remote input or output of data. Some terminals are connected to a video display unit that projects information on a cathode-ray tube. *As many as 30 terminals can be connected at one time, with each user carrying on a direct and in effect uninterrupted dialogue with the computer* (Scientific American). [Latin *terminālis < terminus* terminus] **—ter'-mi|nal|ly,** *adv.*

1. What is an example of a *terminal*?
   _____ a. a keyboard   _____ c. a CRT
   _____ b. a line printer   _____ d. a disk drive

2. In which of the following sentences can *terminal* be correctly placed in the blank?
   _____ a. The keyboard is a _____ that can communicate with the CRT.
   _____ b. The bus _____ is also known as a depot.
   _____ c. The professor required a _____ on the final exam.
   _____ d. Visual output can be seen on the CRT _____.

3. Which of the numbered and lettered dictionary definitions of *terminal* (as a noun) best fits the word's use in the reading selection?
   _____

4. Write a sentence correctly using *terminal*. (Be sure to include context clues to show you understand the meaning of the word.)

   _____

   _____

5. Can more than one *terminal* be connected to the computer? Why or why not? For what purposes?

   _____

   _____

ANSWERS TO CHAPTER 18 EXERCISES

Binary: 1. dd, ee, aa, bb, cc   **2.** b (definition)   **3.** c, d
Byte: 1. d   **2.** (inar) (digi) (ight)   **3.** c
Chip: 1. d   **2.** 10a   **3.** b, d
Cursor: 1. 2   **2.** cc, ee, aa, dd, bb   **3.** c, d

Disk: **1.** a, c **2.** d (function) **3.** 7
Documentation: **1.** b, c **2.** 3 **3.** a, d
Generation: **1.** 4 **2.** a, d **3.** a, b, d
Input: **1.** c, d **2.** 3 **3.** b, d
Interface: **1.** c, d **2.** a, c **3.** 2
Modem: **1.** c **2.** a, d **3.** b (function)
Nanosecond: **1.** d **2.** b **3.** a, d
Output: **1.** b (definition) **2.** a, d **3.** 4
Peripheral: **1.** 4 **2.** a, b, c **3.** a, c
Programming: **1.** cc, aa, dd, ee, bb **2.** a, b **3.** a, b
Terminal: **1.** a, c **2.** a, b, d **3.** 4b

If you missed any of the items in the exercises, return to the exercise and to the dictionary definition to see where you went wrong. Remember: If you get something right, you only affirm that you knew it. If you get something wrong and understand why, *you have learned something.*

COMPUTER SCIENCE POSTTEST

Fill in the blanks with the words from this list.

binary	documentation	nanosecond
byte	generation	output
chip	input	peripheral
cursor	interface	programming
disk	modem	terminal

1. A connection of two or more things brought together in an association such as the computer and peripheral is called a(n) _____.

2. A group of things produced within the same period of time is called a(n) _____.

3. A magnetic _____ on which data can be stored can be floppy or hard.

4. _____ refers to a set of instructions outlining the steps to be performed in a specific operation by an electronic computer.

5. A(n) _____ is a device used in telecommunications to convert digital signals to analog signals, and vice versa, so that computers can interact.

6. A(n) _____ is any part of the electromechanical equipment, such as printers, keyboards, and display units.

7. The _____ is the information supplied by the storage unit of a computer.

8. _____ is a common name for a small piece of silicon on which an integrated circuit is built.

9. A billionth of a second is a(n) _____ .

10. A typewriter keyboard connected to a computer for remote input or output of data is called a(n) _____ .

11. A unit of eight bits in a computer memory is a(n) _____ .

12. A flashing movable pointer on a computer display screen is a(n) _____ .

13. "Involving two" is a definition of _____ .

14. _____ is the collection, processing, and transmission of information related to operating computers.

15. _____ is the coded information entered into a computer.

Answers to this posttest are in the Instructor's Manual.

If you missed any of the words, you may need to return to the exercises and to the dictionary entries to see why your concepts for some words are incomplete.

A P P E N D I X E S:

SUPPLEMENTARY ACTIVITIES

APPENDIX A
GREEK AND LATIN WORD FORMS

APPENDIX B
JUST FOR FUN

APPENDIX C
ADDITIONAL ACADEMIC WORDS

APPENDIX D
SELF-SELECTED VOCABULARY

APPENDIX E
PRETEST ANSWER KEYS/
CROSSWORD PUZZLE KEYS

GREEK AND LATIN WORD FORMS

This appendix presents the combining forms—roots and prefixes—that make up the words introduced in this book. Where several words share the same combining form, all are included with the pertinent root or prefix. Since suffixes are primarily useful to denote the parts of speech, they are not emphasized here.

Below you will find an alphabetical listing of the prefixes and roots, including origins and meanings, the words introduced, and where they can be found in the text. For example,

aequus　　(L.)　　*equal*　　equity　　**17,** 6

indicates that the root **aequus** is of Latin origin, means *equal*, and is in the "family tree" of the word equity, which is word number 6 in Chapter 17.

You will note that prefixes *assimilate*. That is, they vary depending on the root they combine with so that the words can be pronounced. A good example of this is *ad*, meaning "to, toward," which combines variously to form such words as *accessible, adversary, affiliation,* and *assiduous*. Remember, too, that nouns and verbs have various forms, so you may notice what seem to be inconsistencies.

Abbreviations for the languages from which the combining forms are borrowed are the following: **Ar.,** Arabic; **D.,** Dutch; **F.,** French; **G.,** Greek; **L.,** Latin; **M.E.,** Middle English; **Med.L.,** Medieval Latin; **O.E.,** Old English; **O.F.,** Old French; **P.,** Portuguese. Similar English meanings are separated by commas, and dissimilar meanings by semicolons.

PREFIXES

Word Element	Origin	Meaning	Word	Chapter, Word Number
a	(G.)	*not, without; together*	amorphous	**7,** 15
			asymmetry	**15,** 7
ab	(L.)	*off, from, away*	abstract	**5,** 9
ad	(L.)	*to, toward*	accessible	**5,** 11
			adhere	**4,** 13
			adjacent	**5,** 10
			adjunct	**5,** 5
			admonitory	**14,** 8
			adversary	**16,** 14
			aggregate	**11,** 5
			amortize	**17,** 11
			assets	**17,** 4
			assiduous	**5,** 2
			assimilate	**4,** 8
			paramount	**9,** 4
anti	(G.)	*against, opposite*	antipathy	**12,** 9
co	(L.)	intensive	cognition	**10,** 11
			consumption	**11,** 13
			covert	**14,** 9
co	(L.)	*with, together*	coalition	**9,** 14
			cogent	**4,** 11
			compendium	**5,** 4
			competence	**4,** 9
			composite	**8,** 3
			condensation	**7,** 11
			contingency	**16,** 13
			copious	**5,** 13
de	(L.)	*completely; from, down, away*	delineate	**13,** 7
			depreciation	**17,** 9
			derivative	**8,** 13
			distillation	**7,** 9
dis	(L.)	*undoing, reversing, apart*	defamation	**14,** 11
			denouement	**13,** 3
			deploy	**9,** 11
			diffusion	**6,** 6
			diligent	**4,** 2
			discern	**4,** 6
			disclosure	**17,** 15
			distortion	**15,** 6
			diversified	**14,** 2

Word Element	Origin	Meaning	Word	Chapter, Word Number
			diversion	**14,** 14
en	(M.E.)	*to cause to be*	ensconced	**16,** 2
epi	(G.)	*on, upon*	epithet	**13,** 15
			epitome	**13,** 8
ex	(L.)	*out, out of, forth*	eloquent	**13,** 10
			erudite	**4,** 1
			evaporation	**7,** 10
			evolution	**6,** 14
			expedite	**5,** 12
			expenditure	**11,** 15
			exponent	**8,** 5
in	(L.)	*intensive*	innovative	**16,** 10
in	(L.)	*in, into; not, without; on*	empirical	**9,** 10
			entitlement	**16,** 12
			impediment	**4,** 12
			impressionism	**15,** 13
			incentive	**16,** 8
			indictment	**9,** 15
			induction	**7,** 2
			inflationary	**11,** 8
			innate	**10,** 10
			input	**18,** 8
			intangible	**17,** 10
			integral	**8,** 14
			inverse	**8,** 15
inter	(L.)	*between, among*	entrepreneur	**11,** 11
			interface	**18,** 7
intra	(L.)	*into, within*	introspection	**10,** 4
non	(L.)	*not*	nonpareil	**12,** 5
ob	(L.)	*in the way, toward*	ostensibly	**14,** 10
para	(G.)	*side by side*	paradigm	**10,** 15
per	(L.)	*through, by, thoroughly*	paramount	**9,** 4
			perception	**15,** 9
peri	(G.)	*around*	peripheral	**18,** 6
pre	(L.)	*before*	precedent	**12,** 2
			precept	**12,** 12
pro	(L.)	*forward, forth*	procrastinate	**4,** 4
			profound	**13,** 14
pro	(G.)	*before*	programming	**18,** 12
re	(L.)	*back, again*	recession	**11,** 7
			redress	**16,** 6

Word Element	Origin	Meaning	Word	Chapter, Word Number
			reliability	**10,** 12
			remuneration	**16,** 11
			repartee	**13,** 5
			replicate	**5,** 14
			repression	**10,** 6
			requisition	**17,** 13
			retrieval	**4,** 3
			revenue	**11,** 14
se	(L.)	*apart*	sedition	**9,** 9
sub	(L.)	*under; up to*	subjective	**10,** 5
			sublimation	**7,** 13
super	(L.)	*over, above*	sovereignty	**9,** 1
sur	(F.)	*beyond*	surrealism	**15,** 15
syn	(G.)	*together*	asymmetry	**15,** 7
			photosynthesis	**6,** 12
			symbolism	**15,** 5
trans	(L.)	*across*	transaction	**17,** 8
ut	(O.E.)	*out*	output	**18,** 9

ROOTS

Word Element	Origin	Meaning	Word	Chapter, Word Number
aequus	(L.)	*equal*	equilibrium	**7,** 12
			equity	**17,** 6
aesthema	(G.)	*sensation, perception*	aesthetic	**15,** 1
ager, agri	(L.)	*field*	agrarian	**12,** 8
agere, actum	(L.)	*to drive*	cogent	**4,** 11
			transaction	**17,** 8
alere, alitum	(L.)	*to nourish*	coalition	**9,** 14
analogos	(G.)	*proportionate*	analogous	**12,** 3
ancilla	(L.)	*handmaiden*	ancillary	**5,** 1
angere	(L.)	*to choke*	anxiety	**10,** 14
aperire	(L.)	*to open*	overt	**14,** 3
aqua	(L.)	*water*	aqueous	**7,** 6
artic	(L.)	*a joint*	articulate	**4,** 10
audire	(L.)	*to hear*	audit	**17,** 14
augere	(L.)	*to increase*	augment	**14,** 6
avere, avidum	(L.)	*to desire, long for*	avid	**5,** 6
axios	(G.)	*worthy*	axiom	**16,** 3

Word Element	Origin	Meaning	Word	Chapter, Word Number
bakteri	(G.)	*little stick*	bacterium	**6,** 10
ballein	(G.)	*to throw*	metabolism	**6,** 7
			symbolism	**15,** 5
barroco	(P.)	*a rough pearl*	baroque	**15,** 10
bini	(L.)	*two at a time*	binary	**18,** 10
canere, cantum	(L.)	*to sing*	incentive	**16,** 8
capere, cepi	(L.)	*to take, seize*	perception	**15,** 9
			precept	**12,** 12
caput	(L.)	*head*	capitalism	**11,** 6
cedere, cessi	(L.)	*to go, yield, withdraw*	accessible	**5,** 11
			precedent	**12,** 2
			recession	**11,** 7
cernere, cretum	(L.)	*to separate, distinguish*	discern	**4,** 6
charta	(L.)	*leaf of papyrus*	cartel	**11,** 4
chein	(G.)	*to pour*	alchemy	**7,** 1
chroma	(G.)	*color*	monochromatic	**15,** 3
cipp	(O.E.)	*piece cut off a beam*	chip	**18,** 2
claudere, clausum	(L.)	*to close*	disclosure	**17,** 15
congruere	(L.)	*to correspond with*	congruent	**8,** 11
crastinus	(L.)	*tomorrow*	procrastinate	**4,** 4
credere	(L.)	*to believe, entrust*	credit	**17,** 3
currere, cursurum	(L.)	*to run*	cursor	**18,** 5
			cursory	**12,** 6
debere, debitum	(L.)	*to owe*	debit	**17,** 2
deiknynai	(G.)	*to show, point out*	paradigm	**10,** 15
deleesthai	(G.)	*to hurt, injure*	deleterious	**4,** 15
demos	(G.)	*people*	demographic	**14,** 7
densus	(L.)	*thick*	condensation	**7,** 11
despotes	(G.)	*master of the household*	despotism	**9,** 12
dicere, dictum	(L.)	*to say, speak*	indictment	**9,** 15
diskos	(G.)	*discus*	disk	**18,** 12
dividere, divisum	(L.)	*to divide*	dividends	**17,** 7
docere, doctum	(L.)	*to show, teach*	documentation	**18,** 15
domus	(L.)	*house*	domain	**8,** 7
dresser	(O.F.)	*to arrange, straighten*	redress	**16,** 6
ducere, ductum	(L.)	*to lead*	induction	**7,** 2

Word Element	Origin	Meaning	Word	Chapter, Word Number
essentia	(Med.L.)	*essence, sub-stance*	quintessential	**12**, 1
eu	(G.)	*good, true*	eucaryote	**6**, 2
externus	(L.)	*outside, outward*	externality	**11**, 12
facere, factum	(L.)	*to make, do*	facet	**12**, 4
			factor	**8**, 4
			fiat	**16**, 1
			interface	**18**, 7
			liquefaction	**7**, 4
			ramification	**16**, 7
fama	(L.)	*rumor, report*	defamation	**14**, 11
ferre, latum	(L.)	*to carry*	proliferation	**16**, 15
fiscus	(L.)	*purse, woven basket*	fiscal	**11**, 9
flare, flatum	(L.)	*to blow*	inflationary	**11**, 8
formidare	(L.)	*to dread*	formidable	**5**, 3
fundere, fusum	(L.)	*to pour*	diffusion	**6**, 6
fundus	(L.)	*bottom*	profound	**13**, 14
fungi, functum	(L.)	*to perform*	function	**8**, 9
genus, generis	(L.)	*birth, race, kind*	generation	**18**, 1
gnoscere, gnitum	(L.)	*to know*	cognition	**10**, 11
gradus	(L.)	*step, degree*	gradation	**15**, 4
graphein	(G.)	*to draw, write*	demographic	**14**, 7
			programming	**18**, 12
grex, gregis	(L.)	*flock*	aggregate	**11**, 5
haerere	(L.)	*to cling, stick*	adhere	**4**, 13
hiw	(O.E.)	*appearance*	hue	**15**, 12
horan	(G.)	*to see*	theorem	**8**, 1
			theory	**10**, 1
hypo	(G.)	*under*	hypotenuse	**8**, 12
			hypothesis	**10**, 2
ire, iturum	(L.)	*to go*	sedition	**9**, 9
jacere, jactum	(L.)	*to throw*	adjacent	**5**, 10
			subjective	**10**, 5
jungere, junctum	(L.)	*to join*	adjunct	**5**, 5
karyon	(G.)	*nut, kernel*	eucaryote	**6**, 2
			karyokinesis	**6**, 9
kata	(G.)	*down*	cataclysm	**9**, 6
kinein	(G.)	*to move*	cytokinesis	**6**, 8
			karyokinesis	**6**, 9
			kinetic	**7**, 3

Word Element	Origin	Meaning	Word	Chapter, Word Number
klyzein	(G.)	*to wash*	cataclysm	**9,** 6
kybos	(G.)	*cube, a die*	cubism	**15,** 14
kytos	(G.)	*hollow, vessel*	cytokinesis	**6,** 8
			cytoplasm	**6,** 4
legere, lectum	(L.)	*to choose, gather*	diligent	**4,** 2
liber, libri	(L.)	*book*	libel	**14,** 12
libra	(L.)	*balance*	equilibrium	**7,** 12
licgan	(O.E.)	*to lie*	ledger	**17,** 1
ligare, ligatum	(L.)	*to bind, fasten*	liability	**17,** 5
			ligature	**13,** 2
			reliability	**10,** 12
limen	(L.)	*limit, threshold*	sublimination	**9,** 13
linea	(L.)	*line*	delineate	**13,** 7
lingua	(L.)	*tongue, lan- guage*	linguistic	**4,** 5
liquere, liquet	(L.)	*be fluid*	liquefaction	**7,** 4
logy	(M.E.)	*science, system, study*	ecology	**6,** 13
			methodology	**9,** 5
loqui, locutum	(L.)	*to speak*	eloquent	**13,** 10
			soliloquy	**13,** 11
lucrum	(L.)	*gain*	lucrative	**16,** 5
membrana	(L.)	*a covering of skin*	membrane	**6,** 1
meta	(G.)	*change*	metabolism	**6,** 7
			metamorphosis	**12,** 11
methods	(G.)	*method*	methodology	**9,** 5
metros	(G.)	*a measure*	asymmetry	**15,** 7
minutus	(G.)	*small*	minutiae	**16,** 4
miscere, mixtum	(L.)	*to mix*	miscible	**7,** 5
mitos	(G.)	*thread*	mitosis	**6,** 11
modulus	(L.)	*small measure*	modem	**18,** 14
monere, monitum	(L.)	*to remind, advise*	admonitory	**14,** 8
monos	(G.)	*single*	monochromatic	**15,** 3
			monopoly	**11,** 2
mons, montis	(L.)	*mountain*	paramount	**9,** 4
monter	(O.F.)	*to mount*	montage	**13,** 1
morphe	(G.)	*form, shape*	amorphous	**7,** 15
			metamorphosis	**12,** 13
mors, mortis	(L.)	*death*	amortize	**17,** 11
movere, motem	(L.)	*to move*	motif	**11,** 6
munus, muneris	(L.)	*gift, duty*	remuneration	**16,** 11

Word Element	Origin	Meaning	Word	Chapter, Word Number
mutare, mutatum	(L.)	*to change*	mutation	**6,** 15
myrias	(G.)	*countless, ten thousand*	myriad	**5,** 8
nanos	(G.)	*dwarf*	nanosecond	**18,** 3
narrare, narratum	(L.)	*to relate, tell*	narrative	**13,** 12
nasci, natum	(L.)	*to be born*	innate	**10,** 10
			nascent	**12,** 14
neuros	(G.)	*nerve, sinew*	neurosis	**10,** 8
nodus	(L.)	*knot*	denouement	**13,** 3
norma	(L.)	*rule, pattern*	normative	**9,** 7
novus	(L.)	*new*	innovative	**16,** 10
oikos	(G.)	*dwelling*	ecology	**6,** 13
oligos	(G.)	*few*	oligopoly	**11,** 3
operire, opertum	(L.)	*to cover*	covert	**14,** 9
ops	(L.)	*resources*	copious	**5,** 13
optimus	(L.)	*best*	optimum	**4,** 7
organos	(G.)	*instrument, body organ*	organelle	**6,** 3
osis	(M.E.)	*a condition*	metamorphosis	**12,** 11
			mitosis	**6,** 11
			neurosis	**10,** 8
			osmosis	**6,** 5
			psychosis	**10,** 7
osmos	(G.)	*pushing, thrusting*	osmosis	**6,** 5
pala	(L.)	*spade, shovel*	palette	**15,** 2
palpare, palpatum	(L.)	*to feel, pat, stroke*	palpable	**12,** 7
par, paris	(L.)	*equal*	nonpareil	**12,** 5
parcere, parsurum	(L.)	*to spare*	parsimony	**14,** 4
pars, partis	(L.)	*part, side*	repartee	**13,** 5
pater	(L.)	*father*	patron	**13,** 13
pathos	(G.)	*feeling*	antipathy	**12,** 9
pecu	(L.)	*money, cattle*	pecuniary	**16,** 9
peira	(G.)	*experience, experiment*	empirical	**9,** 10
pendere, pensum	(L.)	*to weigh, hang*	compendium	**5,** 4
			expenditure	**11,** 15
personne	(O.F.)	*person*	personify	**13,** 9
pes, pedis	(L.)	*a foot*	expedite	**5,** 12
			impediment	**4,** 12
petere	(L.)	*to seek, drive forward*	competence	**4,** 9

GREEK AND LATIN WORD FORMS

Word Element	Origin	Meaning	Word	Chapter, Word Number
pherein	(G.)	*to carry off*	peripheral	**18,** 6
photos	(G.)	*light*	photosynthesis	**6,** 12
plaga	(L.)	*snare, net*	plagiarize	**5,** 15
plassein	(G.)	*to form, mold, shape*	cytoplasm	**6,** 4
plicare, plicatum	(L.)	*to fold*	deploy	**9,** 11
			replicate	**5,** 14
plus	(L.)	*more*	pluralism	**9,** 13
polein	(G.)	*to sell*	monopoly	**11,** 2
			oligopoly	**11,** 3
polemikos	(G.)	*war*	polemic	**12,** 15
ponere, positum	(L.)	*to put, place*	composite	**8,** 3
			exponent	**8,** 5
postulare	(L.)	*to demand*	postulate	**8,** 10
prassein	(G.)	*to do, act*	pragmatic	**14,** 5
prehendere, prehensum	(L.)	*to take*	entrepreneur	**11,** 11
premere, pressum	(L.)	*to press*	impressionism	**15,** 13
			repression	**10,** 6
pretium	(L.)	*price*	depreciation	**17,** 9
primus	(L.)	*first*	prime	**8,** 2
proles	(L.)	*offspring*	proliferation	**16,** 15
proximus	(L.)	*nearest, next*	proximity	**4,** 14
psyche	(G.)	*soul, mind*	psychosis	**10,** 7
			psychotherapy	**10,** 9
putian	(O.E.)	*to push, thrust*	input	**18,** 8
			output	**18,** 9
quaerere, quaesitum	(L.)	*to seek, inquire*	requisition	**17,** 13
quinta	(Med.L.)	*fifth*	quintessential	**12,** 1
ramus	(L.)	*branch*	ramification	**16,** 7
ranger	(O.F.)	*to array*	range	**8,** 8
realisme	(F.)	*realism*	surrealism	**15,** 15
regere, rectum	(L.)	*to rule, straighten*	regime	**9,** 8
res	(L.)	*matter, thing*	realist	**15,** 8
rivus	(L.)	*stream*	derivative	**8,** 13
rudis	(L.)	*rude, unskilled*	erudite	**4,** 1
satis	(L.)	*sufficient, enough*	assets	**17,** 4
schans	(D.)	*fortification*	ensconced	**16,** 2
schizein	(G.)	*to split*	schism	**12,** 13
secare, sectum	(L.)	*to cut*	sector	**11,** 1

Word Element	Origin	Meaning	Word	Chapter, Word Number
secundus	(L.)	*following, second*	nanosecond	**18,** 3
sedere, sessurum	(L.)	*to sit*	assiduous	**5,** 2
simulare, simulatum	(L.)	*to imitate, pretend*	assimilate	**4,** 8
skandalon	(G.)	*offense*	slander	**14,** 13
skopein	(G.)	*to behold, consider*	scope	**9,** 2
solus	(L.)	*alone*	soliloquy	**13,** 11
solvere, solutum	(L.)	*to dissolve, loosen*	solute	**7,** 7
			solvent	**7,** 8
specere, spexi	(L.)	*to look, examine*	introspection	**10,** 4
stilla	(L.)	*drop*	distillation	**7,** 9
stimulus	(L.)	*a goad*	stimulus	**10,** 3
stringere, strictum	(L.)	*to draw tight*	stringent	**5,** 7
sumere, sumptum	(L.)	*to take up*	consumption	**11,** 13
sur	(F.)	*beyond*	surrealism	**15,** 15
tangere, tactum	(L.)	*to touch*	contingency	**16,** 13
			intangible	**17,** 10
			integral	**8,** 14
tarif	(Ar.)	*information*	tariff	**11,** 10
teinein	(G.)	*to stretch*	hypotenuse	**8,** 12
temnein	(G.)	*to cut*	epitome	**13,** 8
tendere, tensum	(L.)	*to stretch*	ostensibly	**14,** 10
terminus	(L.)	*boundary, limit*	terminal	**18,** 4
thea	(G.)	*a looking at*	theorem	**8,** 1
			theory	**10,** 1
therapeuein	(G.)	*to cure, treat*	psychotherapy	**10,** 9
tithenai	(G.)	*to put, place*	epithet	**13,** 15
			hypothesis	**10,** 2
			photosynthesis	**6,** 12
titulus	(L.)	*title, claim, inscription*	entitlement	**16,** 12
torquere, tortum	(L.)	*to twist*	distortion	**15,** 6
trahere, tractum	(L.)	*to pull, draw*	abstract	**5,** 9
trouver	(O.F.)	*to find*	retrieval	**4,** 3
valere, valiturum	(L.)	*to be strong*	validity	**10,** 13
vapor	(L.)	*vapor, steam*	evaporation	**7,** 10
varius	(L.)	*variegated*	variable	**8,** 6
vastus	(L.)	*immense, empty*	vast	**14,** 1
venire	(L.)	*to come*	revenue	**11,** 14

GREEK AND LATIN WORD FORMS

Word Element	Origin	Meaning	Word	Chapter, Word Number
vertere, versum	(L.)	*to turn*	adversary	**16,** 14
			diversified	**14,** 2
			diversion	**14,** 14
			inverse	**8,** 15
vicis	(L.)	*a turn, change*	vicarious	**14,** 15
viscum	(L.)	*birdlime*	viscosity	**7,** 14
vocare, vocatum	(L.)	*to call*	voucher	**17,** 12
volvere, volutum	(L.)	*to roll*	evolution	**6,** 14

The following words are not listed in the combining forms table:

Word	Source	Location
byte (*b*inary dig*it* *e*ight)	a blend	**18,** 11
deus ex machina	a naturalized foreign phrase	**13,** 4
draconian	a "person word" referring to the Athenian legislator, Draco	**12,** 10
promulgate	from the Latin verb *promulgare,* meaning "to make public." Etymologists are not able to trace it further, so it is said to be "of uncertain origin."	**9,** 3
romanticism	a "place word" referring to Rome	**15,** 11

JUST FOR FUN

Words can come from almost any source, and English has borrowed and created at will, giving us a language that is extensive (one estimate is as high as one million words) and varied (it is hard to find an area where we have *not* borrowed or created). In this chapter we give you a very brief history to show how English has developed, tell you of the interesting origins of several words, and furnish crossword puzzles that use some of the examples.

HISTORY OF ENGLISH

English is not as old as some of the languages on earth, but it is related to the oldest languages and belongs to a family of languages called "Indo-European." If you are interested in seeing how many languages belong to this family and how they are related, look in an unabridged dictionary under "Indo-European languages" for a chart. (Some desk volumes also have this information.)

Very early inhabitants of the British Isles, the Celts, furnished us with a few words, such as *plaid* and *heather*, and influenced the speech of some current inhabitants of the islands—the Welsh, some Scots, and some Irish—but the language of these early settlers had almost no effect on the English of today. A much greater influence came from the Germanic tribes of Angles and Saxons that came from the continent of Europe about A.D. 410. Because the Romans had controlled much of the continent for hundreds of years, the language of the Angles and the Saxons had already been affected by Latin, and keep in mind that Latin had been influenced by Greek a great many years before that. Words used today that come from the Angles and the Saxons include *man, wife,* and *house.* During the Anglo-Saxon period, Christianity spread in England, and some religious words were introduced, such as *candle, church,* and *shrine.* At the same time, Vikings were raiding the coasts of England (called Englalond, where Englisc was spoken) with increasing success. By the eleventh century, the raids had stopped, and the Norsemen (Danes or Vikings) were ruling much of England. Under the Danes, the pronouns *they, their,* and *them* were carried into English from Old Norse, as well as words like *knife, steak, law,* and *husband.*

The next invasion came from the Normans, who lived across the English Channel from the southern coast of England. The Normans were descendants of Vikings who had settled in Normandy about the same time their kin had settled in England. Their language was a blend of Old Norse and Old French; the Old French had been derived from Latin. After this successful invasion of England, the Norman language, French, became the language of the ruling classes for almost 350 years. Despite this, native English survived because the common people continued to use it. A great many words came into the language from French during this period: words from cooking, such as *chef* and *saute*; words from the arts, such as *tapestry* and *design*; and words from polite society, such as *chivalry* and *etiquette.* Borrowings from such intermingled languages resulted in the phenomenon of *doublets.* A language *doublet* is one of two or more words derived from the same original source but coming by different routes. For example, we use the word *chief*, which comes from a Latin word meaning "head," and that Latin word (*caput*) is also the source of *chef.* (You may notice that some of the words introduced in the exercises are *doublets.* A complete definition appears in the material explaining how to use the dictionary entries at the end of Chapter 2.)

During the Renaissance we borrowed again from Latin. This time the borrowings came directly from the older Latin authors, for literary use, instead of by word of mouth as they had in the earlier borrowings of Latin. As travel and trade increased, words were taken from languages around the world. Words from the field of music, such as *stanza, andante,* and *tempo,* were borrowed from Italian; words like *cargo, cigar,* and *vanilla* were borrowed from Spanish; words having to do with the number system, *algebra, cipher,* and *zero,* were taken from Arabic; American Indian words borrowed include *moccasin, raccoon,* and *hickory.* And more, too, from many sources!

You realize that this brief history can give only a few of the borrowings. More information about word origins is revealed as you read the etymologies of words. And English is growing still! It is said to be the richest language in the world.

CREATING WORDS

In addition to borrowing words from other languages, we create words as we need them. For example, we "blend" breakfast and lunch to form *brunch* and smoke and fog to form *smog.* We "compound" words by putting them together to label new concepts like *downtime* and *spinout,* and we make new words from the first letters of other words, as in the acronyms *scuba* (*self-*

contained *underwater breathing apparatus*) and *radar* (*radio detecting and ranging*). Business creates trademark words such as *Xerox* and *Kleenex*, and we use them in a much more general way. Words, words, everywhere! You can see why the language is so rich!

Other words come from literature, classical myths, places, and real people. We borrow these words because new concepts have been introduced or defined in written works, and we need the terms to label those concepts. Then, too, people and places become identified with certain characteristics or objects and become labels for those concepts.

WORDS FROM LITERATURE

Odyssey The Greek writer Homer wrote an epic poem, *The Odyssey*, describing a long and difficult journey of the Greek hero Odysseus to Ithaca at the conclusion of the Trojan War. Now any long wandering or series of adventurous journeys may be called an "odyssey." (It no longer has a capital letter; it is "naturalized.")

Robot Karel Capek, a Czech author and playwright, wrote *R.U.R.* (Rossum's Universal Robots) about machines used to function in place of men. The Czech word *robot* means "worker," but the English translation of the play in 1923 retained the original word and it soon became widely used.

Quixotic (kwik sot'ik) A Spanish novel in two parts that was intended to make fun of contemporary (early 1600s) chivalric romances (books) introduced *quixotic* into English. Miguel de Cervantes created *Don Quixote* (kē hō' tē), a lean elderly man who thought he was a knight and set out on his equally lean horse to right the wrongs of the world. Today the word means romantic, without regard to practicality. (This story also exists as a musical production titled "Man of La Mancha.")

Pandemonium Literature has also given us some "place" words. One of them, *pandemonium*, was created by John Milton in his *Paradise Lost* as the name of the capital of hell and means, literally, "all demons." Now, you may know, it means "a wild uproar."

Utopia Another place name is *utopia*, created by Thomas More in 1516 in his Latin essay describing an ideally perfect community. Translated literally it means "no place," and today it retains a similar meaning, that is, something ideal and nonexistent.

Some other words from written works are *scrooge*, *gargantuan*, and *yahoo*.

WORDS FROM CLASSICAL MYTHS

Aegis (ē′ jis) *Aegis* was the name of a shield associated with the Greek god Zeus and in later mythology was represented as a goatskin hanging over the shoulder of the Greek goddess Athena. Since it was a form of protection for them, it came to mean "protection," and today we say that someone supported or protected by a powerful person or business is "under the *aegis* of" that entity.

Herculean Today, *herculean* describes a task requiring great strength or someone who has great strength and courage. Hercules was the Roman name for the strong and courageous hero who completed numerous difficult tasks (we hear of "the twelve labors" particularly) and who was the only man in mythology to make the full transition from mortal to god.

Nemesis In Greek and Roman myth, a goddess named Nemesis was "the unrelenting avenger of human faults." That is, she saw to it that you got the punishment you deserved. These days you may hear the word used to describe someone, such as a policeman or lawyer, as the *nemesis* of criminals.

Tantalize According to Greek myth, Tantalus was a Lydian king who took advantage of his friendship with the gods, eventually making them very angry. As punishment, he was condemned to the everlasting torment of continual hunger and thirst. He was made to stand in the river Hades with water up to his neck, but it receded when he stooped to drink. Just out of reach, over his head, hung luscious fruits. A *tantalus* today is a stand in which liquor decanters are visible but not available unless one has the key. *Tantalize* is a verb, meaning to tease or torment by presenting something desirable to the view but keeping it continually out of reach.

Protean Proteus was a minor Greek god represented as a wise old man and servant of Poseidon (called Neptune by the Romans—the god of the sea). People, and even gods, would seek advice and favors of him, but he was able to elude them by changing himself from one shape to another. Today we might use the word *protean* to describe an actor who is capable of assuming different characters or to describe anything extremely variable.

Some other words from classical myths are *panic, erotic, echo,* and *atlas.*

WORDS FROM PLACES

Stoic Stoics were ancient Greek philosophers who first met near the Painted *Portico* (*Stoa* Poikile) of the marketplace in Athens. Their founder,

Zeno, taught uncomplaining submission to the vicissitudes of life. Today, someone able to preserve complete indifference to pleasure, pain, or catastrophe is called a *stoic*, or we may say that he meets life's changes with *stoicism*.

Sybarite A *sybarite* is someone who cares very much for luxury and pleasure—a voluptuary. The term comes from inhabitants of the ancient Greek colony of Sybaris, in southern Italy. The fabulous luxury and sensuousness of the colony were known throughout the ancient world. Legend has it that the people of Sybaris taught their horses to dance to the music of flutes or pipes. They were overcome in battle when their enemies discovered the fact and played music during an attack, causing great confusion and defeat.

Laconic When Laconia, a district in ancient Greece, was under attack, its enemy declared "If we come to your city we will level it to the ground." The only Laconian reply was "*If*." This habit of terseness gave the name of the area to our adjective *laconic*, which today describes someone blunt and brief in speech.

Solecism A *solecism* is a blunder or provincialism in writing or speech and takes its name from the Greek colony of Soloi. Located across the Mediterranean Sea from Athens (the capital and considered seat of learning and correct behavior), inhabitants developed a Greek dialect of their own. Visiting Athenians were shocked by the crude, substandard speech they heard and named such errors after the area.

Denim This heavy, coarse, cotton cloth with a diagonal weave has become one of the most popular fabrics in the world. Most of us wouldn't be without our *denims*. The word comes from the town of Nîmes, France, where a durable, twilled fabric with a pronounced diagonal rib called "serge d'Nîmes" was produced. Before long, that special fabric was called *denim*.

Some other words that come from places are *tuxedo, turquoise, jersey, hamburger,* and *spa*.

WORDS FROM PEOPLE

Gerrymander Elbridge Gerry (1744–1814) was a signer of the Declaration of Independence, congressman, governor of Massachusetts, and vice president of the United States. While governor of Massachusetts, he signed a bill into law designed to ensure continuing majorities for his political party. One of the districts so created was used in a political cartoon where the artist added wings, teeth, and claws. Someone suggested that it looked like a salamander, to which a political opponent is said to have replied, "A Gerrymander, you mean!" Today, *gerrymander* is a verb or a noun. The U.S.

Supreme Court has ruled legislative districts must contain roughly equal numbers of people, but legislators are permitted to draw district lines. Wherever the lines are drawn, someone is sure to cry *"Gerrymander!"*

Quisling This is a rather recent "people word" that came into the language in the 1940s. It refers to Vidkum Quisling (1887–1945), a Norwegian facist, who admired Nazi Germany and helped it in its conquest of his homeland during World War II. He served as the Nazi's puppet ruler of Norway until the end of the war, when he was tried, convicted of high treason, and executed. And so, a political traitor, particularly one who serves in a puppet government, is known as a *quisling*.

Maverick Samuel A. Maverick (1803–70) was a Texas politician and a cattleman who declined to brand his calves. Whether this was due to carelessness or laziness is not recorded, but rounding up and branding cattle is a difficult job at best, and given the vast expanse of Texas range lands, it becomes a task of extraordinary proportions. Those who expended the necessary effort found that Maverick's cattle were as good as branded, since they were the ones without a brand! If, on occasion, they branded a stray, or a *maverick*, as their own, who is to blame them? Today the word has extended meanings. One of them describes a person who refuses to affiliate or who breaks with a regular political party as a *maverick*.

Dunce A *dunce* is someone who is dull witted or stupid and may be pictured as sitting in a corner of the school room with a *dunce* cap. But the word stems from someone who was not considered dull witted. John Duns Scottus (d. 1308) was one of the most brilliant thinkers of the Middle Ages. However, after his death his followers held firmly (and loudly) to the doctrines he had endorsed, even in the face of more "modern" thought. Their opponents referred to them as stupid enemies of learning and progress or "Dunsmen," which soon became *dunce*.

Martinet A person who enforces very strict discipline on those under him is labeled a *martinet*. The word comes from Jean Martinet (d. 1672) who served as inspector general of the infantry for Louis XIV of France. Excessively strict, demanding ways made his name synonymous with sharp, military discipline. Martinet was killed at the siege of Duisberg in 1672, accidentally shot by his own artillery.

Many words come from real people. Some others are *fahrenheit, volt, diesel, boycott, guillotine,* and *sadism*.

You can understand from this quick overview that language begins and evolves in diverse ways. Words begin, grow and change, and even die, depending on people's use, or disuse, of them. You have just read of some of the many ways words may begin. Then they may change—in pronunciation, spelling, and meaning—not just once but several times. And sometimes when the times change and we no longer need to express certain concepts, words fall out of use and become obsolete. (For example, according to the Oxford English Dictionary, *auripotent*, or "rich in gold," hasn't been used in a written work since 1560.) If it were not for written language and record books, these words would be forgotten. Think of the words that must have come and gone in prehistoric times! But that's another story.

On the following pages are some crossword puzzles for you to enjoy. They employ many of the words used in this appendix as examples. Of *course* you may look back into the appendix! Answer keys are in Appendix E.

Puzzle 1

Across Clues

3. a late breakfast or early lunch
5. an independent individual
8. protection
11. forms of behavior to be observed in social life
12. having impossibly ideal conditions
15. one of two or more words, same source, different route
16. tree of the walnut family
17. an adult male human
18. to tease or torment
21. the qualities of the ideal knight
23. a cutting instrument
25. in music, moderately slow
26. a formidable, usually victorious, opponent
28. objective case of *they*
30. using a minimum of words
32. of extraordinary power or difficulty
33. a soft leather heelless shoe
34. a long journey full of adventure

Down Clues

1. a rule of conduct enforced by authority
2. self-contained underwater breathing apparatus
4. a married man
6. a machine that performs acts much like a human
7. ungrammatical combination of words
9. a political traitor
10. trademark of a copy machine
13. readily assuming different shapes
14. a division of a poem
19. a skilled cook
20. a plant with tiny purplish pink flowers
22. tropical American climbing orchid
24. goods conveyed in a vehicle
27. to plan out in the mind
29. to fry in a small amount of fat
31. a small roll of tobacco leaf for smoking

Across Clues

1. objective case of *they*
3. goods conveyed in a vehicle
8. building that serves as living quarters
9. rate of speed of a musical piece
11. to plan out in the mind
12. a formidable, usually victorious, opponent
13. readily assuming different shapes
14. one of two or more words, same source, different routes
15. to fry in a small amount of fat
17. a long journey full of adventure
22. a rotational skid by an automobile
24. tropical American climbing orchid
25. radio device for locating a object
27. heavy woven textile used for wall hangings or upholstery
28. place in which devotion is paid to a saint or diety

Down Clues

2. a married man
3. zero
4. time during which a machine is inactive in normal working hours
5. a cutting instrument
6. a strict disciplinarian
7. having impossibly ideal conditions
10. tree of the walnut family
13. pattern of unevenly spaced stripes crossing right angles
16. to tease or torment
18. self-contained underwater breathing apparatus
19. one indifferent to pleasure or pain
20. a slice of beef
21. a married woman
22. ungrammatical combination of words
23. a machine that performs acts much like a human
26. relating to themselves as possessors

Puzzle 3

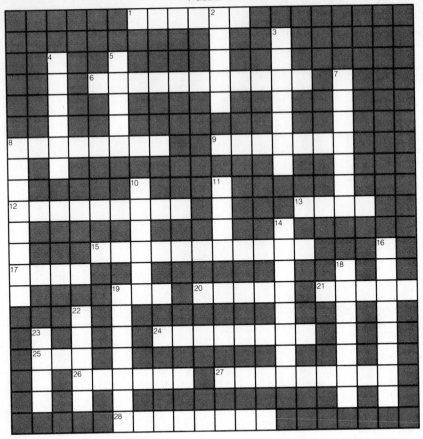

Across Clues

1. a building for public worship
6. to divide area into political units to give special advantages to one group
8. a soft leather heelless shoe
9. arithmetic in which letters representing numbers are combined according to rules of arithmetic
12. forms of behavior to be observed in social life
13. those ones
15. a wild uproar
17. a skilled cook
19. a rule of conduct enforced by authority
20. trademark of a copy machine
21. a firm, durable, cotton fabric
24. voluptuary
25. an adult male human
26. wax containing a wick, burned to give light
27. of extraordinary power or difficulty
28. the qualities of the ideal knight

Down Clues

2. a small roll of tobacco leaf for smoking
3. trademark of a cleansing tissue
4. a late breakfast or early lunch
5. protection
7. in music, moderately slow
8. an independent individual
10. a division of a poem
11. arithmetic: the absence of all quantity
14. idealistic to an impractical degree
16. a political traitor
18. a plant with tiny purplish pink flowers
19. using a minimum of words
22. one who is dull-witted or stupid
23. fog made heavier by smoke

ADDITIONAL ACADEMIC WORDS

This chapter contains additional words and phrases for each discipline. You can locate the definitions in the glossaries of textbooks in each field, or you can look the words up in a dictionary. If you use a regular dictionary, be sure to read the definitions carefully so that you select the one most appropriate to the field of study. Sometimes the dictionary will have a subject label to assist you.

CHAPTER 6—SCIENCES: BIOLOGY

absorption	homeostasis
anaerobic	leukoplast
anaphase	medulla
anthropoid	mutagen
antibody	nucleotide
biosynthesis	omnivorous
capillary	phenotype
catalyst	polymorphism
cyclosis	recombination
endoderm	substrate
glycogen	transpiration
herbivore	vacuole

CHAPTER 7—SCIENCES: CHEMISTRY

absolute zero	manometer
alpha particle	monomer
Avogadro's number	noble gas

catalyst
colligative properties
dispersion forces
energy
halogen
inhibitor
isomer
ketone
limiting reagent

octet rule
oxyacid
Pauli Exclusion Principle
redox
specific gravity
spectroscope
stoichiometry
valence electrons
water of hydration

CHAPTER 8—SCIENCES: MATHEMATICS

axis
complementary angle
constant
coordinates
disjunction
equilateral
equivalent sets
histogram
intercepts
interval
linear equations
plane

polynomial
powers
probability
quadrant
sample
scientific notation
slope
subscript
symmetry
tangent
Venn diagram
volume

CHAPTER 9—SOCIAL SCIENCES: POLITICAL SCIENCE

balance of power
coexistence
collective security
conservative
containment
disengagement
facism
Federalist Papers
historical irony
humanism
International Monetary Fund
isolationism

liberalism
Machiavellian
manifest destiny
Marxist theory
natural law
pragmatism
purges
reactionary
secularism
totalitarian-socialism (communism)
traditionalism
welfare-capitalism

CHAPTER 10—SOCIAL SCIENCES: PSYCHOLOGY

accommodation
behavior determinants
canalization
cathexis
contingencies of reinforcement
distal events
dysplasia
ectomorphy
endomorphy
entropy
extraversion/introversion
figure-ground

goal gradient
inhibitory potential
isomorphism
latency stage
latent learning
mesomorphy
operant behavior
psyche
schema
self-actualization
transcendent function
unity-thema

CHAPTER 11—SOCIAL SCIENCES: ECONOMICS

agribusiness
allocation
coalition
consumption
disequilibrium
elasticity
expansionary
Federal Reserve system
forecast
free enterprise
liability
mercantilism

perpetuity
portfolio
premium
productivity
quota
resource allocation
securities
synergism
trademark
trusts
value-added tax
yield

CHAPTER 12—HUMANITIES: HISTORY

abolition
abrogation
Alien and Sedition Acts
caucus
commonwealth
consortium

impeachment
manifesto
nullification
referendum
secession
spoils system

Emancipation Proclamation
embargo
expansionism
filibuster
gold standard
Homestead Act

suffrage
temperance movement
tenure of office
Truman Doctrine
Wilmot Proviso
xenophobia

CHAPTER 13—HUMANITIES: ENGLISH

allegory
alliteration
apostrophe
assonance
blank verse
canto
caricature
controlling image
dactyl
dramatic personae
elegy
epic

farce
genre
haiku
iamb
metonomy
onomatopoeia
proscenium
quatrain
rondeau
scansion
spondee
trope

CHAPTER 14—HUMANITIES: COMMUNICATIONS

analog recording
arbitron
blacklist
canons of journalism
cease-and-desist order
conglomerate
daguerreotype
digital recording
disclaimer
diurnal
electromagnetic spectrum
fairness doctrine

format
gramophone
hologram
inverted pyramid
multitrack recording
nonduplication rule
ombudsperson
payola
prime time access rule
rack jobber
simulcast
underground press

CHAPTER 15—HUMANITIES: ART

analogous
art nouveau
brushwork
contrapposto
Dada
fauves
focus
glaze
grottoes
illusionism
intensity
kinetic sculpture

mobile
optical art
organic
perspective
portraiture
reductionism
Romanesque
silhouette
synchronism
terra-cotta
value
wood cut

CHAPTER 16—BUSINESS: BUSINESS ADMINISTRATION

actuary
affirmative action programs
arbitration
bait pricing
bargaining unit
blue-sky laws
callable bond
cartel
chattel mortgage
corporate financial model
debenture bond
excise tax

fair trade laws
f.o.b. destination
garnishment
Green River Ordinances
implied warranty
intangible assets
jurisdictional strike
letter of credit
preemptive right
rule of reason
stare decisis
trade barriers

CHAPTER 17—BUSINESS: ACCOUNTING

accelerated depreciation
accrual basis
allowance
by-product
consolidation
controller

job order
market value
obsolescence
petty cash
premium
reserves

default
deferred credit
gross margin
gross national product (GNP)
indirect cost
inventory

revenue
securities
surplus
tax shield
working capital
value-added tax

CHAPTER 18—BUSINESS: COMPUTER SCIENCE AND DATA PROCESSING

analog
array
BASIC
batch
branching
buffer
COBOL
compiler
formatting
form feed
FORTRAN
logic

loops
matrix
megabyte
password
prompt
scrolling
spreadsheet
subroutine
timesharing
tutorial
utility program
word processing

SELF-SELECTED
VOCABULARY

The purpose of this appendix is to provide forms for you to record your own self-selected vocabulary related to the exercises and essays in the chapters. You can also use this vocabulary in context in an original sentence.

ESSENTIALS FOR COLLEGE SUCCESS WORKSHEET

Record words here that you need to know or have discovered as you were reading the essay and doing the exercises. These words can also be ones that you have encountered in your daily activities and which you *need* to be both an effective student and a knowledgeable person. Provide an original sentence using each word in appropriate context.

Word	Pronunciation	Meaning(s)	Sentence

FIELDS OF STUDY WORKSHEET

Record words here that you need to know or have discovered as you were reading the essay and doing the exercises. These words could also be ones that you have encountered in your daily activities and which you *need* to be both an effective student and a knowledgeable person. Provide an original sentence using each word in appropriate context.

Discipline	Word	Pronunciation	Meaning(s)	Sentence

APPENDIX E

PRETEST ANSWER KEYS, CROSSWORD PUZZLE KEYS

CHAPTER 4 PRETEST ANSWER KEY

1. competence
2. assimilate
3. erudite
4. linguistic
5. proximity
6. diligent
7. adhere
8. impediments
9. retrieval
10. procrastinate
11. discern
12. deleterious
13. articulate
14. cogent
15. optimum

CHAPTER 5 PRETEST ANSWER KEY

1. compendium
2. myriad
3. avid
4. assiduous
5. plagiarize
6. accessible
7. replicate
8. adjunct
9. stringent
10. adjacent
11. copious
12. abstract
13. formidable
14. ancillary
15. expedite

CHAPTER 6 PRETEST ANSWER KEY

1. eucaryote
2. diffusion
3. membrane
4. organelle
5. osmosis
6. ecology
7. mutation
8. metabolism
9. bacterium
10. mitosis
11. evolution
12. photosynthesis
13. karyokinesis
14. cytoplasm
15. cytokinesis

CHAPTER 7 PRETEST ANSWER KEY

1. aqueous	6. alchemy	11. amorphous
2. induction	7. condensation	12. kinetic
3. miscible	8. equilibrium	13. liquefaction
4. sublimation	9. viscosity	14. evaporation
5. solute	10. solvent	15. distillation

CHAPTER 8 PRETEST ANSWER KEY

1. function	6. postulate	11. factor
2. exponent	7. range	12. domain
3. prime	8. inverse	13. hypotenuse
4. derivative	9. composite	14. congruent
5. variable	10. theorem	15. integral

CHAPTER 9 PRETEST ANSWER KEY

1. coalition	6. pluralism	11. sovereignty
2. promulgate	7. cataclysm	12. indictment
3. scope	8. sedition	13. paramount
4. deploy	9. despotism	14. regime
5. methodology	10. empirical	15. normative

CHAPTER 10 PRETEST ANSWER KEY

1. innate	6. introspection	11. psychosis
2. hypothesis	7. paradigm	12. stimulus
3. theory	8. subjective	13. anxiety
4. psychotherapy	9. repression	14. neurosis
5. reliability	10. cognition	15. validity

CHAPTER 11 PRETEST ANSWER KEY

1. sector	6. fiscal	11. entrepreneur
2. monopoly	7. recession	12. consumption

3. oligopoly
4. aggregate
5. tariff

8. inflationary
9. externality
10. capitalism

13. revenue
14. expenditure
15. cartel

CHAPTER 12 PRETEST ANSWER KEY

1. analogous
2. cursory
3. nascent
4. palpable
5. precedent

6. agrarian
7. schism
8. precept
9. nonpareil
10. antipathy

11. draconian
12. polemic
13. metamorphosis
14. quintessential
15. facet

CHAPTER 13 PRETEST ANSWER KEY

1. deus ex machina
2. personify
3. motif
4. ligature
5. patron

6. denouement
7. delineate
8. eloquent
9. repartee
10. montage

11. narrative
12. profound
13. soliloquy
14. epitome
15. epithet

CHAPTER 14 PRETEST ANSWER KEY

1. covert
2. demographic
3. admonitory
4. vast
5. parsimony

6. overt
7. augment
8. diversion
9. pragmatic
10. libel

11. vicarious
12. ostensibly
13. defamation
14. diversified
15. slander

CHAPTER 15 PRETEST ANSWER KEY

1. hue
2. aesthetic
3. realist
4. baroque
5. surrealism

6. cubism
7. monochromatic
8. distortion
9. perception
10. symbolism

11. asymmetry
12. palette
13. romanticism
14. gradation
15. impressionism

CHAPTER 16 PRETEST ANSWER KEY

1. entitlement
2. innovative
3. ensconced
4. ramification
5. lucrative
6. adversary
7. pecuniary
8. fiat
9. contingency
10. redress
11. incentive
12. proliferation
13. axiom
14. remuneration
15. minutiae

CHAPTER 17 PRETEST ANSWER KEY

1. ledger
2. debit
3. equity
4. assets
5. dividend
6. liabilities
7. transaction
8. credit
9. depreciation
10. intangible
11. amortize
12. voucher
13. requisition
14. audit
15. disclosure

CHAPTER 18 PRETEST ANSWER KEY

1. chip
2. nanoseconds
3. output
4. terminal
5. peripheral
6. byte
7. modem
8. cursor
9. programming
10. binary
11. disk
12. documentation
13. generation
14. input
15. interface

Puzzle 1 Answers

			¹L				²S				³B	R	U	N	C	H	⁴H
		⁵M	A	V	E	⁶R	I	C	K								U
⁷S			W		O	U					⁸A	E	G	I	S		S
O	⁹Q				B	B											B
L	U		¹⁰X		O	A											A
¹¹E	T	I	Q	U	E	T	T	E			¹²U	T	O	¹³P	I	A	N
C	S		R				¹⁴S							R			D
I	L	¹⁵D	O	U	B	L	E	T		¹⁶H	I	C	K	O	R	Y	
S	I		X				A			T							
¹⁷M	A	N				¹⁸T	A	N	T	A	L	I	Z	E			¹⁹C
	G						Z			A							H
			²⁰H		²¹C	H	I	²²V	A	L	R	Y		²³K	N	I	F	E
²⁴C			E					A				²⁵A	N	D	A	N	T	E		²⁶N	E	M	E	S	I	S			²⁷D

Puzzle 2 Answers

Puzzle 2 Answer Key

CARGO
CIPHER
DESIGN
DOUBLET
DOWNTIME
HICKORY
HOUSE
HUSBAND
KNIFE
MARTINET
NEMESIS

ODYSSEY
PLAID
PROTEAN
RADAR
ROBOT
SAUTE
SCUBA
SHRINE
SOLECISM
SPIN-OUT

STOIC
STEAK
TAPESTRY
TANTALIZE
TEMPO
THEM
THEIR
UTOPIAN
VANILLA
WIFE

Puzzle 3 Answers

Puzzle 3 Answer Key

AEGIS	DUNCE	MOCCASIN
ALGEBRA	ETIQUETTE	PANDEMONIUM
ANDANTE	GERRYMANDER	QUIXOTIC
BRUNCH	HERCULEAN	QUISLING
CANDLE	HEATHER	SMOG
CHURCH	KLEENEX	STANZA
CHEF	LAW	SYBARITE
CHIVALRY	LACONIC	THEY
CIGAR	MAN	XEROX
DENIM	MAVERICK	ZERO

INDEX

Note: Vocabulary words appear in bold. Numbers in bold indicate pages where the word definitions can be found.

blends, 316
Braque, Georges, 230
business:
   accounting, 264–282
   business administration, 246–263
   computer science and data processing,
     283–301
business cycles, 156
byte, 284, 286, **289,** 300, 314

calculus, 96, 97, 99–100
Capek, Karel, 317
capitalism, 155, 156, 157, **159**–160,
   172, 308
cartel, 155, 156, 157, **160**–161, 172, 308
cash account, 266
cataclysm, 118, 119, 120, **121,** 133, 309,
   310
cell, 61–62, 65
Cervantes, Miguel de, 317
chemistry, 78–95
chip, 283, 284, 285, 287, **289**–290, 300,
   308
classical myths, words from, 317, 318
coalition, 118, 119, 120, **121**–122, 133,
   305, 307
cogent, 24, 26, **30**–31, 40, 305, 307
cognition, 136, 138, **140**–141, 153, 305,
   309
Columbia University School of Government, 118–119
communications, 209–227
compendium, 41, 42, 44, **50**–51, 57,
   305, 311
competence, 24, 26, **31,** 40, 305, 311
competition, 156
composite, 97, 100, **101**–102, 115, 305,
   312
compound words, 316
computer functions
   input, 285–286
   memory, 285–286
   output, 285–286
   processing, 285–286
computer hardware, 285
computer science and data processing,
   283–301
computer software, 286

condensation, 79, 80, **84**–85, 95, 305,
   308
congruent, 97, 99, 100, **102**–103, 115,
   308
connotations, 8–9
consumption, 155, 156, 157, **161**–162,
   172, 305, 313
context clues, 15–18
   contrast, 16
   example, 16
   general information, experience, 16
   graphic, 16–17
   restatement, 16
contingency, 247, 249, **252**–253, 263,
   305, 313
copious, 41, 43, 44, **51**–52, 57, 305, 311
covert, 210, 211, 212, **215**–216, 226,
   305, 311
CPA (certified public accountant), 264,
   266
credit, 265, 266, **271**–272, 282, 308
critical thinking, 25
cubism, 229, 230, 231, **234**–235, 244,
   310
cursor, 284, 285, 287, **290**–291, 300,
   308
cursory, 175, 176, 177, **180**–181, 191,
   308
cytokinesis, 61, 62, 63, **65,** 76, 309, 310
cytoplasm, 61, 63, **65**–66, 76, 310, 312

Dali, Salvador, 230
DDT (dichloro-diphenyl-trichloroethane), 62
debit, 265, 266, **272**–273, 282, 308
DeBow, John, 176
defamation, 210, 212, **216,** 226, 305,
   309
Degas, Edgar, 230
Delacroix, Eugene, 230
deleterious, 24, 26, **32,** 40, 308
delineate, 193, 194, **195**–196, 208, 305,
   310
democratic renaissance, 175
demographic, 210, 211, 212, **217,** 226,
   308, 309
denotations, 8–9
denouement, 193, 194, **196**–197, 208,
   305, 311

Pronunciation Key*

a	hat, cap	oi	oil, voice		Non-English sounds
ā	age, face	ou	house, out	Y	as in French *du*. Pronounce ē with the lips rounded as for English ü in *rule*.
ã	care, air	p	paper, cup		
ä	father, far	r	run, try		
b	bad, rob	s	say, yes		
ch	child, much	sh	she, rush	œ	as in French *peu*. Pronounce ā with the lips rounded as for ō.
d	did, red	t	tell, it		
e	let, best	th	thin, both		
ē	equal, see	TH	then, smooth	N	as in French *bon*. The N is not pronounced, but shows that the vowel before it is nasal.
ėr	term, learn	u	cup, butter		
f	fat, if	u̇	full, put		
g	go, bag	ü	rule, move		
h	he, how	v	very, save		
i	it, pin	w	will, woman	H	as in German *ach*. Pronounce k without closing the breath passage.
ī	ice, five	y	young, yet		
j	jam, enjoy	z	zero, breeze		
k	kind, seek	zh	measure, seizure		
l	land, coal			à	as in French *ami*. The quality of this vowel is midway between the a of *hat* and the ä of *far*, but is closer to the former.
m	me, am	ə	represents:		
n	no, in	a	in about		
ng	long, bring	e	in taken		
o	hot, rock	i	in pencil		
ō	open, go	o	in lemon		
ô	order, all	u	in circus		

* © 1986 by Doubleday & Company, Inc. By permission of World Book, Inc.